THE BALKANS
THE SECOND WORLD WAR

The Postwar World
General Editors: A. J. Nicholls and Martin S. Alexander

As distance puts events into perspective, and as evidence accumulates, it begins to be possible to form an objective historical view of our recent past. *The Postwar World* is an ambitious series providing a scholarly but readable account of the way our world has been shaped in the crowded years since the Second World War. Some volumes will deal with regions, or even single nations, others with important themes; all will be written by expert historians drawing on the latest scholarship as well as their own research and judgements. The series should be particularly welcome to students, but it is designed also for the general reader with an interest in contemporary history.

THE BALKANS
SINCE THE SECOND
WORLD WAR

R. J. CRAMPTON

An imprint of **Pearson Education**

London · New York · Toronto · Sydney · Tokyo · Singapore · Hong Kong · Cape Town
New Delhi · Madrid · Paris · Amsterdam · Munich · Milan · Stockholm

PEARSON EDUCATION LIMITED

Head Office:
Edinburgh Gate
Harlow CM20 2JE
Tel: +44 (0)1279 623623
Fax: +44 (0)1279 431059

London Office:
128 Long Acre
London WC2E 9AN
Tel: +44 (0)20 7447 2000
Fax: +44 (0)20 7240 5771
Website: www.history-minds.com

First published in Great Britain in 2002

© Pearson Education Limited 2002

The right of R. J. Crampton to be identified as Author
of this Work has been asserted by him in accordance
with the Copyright, Designs and Patents Act 1988.

ISBN 0 582 24883 3

British Library Cataloguing in Publication Data
A CIP catalogue record for this book can be obtained from the British Library

Library of Congress Cataloging in Publication Data
A CIP catalog record for this book can be obtained from the Library of Congress

10 9 8 7 6 5 4 3 2 1

Typeset in 10.5/12pt Bembo by Graphicraft Limited, Hong Kong
Printed in Malaysia

The Publishers' policy is to use paper manufactured from sustainable forests.

To David and Hilary Harkness

————————————

CONTENTS

LIST OF TABLES

LIST OF MAPS

PREFACE

Their very diversity makes the Balkans impossible to define confidently or precisely. Topographically the region varies from the mountain fastnesses of northern Albania and the higher peaks of the Carpathians, through the fertile valley of the lower Danube, to the Mediterranean coastline of Greece and its islands.

The *Oxford English Dictionary*, second edition 1989, has the following entry for the adjective 'Balkan': 'Of or pertaining to the peninsula bounded by the Adriatic, Aegean and Black Seas, or to the countries or peoples of this region: *spec.* with allusion to the relations (often characterized by threatened hostilities) of the Balkan states to each other or to the rest of Europe . . .' The *Encyclopaedia Britannica*[1] confines itself to a more political definition: 'In contemporary usage the term "Balkans" signifies the territory of the states of Albania, Bosnia and Hercegovina, Bulgaria, Croatia, Greece, Macedonia, Moldova, Romania, Slovenia, and Yugoslavia (Montenegro and Serbia)', but even this authoritative source cannot have complete confidence in its definition, adding, 'though there is considerable doubt as to whether Slovenia and Romanian Transylvania are Balkan in any meaningful sense'. The encyclopaedia then notes that 'The term also includes the European portion of Turkey, although Turkey is not a Balkan state.'

The *Encyclopaedia Britannica* uses political criteria in defining the area but, when first coined in 1808 by the German August Zeune, the phrase 'Balkan peninsula' was used as a purely geographic term and had even less political weight at that time than the word 'German'. 'Balkan' was a Turkish word meaning 'wooded upland', and was applied to what the ancients had called the Haemus mountains, that is the range which runs east–west through the centre of present-day Bulgaria. This geographic usage persisted throughout most of the nineteenth century; when a political phrase was needed it was usually 'Turkey in Europe', the Ottoman empire, for much of the century, being the largest political unit in the area.

That the dismemberment of Turkey in Europe took place in conflicts which became known as the 'Balkan wars' (1912–13) indicated that the term had been given a political as well as a geographic loading. The association of 'the Balkans' with the phenomena of political fragmentation and hostility was well-established by the end of the First World War, Harold Nicolson noting in his classic memoir of the Paris peace negotiations that 'We succeeded in Balkanizing Europe although we europeanized the Balkans.'[2] Given what was to occur in Europe within the next quarter of a century one might ask who got the better of such an exchange, but the *bien pensant* intelligentsia of the western world were, as they generally still are, supremely unselfknowing in such questions; no matter what might have happened on the prairies of north America or in the interior of Tasmania, or what was about to happen in the death camps of central Europe and the Eurasian Gulag, the Balkans were frequently dismissed as irredeemably divided and violent; they were still, to use the title of a pre-First World War travelogue, 'Savage Europe'.[3] The pejorative connotations have remained and intensified. In recent months there has been a tendency among the more slip-shod of British journalists to use the term 'Balkan' to mean those areas of the peninsula which have fallen, or which seem in danger of falling, prey to anarchy and violence; in this definition, Albania, Kosovo and Macedonia are 'in' and Bulgaria and Greece are 'out'.

It is generally acknowledged that 'like all great European peninsulas, the Balkans are a world apart';[4] but wherein lie the differences? Certain characteristics are discernible in a number of areas; Orthodox Christianity, economic backwardness, ethnic intermixture are three of them, but these are found elsewhere in Europe and none of them can be taken as a single, diagnostic feature. Not even subjection to a great empire, Habsburg, Ottoman or Soviet, will suffice, because Montenegro and northern Albania were never fully conquered. An American historian has defined the Balkan world as a relict of 'the first Europe', that is a world which, since Neolithic times, was 'bound religiously, psychologically, and economically to the soil and the surrounding space'.[5] But this does not take fully into account the mercantile communities which were established in Ragusa (Dubrovnik) and at other points on the coast. Even where it did exist the 'first Europe' began to decay from the mid-nineteenth century as production-orientated systems began to make their impact, as, soon after, did western ideas of nationalism and the nation-state. The problem was that the economic and the political odds were stacked against the Balkans. Most of the area did not have easy communication with either the great centres of consumption in central and western Europe or the oceans linking it with the wider world, and the construction of nation states was hideously difficult in areas which were not only ethnically diverse but in which ethnic divisions often coincided with social ones, meaning that the urban commercial or manufacturing bourgeoisie was frequently of a different ethnic group to the surrounding countryside. The situation was made worse by the fact that individual European great powers had their own fish to fry and invariably did all they could to ensure that it was their fish which was best cooked.

In the early twenty-first century the least unsatisfactory means of defining the Balkans is to follow the *Encyclopaedia Britannica* and rely on political boundaries. This is even more the case in a study such as this which is intended to provide a political narrative of the area. This book will therefore concentrate on the political evolution of what in the United States is frequently called 'South-Eastern Europe', a term which has cognates in French and German. It includes the present states of Albania, Bulgaria, Greece and Romania, together the territories which between 1944 and 1992 made up the Federal Republic of Yugoslavia; all the states covered were once part of, or limitrophe with, post-Second World War Yugoslavia. All were dominated by the peasantry and preoccupied with the problems of modernization. And at the beginning of the period covered by this book all the states concerned had to face the myriad political and moral questions posed by the experience of foreign occupation or domination. For all the states but Greece the modernizing drive for most of the second half of the twentieth century was Marxism-Leninism which was imported from the Soviet Union. In political terms they all faced the difficulties of clientalism and corruption.

The book does not include Moldova, a member of the Confederation of Independent States, and a country which looks more to what were once its sister republics in the former Soviet Union than to the west and the southwest. Nor does it include Cyprus, except when that island affects the affairs of Greece, although in terms of culture and historical experience Cyprus has many similarities with Crete and other islands now included in Greece. Nor does the book include the area which in terms of population is second only to Romania in size, European Turkey, the destiny of that area being primarily determined, despite Turkey's European aspirations, in the Turkish capital in Asia Minor.

This definition is as open to question and debate as any other attempt to draw boundaries around 'the Balkans'. Greece's position as a Balkan state is questionable. Some would argue that Greece was in essence a Mediterranean rather than a Balkan country; it is the case that Greece, with European Turkey, is singular in the region in having a coastline which is longer than its land frontier. Unlike Turkey, Greece has a long mercantile and maritime tradition. This it shares with Croatia but the Greeks have in addition to this a more influential and more widespread diaspora which enabled the Greeks to develop close links with cultures and states outside the Balkan peninsula, though in very recent times Croatians abroad have exercised a huge and important influence on Croatia itself. On the other hand, Greece has many of the features which are frequently found in the Balkans. It is an Orthodox Christian society. Its economy, a few coastal areas excepted, remained backward until the third quarter of the twentieth century. The Greek state and political system fell victim to the clientalism found in, but by no means confined to, the other Balkan states. And in its foreign policy Greece was inevitably influenced by events in the states immediately to its north.

Romania was part of the Ottoman system, though under conditions very different to those in areas such as Bulgaria and Macedonia at the core of that empire in Europe, but again it, or much of it, was an integral part of Orthodox Christianity, it has suffered from political clientalism and has had to adjust its foreign policy to take into account the actions of its neighbours to the south.

Unlike the other southern European peninsulas, Iberia and Italy, the languages spoken in the Balkans do not belong predominantly to one linguistic family, and are of widely differing origins. The oldest is Albanian. The Albanians are descendants of the ancient Illyrians and are of Indo-European origin, but their language does not fall into any of the major Indo-European families. The Greeks who arrived from Asia Minor in prehistoric times are the second oldest group and are also Indo-European. The Romanians, too, speak an Indo-European language, though theirs is Romance, being derived from the Latin spoken by the legionaries who conquered the area to the north of the Danube in the second century AD. The Slavs arrived in a series of incursions and migrations between the third and seventh centuries. Another people of Indo-European origin they divided into various groups which can now be identified as Croat, Macedonian, Serbian and Slovene. The Bulgarians also speak a Slavonic language though they are not of Slav ethnic origin, the original Proto-Bulgars who arrived in the seventh century having absorbed the Slav culture of the people they conquered.

Most of the peninsula had been under Roman and then Byzantine domination and its peoples had become Christian. In the eleventh century, however, they divided between Christianity's Roman, or Catholic, and eastern, or Orthodox, versions based in Rome and Constantinople respectively. The division did not follow ethnic lines but was determined more by geography and propinquity to one of the two great religious centres. The Croats and Slovenes adhered to Rome, while the Bulgarians, Romanians, Serbians and Greeks opted for Orthodoxy. The Albanians were divided between the two. The division was deep and was made deeper by the Fourth Crusaders who seized and despoiled Constantinople, the centre of Orthodoxy, in 1204.

In the fourteenth century the conquering Ottoman armies bought a new religion, Islam, and a new people, the Turks, to the area. The Ottoman system of government, however, paid little heed to ethnicity, religious affiliation being the main dividing line. The new rulers seldom indulged in forced conversion though some landowners, particularly in Albania and Bosnia, adopted the new faith in order to preserve entitlement to their lands, and forcible conversion was occasionally meted out as a punishment to communities which had attempted to rebel. When the upheavals of the conquest subsided the Balkans became part of an economic system which was strongly tied to the remainder of the Ottoman empire in Anatolia, Mesopotamia, the Levant, Arabia and north Africa. With inclusion in this system came merchant communities of Armenians, Jews and others who settled throughout the empire. By the time the Ottoman empire entered into serious decline in the eighteenth century the ethnic composition of at least the urban centres of the Balkans was more varied than that of any other part of Europe. Not until European notions of nationalism spread into the area after the French Revolution did this become a serious problem. It is a problem which as yet is far from resolved.

This book is intended to provide an introduction to the political evolution of an area which has seldom been out of the headlines in the last dozen or more years. Familiarity with its history will not provide solutions to its problems, but it should help in the search for such solutions, if only by pointing out the mistakes which have already been made. The book is therefore intended not only for students but for journalists, politicians, professional people and those in the business world, all of whom will play a part in the future of Balkans.

The book is divided into three, chronological sections. The first deals with the turbulent years from 1944 to 1949/50, the period of 'shake-down' from the Second World War. In this period the driving force, in all countries, was the communist party, which was successful in all of them except Greece. The second period covers the years when the communists remained dominant in the area, Greece excepted, and therefore ends with the climactic events of 1989. Since then the region has been undergoing another period of turbulent 'shake-down', this time from the era of communist domination. This period has been dominated by the attempted transitions to pluralism and the market economy as well as by the collapse of the former Yugoslavia and by all that flowed therefrom.

Each section begins with a short introduction which is followed by an examination of events in Yugoslavia. Yugoslavia is given this prominence primarily because it was this state which had the major impact on the peninsula as a whole. In the very early post-Second World War years Marshal Tito appeared as the most popular communist figure in the Balkans, and elsewhere in the Soviet bloc, and it was the rupture between him and Stalin which set the stage for the purges in Eastern Europe, while his rehabilitation by Khrushchev did much to precipitate the unrest which shook Eastern Europe in the mid-1950s. The fact that Yugoslavia had, perforce, to plot its own path to socialism, did much to determine the international configuration of the Balkans between the mid-1950s and the mid-1980s. Albania feared Yugoslav expansionism and sought friends who would safeguard it against such a danger; Romanian aspirations to greater freedom within rather than from the Soviet bloc were much encouraged by the Yugoslav example, while Bulgaria found its safety and protection in becoming the only fully pro-Soviet state in the area. Greece, firmly locked into the western system, was less affected by developments in Yugoslavia.

After examining Yugoslavia each section then discusses developments in the remaining communist states, Albania, Bulgaria and Romania, before ending with a survey of affairs in Greece.

All books on this area face the problems of nomenclature, translation and transliteration. With regard to the first, the current usage is general employed, though there is a certain degree of historical licence. Where a variety of names exists for one particular location, which is almost always the case in the Balkans, the one used is that considered likely to be most familiar to the English-language reader, hence Salonika rather than Thessaloniki and Belgrade rather than Beograd. Perversely, my preference is for 'Hercegovina' rather than 'Herzegovina', the former being the variant used in the local latin script, and the latter being pointless because the 'z' should be 'ts'. For the most part initials of institutions are of their English-language version but some have become so well-known by their original-language initials that the latter have been retained, as for example in NDH for the wartime Independent State of Croatia, and PASOK for the Pan-Hellenic Socialist Movement. Occasionally original language initials have been retained because in translation they have the same letters as other organizations: the Serbian Democratic Party, for example, is referred to as the SDS to avoid confusion with the Social Democratic Parties which existed in many states. Communist parties usually pertained to territories rather than nationalities or ethnic groups, the more so when the states in question were federations such as Yugoslavia and the Soviet Union. In other instances, however, I have followed what has become common practice in historical writing and used the adjectival form, as in the Bulgarian Communist Party, the Romanian Communist Party, etc.

A major problem in translation from Slav languages is the word 'narod' which in English can mean both 'people' and 'nation'. There is no entirely satisfactory rule for which English equivalent should be used; a rough guide to my own practice is to be found in footnotes on pages 13 and 239.

The transliteration of Cyrillic and Greek names is an unending nightmare. In the case of Serbian names diacritic marks have generally been used because this has become increasingly commonplace in the English-speaking world where one finds 'Milošević' more frequently than 'Miloshevich'; with Bulgarian, Macedonian and Greek words consistency has at least been the objective. In general I have adapted the spelling and sometimes the punctuation of quotations to conform to what I hope is the standard British-English pattern.

Footnoting has been kept to a minimum and used generally only for direct quotations.

The writer of contemporary history, like the politician, is always at the mercy of 'events', and nowhere has this been more true than in the affairs of Eastern Europe and the Balkans in the last decade and a half. I have attempted to incorporate and evaluate the most recent developments but no doubt others will occur before this text reaches its readers.

Of the many people who have helped in the preparation of this text five deserve my especial thanks in that they have read and passed enormously helpful comment on part of it; they are: John Allcock of the University of Bradford; Richard Clogg of St Antony's College, Oxford; Snježana Šakić, also of St Antony's College, Oxford; Robin Burleigh of Ascott-under-Wychwood; and my son, Ben Crampton, of the Research Analysts in the Foreign and Commonwealth Office. Others whose company, friendship and expertise have made my task easier and more pleasurable include: Stevan K. Pavlowitch, University of Southampton; John R. Lampe, University of Maryland; Robert Evans, Oriel College, Oxford; John Dunbabin, St Edmund Hall, Oxford; Anne Deighton, Wolfson College, Oxford; Dennis Deletant, University of London; Timothy Garton Ash, St Antony's College, Oxford; Michael Hurst, St John's College, Oxford; Kyril Drezov, University of Keele; Ivan Krŭstev, Centre for Liberal Strategies, Sofia; Sir Ivor and Lady Elizabeth Roberts, Louis Sell and many others. It would be churlish not to mention some of my graduate students, past and present, who have worked on this area and added greatly to my knowledge and understanding of it, and so I thank Nada Alaica, Peter Palmer, Teodora Parveva, Marietta Stankova, Dimitris Livanios and Daniella Kalkandjieva.

The remaining imperfections in this work can be the responsibility of me alone.

My editor, Heather McCallum, has been a model of professionalism and has proved beyond any doubt that patience is indeed a virtue.

The debt to my wife, accumulated over nearly forty years, is as incalculable as it is invaluable.

St Edmund Hall, Oxford,
October 2001

Notes

1. CD ROM 1997. There has been much excellent discussion on the use and meaning of the term 'Balkan' in recent years. See, for example, Maria Todorova, *Imagining the Balkans*, Oxford: Oxford University Press, 1997; Mark Mazower, *The Balkans, a Short History*, New York: the Modern Library, 2000, pp.xxv–xliii; Misha Glenny, *The Balkans 1804–1999: Nationalism, War and the Great Powers*, London: Granta Books, 1999, pp.xxi–xxv; and John B. Allcock, 'Constructing the Balkans', in John B. Allcock and Antonia Young (eds), *Black Lambs and Grey Falcons: Women Travellers in the Balkans*, Bradford: Bradford University Press, 1991, pp.170–91.
2. Harold Nicolson, *Peacemaking 1919*, revised edition, London: Methuen, 1964, p.xix.
3. Harry de Windt, *Through Savage Europe*, London: T. Fisher Unwin, 1907.
4. Z. A. B. Zeman, *Pursued by a Bear*, London: Chatto & Windus, 1989, p.2.
5. Traian Stoianovich, *Balkan Worlds; the First and Last Europe*, Armonk, NY; London: M. E. Sharpe, 1994, p.42.

ACKNOWLEDGEMENT

The publishers are grateful to the following for permission to reproduce copyright material:
Map 7 adapted from *To End a War* by Richard Holbrooke, copyright © 1998 by Richard Holbrooke; Maps copyright © 1998 by David Lindroth, Inc. Used by permission of Random House, Inc.

In some instances we have been unable to trace the owners of copyright material, and we would appreciate any information that would enable us to do so.

LIST OF ABBREVIATIONS

ACC	Allied Control Commission
ACP	Albanian Communist Party
ADF	Albanian Democratic Front
AIC	Agro-Industrial Complex (Bulgaria)
ANLA	Albanian National Liberation Army
ANS	Alliance for National Salvation (Bulgaria)
APL	Albanian Party of Labour
ARF	Alliance of Reform Forces (Yugoslavia)
AVNOJ	Anti-Fascist Council for the National Liberation of Yugoslavia (Second World War)
BANU	Bulgarian Agrarian National Union
BANU–NP	Bulgarian Agrarian National Union – Nikola Petkov
BBC	British Broadcasting Corporation
BCP	Bulgarian Communist Party
BDP	Bloc of Democratic Parties (Romania)
BK	Balli Kombetar (non-communist resistance movement, Albania, Second World War)
BMO	Bosnian Muslim Organization
BNB	Bulgarian National Bank
BOAL	Basic Organization of Associated Labour (Yugoslavia)
BSP	Bulgarian Socialist Party
BWP	Bulgarian Workers' Party
CC	Central Committee
CG	Contact Group
CITUB	Confederation of Independent Trade Unions in Bulgaria
Cocom	The Coordinating Committee for Multilateral Export Controls
CPC	Croatian Communist Party
CPP	Croatian Peasant Party
CPSU	Communist Party of the Soviet Union
CPY	Communist Party of Yugoslavia
CSCE	Conference on Security and Cooperation in Europe
DAG	Democratic Army of Greece (communist, Greek civil war)
DCR	Democratic Convention of Romania
DLK	Democratic League of Kosovo
DNSF	Democratic National Salvation Front (Romania)

DP	Democratic Party
DPA	Democratic Party of Albania
EAM	National Liberation Front (left-wing political resistance organization, Greece, Second World War)
EC	European Community
EDA	United Democratic Left (Greece)
EDES	National Democratic Greek League (non-communist military resistance organization, Greece, Second World War)
EDIK	Union of the Democratic Centre (Greece)
EEC	European Economic Community
EKKA	National and Social Liberation (non-communist political resistance organization, Greece, Second World War)
ELAS	National Popular Liberation Army (left-wing military resistance organization, Greece, Second World War)
EMU	European Monetary Union
EOKA	National Organization of Cypriot Fighters
EPEK	National Progressive Union (Greece)
ERE	National Radical Union (Greece)
EU	European Union
FADURK	Fund for the Development of Underdeveloped Republics and Regions (Yugoslavia)
FEC	Federal Executive Council (Yugoslavia)
FF	Fatherland Front (Bulgaria)
FRG	Federal Republic of Germany
FRY	Federative Republic of Yugoslavia
FYROM	Former Yugoslav Republic of Macedonia
GATT	General Agreement on Tariffs and Trade
GDP	Gross Domestic Product
GDR	German Democratic Republic
GNA	Grand National Assembly (Bulgaria)
GRP	Greater Romania Party
HAR	Hungarian Autonomous Region (Romania)
HDUR	Hungarian Democratic Union of Romania
HDZ	Croatian Democratic Union
HNS	Croatian People's Party
HR	High Representative (Bosnia)
HRU	Human Rights Union (Albania)
HSLS	Croatian Social Liberal Party
ICFY	International Conference on the Former Yugoslavia
ICTFY	International Criminal Tribunal for the Former Yugoslavia
IDEA	Sacred Bond of Greek Officers (right-wing conspiratorial group)

IFIs	International Financial Institutions
IFOR	Implementation Force (Bosnia)
IMF	International Monetary Fund
IMRO-DPMNU	Internal Macedonian Revolutionary Organization – Democratic Party for Macedonian National Unity
ISDP	Independent Social Democratic Party (Romania)
JNA	Yugoslav National Army
JUSMAPG	Joint United States Military Advisory and Planning Group (Greece)
K-FOR	Kosovo Force
KGB	Committee for State Security (Soviet political police)
KKE	Communist Party of Greece
KLA	Kosovo Liberation Army
LC	League of Communists
LCC	League of Communists of Croatia
LCK	League of Communists of Kosovo
LCS	League of Communists of Slovenia
LCS-PDR	League of Communists of Slovenia – Party of Democratic Renewal
LCY	League of Communists of Yugoslavia
LM	Legality Movement (royalist resistance movement, Albania, Second World War)
LP	Liberal Party (Romania)
MHAR	Mureş Hungarian Autonomous Region (Romania)
MRF	Movement for Rights and Freedom (Bulgaria, mainly ethnic Turkish party)
MTS	Machine Tractor Station
NATO	North Atlantic Treaty Organization
ND	New Democracy (Greece)
NDF	National Democratic Front
NDH	Independent State of Croatia (Second World War)
NDLK	New Democratic League of Kosovo
NEFM	New Economic and Financial Mechanism (Romania)
NEM	New Economic Mechanism (Bulgaria)
NKVD	National Commissariat for Internal Affairs (Soviet political police, forerunner of KGB q.v.)
NLF	National Liberation Front (Albania)
NLP	National Liberal Party
NPP	National Peasant Party (Romania)
NPPCD	National Peasant Party – Christian Democratic (Romania)
NSF	National Salvation Front (Romania)
OPEC	Organization of the Petroleum Exporting Countries
OSCE	Organization for Security and Cooperation in Europe
OZNa	Department for the Protection of the People (political police, Yugoslavia)

PASOK	Panhellenic Socialist Movement
PDA	Party of Democratic Action (Bosnia)
PDF	People's Democratic Front (Romania)
PDG	Provisional Democratic Government (communist, Greek civil war)
PEEA	Political Committee of National Liberation (left-wing political resistance organization, Greece, Second World War)
PF	Ploughmen's Front (Romania), and Peoples' Front (Yugoslavia)
PKK	Kurdish Separatist Organization
PLA	People's Liberation Army (Yugoslavia)
PLC	People's Liberation Council (Yugoslavia)
PLF	People's Liberation Front
PP	People's Party (Greece)
PR	Proportional Representation
PRC	People's Republic of China
PRM	People's Republic of Macedonia
PRNU	Party of Romanian National Unity
PSDR	Party of Social Democracy in Romania
RCP	Romanian Communist Party
RIS	Romanian Intelligence Service
RRF	Rapid Reaction Force
RS	Republika Srpska (Bosnia)
RWP	Romanian Workers' Party
SAWPY	Socialist Alliance of the Working People of Yugoslavia
SDP	Social Democratic Party
SDS	Serbian Democratic Party
SDU	Social Democratic Union (Romania)
S-FOR	Stabilization Force (Bosnia)
SLP	Socialist Labour Party (Romania)
SPA	Socialist Party of Albania
SPH	Social Democratic Party of Croatia
SPP	Socialist People's Party (Serbia; Milošević's party)
SPS	Socialist Party of Serbia
SRM	Serbian Renewal Movement
SRZ	Peasant Work Cooperative (collective farm, Yugoslavia)
SSNM	Simeon II National Movement (Bulgaria)
TDF	Territorial Defence Force (Yugoslav republics)
TKZS	Labour-Cooperative Agricultural Economic Unit (cooperative/collective farm, Bulgaria)
UDBa	State Security Administration (political police, Yugoslavia, successor to OZNa, q.v.)
UDF	Union of Democratic Forces, also United Democratic Forces (Bulgaria)

UK	United Kingdom
UN	United Nations
UNHCR	United Nations High Commissioner for Refugees
UNMIK	United Nations Interim Administration in Kosovo
UNPREDEP	United Nations Preventive Deployment Force (Macedonia)
UNPROFOR	United Nations Protection Force (Croatia and Bosnia)
UNRRA	United Nations Relief and Rehabilitation Administration
UNSC	United Nations Security Council
UNSCR	United Nations Security Council Resolution
UNTAES	United Nations Transitional Administration in Eastern Slavonia, Baranja and Western Sirmium
USA	United States of America
USSR	Union of Soviet Socialist Republics
UWF	United Workers' Front (Romania)
WEU	Western European Union
WSDP	Workers' Social Democratic Party (Bulgarian, anti-communist)
WTO	Warsaw Treaty Organization (Warsaw pact)

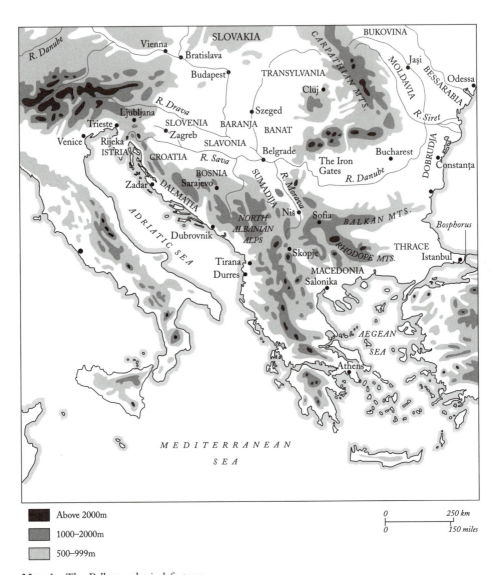

Above 2000m

1000–2000m

500–999m

0   250 km

0   150 miles

Map 1   The Balkans, physical features

Map 2 The Yugoslav lands

Map 3   Albania

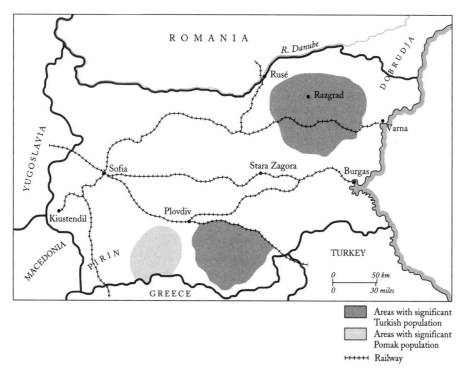

Map 4 Bulgaria

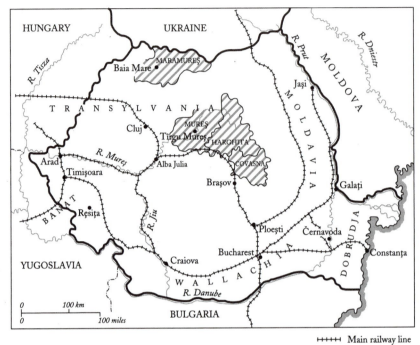

H+++H Main railway line

Map 5   Romania

Map 6 Greece

Map 7   The wars in Croatia and Bosnia

Map 8 Bosnia–Hercegovina and the Dayton Accord

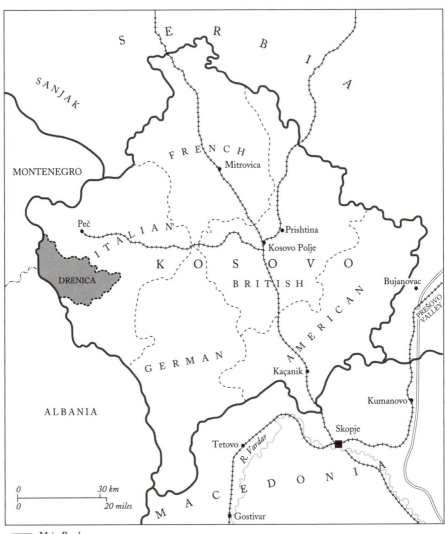

Map 9 Kosovo and north-west Macedonia, 2001

Part I

COMMUNIST TAKEOVERS
AND CIVIL WAR:
THE BALKANS 1944–1949

Chapter 1

INTRODUCTION

If they are to avoid infinite regression all histories must have a starting point. These are never totally satisfactory because no single starting point can be fully explained without some introduction to its own historical background. The starting point for this history is the end of the Second World War yet what happened after the end of that conflict was largely conditioned by the war itself and also the period before it. By the mid-1930s in the Balkans, as in much of Europe and beyond, there was little left of the Versailles system created at the end of the First World War. The League of Nations and collective security were soon to collapse while on the domestic front authoritarianism progressed inexorably, not least because the disastrous economic recession and its social consequences were rapidly increasing the power of central government. By 1939 political power was vested in a centralized executive and political activity confined to what that power deemed acceptable. The battle against the depression and its effects had concentrated an unprecedented amount of economic and social control with the central authorities.

The Second World War intensified these processes. Occupation by or association with Nazi Germany and fascist Italy increased and sanitized the build-up of central power just as it further restricted political and other freedoms. During these years what little remained of the political left was destroyed. When the war ended, in all states except Greece the previously dominant political right was then liquidated. Practically all that remained as an organized political force were those groups which had fought in the anti-fascist resistance or which were imported in the baggage train of the liberating Red Army. The latter consisted almost entirely of communists, the former were heavily under their influence.

The massive destruction brought about by the war itself shattered economies which had only just begun to recover from the depression. What was needed, it was generally believed after the fighting was over, was an energetic, coordinated force to plan and carry out massive programmes of economic and social renewal. Furthermore, few people in 1944–5 believed that capitalism had any future. Its record was one of failure. It had produced the great depression which in turn had fostered aggressive right-wing nationalism and war. The only state, it seemed, which had weathered the economic hurricane was the Soviet Union. No one could envisage the successful consumer capitalism which emerged in the west in the 1950s and 1960s and the economic future seemed to lie with socialism.

So too did the political future. The right had been discredited by its association with aggressive fascism, liberalism by its appeasement of it. The path was open for the left. Within it, the communists, with their strong anti-fascist credentials bolstered by the sacrifices of the Soviet Union and the Red Army, and with their passionate energy, their ferocious internal discipline and their impregnable determination, were the dominant force. They had another advantage which was much enhanced by the war. The fighting between 1941 and 1945, in the Balkans as elsewhere, had involved a brutality unequalled perhaps since the Thirty Years War of the seventeenth century. The resort to force for political means and the willingness to assume that the ends justified the means had become the norm rather than the exception.

The authoritarianism of the 1930s and the brutality of the Second World War did much to shape the destiny of the Balkans.

Even before the German attack on Poland in September 1939 one Balkan state, Albania, had fallen to the Axis when Italian troops invaded the country on Good Friday 1939. Fighting resumed in the Balkans in October 1940 when Italian troops operating from occupied Albania attacked Greece. They were soon driven back, but in April 1941 the German army entered Yugoslavia and after conquering that country moved into Greece. Yugoslavia ceased to exist; a rump Serbia was set up under total German domination; a supposedly independent Croatian state, which included Bosnia, was established; and the remainder of the former Yugoslavia was partitioned between Italy, Germany and Bulgaria. Greece was occupied by the same three powers, although the Greek state continued to exist in nominal form. In Albania, Greece and Yugoslavia powerful resistance forces emerged during the war though in all these countries there was fierce rivalry and often open warfare between the different resistance groups. The other two Balkan states, Romania and Bulgaria, both sided with the Axis and both received territorial compensation for doing so, Romania east of the Dniestr and Bulgaria in Macedonia and Thrace. The nature of the war in the Balkans was transformed first by the surrender of Italy in September 1943 and then by the rapid advance of the Red Army which entered Romania in April 1944. By the summer of that year it was obvious that Germany was destined for defeat and that it would soon be forced out of the Balkans. The struggle for the succession began long before the Wehrmacht had withdrawn, but the D Day landings in northern France on 6 June dashed the hopes of the anti-communists that western forces might be landed in the Balkans and thereby block the advance of the Red Army into the peninsula.

In the ensuing half decade in all Balkan states, with the exception of Greece, it was the communists who emerged victorious from that struggle. At the same time all communist states, with the exception of Yugoslavia, fell under Soviet domination. Although the speed of the communist takeover varied there were common features in each state, some of them also being found in Greece.

The first was the decisive influence of the great powers and the evolving confrontation between the western allies and the Soviet Union. In Moscow in October 1944 Winston Churchill, desperate to find ground on which he and Stalin could compromise before tackling the critical question of Poland, had put forward his famous, or infamous, percentages agreement. It offered Stalin a majority influence in Romania and Bulgaria and an equal share in Yugoslavia and Hungary; in return he was to acquiesce in western preponderance in Greece. At the Yalta conference in February 1945 Britain, the Soviet Union and the United States agreed that in liberated territories there were to be free and fair elections in which all non-fascist parties could take part. At Potsdam in July and August of the same year Britain and the United States made it clear that they would not recognize any government which, they believed, had not come to office by free and fair elections. After the Potsdam conference the primary forum for the powers' discussions was the periodic foreign ministers' conferences, with those in London in September-October 1945 and in Moscow in December of the same year being of particular significance. In the two former enemy states, Bulgaria and Romania, the victorious powers established Allied Control Commissions to supervise the administration until the signature of a peace treaty.

In all states the communist parties took inspiration and encouragement, if not always material assistance from the Soviet Union, though the Red Army, which had so influential a role in central Europe, was of major significance only in Romania and Bulgaria. The communists' opponents in turn looked westwards for political succour but none, except those in Greece, found it.

The Allied Control Commissions were disbanded after the signature of peace treaties with Romania and Bulgaria in February 1947. By that time the rifts between the Soviets and the west were deepening rapidly, the Truman Doctrine being expounded in the following month to save Greece, it was believed, from communism and Soviet domination. In September 1947 the ruling communist parties, minus that of Albania but plus those of France and Italy, met at Szklarska Poręba in Poland to create The Communist Information Bureau, or Cominform, whose task was to sharpen communist policies in the struggles to achieve power and to create a socialist system. Cominform was also intended to increase Soviet control over the junior parties, a fact which became apparent when the Soviet Union and Yugoslavia parted company in 1948. With the formation of NATO in the following year the divisions which characterized the era of the cold war had been drawn.

If Greece had been threatened by communism then that threat came more from within than from without. The deepening rift between left and right in the country led finally to a civil war which raged from 1947 to 1949 but throughout the period after October 1944 Stalin kept to the percentages agreement.

Stalin's determination not to provoke the west over Greece was a contributory factor in the split between the USSR and Yugoslavia in 1948. That split was to have profound repercussions in the internal politics of all communist states; it was, after the separation of Greece from the rest of the Balkan states, the first example of the process of tessellation which, by the end of the 1960s was to mean that each Balkan state had an individual foreign policy alignment.

Before the Soviet-Yugoslav split, however, the Balkan states other than Greece seemed destined to become communist satrapies of the Soviets. The part played by the indigenous party in a state's evolution towards communist rule depended largely on that state's recent past. In the countries where a strong resistance movement had developed, Albania, Yugoslavia and Greece, the local communist parties were strong while in Bulgaria the communists could cash in on a long history of activity and organization even if their resistance efforts during the war could not be compared with those of communists in occupied countries. In Romania the local communist party had almost no local support or standing.

In the political struggle the communists operated mainly through National or Popular Fronts, loose coalitions of leftist, anti-fascist forces. The struggle was ruthless. In a frenetic and savage assault the fronts eliminated right-wing or even centrist opposition immediately after the war. On the other hand, the destruction of leftist forces, many of them within the coalition, was piecemeal, gradual and studiously crafted. This slicing off of one opponent group after another was, in a phrase later made famous by the Hungarian communist leader, Mátyás Rákosi, 'salami tactics'. But it was not just political parties and groupings which were attacked.

The communists persecuted and neutralized all individuals and organizations with connections to the west, and they undermined all public institutions and social groups which might serve as a basis for opposition. Of the former the most important was the Catholic Church. All communist parties crossed swords with the Church, though the ferocity of the struggle varied considerably. The conflict with the Church meant disputes over education and the property rights of religious institutions, and also disagreement on the rights of organizations such as the Boy Scouts and Girl Guides. As the communist drive for total authority intensified, suspicion of those with external, non-Soviet connections grew almost to the point of paranoia; minor religious sects and even hapless esperantists, seldom seen as a threat to the established order, were persecuted with demonic fury. Inevitably in such an atmosphere the links to western culture became attenuated. Western films, plays and books were much rarer than their Soviet equivalents, and links between Balkan communist and western scientific and academic institutions withered on their already slender vines. The corollary of breaking ties with the west was to strengthen those with Moscow. Soviet Friendship Societies became powerful social institutions and, more especially after the full assumption of communist political control, the Soviet model was copied in the army, police, education, in the organization of the trade unions and in almost all aspects of social life.

The weakening and eventual destruction of public institutions and social groups which were deemed hostile was a long and complex process in which subtlety as well as brutality played its part. At the top of the social and political system of the pre-war Balkan states had been the monarchs. They posed few problems for the communists. Those of Albania, Greece and Yugoslavia had obligingly absented themselves, and their return was easily prevented; even the Greek monarch had to wait almost two years before his sponsors felt it was safe enough to allow him back. In Bulgaria the reigning monarch was a minor of nine years and could therefore be undermined by attacking the regency rather than the king. Only in Romania did the monarch present a serious obstacle to communist designs.

Closely associated with the monarchy was the army. In the states defeated by the Axis the old armies had been largely discredited and disbanded; when reformed they could be shaped very much after the image of the locally dominant great power. In the two Balkan states which had aligned with the Germans and Italians, Romania and Bulgaria, the military presented a greater problem. It was largely but not entirely overcome by sending the standing army into battle against the Germans in the final stages of the war.

Of great importance in the post-war political configuration of forces were the local police forces. In all states where the communists took power the pre-existing police forces were entirely disbanded and new ones, usually known as people's militias, formed, while in Greece the British enlisted auxiliary police elements in the struggle against the local communists. In addition to people's militias there were people's courts in which swift and retributory justice was meted out to political opponents, real or suspected. The ability of the anti-communist press to comment on such tactics was diminished by a variety of methods such as the control of newsprint, the refusal of communist-dominated print unions to set the type of anti-communist articles, and the outright intimidation of everyone involved in such newspapers from owners and editors to the boys who sold the papers on the street.

Of the communists' social rivals the landed aristocracy was easily neutralized as it had had little influence in Balkan political life; where it had existed its power had been greatly reduced by land redistribution in the inter-war period. Its remaining economic and social powers were dissolved by further land reforms which also affected the Orthodox and Catholic Churches whose lands had frequently supported the Churchs' charitable institutions.

The middle classes were considerably weaker than their western or central European equivalents. In much of the Balkans, as in central and Eastern Europe, the urban bourgeoisie and state employees were frequently of a different ethnic group to the surrounding peasantry and, even if the predominance of Jews and Germans in the Balkan urban communities was not as pronounced as in those of central Europe, the slaughter of the former in the war and the flight of the latter after it inevitably weakened the established bourgeois elements. These elements also suffered from other pressures. Living space was limited because of housing shortages caused by wartime damage, but whatever the reason for these limitations middle-class life was unalterably changed when it became impossible to house treasured collections of books or paintings, or to retain the servants upon whom so much of previous life had depended. A blow at least equally as severe was delivered by swingeing taxation of middle-class wealth. Accumulated wealth, especially in liquid assets, was hard hit by post-war inflation, a phenomenon which also weakened educational and charitable institutions which relied upon investment income; many a private school, hospital or nursing home collapsed for this reason long before the communists had the opportunity to destroy it. If any savings did manage to survive inflation they were defenceless against taxation and even more so against government policies over banking and currency; the introduction of a new currency, often made necessary by inflation, was almost always accompanied by restrictions on savings and the exchange rates for new and old currencies were invariably tilted against those who had sizeable or even moderate bank accounts.

The intelligentsia, despite its generally left-leaning characteristics, was as much a victim of these policies as the commercial or industrial bourgeoisie. For the latter there were additional burdens. The Soviets had, with general allied approval, made it known that they would seize as booty any German property or any property used to further the German war effort. As the Germans had in general conscripted all industry in occupied or allied territories this meant that the Soviets believed they had the right to confiscate virtually all local industry. And where industrial or commercial property did remain in corporate or private hands the freedom to use it was rapidly diminished. Again fiscal policies were important in restricting private enterprise, but so too was state direction of the economy, frequently expressed in the form of state plans, initially usually for one or two years then, later, in the classic Stalinist five-year plan. State direction of the economy was by no means a new phenomenon and it was one which in the face of the massive destruction and dislocation of the war seemed to have a sound economic rationale. It was also, however, grist to the communist mill and eventually made it much easier to extend not only state control but also state ownership.

At the end of the Second World War the Balkan lands were still peasant societies. And in most it was the small independent proprietor who predominated. Here the communists had to tread warily. In most areas the peasant was fiercely independent, devoted to his small plot and suspicious of a political ideology which denigrated his class and vilified his religion. Furthermore, in many states the peasant had behind him the strength of well-established if not always united peasantist political parties which were rigorously opposed to any notions of collectivization on the Soviet pattern. Communist tactics were subtle. Left-wing groups within the peasant parties were cultivated; frequently they were lured into coalition and then suborned from within. Collectivization was seldom mentioned and never featured as a policy goal of the communists; quite the contrary, in some areas early schemes for land redistribution bolstered the small proprietor and in many cases communists took an active part, with peasantists and others, in drawing up and implementing the redistribution schemes; the committees which carried out this complicated task showed that the communists were well-intentioned reformers and were willing to cooperate with their former political adversaries. Land redistribution made social as well as political sense. An immediate consequence of collectivization was the displacement of surplus peasant population but with cities, infrastructures and agriculture damaged by the war the Balkans could not yet absorb any displaced populations. Furthermore, there was a desperate need for food and the quickest way to ensure agriculture began to function again was to keep the land in the hands of those who were then using it; immediate millenarian experiments in social reconstruction were the last thing devastated and starving Europe could afford.

In some areas the communists enjoyed the bonus of having considerable areas of land to distribute. As in Czechoslovakia, the Soviet zone of Germany and western Poland, there were parts of the Balkans where ethnic redistributions released land for resettlement. This was the case in the Yugoslav regions of Istria, Dalmatia, Slovenia and Vojvodina in particular, where the local Italian or German population had fled or been expelled, and it was also seen in northern Transylvania where, after Hungary repossessed the area in 1940, the former landlords had been reinstated. As in central Europe the communists did all they could to ensure that the patronage which this redistribution process created was in their hands.

The remaining social group, the industrial working class, offered no threat to the communists. The Balkan working class was small. It had on occasions flexed its muscles in strikes but they had generally been of short duration. The trade unions had little power and were as focused on rural problems as on those of the urban centres. In political terms few socialist movements had real strength; they tended to be intelligentsia-dominated; in some cases they had never managed the synthesis between European Marxism and Russian-Slav populism; and in all too many instances they were critically weakened by disunity. And perhaps the communists' greatest asset with regard to the working class and the socialist movement was that in the general pro-left climate of the immediate post-war years the intelligentsia and the grass-roots socialist activists were prepared to give the communist party the benefit of their manifold doubts.

In some instances the communists did not need such indulgence. In countries where cities and towns had to be rebuilt, infrastructures repaired, and land cleared of the detritus of war – including bodies, wrecked vehicles and mines – energy and discipline were of the essence and those who displayed them earned and deserved considerable credit. In the many cases where the communists were frequently the best organized, the best disciplined and the most energetic of local political forces it was they who earned most credit in this reconstruction process.

The credit so earned was one reason for the rapid growth in communist party membership in the post-war years. Another was simple careerism. Balkan populations needed few lessons in the relationship between party allegiance and social power; clientalism had flourished in the region since at least the final quarter of the nineteenth century. In all states, Greece included, political reliability was essential for social advancement and personal security.

By the end of the 1940s the reconstruction of the political system had been completed. The elimination or emasculation of non-communist left-wing forces had been symbolized in most cases in the fusion of those forces with the communists. The resulting organization was not always known as a communist party but it was always under the domination of the communists and openly acknowledged Marxism-Leninism as the ruling ideology. Recognition of this came with the clauses allowing the ruling party, whatever its name, a leading role in the state and society, this being included in the Soviet-style constitutions adopted in all communist states at the end of the takeover process.

Having secured itself in power the party would press ahead with imposing social revolution from above.

Chapter 2

YUGOSLAVIA, 1944–1948

The Yugoslav state had been created after the First World War. Its core, Serbia, was a victor state in that war; it had emerged as an independent political entity after a revolt against Ottoman rule in 1804, though full recognition of that independence had not been granted by the international community until the treaty of Berlin in 1878. Yugoslavia's other main component areas were Croatia, Bosnia-Hercegovina, Kosovo, Macedonia, Montenegro, Slovenia and Vojvodina. They had experienced widely differing forms of social and political evolution and this, together with significant ethnic and religious differences, made cohesion within the new unit after the First World War difficult. The process was hindered by a widespread feeling outside Serbia that the new state was little more than an extended Serbia, as its dynasty was Serbian and Serbs dominated the critical institutions of the state, the administration and above all the army. Resentment at what was perceived as Serbian domination was most strongly felt and articulated in Croatia and it was to a large degree the Serbian-Croatian divide which crippled parliamentary democracy in the 1920s.

In 1929 a royal *coup d'état* attempted to create a system in which regional and particularist allegiances would be replaced by a new 'Yugoslav' consciousness. It did not work. By the mid-1930s, the royal architect of the new edifice having been assassinated in 1934, the social and economic problems created by the depression and the diplomatic difficulties posed by the rise of Nazi Germany preoccupied Yugoslavia's rulers. In the atmosphere of increasing international tension an 'agreement', or *sporazum*, was finally reached between the central government and the Croats under which the latter were to enjoy a considerable degree of home rule. When, in March 1941, the government agreed to join the tripartite pact of Germany, Italy and Japan, a popular military coup in Belgrade reversed the decision. The popularity of the coup in Serbia derived not only from its foreign-policy implications; many Serbs saw it as a step towards the dissolution of the *sporazum*.

Germany attacked Yugoslavia after the coup and after the new government had shown signs of friendship towards the Soviet Union. The Yugoslav army had no chance against the mechanized forces of Nazi Germany the more so because in some parts of the country, above all in Croatia, there was little disposition to fight for the old Yugoslavia. After the conquest, Yugoslavia was partitioned. A rump Serbia remained under the rule of a German general who appointed the Serb General Milan Nedić president of a Serbian administration, Kosovo was incorporated into Italian-occupied Albania, Montenegro was given to Italy, Hungary took the Baranja and Bačka regions of north-western Serbia, Macedonia was divided between Bulgaria and Italy-Albania, Slovenia was partitioned between Germany and Italy, and Croatia became a nominally independent state, the Independent State of Croatia (NDH) which also incorporated Bosnia and Hercegovina. The government of Croatia was in the hands of extreme-rightist elements led by Ante Pavelić.

Resistance to the German occupation began almost immediately in Serbia under the direction of a royalist general, Draža Mihailović. After the German invasion of the Soviet Union on 22 June 1941 communist forces also organized resistance groups. Before long the fighting between the two main resistance forces was as fierce as that against the occupiers and their local accomplices.

THE SECOND WORLD WAR AND FOUNDATION OF COMMUNIST POWER

Communist power was rapidly entrenched in Yugoslavia after the Second World War. This was primarily due to the fact that during the war the communist-dominated partisan resistance army had emerged victorious in the savage war against Mihailović's chetniks.

The partisans had benefited from the fact that they were the main resistance force in areas under Italian occupation and therefore when the Italian army capitulated in September 1943 much of its weaponry was seized by the partisans. They benefited even more from the fact that at the end of that year the allies became convinced that more Germans were being killed by the partisans than by the chetniks and as a result all allied aid was switched from the latter to the former. The chetniks were victims of a strategy, recommended by allied commanders to resistance movements in Poland, France and elsewhere, of keeping their powder dry for use in the uprising to be staged when the liberating allied armies approached the borders. Also the partisans were prepared to tolerate the hideous reprisals resistance involved; the reprisals, they calculated, would increase popular antipathy to the occupiers and quislings.

The partisans had other advantages. Shocked by the savagery with which the NDH had persecuted Serbs on its territory, the partisans insisted that their movement was 'Yugoslav' and that any post-war political settlement had to grant equality of status to and guarantee the safety of all the ethnic groups of Yugoslavia. At the same time the partisans promised social and political reform in the post-war state. In the meantime they emphasized the lack of ethnic identity in their movement by calling the partisan army the 'Peoples'

Liberation Army'* and in areas under their control they attempted to prove their ability to govern by taking charge of local government.

The partisans also benefited from efficient organization. Their political wing, the Peoples' Liberation Front (PLF) again emphasized unity, bringing together a number of anti-fascist parties many of whom were content to hand real authority to the communists whose discipline and experience in clandestine activity were unparalleled. Cooperation with the communists was made easier by the fact that Stalin, fearing the reaction of the west, ordered the Yugoslav comrades to play down their long-term socialist objectives and to concentrate on the struggle against the fascists. The boss of the Yugoslav Communist Party and partisan leader, Josip Broz, or 'Tito', a former Comintern activist of mixed Slovene and Croat origin, obeyed his orders, if not always with a good grace.

The partisans' organization operated at a variety of levels. At the local level 'peoples' councils' in liberated areas attempted to return life to as great a degree of normality as conditions allowed, organizing education, levying taxes, setting up postal services, restoring or improving transport facilities, encouraging improvements in agriculture and even attempting at one point to stage a 'partisan Olympic games'. They also burned local police records. In the peoples' councils many peasants first learned to have a grudging trust in the communists. Liberation Councils at a regional level also appeared. Their emergence was spasmodic and although in the post-war state there was one for each of the constituent republics their configuration during the war did not always coincide with the internal boundaries to be drawn up in post-war Yugoslavia. In November 1942 the communists organized the first meeting of the Anti-Fascist Council for the National Liberation of Yugoslavia (AVNOJ) at Bihać, western Bosnia. A second AVNOJ meeting was convened in Jajce in southern Bosnia a year later. It was larger than the Bihać meeting because delegates from Slovenia and Macedonia were included, and it also went much further in staking a political claim on the post-war state; it now claimed it was a legislature representing all regions of Yugoslavia and a variety of anti-fascist political parties. The Jajce meeting also invested executive power in a new all-Yugoslav Peoples' Liberation Council (PLC). It further enacted that post-war Yugoslavia would be a federation and that the king would not be allowed to return until after a referendum had been held on the future of the monarchy. AVNOJ had in effect elevated itself into a provisional government.

---

* The word 'Peoples'' is somewhat ambiguous. Most Slavonic languages cannot distinguish between the English nouns 'nation' and 'people', or their respective adjectives; the name of the partisan army, or any other 'national' organization could equally well be translated as 'popular', 'people's' or 'peoples''. The official translation in Yugoslavia was 'peoples'' and this I have used in most cases, the exceptions being when using the technical term *narodi* and for the Chamber of Nationalities, the National Bank, the Anti-Fascist Council for the National Liberation of Yugoslavia and the Yugoslav National Army, the latter two because they have become common usage in the west.

One of the first acts of that 'government' was to attempt to boost its support in Croatia by laying claim to the Slovene littoral and to Istria, areas contested between Yugoslavia and Italy throughout the inter-war years.

By the summer of 1944 the partisans were clearly the dominant force in Bosnia, Hercegovina, Montenegro and Slovenia. In Croatia the strength of the NDH was declining and in areas no longer under its control the partisans were soon established as the most powerful group. The position in Macedonia was unclear because of Bulgarian interests and presence in the area. In Kosovo support for the partisans was almost non-existent; here the majority Albanian population preferred to retain the wartime frontier which had included them in the Albanian state. In Serbia, especially in the rural areas, the conservative, royalist and nationalist chetniks remained predominant.

The partisans represented a new authority which would inevitably clash with the king and the government in exile, but Tito and his associates knew that whatever their internal strengths their contest with the old order could not be resolved by internal forces alone. Neither Stalin nor the western allies were yet prepared to see a Yugoslavia totally under partisan and communist domination. Tito therefore announced he was ready to cooperate with the former regime, and when a new government in exile was formed in July 1944 under Ivan Šubašić it included two nominees of Tito. The new cabinet not only appeared to bridge the gap between the old Yugoslavia and the new but also to reintegrate the Croats into Yugoslavia in that Šubašić, a Croat, had a sound Yugoslav pedigree having deserted from the Habsburg army during the First World War and then served with the Serbian forces where he was awarded the highest decoration for bravery, after which he had become a confidant of the king and his advisor on Croat affairs.

COMMUNIST POWER ENTRENCHED: OCTOBER 1944 TO NOVEMBER 1945

The compromise with the government in exile left the partisans free to concentrate on military activities and in October 1944 Tito's élite First Proletarian Brigade helped the Red Army liberate Belgrade. Although Yugoslavia was not to be completely freed from Axis troops until the very end of the Second World War in Europe the liberation of Belgrade returned to the forefront of national discussion the question of the relationship between the PLC and the government in exile. It also threw into sharper focus the relations between the partisans and other political groups in Yugoslavia. From the liberation of Belgrade until the summer of 1945 Yugoslav affairs were characterized by apparent compromise in the former issue, and an elemental, savage violence in the latter.

The authority of the PLC in Belgrade was never seriously threatened by either the government in exile in London or the king; neither any longer had an effective nationwide power base and both were widely regarded as representatives of the old machinery of state which had proved incapable of defending the country in 1941. Nevertheless, to preserve the appearance of unity and to placate the great powers Tito had concluded an agreement with Šubašić in November. It stated that the king would not return to Yugoslavia until after a referendum on the future of the monarchy and that until then the official head of state would be a three-man regency. The three regents appointed were all nominees of Tito; one was a Croat, one a Serb and one a Slovene, but not one of them was a member of the Communist Party. Meanwhile, the king did little to further his own cause. In January 1945 he questioned both Tito's right to nominate the regents and the legislative powers still enjoyed by the AVNOJ assembly; in this the king was constitutionally correct but politically unwise. He compounded his folly by dismissing Šubašić as head of the government in exile and refusing to allow any member of that government to leave London for Belgrade. Tito welcomed the king's ineffectual interventions which further diminished the monarch's prestige and influence both in London and in Yugoslavia. At Yalta in February the three allies confirmed their support for the Tito-Šubašić agreement, though it was suggested that the AVNOJ assembly should be enlarged and given a broader political base. In March the regency took office, the government in exile in London surrendering its authority to the regents, and Tito his to ANVOJ. A new, 28-member cabinet was formed, all but five of whom were partisans. The five included Šubašić and another prominent non-communist, Milan Grol, the leader of the Democratic Party whose members were overwhelmingly Serbian but whose aspirations were Yugoslav.

If the partisans had little difficulty in neutralizing any threat from the government in exile and the king, the communists were almost equally unthreatened by rival parties within Yugoslavia. Serbia, and especially its rural areas, remained mostly loyal to the king but there was no strong party within Serbia to further the royal cause and its chief protagonist, Draža Mihailović, was a hunted man whom communist propaganda had condemned as a collaborator. The major potential political challenge to the communists from within Yugoslavia came from the Croatian Peasant Party (CPP). The CPP which had dominated the Croatian political scene in the inter-war years had kept its head down during the war, refusing to have anything to do with the NDH apparatus and taking little part in the resistance. In so doing it retained the support of the majority of the Croatian peasantry and in the final stages of the war felt strong enough to decline communist approaches for cooperation; Tito and other communist leaders admitted that the CPP leader, Vladko Maček, was the only man in Yugoslavia they feared. They were lucky. During the war Maček had been summoned by the NDH leader, Ante Pavelić, who proposed a deal which would have placed both of them under allied protection. Maček had refused the offer but knew that its having been made was enough for the communists to condemn him; in May 1945 he escaped from Croatia, driving across Germany to deliver himself to the allies at Rheims. The leadership of the historic CPP passed to Šubašić who was already an ailing man who was not popular within his own party. The CPP remained locally popular but effectively leaderless.

The contest between the communists and other potential opponents was not settled so peacefully. Party political activity was not impossible in Yugoslavia between October 1944 and the summer of 1945 but, to say the least, it was not encouraged. Legislation passed by AVNOJ in 1944 had stated that pre-war parties could legalize themselves either by declaring that they would join the PLF or by applying to the relevant authorities for permission to engage in political activities. The partisan leadership, however, made no secret of the fact that such activity was not welcome, at least while there was the overriding need for a combined, non-party, national effort to smash the Hitlerites.

Behind the scenes the communists were prepared to take extreme measures against opponents past, present and future, real and potential. In this they were helped by their international standing. Because the Tehran conference in November 1943 had recognized it as an allied force Yugoslavia was not saddled with an Allied Control Commission to supervise its administration. Nor were there any allied troops in occupation, the Red Army moving northwards and westwards in its relentless, slogging pursuit of the Germans. The new rulers of Yugoslavia were therefore left a free hand. They used it. Even during the war they had fought not only against the occupiers and local fascists but also against rival resistance groups, and after the war the campaign against them continued. In Croatia and Slovenia members of the military, together with the quasi-military and police units formed during the war, had generally gone into hiding or fled westwards into the arms of the advancing British armies. Those who remained behind were flushed out and subjected to summary justice; those who fled were returned by the British usually to meet a similar fate, the leading Yugoslav communist Milovan Djilas estimating that 50,000 such returnees died.[1]

A similar number of lives were lost in Kosovo where the local Albanians' determination not to be returned to Yugoslav rule was sharpened by the fear that this would mean the conscription of local men to fight the Germans in northern Yugoslavia and beyond. The communists were under no illusion as to the problems facing them in Kosovo; in December 1944 General Tempo (Svetozar-Vukmanović) told Colonel Deakin, the senior British Liaison Officer with the partisans, that the Albanians were the one ethnic group which would probably not be brought into the new Yugoslavia except by force, and that the Bulgarians might be used to do this so as to shift the blame from the Yugoslav partisans.[2] Before this could be done Kosovo had dissolved into rebellion and in February 1945 martial law and military administration were imposed. Although the political aims of the rebels were not clearly spelled out fighting continued with much savagery for six months.

In addition to liquidating would-be refugees in the north and the insurgents of Kosovo the communists also launched a more sustained and wide-reaching persecution through the peoples' courts which had been established in all areas under partisan control and were then extended to the entire country after October 1944. These courts tried hundreds of alleged collaborators. As elsewhere in Europe, collaboration was an elastic term; it included many low-grade civil servants, traders, teachers or priests and could be stretched to catch those who had merely tried to live normally in the abnormal conditions of the occupation. They were seldom afforded the services of a defence lawyer which in any case made little difference for few were acquitted and most were given long sentences in labour camps or even executed.

The new rulers were able to act with such dispatch against their internal enemies because an intricate and pervasive police system had been built up during the war. After liberation it was organized on a Yugoslav-wide scale in The Department for the Protection of the People, OZNa. OZNa was directly responsible to the ministry of national defence and neither the central nor the republican* governments had any control over it. That privilege resided with Aleksandar Ranković, a Serb who was one of the three or four closest associates of Tito.

The communists also used the army to entrench their power. They had always controlled the Peoples' Liberation Army (PLA) and after the war they exploited this position with considerable skill. Just before the end of hostilities in Europe they declared mass mobilization. The ostensible reason for this was the prosecution of the war against German fascism but there were other equally compelling though unadmitted causes, not least the need to contain separatism in Kosovo or anywhere else where it might raise its head. The creation of a large army would increase both Yugoslavia's prestige abroad and the country's ability to defend – or extend – its borders. Extensive mobilization would also ease pressures on domestic food and housing resources. More importantly, putting large numbers of young people into the partisan-controlled military would provide the opportunity to indoctrinate them in the new ideology. Furthermore, the civilian authorities were inexperienced and had demobilization taken place many returning soldiers would not have accepted unquestioningly these new authorities.

It was also in this first period of post-war Yugoslav development that the social transformation of the country began. Tito declared in a radio broadcast in March 1945 that the destruction caused by the war made state intervention in and planning of the economy essential. This was an idea common throughout Europe, east and west, but in the east the communist-dominated regimes

---

* From January 1946 Yugoslavia was divided into six republics: Bosnia and Hercegovina, Croatia, Macedonia, Montenegro, Serbia and Slovenia. Serbia consisted of Serbia itself together with Vojvodina and Kosovo; the latter had certain rights and were usually referred to as 'provinces'. For the sake of convenience the words 'republic' and 'province' will be used throughout to describe the individual territories which made up Yugoslavia for the majority of the period from the end of the Second World War to the wars of Yugoslav succession in the 1990s.

adopted a policy seldom used in the west and the Yugoslav communists were among the first to use it. This was to turn over to public ownership all property of the enemy. On 21 November 1944 a decree expropriating the property of the German state, of war criminals and of obvious collaborators, brought into state ownership some 55 per cent of Yugoslav industry, including the former British lead and zinc mines in Trepča in Kosovo and the Czechoslovak Bata leather works. The decree created the core of the postwar nationalized economy of Yugoslavia. The decree on industry also further weakened the haute bourgeoisie. When a special tax on war profits was introduced in March 1945 the petite bourgeoisie was equally affected; war profits were defined as including all income made from selling goods to the occupiers and even petty-shopkeepers or small farmers could be caught in this trap. At the same time general taxes on small businesses were increased tenfold, while new price controls frequently meant companies had to sell at prices which would not cover production costs and therefore declared themselves bankrupt whereupon they were subsumed into the public sector.

The months between October 1944 and August 1945 also saw major changes in the countryside. Large tracts of land changed hands in areas where population movements took place. In Istria and Dalmatia Italians left or were driven out and were replaced by Slovenes and Croats while many Croats moved from western Hercegovina as did equal numbers of Serbs from around Knin; both groups were resettled in eastern Slavonia, Baranja and Vojvodina. Here large tracts of land had become available because its previous German owners had fled, been killed or had been conscripted for unpaid labour. Vojvodina then became an area for a large-scale social and ethnic experiment. The communists were anxious to encourage all groups to move in to create a new ethnic mosaic which would become a model for and encourage the development of a Yugoslav national consciousness. It did not work. In the period up to 1948 80 per cent of the applicants were ethnic Serbs, many of them fleeing or being excluded from other parts of Yugoslavia, especially Croatia, Macedonia and Kosovo.

Major land reform was enacted in August 1945. The law was based on the principle that the land belonged to those who cultivated it. The law expropriated: large holdings over 45 hectares (ha), or 25–35 ha of best agricultural land if worked by tenants; land held by banks and enterprises, except that intended for industrial, building, scientific, cultural and other socially useful purposes; land held by churches, monasteries, church institutions and charitable foundations; holdings over 3–5 ha worked by hired labour; and any land which became ownerless during the war or for which there was no legal succession. No compensation was to be paid while tractors and farm machinery were to be given to the Machine Tractor Stations (MTSs) established the previous month. The amount of land left in private holdings was to vary according to its quality but was generally not to be less than 20 ha or more than 35 ha per unit, and it was to be worked by one family. Churches and monasteries were to be left with 10 ha, except churches of major importance or historic worth which would be allowed 30 ha of arable land and 30 ha of woodland, the state determining which churches were of historic worth. Confiscated land was not to be nationalized but passed to the peoples' land fund and then redistributed to the benefit of the landless peasants and dwarf holders. In fact only just over half the redistributed land (51 per cent), went to individual peasant farmers; 316,415 families received land of whom 136,454 (43.13 per cent) were landless or were colonists, primarily though not exclusively in Vojvodina. The remainder of the land was put aside for state farms, MTSs, breeding, seed and seedling stations, cooperatives and the new state farms introduced by another law in the summer of 1945.

In the year following the liberation of Belgrade the partisans had sidelined the king, neutralized or liquidated most of their internal political opponents, and begun a social transformation which was intended to destroy private ownership and banish foreign capital. It was time to consolidate and institutionalize these changes.

COMMUNIST POWER LEGITIMIZED: THE NOVEMBER 1945 ELECTIONS AND THE JANUARY 1946 CONSTITUTION

The industry law had been passed and the agrarian reform bill drafted by an explicitly provisional assembly which was virtually unchanged since AVNOJ's Jajce meeting in November 1943, despite the fact that the Yalta Declaration of February 1945 had said that AVNOJ should be expanded. In August 1945 the communists agreed to make concessions, though it took long and intense debate before the fine print was agreed. AVNOJ was expanded by over a hundred to make it more representative, some of the 'new' deputies having been members of the pre-war parliament. The enlarged assembly, which was still under effective communist control, was known as the peoples' provisional parliament. At the same time the PLF recognized that its function had changed by altering its title to Peoples' Front (PF).

On 11 August the peoples' provisional parliament passed an electoral law. It promised that elections for a constituent assembly would be held on 11 November. The law enfranchised all Yugoslav citizens over eighteen years of age and, regardless of age, all past and present members of the PLA and partisan units. It excluded from the vote all members of military formations which had fought against Yugoslavia, all members of German and Italian fascist organizations, all active officials and prominent members of former Yugoslav fascist organizations, and all alleged military and economic collaborators. The electoral law also provided that no decisions of AVNOJ could be changed by the constituent assembly.

The announcement of the elections did produce some easing of political controls by the PF. Censorship was relaxed somewhat and a number of political detainees were released. Some criticism of government policy was expressed from within the PF, particularly by the Agrarian Union whose leader, Dragoljub Jovanović, drew attention to the fact that every public prosecutor was a member of the communist party, a condition which, he said, was the incarnation of one-party dictatorship. He also embarrassed the communists by reminding them of the legitimacy in the Leninist canon of an alliance between peasant and worker. But any party which joined the PF agreed upon doing so that it would always support the government in parliament which meant that the communists had to take seriously only those parties which remained outside the PF. The main ones were Grol's Democratic Party and a faction of the CPP led by Marija Radić, the widow of the party's founder, Stjepan. Grol's Democrats were strong in Serbia, where the communists were weak; they argued for close relations with other Balkan states, especially Bulgaria, and reflected Serbian, and especially Belgrade bourgeois opinion in that while they were prepared to recognize Croatia, Slovenia and perhaps Bosnia-Hercegovina as full republics equal with Serbia, they were not prepared to extend that recognition to either Montenegro or Macedonia.

The party contest was an unequal one. The communists were greatly strengthened by the fact that they were the only national, Yugoslav party. They were also considerably helped by divisions within the other parties, and where these did not exist the communists created them. If a party were split between factions within and outside the PF those without would be branded as enemies of the people, on the ground that the PF represented the people. In the long term parties outside the PF would be destroyed, after which their cognates within the PF would wither and eventually cease to exist. Where political activity continued, especially in the case of Grol and Marija Radić, the anti-communists would be subject to constant vilification through the official media, the most frequent accusation being that of collaboration. Opposition newspapers were heavily censored; their newsprint allowances were restricted and their distribution network subjected to disruption; *Demokratija*, a popular newspaper in Belgrade, appeared only seven times before 'outraged' print workers refused to set the type. The PF, in addition to intimidating the opposition press, had a monopoly over the radio which it used to denounce critics of the government in terms usually used for war criminals and traitors.

The intimidation of opposition newspapers was only one way in which the election campaign of 1945 was influenced by the communists. Grol had already resigned from the government in August because it refused to enact laws guaranteeing civil rights before the electoral law was passed and the election campaign launched. Grol's was a serious point because throughout the election campaign the oppositionists, and even neutrals, complained that OZNa was intimidating everyone; Grol further insisted that if free elections were to take place OZNa had to be replaced by ordinary civilian police and that the army had to be demobilized.

The opposition also faced technical difficulties. All potential candidates had to find fifty persons to nominate them. This had been the case before the war but now the regulations required that the fifty sponsors must appear in person before the local election committees where they were likely to be closely questioned, with no doubt at least one OZNa agent among the questioners. Very small parties were effectively debarred from the electoral contest by regulations demanding that all parties wishing to present a national list must have candidates in at least half the constituencies. There were also complaints that accusations of collaboration were used to disenfranchise known opponents, though in comparison with some other countries this weapon seems to have been sparingly used in Yugoslavia where no more than 3.5 per cent of the electorate were excluded in any of the republics. Another complaint by non-PF parties was that the time granted for registration of candidates, ten days, was too limited. But the most fundamental grievance was that every stage of the electoral process, from the registration of candidates to the counting of votes, was in the hands of the local committees of the PF.

The mounting frustrations of the campaign persuaded the main opposition parties to boycott the elections. The results of the 11 November poll were therefore hardly surprising; in round terms the PF received 90 per cent of the vote and the opposition parties 10 per cent. The turnout was in the region of 90 per cent.

The constituent assembly convened on 29 November and rapidly set about its business. A federal republic was declared on the opening day and Dr Ivar Ribar nominated president. A widely respected figure, and a non-communist, Ribar had lost a son in the partisan ranks. The constitution was enacted on 31 January 1946 after which the constituent assembly transformed itself into the peoples' assembly of the Federative Republic of Yugoslavia (FRY). The assembly was bicameral. The FRY was to comprise the six republics of Bosnia and Hercegovina, Croatia, Macedonia, Montenegro, Serbia and Slovenia. The new constitution made all six republics equal in status; Serbia was nevertheless weakened by making Vojvodina an autonomous province and Kosovo an autonomous territory. The federal capital was to be Belgrade. There had been calls to locate it in multi-ethnic Sarajevo in the centre of the country but it was too small, communications with it were too difficult, and there were fears that to move the capital away from Belgrade would be seen as a humiliation by the Serbs.

During the war the PLF leaders had paid relatively little attention to the question of internal borders. This was in part because of other pressing concerns but it was also because they did not believe the issue would be of enormous importance in the new Yugoslavia they were to create. They had built their partisan army on the basis of cooperation between all ethnic groups and in the new post-war Yugoslavia 'brotherhood and unity' became one of the basic official tenets; it was to remain one until the late 1980s. In these circumstances those nationalists who felt passionately about internal borders dared not express their feelings in public. But the question of internal boundaries was important, and nowhere more so than in Croatia. Andrija Hebrang, the Croat communist leader until the end of 1944, spoke of Croatia regaining the territory it had had in Habsburg days, a claim which would have brought the Croat–Serb border to Zemun on the outskirts of Belgrade. The Communist Party of Croatia (CPC) knew such claims were unrealistic but it did support Hebrang's demand that Srem should go to Croatia. Situated between the Sava and the Danube, Srem was historically part of Slavonia but the area had a Serb majority and there was strong distaste for Hebrang's ideas. The border in Srem was eventually drawn as far as possible on ethnic lines, leaving only the western extremities to Croatia; it was to become a major factor in the wars of the early 1990s. There was also a dispute, kept quiet, between Croatia and Montenegro over the Bay of Kotor; it went to Montenegro, as its population wished, the Croat claim being based mainly on the fact that the area had been part of the Habsburg province of Dalmatia which went to Croatia. In another adjustment Bosnia was given a tenuous foothold on the coast at Neum, which it had lost in 1908 when Austria-Hungary annexed the province. The most arbitrary of the new boundaries was that between Serbia and Macedonia.

The constitution defined the individual republics as the sovereign homelands of sovereign nations. There were five nations: Serb, Croat, Slovene, Macedonian and Montenegrin; the Muslims were not recognized as a nation until 1981.* Those members of the five nations living outside their own republic were to be treated as part of their own nation; this ethnic rather than territorial definition therefore made the Serbs living in Croatia part of the Serbian rather than the Croatian nation. A citizen of one republic was to have full political and civil rights in another republic should he choose to live there. The boundaries between the republics were not to be altered without the consent of the republics concerned. In addition to the nations (narodi) there were also the nationalities (narodnosti). The differences between these two concepts were of great constitutional importance throughout the history of the FRY but for concision it might be said that the nationalities were the minorities, most of whom were non-Slav and none of which had their own republic. The nationalities included Albanians, Hungarians, Turks, Bulgarians and Jews.

The January 1946 constitution promised Yugoslavia's citizens equality irrespective of race, nation, language, creed, education or social position; it guaranteed individual freedom, freedom of religion and conscience, freedom of speech, the press, assembly and association, as well as the right to private property and private enterprise. There was no mention of socialism or of the communist party. The constitution did not allow the right to strike; this was considered necessary only in capitalist states whereas those blessed with control by the people did not need such a right. The right to a free press, though guaranteed in the constitution, was in reality negated by the state's monopoly

---

* In 1961 a category of 'Muslims in the ethnic sense' was recognized and in 1971 this was replaced by 'Muslims by nationality', but not until 1981 did the Yugoslav authorities accept that 'Muslim' was itself a national identity.

of the means of printing, and by a clause which gave the government the right to ban the distribution of any material which incited changes in or violation of the constitution.

UNRESTRAINED COMMUNIST POWER IN YUGOSLAVIA, 1946-8

Once they had secured the legitimizing comfort of the new constitution the communists felt under even less constraint. That they were determined to pursue their former enemies relentlessly was made clear in March 1946 when at last they ran to ground the chetnik leader, Mihailović. Many of his supporters had already been subjected to summary justice but Mihailović himself was made to undergo a public trial in which the communist prosecutors and press lambasted the wartime record of the Serbian royalists, highlighting every instance of alleged collaboration while denying a hearing to British military witnesses prepared to defend the general's wartime record. Mihailović was found guilty and executed on 17 July.

The communist undermining of the other parties continued. The election campaign had seen the virtual neutralization of parties outside the PF and communist pressure was now put on other parties within the Front. In July 1946 an offensive was launched against Dragoljub Jovanović of the Agrarian Union when his status as a deputy was suspended; after a series of harassments he was finally put on trial charged with sabotaging the resistance and colluding with the occupiers. Other leaders were also targeted so that by the time the second congress of the PF met on 26 September 1947 there was almost nothing left of party life outside the PF. From 1943 until 1947 the pretence had been that the PF was a broad, popular movement whose programme the Communist Party of Yugoslavia (CPY) supported; after 1947 the PF rapidly became a means for implementing the CPY programme, a programme which the PF accepted as its own in April 1949.

The new authorities also stamped their authority on groups and organizations outside the PF. In July 1947 a show trial of fourteen prominent Slovene intellectuals was staged, some of them members of the 'Pravda' group who had joined the resistance as early as August 1941. All the accused were charged with organizing espionage and with having contacts with a spy centre in Austria. Three of them were sentenced to death and the others to long terms of imprisonment. It was sharp warning both to intellectuals in general and to those with a national association in particular. It was also an example of the communists' willingness to attack those whom they considered to be a potential rather than an actual danger.

The Roman Catholic Church and the communists had always regarded each other as dangerous. Conflict between them had never been absent, but it was not brought to a climax until after the promulgation of the new constitution. The strongholds of the Catholic Church were Slovenia and

Croatia. In Slovenia, initially at least, relations between church and state were easily managed. Because Slovenia had been divided and occupied many priests had found it easy to side with the resistance, and immediately after the war the senior resident cleric, Bishop Rožman, who had perforce to work with the wartime authorities, had fled. Immediately after the war it appeared the Church in Slovenia was seeking an accommodation with the state because it was the Church rather than the political powers which requested discussions between the two. In 1946, however, as the government tightened its hold on the country, relations deteriorated. A number of priests were arrested on charges of collaboration and in August 1946 Rožman was tried *in absentia*. By the end of the year little remained of the apparent willingness for compromise between church and state in Slovenia. In Croatia it hardly ever existed.

Catholicism had always been a part of Croatian nationalism. The NDH had seen in the Catholic Church if not an ally or an accomplice, then at least a natural supporter. The head of the Croatian Church, Archbishop Stepinac, had trodden a very difficult path very carefully. He had not been personally associated with the worst excesses of the ruling fascists, the Ustaše, but his relationship with the Pavelić government had inevitably been too close for post-war comfort. Some of his priests had been less restrained. Many of them were liquidated in the retribution of the immediate post-war weeks; hundreds more were arrested and tried in 1945 and 1946. Immediately after the war Stepinac had attempted to build bridges with the communists, who were not entirely unreceptive, but the legacy of the war created chasms wider than any bridge could span. Land reform widened the chasm because it weakened the Church financially and therefore impaired its ability to run charitable institutions; the Church was also angered by the constitutional provision which made marriage a civil union and it complained that its press was given insufficient newsprint; but, as in so many church–state clashes, the most intense feelings were aroused over education. And at this period there was an especial urgency in the education conflict. There was enormous pressure on school space and time because of the destruction of school buildings, because of the influx into the schools of large numbers of children who had not been able to receive a proper education during the war, and because the period of compulsory education had been increased. If the Church did not act it would be the communists who would mould the minds of the new generation.

Any hope that a modus vivendi between the new state and the old Church might be found disappeared in September 1945 when the conference of bishops complained at the persecution of the clergy of whom, it said, five hundred were dead, imprisoned or missing. So stern was the bishops' letter that some priests, especially in areas with mixed Croat and Serb populations, refused to read it to their congregations. Tito waited a month before responding. When he did so he did not pull his punches. He castigated the bishops for not speaking out when Serbs were being butchered by Pavelić's thugs, insisted that there was no anti-church persecution but only the lawful prosecution of guilty individuals, and warned the bishops that there were laws against chauvinism. At the same time the government tried to split the Church by insisting that the criticisms of the new regime came from the hierarchy and not the rank and file priests. Relations became even more strained after the elections in November when clerics in Zagreb attempted to justify the wartime record of the Church; in January 1946 a protest against black marketeers turned into a demonstration demanding the arrest and trial of Stepinac. He was arrested in September and tried for collaboration and resisting the communist government of Yugoslavia. He was sentenced to sixteen years hard labour.* With the imprisonment of Stepinac the state had established its supremacy over the Catholic Church, though the persecution of leading clerics continued for some years.

The conflict between the state and the Orthodox Church was less intense. The Serbian Orthodox Church had a respected leader in Patriarch Gavrilo who at the end of the war was in Dachau. On the other hand it was weakened by losses in personnel, especially in Croatia and Bosnia, and by the destruction of its properties in the same areas. Furthermore, the Serbian Church faced a difficulty in Macedonia where a number of young priests were anxious to split away and form a new Macedonian Church: were the Serbian Church to show too much hostility to the government the latter might throw its support behind the secessionists in Macedonia. The government might also back another faction which troubled the Serbian Orthodox hierarchy, its own radical priests. A number of priests' associations, bodies which by implication questioned the authority of the bishops and the established hierarchy, had been formed during the war by Orthodox priests who had joined the partisans. One point at issue was that the radicals wanted the associations to be coterminous with republican boundaries while the Synod wanted them to be based on existing dioceses; were the former to prevail the formation of a Macedonian priests' association would be possible.

Initially the communists attempted not to offend the Muslim community in Yugoslavia, but in 1946 the Islamic courts were abolished; the new rulers could not afford to have an alternative system of justice. In 1947 the government suspended financial help to Muslim religious institutions. They could not survive on their own resources or on voluntary contributions and therefore they 'capitulated and exchanged any possibility of political autonomy for the renewal of state financial support'.[3]

The enactment of the new constitution in 1946 initiated an intensification of the communists' attacks upon its class as well as its ideological enemies. What remained of bourgeois economic wealth was soon undermined by further nationalization measures, a law of 6 December 1946 taking forty-two branches of industry, including printing, into state ownership. In 1948 the

---

* He twice refused offers of release on condition that he left the country. He was removed from prison in December 1951 and allowed to live in the priest's house of his home village. He was made a Cardinal in 1952 and died in February 1960. Tito allowed a full ceremonial funeral in Zagreb cathedral.

state sought to eliminate what remained of the private and unofficial traders who, said the authorities, were evading the socialized trading network and charging higher prices. Anyone trading without a licence was liable to prosecution and in April a law transferred to social ownership what was left of private or local authority retail trade. This affected small industrial and construction enterprises, all printers and warehouses, 500 hotels, 30 hospitals and sanatoriums, 100 cinemas and 530 dairies; over 3,000 private shops and enterprises closed immediately. The party heralded the April law as the 'road to liquidating the bourgeoisie'.

In agriculture the power of the peasantry, who were still by far the largest social group in the country, dictated a more cautious approach. The 1945 agrarian reform act had provided that large areas of land should be passed to the state land fund. This was because the main architect of the reform, Moša Pijade, wished to use the area for social engineering. He believed that state farms, staffed and run by communists and war veterans, would be the ideal vehicle for promoting modern techniques and mechanization. Pijade also hoped that the war veterans would, on their own initiative, establish collective farms which would serve to convince other peasants of the benefits of communal ownership and work. The results were disappointing. By the end of 1945 only 35 cooperative farms had been formed, all of them in Vojvodina. The communists decided that they would proceed cautiously, hoping still that the agricultural cooperative would prove its economic and ideological worth, and hoping too that the development of retail cooperatives would also promote collective attitudes. In the summer of 1946 in recognition of the power and the growing discontents of the peasantry, the government passed a law amnestying all those who had not yet completed or begun sentences imposed for the violation of compulsory delivery orders, a concession which showed how far the authorities were still dependent on the good will of the peasantry. Conciliation was more difficult, however, in times of food shortage. In the first quarter of 1947 when there were serious shortages in the mountains of Bosnia and Hercegovina the authorities did not shrink from tough measures, forcibly requisitioning grain, reducing rations for humans and animals, and punishing hoarders. In the following year the ideological battle against the peasant was intensified and the April laws which restricted private traders also prohibited the sale of fixed assets, including land, even if the area involved were less than the minimum permitted holding. At the same time the private purchase of agricultural machinery was made illegal and cumbersome mechanisms were introduced for anyone wishing to employ village labour.

EXTERNAL AFFAIRS FROM THE END OF THE WAR TO THE BREACH WITH STALIN, 1944–8

By 1948 Yugoslavia was moving more rapidly than any other state in Eastern Europe, with the possible exception of Albania, to the creation of a Soviet-style system. Its external policies were equally well-aligned with those of the

USSR, or so it seemed from outside the very closest quarters of the Soviet and Yugoslav leaderships. Yugoslavia was an energetic critic of the western powers and it was to play a prominent part in the foundation of Cominform in September 1947. Yet, ironically, its extreme, unrestrained and at times apparently uncontrollable anti-westernism was one of the most important factors in precipitating Yugoslavia's expulsion from Cominform in June 1948. As will be seen, the process by which this took place was complex in the extreme and was affected by the politics and personalities of the Yugoslav leadership, of the Balkans, of the international communist movement and of the great powers.

Yugoslav criticism of the western powers was trenchant, persistent and by no means unpopular at home. Government propagandists made much of alleged western connections with or backing for the communists' defeated domestic enemies, criticizing the British support for Mihailović and the Vatican's alleged toleration of the Pavelić regime; nor would official Yugoslavia believe the repeated, and truthful, assurances of the western powers that they did not have the offending Croatian leader in their custody. Communist propaganda deftly manipulated problems in supplying food relief. There was actual starvation in 1945 in parts of Yugoslavia, especially Dalmatia. The communists complained that while the west was willing to feed the former enemy population in Italy it would not send relief to its erstwhile comrades in arms in Yugoslavia, whereas in reality UNRRA (the United Nations Relief and Rehabilitation Administration) was desperately trying to do just that despite the difficulties caused by incessant communist accusations that its workers were western spies. Even when UNRRA food was flowing into the country the communist press still gave much more attention to the paltry quantities sent from the Soviet Union. And above all there was huge resentment at the west's refusal to allow Yugoslav possession of Trieste which was to remain the chief bone of contention between Yugoslavia and the west until the early 1950s.

In its relations with its Balkan neighbours other than Greece, whose government was drifting towards civil war with the Greek communists, Yugoslavia seemed to have few serious problems. With Enver Hoxha's communist leadership in Albania there were few differences or difficulties, once the Albanians had accepted the reintegration of Kosovo into Yugoslavia. The Albanians looked to Yugoslavia for economic advice and assistance and in 1947 a number of joint Albanian-Yugoslav companies were established in banking, foreign trade, railways, shipping, electricity generation, minerals and petroleum. In 1946 Stalin and Tito had agreed on the desirability of a Yugoslav-Albanian federation but not on its timing. Early in 1948 Tito, in what was largely a personal and secret decision, ordered that a Yugoslav division should be sent to Korça in southern Albania to protect the area against a possible incursion by Greek royalist forces.

Yugoslavia's relations with Bulgaria were more complex. In the autumn of 1944 Bulgarian forces had joined the Red Army in the war against the

Germans and had therefore fought in and through Yugoslavia. Their conduct gave rise to some misgivings but there was cooperation as well as tension between Yugoslavia and Bulgaria. The Yugoslav communist government established diplomatic relations with Bulgaria before it did with the Soviet Union, and despite the criticisms of their behaviour Bulgarian troops were allowed to take part in the victory parade in Belgrade. The Bulgarians also gave considerable sums in humanitarian aid, including medical supplies, support for some ten thousand children, and care for a number of orphans, the first of whom arrived in Bulgaria in January 1945.

Inevitably Macedonia played a prominent part in Yugoslav-Bulgarian relations and the issues at stake were large. In 1945 a Macedonian national consciousness hardly existed beyond a general conviction, gained from bitter experience, that rule from Sofia was as unpalatable as that from Belgrade. But if there were no Macedonian nation there was a Communist Party of Macedonia. It had been the Communist Party of Macedonia which had organized resistance activity during the war and it was therefore around the Communist Party of Macedonia that the first modern Macedonian state, the People's Republic of Macedonian (PRM) was built. It was in the PRM that the modern Macedonian nation was to be born in terms of the creation of a national alphabet and the rapid growth of a sense of Macedonian national identity. During the war the Bulgarian and the Yugoslav parties had been reluctant to allow the other domination over the Macedonian comrades and the Comintern had passed the buck by ruling that the solution had to be found on the basis of the self-determination of the Macedonian people. But as the Macedonian people did not have sufficient sense of national unity to express a definite opinion on this issue the Comintern ruling in effect handed predominance in Macedonia to whichever faction would emerge as the strongest at the end of the war; that turned out to be the Yugoslav partisans. This point was emphasized when two complete Yugoslav army corps were moved from central Yugoslavia to Macedonia. They were stationed near the Greek border but their presence was a powerful reminder to Sofia as well as to Athens that Vardar Macedonia at least was Yugoslav territory.*

Immediately after the end of fighting in Macedonia a number of immediate points at issue between Yugoslavia and Bulgaria were settled at a Soviet-sponsored meeting between Tito and a Bulgarian delegation at Craiova in Romania in October 1944. A possible escape from longer-term disagreements over Macedonia was believed to be a Balkan federation. This notion was

---

* After the collapse of the Ottoman empire in Europe during the first Balkan war of 1912–13 Macedonia was partitioned by Greece, Bulgaria, and Serbia. A further partition took place after the second Balkan war in 1913 which greatly reduced Bulgaria's share of the spoils. The Serbian portion of Macedonia became known as Vardar Macedonia from the river which runs through it; Bulgaria's was Pirin Macedonia, named after the mountains in that region; and Greece's coastal strip, which included Salonika, was referred to as Aegean Macedonia.

discussed a number of times between 1944 and 1948 though the federation proposed differed considerably from one discussion to the next. In late 1944 Stalin, meeting Tito for the first time, suggested a federation between Yugoslavia and Bulgaria. The idea was supported by the leader of the Bulgarian communists and former head of Comintern, Georgi Dimitrov, although he was not convinced that much could be done before the end of the war. Nevertheless, in November the Bulgarian party leadership, in a letter to the Yugoslav party central committee, announced that the party organization in Gorna Djumaya (now Blagoevgrad), the chief town in the Pirin region, was to be redefined as a Macedonian party organization, schools and other institutions were to be given the names of Macedonian heroes, and a Macedonian newspaper was to be established. This caused some excitement in Belgrade. A senior Yugoslav politburo member, Edvard Kardelj, scuttled off to Sofia with high expectations which were immediately disappointed. Although federation would have enabled Bulgaria to slough off the stigma of being the only pre-war Slav state which joined the Axis and might even have allowed it to escape a punitive peace treaty, Dimitrov's apparent enthusiasm for the federation was not shared by other leading Bulgarian communists, especially the influential Traicho Kostov. Kardelj himself was not pleased when his hosts suggested that if there were a federation Sofia should be its capital, Dimitrov its party leader, and Tito its president; that would have left real power in Dimitrov's hands. Nor was there agreement on the nature of the federation. The Bulgarians assumed it would be an association of the two states, whereas the Yugoslavs thought this would belittle the Slovenes and Croats, and even more so the Serbs; the Yugoslavs' assumption was that Bulgaria would become another constituent unit of Yugoslavia equal to and no greater than any other. By January 1945 Stalin had lost his ardour and was telling both parties to keep matters vague and confine any agreement to economic affairs. His caution followed indications from London that Britain would not accept any federation which might threaten Greece and the Aegean littoral.

By the early summer of 1945 the idea of federation was less popular both in Belgrade and Sofia. The Yugoslavs said they could not conclude an economic agreement with Bulgaria until the latter had signed a peace treaty with the allies and the Bulgarians were sounding less accommodating over Pirin. When Tito visited Stalin in May 1946 the latter urged the conclusion of a federation but Tito disagreed. Nothing would come of the idea, he argued, because the two states were at different stages of economic and political development; in Bulgaria, he said, the government was strongly influenced by other parties whereas in Yugoslavia, though the other parties existed technically, power was essentially in the hands of the communists. Little came of the conversations and when Yugoslav-Bulgarian discussions took place in Moscow in June 1946 it was agreed that the question of federation must be left until after the signature of a peace treaty.

A month later the situation was transformed. Dimitrov told the Yugoslav ambassador to Bulgaria that Pirin would become part of Macedonia. When

Dimitrov addressed a plenum of the Bulgarian central committee on 9 August he said there were not three Macedonias but one, that the PRM represented the Macedonian nation, and that the other Macedonias, Pirin and Aegean, would join it. Pirin Macedonia had already expressed a willingness to join the PRM and this would happen, said Dimitrov, as part of a general Bulgarian-Yugoslav agreement. These explosive views were not relayed by the press and party members were informed confidentially via internal party documents. The Yugoslav comrades were told by letter. In February 1947 a major obstacle on the road to federation was removed when Bulgaria signed a peace treaty with the allies. In August of that year an agreement between Yugoslavia and Bulgaria was concluded in the Slovene town of Bled. The Bled agreement called for the fastest and deepest possible strengthening of economic ties, the abolition of customs dues, and moves towards the simplification of border controls. The two states were to take a common stance against Greek frontier provocations. Cultural ties were to be encouraged and Yugoslavia agreed to forgo the $24 million reparations from Bulgaria awarded to it under the terms of the February peace treaty. After Bled came an agreement in October on economic cooperation; Bulgaria was to specialize in the production of vegetables, fruits, fats and a number of other mainly primary products, while Yugoslavia was to concentrate on metallurgy, machine building, chemicals and the fish and meat preserving industries. The question of Pirin also appeared to be solved. In August the Bulgarian parliament had approved legislation introducing the teaching of Macedonian history and language in local schools and Bulgaria was to pay for 87 teachers to be brought from the PRM to Pirin for three years, and with the help of the National Theatre in Skopje a Macedonian Theatre was opened in November in Gorna Djumaya. November was also the month in which Tito paid a celebratory visit to Bulgaria, signing the official treaty of friendship and cooperation at Evksinograd, the former summer palace of the Bulgarian kings, on 27 November.

Uncharacteristically, and perhaps because Dimitrov was in poor health, the Bulgarians had not kept Moscow fully informed of developments leading up to the signing of the treaty. Dimitrov compounded this error in late January 1948. Returning from what he regarded as a successful visit to Bucharest he gave an interview to a journalist in the train. Dimitrov talked of the formation of a large federation which would include not only Bulgaria and Yugoslavia but also Hungary, Romania, Czechoslovakia, Poland, Albania and Greece. The inclusion of Greece, which Dimitrov especially emphasized, was significant in that on 24 December 1947 the Greek communist leader, Markos Vaphiadis, had declared the provisional democratic government of Greece. Details of the interview appeared in *Pravda* on 28 January 1948. On the following day *Pravda* carried another article, this time stating that it disagreed with Dimitrov and arguing that there was no need for a Balkan federation. It was not usual for *Pravda* to reverse its opinion overnight. Clearly large issues were at stake, though as yet few realized how large they were.

The extent of Stalin's anger was soon known to the Bulgarian and Yugoslav leaders. They were summoned to a meeting in Moscow. Tito refused to go and the Yugoslav delegation was headed by Kardelj. When the delegations arrived in Moscow they faced three main allegations: the publication of the proposed treaty of union without prior consultation with the Soviets; Dimitrov's inclusion of Greece in his projected federation; and Tito's decision to send a division to Korça in Albania. The Yugoslavs immediately conceded on the last question. Stalin then stunned the delegates by announcing there should be a federation, but of Bulgaria and Yugoslavia alone. The Yugoslavs aborted this discussion by stating they were not authorized to make decisions on the issue. From the conversations it was clear that Stalin's main concern was to avoid provoking the west and giving grist to the mill of the 'reactionaries' in the United States. At the end of the visit he insisted that the Yugoslavs sign an undertaking always in future to consult with Moscow on issues of foreign policy. As Dimitrov had already promised to do this, a beleaguered Kardelj felt he had little choice but to comply.

After the confrontation over the question of the federation small signs of a change in Soviet-Yugoslav relations began to appear to the discerning, as when *Le Figaro* reported on 12 February that Tito's portrait was being taken down from official places in Romania. By March the Yugoslav leadership knew that it was facing a serious crisis. When an expanded politburo meeting convened in Belgrade on 1 March the first item on its agenda was relations with the Soviet Union; the second was relations with Bulgaria. Relations with Moscow, said the Yugoslav supremo, were at an impasse and if they could not be improved he would have to resign. This may have been little more than a histrionic gesture but when the excitement subsided others added to the bleak picture, Kardelj giving a graphic account of Stalin's boorishness at the February meeting, and the new head of the economic programme, Boris Kidrič, describing the problems with the Soviet Union on the economic front. As to Bulgaria, Tito said the Bulgarian party was distancing itself from Yugoslavia, and that if federation were to take place it would be little more than a Trojan horse inside the CPY; 'In Bulgaria', he said, 'the Russians have their fingers in every pie. The ministry of the interior is entirely in their hands.'[4]

From March the descent to the final rupture in June was rapid but almost entirely private. On 18 March the Soviets suddenly announced they were to withdraw all their military instructors from the country and two days later the economic advisors followed them. On 27 March a letter signed by Stalin and Molotov, the Soviet commissar for external affairs, arrived giving detailed criticism of Yugoslav policy. On 12 April a plenum of the CPY central committee was called, the first since the committee's election in October 1940, to debate the Soviet note and the reply drafted by Djilas. Any hope that the breaches might be mended was dashed on 4 May with the arrival of a thirty-page letter from the Soviet central committee in which Hebrang and Sreten Žujović, the only two leading Yugoslav communists who had spoken on the Soviet side, were defended and Tito and Kardelj branded as sinners. Another Yugoslav plenum met on 9 May. It decided not to attend the forthcoming meeting of Cominform and expelled Hebrang and Žujović who were both now under house arrest; a few days later, on Tito's orders, they were imprisoned. On 18 May the Yugoslav expert from the Soviet central committee arrived and tried to argue for Yugoslav attendance at the Cominform meeting. On 19 June the official Cominform invitation arrived and a meeting of the expanded politburo the following day reaffirmed the decision not to attend. Yugoslavia's expulsion from the Cominform was announced on 28 June. The following day a plenum of the Yugoslav central committee met and accepted a draft response prepared by the leadership. To emphasize that the latter had not closed the door on reconciliation Tito ended his speech with the cry 'Long Live the Soviet Union, Long Live Stalin'. The issue was discussed again at the fifth congress of the CPY which met from 21 to 29 July. Tito's opening speech, all eight hours of it, was broadcast live to the nation and the endorsement given the party leadership by the congress confirmed legitimacy in its stance against the Soviet Union. There were those in the party, the most prominent being Hebrang and Žujović, who wished to avoid the split and were therefore willing to accommodate the Soviet Union, and thousands of these so-called 'cominformists' were to spend years in detention on the notorious island of Goli Otok. The cominformist threat was serious and gave added purpose to the police apparatus. At the same time, Tito's defiance of Moscow reconciled some non-communists to the regime for the first time.

The outside world was stunned. In the communist community there was confusion, consternation and fear. There was every reason for fear and within a short period the accusation of 'nationalist deviation' or 'Titoism' was to be used as a charge in purges in almost every ruling communist party. In the Yugoslav leadership there was anger, puzzlement and a kafkaesque sense of unreality. They had seen themselves as among the most loyal and assiduous of Stalin's pupils, and when Tito visited Moscow in May 1946 he had been treated virtually as the heir apparent in the international communist movement.* This had greatly flattered the Yugoslavs and could perhaps have further encouraged that tendency to *excès de zèle* already born of the Yugoslav communists' wartime exploits and successes. This feeling was reinforced by the founding meeting of Cominform in Poland in September 1947 where the Yugoslav had seemed to be a much favoured party to which the Soviets had allotted the leading role in criticizing those parties which had not displayed

---

* Stalin had declaimed that 'Tito must take care of himself, that nothing would happen to him . . . for I will not live . . . laws of physiology . . . but you will remain for Europe'. See Leonid Gibianskii, 'The Soviet Bloc and the Initial Stage of the Cold War: Archival Documents on Stalin's Meetings with Communist Leaders of Yugoslavia and Bulgaria, 1946–1948', in David Wolff (ed.), *International History Project Bulletin* (Woodrow Wilson International Center for Scholars, Washington DC), no. 10 (March 1998), pp.112–34, p.123.

sufficient zeal and aggression. So great a transformation must have had profound causes.

Some of these can be traced back to the Second World War. As the partisans gained strength and confidence they asked for, and expected, more help from the Soviet Union, and were frustrated and puzzled when they did not receive it. For his part Stalin began to feel uncomfortable with Yugoslav adventurism which he feared might alienate the west, and he was furious with the Jajce proclamation of a provisional government which came on the eve of the Tehran conference and of which the Yugoslav leadership quite deliberately gave him no prior warning. Once again he feared western reaction. In the final stages of the war Stalin, again to avoid alarming Britain and the United States, angered Tito by urging him to bring King Peter back to Yugoslavia; when Tito demurred and said there was no public support for the king, Stalin said he should be brought back anyway and then Tito could slip a knife into his back at the appropriate moment.

After the war the Yugoslav communists, as victorious allies, felt free to express their own, socialist and anti-imperialist sentiments. At times this too caused friction with the Soviets who were not used to free speech from those they regarded as underlings rather than equals. In return the Yugoslavs were angered by patronizing attitudes on the part of Moscow and even more so by its interference in internal Yugoslav affairs, as when it pressed, unsuccessfully, against the inclusion of Grol in the government or when it argued, successfully, that the Yugoslav plan to include in the 1946 constitution a clause allowing medical, disability and pension insurance for peasants be dropped because the Soviet constitution did not include such a provision.

A much more serious issue had arisen at the end of the war over the conduct of Red Army troops. Their raping and looting hardly helped the communist image but Yugoslav complaints on this issue outraged both local Red Army commanders and Stalin himself. Another cause of Yugoslav resentment was the behaviour of Soviet advisors sent to Yugoslavia after the war. Many of them, especially those working on the railways, recruited agents for the Soviet intelligence services. On a wider scale the advisors caused resentment among the general population because they were much more highly paid than their Yugoslav counterparts, and the military officers all had personal servants, a custom not known in the austere, partisan-based Yugoslav forces. Soviet officers attached to Yugoslav units also caused a promotion blockage.

An equally serious difference arose in the sphere of the economy. Hebrang, who had been given charge of economic planning and development after the war, favoured cautious expansion and argued that Yugoslavia did not itself have sufficient resources or capital to float large-scale industrialization. Soviet help, he argued, was essential. In February 1946 he approached the Soviets with a plan for joint operations in the extraction and refining industries, in the construction of power plants and in transportation. The Soviets' response was measured. Not till April did they show any interest in the Yugoslav proposal. It was eventually agreed to establish joint enterprises for navigation on the Danube and for air transportation; there was also to be a jointly run Yugoslav-Soviet bank. The joint enterprises were a political disaster. The Yugoslavs refused to allow the joint bank to indulge in normal banking business and also refused to agree that a Soviet citizen, appointed by Moscow, should be its director. The most serious problem, however, was that the Yugoslav contribution to the joint enterprises was valued at 1938 prices and the Soviet at 1945–6 levels which were much higher. In 1947 the enterprises were abandoned, Stalin saying they were appropriate only for defeated nations. Nevertheless, this did not remove the difficulties over trade agreements where price differentials were again a bone of contention. These agreements required Yugoslavia to sell to the USSR at modest prices goods such as hemp and non-ferrous ores which on the open market could command high prices in hard currencies. Even so, the Soviets were slow to fulfil their side of the bargain and by the beginning of 1948, just as in the war, when help was most desperately needed little was forthcoming. There were huge opportunity costs in ideological loyalty.

High politics could not be differentiated from political intrigue. In the economic negotiations Hebrang had made himself the proponent of close relations with the Soviet Union and this in part explained his behaviour in 1948. But there were other reasons why Hebrang was distrusted in leading party circles. Towards the end of the war he had alarmed other senior communists not only with his territorial extravaganzas but also by pursuing a distinctly Croatian policy, courting the Catholic Church and even at one point trying to set up a separate Croatian news agency. Croat nationalism was suspect even in a proven communist. To prevent his becoming too mighty a subject in his native region Tito removed Hebrang from the leadership of the Croat party in late 1944 and made him minister of industry. Having been condemned for Croat nationalism inside Yugoslavia, Hebrang sought to condemn Tito for Yugoslav nationalism within the international socialist system.

The final break between Belgrade and Moscow cannot be divorced from the contemporary global situation. In 1948 the communist takeover in Czechoslovakia had greatly exacerbated the east–west divide in Europe, and the Berlin crisis began in the very month in which the Yugoslavs were expelled from Cominform. In such circumstances adventurism could be dangerous, especially before the Soviet Union had developed its own nuclear potential.

What Stalin saw as Yugoslav adventurism had been apparent even in the last days of the war. Tito was determined to take what the Italians called Venezia Giulia, an area which included Fiume and Trieste. Partisan units had entered the latter city in early May 1945. They occupied and administered a part of it until mid-June when they left under pressure from the western allies; Yugoslav troops, however, remained in control of most of the rest of Istria and the Slovene littoral, Tito insisting that the honour of his army and his country demanded they do so. The Trieste question, which was not to be finally settled until 1954, was second in importance only to Poland in the inter-allied discussions at Potsdam in the summer of 1945 and that it was on the agenda at all was mainly the responsibility of the Yugoslav communists.

Yugoslavia's determination to assert its own interests, in Trieste and elsewhere, was plainly stated by Tito in a speech in Ljubljana on 27 May 1945.

> Our goal is that everyone be the master in his own house. We are not going to pay the balance on others' account, we are not going to serve as the small change in anyone's currency exchange, we are not going to allow ourselves to become entangled in political spheres of interest. . . . Today's Yugoslavia is no object for bartering and bargaining.[5]

Tito's words were directed against the western powers but the Soviets were enraged and sent a protest note describing the speech as 'an unfriendly act'.

If Trieste were the most contentious of Yugoslavia's territorial claims it was by no means the only one. The others included: from Hungary, the Baja Triangle and the area around Pécs where the population included a large number of Slovenes but which also had valuable reserves of coal; from Italy, Trieste, Pula and Fiume which were mainly Croat and Slovene, and part of the Korucs region, which again was mainly Slovene; from Austria, southern Carinthia and part of Styria with their Slovene minorities; and from Romania the area around Timișoara which contained a number of ethnic Serbs, and the area of Reșița with its iron and steel works. Stalin was worried by Yugoslav appetites; when Dimitrov told him he thought the Yugoslavs wanted, in addition to the above claims, the whole of Macedonia and most of Albania, Stalin responded, 'That's crazy; I don't like the way they are going about things.'[6] Yet despite such worries Stalin was capable of encouraging the Yugoslavs in their territorial dreams. When Tito visited Moscow in May 1946 and mentioned that Yugoslavia would like to have Aegean Macedonia and Salonika, Stalin's reply was, 'Yes, Salonika is an old Slavic city. You need access to the Aegean.'[7]

Despite such encouragement the Yugoslavs received little real support from the Soviet Union in any confrontation with the west. When, in 1946, Yugoslav forces shot down two United States transport planes over Yugoslav territory Belgrade was left alone to face the wrath of Washington and was forced to pay compensation. The Yugoslavs proved keen supporters of the communist cause in neighbouring Greece but once again Moscow was of a different mind, Stalin consistently arguing that the communists would not win in Greece and urging the Yugoslavs not to become involved. There was even less enthusiasm in Moscow for Yugoslav territorial designs. Moscow gave formal support to Yugoslav claims on Austria not because it believed in the justice of those claims but mainly because they were a useful weapon or bargaining counter in discussions within the inter-allied administration of Austria. But the most dramatic snub to the Yugoslavs came over Trieste. On the evening before the issue was to be discussed in the Paris peace conference in 1947 the Yugoslav delegation arranged with the Soviets that they would agree that Trieste should be a free territory and Gorizia should go to Yugoslavia.

But when the discussion took place Molotov never raised the question of Gorizia; a British diplomat told Kardelj, the chief Yugoslav negotiator, that the British would have agreed to Yugoslavia having Gorizia.[8]

If Tito's capacious territorial appetites were perceived as a threat to Stalin so was the huge popularity the Yugoslav leader enjoyed in the other satellite states. By 1948 he had visited all of them, the Soviet zone of Germany excluded, and had everywhere been given a hero's welcome. Some local communists had even been known to express the view that Tito's revolution was more relevant than the Soviet one to their own situation. At a time of rapidly sharpening division in Europe Stalin could not afford any potential alternative source of loyalty or authority. This would smack of ideological diversity which in a monolithic system is accounted heresy. When the Soviets attacked the Yugoslav communists they accused them therefore of a range of ideological sins. The assertion that the CPY was Trotskyist was absurd but a more realistic accusation was that which focused on the rural rather than the urban nature of the CPY and on its position within and relations to the PF. That the CPY was predominantly a rural organization could hardly have been otherwise. The party had expanded rapidly with the development of the partisan movement but that had been based in the mountains and rural areas. This did not seem to concern the Yugoslav party leadership which proudly proclaimed that 'The peasant is the most stable foundation of the Yugoslav state.' This did not chime with Moscow orthodoxy. The Soviet propagandists argued that the CPY was so much dominated by the peasantry that it was neglecting the interests of the proletariat. Furthermore, said Moscow's propagandists, the CPY had not asserted itself sufficiently within the PF. Although Tito had convinced Stalin in May 1946 of the irrelevance of the other political parties in Yugoslavia two years later the Soviets criticized the CPY for submerging itself into the PF rather than asserting full control over it. And in the PF, said Moscow, peasant interests ruled supreme.

These arguments were important in a much wider context. The Yugoslav revolution had been made by partisans in a struggle which was both a civil war and a resistance campaign against a foreign occupier. It was furthermore a struggle which had begun essentially with the partisans' march from Serbia to Bosnia in 1941–2. The Yugoslav revolution was also one which, in its own definition, was highly dependent on the peasantry. In China too the communists had staged their 'Long March'; in China too they had struggled to victory against both an invader and their own domestic enemies; and in China too they proclaimed that the revolution was based upon the peasant. In disciplining Tito Stalin was also stating that the Soviet model was the only one to be tolerated for the organization of the party and the building of socialism; in effect the Soviet Union was to remain undisputed master of the world socialist movement. On 4 October 1948 Kardelj, who was attending a meeting of the UN General Assembly in Paris, wrote to Tito after talking to a number of left-wing intellectuals and communists:

Our case, say these people, is crucial in the International Workers' Movement because of the similar situation regarding the Chinese Communist Party and Mao Tse-tung. They say that the Chinese Communist Party's views, which they call 'Maoism', have long been considered a 'worrying' development.[9]

The Yugoslav–Soviet split had worldwide significance. For Yugoslavia it meant that a new path had to be found, one which retained the essentials of socialism but avoided reliance upon the Soviet Union and its minions.

Notes

1. Milovan Djilas, *Tito: The Story from Inside*, translated by Vasilije Lolic and Richard Hayes, London: Weidenfeld and Nicolson, 1981, p.77.
2. See Public Record Office, Kew. FO 371/48149.
3. Duncan Wilson, *Tito's Yugoslavia*, Cambridge: Cambridge University Press, 1979, p.43.
4. ' "In Bulgarien haben die Russen ihre Hände in allen Angelegenheiten. Sie halten das Innenministerium vollständig in ihrer Hand." ' In Magarditsch A. Hatschikjan, *Tradition und Neuorientierung in der bulgarischen Aussenpolitik 1944–1948; die 'nationale Aussenpolitik' der Bulgarischen Arbeiterpartei (Kommunisten)*, Munich: R. Oldenbourg, 1988, p.360.
5. Milovan Djilas, *Rise and Fall*, London; Basingstoke: Macmillan, 1985, p.91.
6. Georgi Daskalov, *Bŭlgaro-yugoslavski politicheski otnosheniya, 1944–1945*, Sofia: Universitetsko izdatelstvo 'Kliment Ohridski', 1989, p.288.
7. Leonid Gibianskii, 'The Soviet Bloc and the Initial Stage of the Cold War: Archival Documents on Stalin's Meetings with Communist Leaders of Yugoslavia and Bulgaria, 1946–1948', in David Wolff (ed.), *Cold War International History Project Bulletin* (Woodrow Wilson International Center for Scholars, Washington DC), no.10 (March 1998), pp.112–34, see p.122.
8. Edvard Kardelj, *Reminiscences: the Struggle for Recognition and Independence: The New Yugoslavia, 1944–1957*, London: Blond & Briggs in association with Summerfield Press, 1982, p.85.
9. Ibid. p.120, note 9.

Chapter 3

ALBANIA, 1944–1948

Although the longest-established people in the Balkans the Albanians are the most remote and the least-known. The mountainous terrain has largely isolated them from the outside world. Greek settlements were established on the coast and the Romans dominated the region from the second century BC to the fifth century AD, one of their most impressive achievements being to drive a road, the Via Egnatia, from Dyrrachium (present-day Durres) through the mountains to Macedonia, the Aegean coast and Constantinople. The only other force to establish itself in the interior of the country was the Ottoman empire, though it never fully dominated the northern mountains. The Ottomans brought Islam which was adopted by approximately 70 per cent of the population, the remainder being divided between Orthodoxy, around 20 per cent, and Catholicism, approximately 10 per cent, though in Albania there is less of a division between the religions than between the two main dialect groups, the Ghegs of the north and the Tosks of the south. In general, Albania remained loyal to the Ottoman sultans in return for which the Albanians were exempted from many central government exactions. Albanian traditional culture continued. This was based upon the clan, particularly in the northern mountains, and in it the blood feud played an important part.

Political awakening came with the gradual decay of the Ottoman empire, a process which exposed the Albanians to the danger of incorporation into one or more of the neighbouring, successor states, none of which was so culturally indulgent as the empire had been. A second threat came from modernizing tendencies in the Ottoman empire itself. It was these which persuaded Constantinople to subject the Albanians to central taxation, conscription and a ban on the carrying of firearms. The Albanians had other ideas. In the late 1900s and early 1910s they staged a series of revolts. In 1912 Albanian rebels took Skopje and thereby threatened the stability of the entire central Balkans. The surrounding states moved in before the great powers could do so. As a result of the ensuing Balkan wars of 1912–13 a new Albanian state was created but it had little or nothing in the way of an infrastructure, and Kosovo, despite a widespread uprising in the autumn of 1913, had been assigned by the great powers to Serbia. The new Albania was still dominated by the tribal chiefs, all of whom guarded their local powers jealously and were as resentful of central authority based in Tirana or Durres as that based in Constantinople. The first head of the new Albania, Prince Wilhelm zu Wied, was in the country only a few months before it collapsed under the impact of the First World War.

After the war Albania was reconstituted but it was still woefully lacking in modern institutions. The power of the tribal chiefs seemed undiminished and it was one of them, Ahmed Zogolli, from the northern Mati clan, who rose to prominence, finally declaring himself King Zog in 1928. He attempted to modernize his kingdom but was hugely hampered by its backwardness and poverty, factors which forced him to rely on Italy for assistance. Finally, Mussolini decided that Albania was a fitting object of fascist Italy's European expansion; he invaded on Good Friday 1939.

Zog fled with his wife and newborn son, Leka. Italian rule proved incompetent and unpopular but what should take its place was in dispute and, as in Yugoslavia, a number of resistance groups emerged, one of them being dominated by the communists.

THE FOUNDATION AND GROWTH OF THE COMMUNIST MOVEMENT

The Albanian Communist Party (ACP) was founded in November 1941 under the leadership of Enver Hoxha. Born in 1908 Hoxha had been educated in France and was to become, with the possible exception of Rákosi of Hungary, the only intellectual among the communist leaders of Eastern Europe. His was not a promising terrain for the development of a Marxist party acting as the vanguard of the proletariat. Not only was there was no proletariat, there was little else beyond peasant subsistence agriculture; the country had no railways and no towns larger than 20,000. Yet Albania was one of the first states in Europe to adopt a communist system and 'no Communist party has ever achieved such swift success as the ACP under Hoxha'.[1] Initially, during the war years the Albanian communists were much influenced by their Yugoslav comrades; the warmth of that relationship was equalled, perhaps, only by the heat generated when it was ruptured.

After November 1941 the communists rapidly established anti-Italian guerrilla units but initially they attracted few adherents. The communists' response was to emphasize the nationalist rather than the social nature of their movement and to seek cooperation with other resistance forces on the basis of a common national cause. It was therefore on communist initiative that ACP chiefs met leaders of the other major resistance force, Abas Kupi's Balli Kombetar (BK) at Peze near Tirana in September 1942 and formed the National Liberation Front (NLF)[2] which was to be run by a general council which was firmly under communist control. When the Italians laid down their arms in Albania in July 1943 and were replaced by the Germans, the

NLF met again, this time in Labinot, to form a joint military organization, the Albanian National Liberation Army (ANLA). Cooperation seemed to extend further in the following month when the leaders met again, this time at Mukje. Here it was agreed to set up a Committee for the Salvation of Albania which was to consist of six members from the NLF and six from the BK. It was further agreed that both organizations would fight jointly against the occupiers and that after liberation Albania's form of government would be decided by the people. Almost immediately, however, the Mukje agreement was renounced by the general council of the NLF, causing Kupi to leave the alliance and to reactivate his own group as an independent force. The situation was further complicated by the emergence of a third sizeable group, the royalist Legality Movement (LM), which wanted to bring back King Zog.

Competition between the NLF, the BK and the LM escalated rapidly and within a year had assumed the proportions of virtual civil war. The odds were heavily stacked in favour of the NLF. Their mobility plus their ruthlessness meant that they could kill more Germans, notwithstanding the fierce reprisals that this provoked. The other groups seldom found it easy to bury their differences and frequently cooperated with the Germans against the communist-dominated NLF. This meant that they lost credibility both with the younger, nationalist elements of the population, and, more importantly, with the allies who supplied much of their equipment and most of their money.

One reason for the NLF's unwillingness to continue cooperation with the other resistance forces was its fear that the western allies were about to land in the Balkans; had they succeeded in doing so the political balance would have swung rapidly in the direction of the non-communists. In September 1943 the NLF therefore ordered its local organizations, the national liberation councils, to mobilize the local population and ensure that it did not look to the BK: 'The administration of Albania' read a document of 9 September 1943, 'should be entirely in the hands of the liberation councils.'[3] There was no doubt in the minds of the NLF leaders, however, that domination of the national liberation councils was not merely a tactic to cope with a possible landing; it was a stratagem for taking power in post-war Albania as a circular of 3 November 1943 to the councils made clear:

> It must be understood thoroughly that the national liberation councils are the backbone of the future democracy of Albania; therefore, the best of our comrades must be placed at the head of these councils, and the most strenuous activity must be performed in order to give them the necessary status. . . . It is through these councils that the people become conscious of our war and come close to us in our struggle.[4]

By the spring of 1944 the NLF seemed to be heading for victory in its civil war against the other resistance groups. This was signalled on the political front in May 1944 in Permet when the NLF held the first Anti-Fascist

Congress for National Liberation. Following the lead set by the Yugoslav partisans at Bihać and Jajce, the congress elected a permanent Anti-Fascist Council for National Liberation which in turn elected a 13-man Anti-Fascist National Committee for National Liberation as a temporary government for liberated areas; it was headed by Hoxha who was also made commander in chief of the armed forces. In October 1944, at Berat, a second congress declared the Anti-Fascist Committee for National Liberation to be the democratic government of Albania with Hoxha as its president. On 28 November, the anniversary of the creation of the Albanian state in 1912 and the country's national day, Hoxha entered Tirana which had been liberated from the Germans eleven days previously.

THE CONSOLIDATION OF COMMUNIST POWER, NOVEMBER 1944 TO MARCH 1946

In the year and a half after their entry into Tirana the communists did much to weaken their potential opponents, particularly through new legal institutions. They also took measures to weaken the economic and social strength of opposing groups. By the spring of 1945 they felt strong enough to hold local elections which were followed at the end of the year by elections for a national constituent assembly. The latter devised a new constitution which came into effect in March 1946.

The creation of the Anti-Fascist Council for National Liberation had not meant the demise of the communist-controlled general council of the NLF. This dual power was replicated through every level of the government and the administrative apparatus. Yet while there was no doubt that the ACP was firmly in the control of the central government, Albania was still, as it had always been, a country which did not take readily to central control. In the north there remained considerable opposition to communist domination. This opposition stemmed in part from strong, local tribal affiliations, but also from loyalty to the Catholic Church, especially in the Shkoder area. It also stemmed from the fact that the majority of the communists were Tosks from the south of the country, whereas Zog and his followers had been of northern, Gheg origin. For much of their first months in power the communists concentrated on neutralizing this opposition and paying off old, wartime scores under the slogan of 'revolutionary justice'.

At times revolutionary justice meant nothing more sophisticated than murder. From the liberation of Tirana on 17 November to the entry of Hoxha eleven days later four hundred of the city's population were executed and in Shkoder, a smaller town, the number was higher. Soon after October 1944 there was a series of trials of war criminals, collaborators and enemies of the people. As usual these were elastic terms and the newly established 'People's Courts' could stretch them to include even those stallholders, shopkeepers or merchants who had traded with the occupying forces. In January 1945 a law allowed military courts to try as enemies of the people 'all those who disobey the people's power and work against it'.[5] 'Audience participation' was frequent in such courts with the gallery calling out what they thought, or had been told to think, were the appropriate sentences. So-called 'People's Counsellors' were attached to the courts to supervise the execution of sentences; there were no public prosecutors until 1946, members of the communist party usually fulfilling their functions, while the accuseds' rights to a defence counsellor were dependent on the will of the court. There were also special courts for the prosecution of so-called political offenders, that in Tirana being of particular importance.

In their first few months in power the communists also launched a sustained attack upon the economic and social position of their opponents. Convicted 'enemies of the people' were dispossessed but many others were affected by fiscal measures. March 1945 saw the introduction of a swingeing tax on war profits, a term which, as in Yugoslavia, could be held to include the income made from selling goods to the occupiers. Revenue from this tax soon amounted to half of all state income and those who could not pay had their property confiscated. In January of that year all banking and credit institutions had been nationalized and the import or export of currency forbidden, while in June the right to buy and sell foreign currency became a state monopoly.

State power over the economy had been expanding since December 1944 when central control was imposed on all industries and corporations, and a prohibition placed upon the export of precious metals, mining products and Albanian manufactured goods, such as they were. By August 1945 the state had eliminated private enterprise in the wholesale trade, had assumed control of most larger retail concerns and had nationalized all water resources. There were also significant moves towards land reform. In January 1945 all agricultural debts had been cancelled and rents reduced by as much as three quarters. A decree put into effect in September stated that all land not worked by its owner was to be confiscated without compensation; owners who employed modern methods could retain up to forty hectares (ha) of which a quarter had to be pasture. For other owners and for religious institutions which worked the land themselves the allowances were halved. The landless and those with holdings of less than five hectares were given five further hectares per family unit with additional amounts for married sons who were members of the household. The 1945 reforms were moderate but they brought to virtual completion the process, begun in the inter-war period, of destroying the power of the landowners who had dominated Albania for generations. The reforms could do little, however, to remedy the food shortages which were so severe that the country had to rely for survival on food aid from UNRRA, a condition which limited the communists' freedom of action; any sign of real radicalism, especially if it involved property seizures, would have alarmed the USA which provided most of UNRRA's food, and could have driven the small independent farmers, the main producers in Albania itself, to destroy crops and slaughter cattle. The following year was to see much more extensive and contentious change.

There were important political as well as social and economic changes. In April 1945 elections were held for local councils which were to replace the national liberation councils. The polls were reasonably open and the solid NLF majority reflected popular opinion in the south and among the young. In August the NLF converted itself into a political organization, the Albanian Democratic Front (ADF), in which the ACP played a dominant role. In December elections were held for a national constituent assembly. They too were held secretly and without obvious government intimidation. But there was little need for this because the opposition did not field candidates; it had been technically free to do so but the time allowed for the registration of candidates had been very short. There was, however, in each polling booth a special ballot box in which those who wished to oppose the government candidate could place their ballot slips. Few did so. Of the 90 per cent of the electorate who turned out to vote, 93 per cent did so for the government list. Of the 82 elected members 78 were from the ADF and 4 were classed as independents; 79 were men and 3 women; there were 56 Muslims, 22 Orthodox and 4 Catholics. The assembly convened on 10 January 1946 and on 14 March enacted a new constitution. It was based on the 1936 Soviet model, though without its federal features and also without any mention of the leading role of the party. It did, however, declare Albania to be a People's Republic. Following the enactment of the constitution the assembly turned itself into a legislative parliament.

Before the new constitution had been introduced the NLF/ADF had held its fifth plenum on 21 February 1946. The plenum was the supreme policy-making body and it pointed clearly to the way in which the ADF intended the country should develop, calling for further nationalization, intensified agrarian reform and a more clearly pro-Soviet orientation in foreign policy.

THE BEGINNINGS OF THE REVOLUTION FROM ABOVE, MARCH 1946 TO JUNE 1948

The first stages of Albania's post-war social revolution were determined by the decisions of the fifth plenum and involved an all-out attack on what remained of individual wealth and private enterprise outside the agrarian sector. There were also reforms in the countryside but the government was not yet confident enough of its authority to move towards compulsory collectivization. To entrench their power the communists also launched an offensive against organized religion.

The constitution makers took the hint laid down by the fifth plenum and enacted that the state should direct the economic life of the nation. Accordingly in June the new procurement branch of the trade directory in the ministry of the economy was granted the exclusive right to purchase, stockpile and sell agricultural, dairy and industrial products. At the end of 1945 about 7 per cent of Albania's industrial enterprises had been nationalized; by the end of 1946 the figure was 79 per cent and a year later it was 100 per cent. State direction came in 1948 with a one-year plan for economic development, followed in 1949 by a two-year plan and then by 1951 Albania's first five-year plan.

What remained of Albania's small bourgeoisie had already been blasted by tough taxation policies and rulings that anyone who defaulted on tax payments could be jailed or sent to a labour camp and their property confiscated. Currency reform was a greater and more extensive blow. On 11 July 1946 all existing banknotes were withdrawn from circulation. New notes were issued at a rate of one new for five old francs. The real blow for the wealthier elements was the ruling that no family could exchange more than five thousand old francs; if a family held more than that amount then the excess had to be placed on deposit in the bank and utilized for national reconstruction. In 1948 an entirely new coinage, the lek, replaced the 1945 franc and in 1949 yet another reform was necessary to separate the Albanian from the Yugoslav currency.

In addition to stating that the economy should be under state direction the March 1946 constitution had also decreed that the land belonged to those who tilled it. But landed property was soon to be subjected to attacks as devastating as those directed at industrial, commercial or fiscal holdings. On 2 February, even before the fifth plenum, it had become necessary to secure government permission to slaughter cattle. To some extent this ruling had resulted from the continuing shortage of food, as did a decision in April to give military tribunals powers to imprison anyone found hoarding grain. But further reforms soon revealed the hard ideological content of government policy as laid down in the March constitution. Farm implements and draught animals were made state property and in June orchards, vineyards and olive groves, as well as the buildings and equipment of all those who did not work the land, were expropriated without compensation. Before the 1946 harvest was taken in peasants were given high quotas at low prices for compulsory deliveries to the state purchasing agencies of the staple crops of wheat, maize, barley, rye and oats. In November the sale of municipal land to individuals was forbidden and land already so transferred had to be returned without compensation. In a further restriction of their rights individual farmers now had to lease pasture from the state and if they wished to turn any land into meadows they would not be given a compensatory decrease in their delivery quotas for grain and other arable products. In December 1946 producers who had failed to deliver their quotas were denounced and severe retribution, widely publicized, was meted out to them and to those who had criticized the regime. In May 1947 the government was given absolute power to confiscate the property of any defaulting individual producer while at the end of that month a warning was issued that anyone delivering grain containing more than 4 per cent of moisture would be considered a saboteur and an enemy of the people. These pressures on agriculturalists produced considerable redistribution of land. In all some 173,000 ha, 59 per cent of the cultivated area of 1938, was expropriated; 150,000 ha was given to some 70,000 landless families in plots of 5 ha, the remainder becoming state property.

Yet despite these measures the new authorities did not feel they had complete mastery over the rural masses and on the major issue of collective land ownership the communists proceeded with extreme caution. In 1947 they began to offer tax incentives to those who were prepared to merge their holdings into collectives, but there was little response with only 2,428 families joining the collectives in 1948. Propaganda in favour of the new system continued but was equally ineffective and no systematic collectivization drives were attempted until the first half of the 1950s.

The shifts and changes in policy initiated by the fifth plenum and the constituent assembly were political as well as economic. The ACP was itself in the firing line – sometimes literally. In the summer of 1943 the party had had about 700 members. This had grown to 2,800 by November 1944 and in November 1948 was to stand at 45,382. In between, however, the party had conducted a minor purge. Between November 1945 and June 1946 some 1,246 party members, or about a tenth of the existing ranks, lost their party cards, many of them after the fifth plenum. A sterner, more disciplined party was needed to carry through the impending social revolution.

Outside the ranks of the communists there were growing restrictions on personal and political freedoms. After the fifth plenum members of the Kokoshi-Aslani group, who had attempted to create a separate political party before the recent elections, were all arrested and imprisoned. Pro-ADF propaganda was at the same time intensified with schoolchildren being given prizes for spying on their teachers and even on their parents. Much more threatening was order No. 4 of the ministry of the interior, issued in 1946, which allowed the authorities to evacuate entire communities, urban as well as rural, under certain circumstances. This was an effective threat in a society in which opposition to the central government was traditional and strongly localized. In December 1946 law No. 371 gave the security police the power to arrest, detain, confine or deport to labour camps without process of law. In 1948 a new legal code based on that of Yugoslavia replaced all existing laws; it lasted until 1952 when, because of the break with Yugoslavia, it had to be superseded by one based on the Soviet model.

Political containment in the Balkans can seldom be entirely free from an ethnic dimension and in Albania considerable pressure was exerted on the Greeks in the south of the country, especially those who had retained their Greek citizenship; some eight thousand Greeks were estimated to have fled from southern Albania in 1945 and the first half of 1946, Albania's frontiers, like most in Europe, being relatively porous, at least for the first year or two after the war. The traffic in refugees and expellees was two-way and as

Greeks left Albania they were replaced by Albanians and Chams, Muslim Albanians resident in Greece. The fact that the Greek government frequently raised the question of the frontier with Albania provided the Tirana regime with a convenient excuse for maintaining a strong military presence in the area which in turn made it easier to wield a heavy hand there.

Religious persecution increased markedly after the fifth plenum. The close association of anti-government sentiment with Catholic allegiance had already produced attacks on Catholics and Catholic institutions in northern Albania in late 1944 and in 1945. There were persistent efforts to expel Catholic priests of Italian origin and the Church's activity in the social sector was limited by the closure of church schools and orphanages. By the spring of 1946 these pressures were also being applied to the Orthodox Church and to the Bektashi and other Muslim sects. In 1946 the area of land allowed to religious institutions was halved to ten hectares which limited their capacity to finance charitable institutions or to sustain contemplative monastic communities. It was not until 1949, however, that the campaign against the religious institutions reached its climax, a law of 26 November requiring religious institutions to develop among their flocks a sense of loyalty to 'People's Power'. The law also forbade religious communities with headquarters abroad to have branches in Albania and existing ones had to close within a month. The election of religious heads was to be confirmed by the council of ministers and communist stooges were installed in most organizations. This was not always a peaceful process. A number of prominent Sunni Muslim leaders were killed or imprisoned, as was a pro-communist placed at the head of the Bektashis, while three leading Orthodox clerics were interned. By 1953 of the 93 Catholic priests in Albania in 1945 only ten remained at work in the country and of the 253 Catholic churches only one hundred had survived.

ALBANIA'S EXTERNAL ALIGNMENT, 1944–8

The Albanian communists were acutely aware that their country was backward, impoverished and, they believed, threatened by enemies in Greece and across the Adriatic. In the circumstances the need for an external patron and protector was assumed. The problem, and it was one which was to remain with Albania throughout its post-war history, communist and post-communist, was which one. The fifth plenum of the ADF central committee produced a marked change in Albanian foreign policy. Until then it was clear that Soviet and communist influence were growing. In September 1945 Albania and the Soviet Union had signed an agreement whereby the Soviets would supply grain and technical expertise in the oil and mineral extraction industries in return for Albanian tobacco, preserved fruits, copper ore and oil. As yet, however, pro-sovietism did not automatically mean anti-westernism and western literature circulated freely while American and British films were shown to civilian and military audiences. This was not unwise in a country in which several thousand citizens had been educated in American schools in the country, and where 'It is estimated that about 25 per cent of the population have either been in [the] US or have friends and relatives who have been there.'[6]

The February 1946 plenum changed this. It had called for a policy of close alignment with Moscow which, in the context of 1946, also meant close ties with Tito's communist regime in Belgrade. Albanian communists had fought with Tito's partisans in Kosovo and elsewhere during the war and, the disagreements over Kosovo notwithstanding, the Albanian communists needed and sought patronage and assistance from the larger, neighbouring party. It is not certain that Tito was so keen. He considered Albania easy picking and preferred to concentrate on the more difficult task of including Trieste in his federation, but the Albanians were persistent; three times they had attempted to come to Belgrade, Tito had told Stalin in May, and in June they at last succeeded, Hoxha visiting the Yugoslav capital and signing a treaty of friendship and mutual assistance.

The swing to closer relations with the Soviet Union and Yugoslavia brought increasing anti-westernism. Although all three major powers had agreed to recognize the Albanian government on 10 October 1945 only the Soviets established a full diplomatic mission in Tirana.[7] The Albanians resented as an 'insult' both the western proposal that international observers should be sent to the Albanian elections in December, and the suggestion that the exchange of full diplomatic missions should be dependent upon western satisfaction that the election results fairly represented popular opinion. There was further Albanian resentment at persistent western blocking of Albanian attempts to join the new international bodies which were being established in the immediate post-war period, while the west was increasingly frustrated by Tirana's continuing refusal to accept responsibility for the financial liabilities incurred by previous Albanian regimes. In the event neither Britain nor the United States sent diplomatic missions to Tirana. British action was suspended after Albanian shore batteries had fired ineffectively at two British warships in the Corfu Channel on 15 May 1946. Far more serious was the second Corfu Channel incident on 22 October when two British vessels were mined in waters already swept clean of mines. Forty British seamen died; it was the longest casualty list reported by British forces since the end of the war. The incident effectively ended any chance of Britain recognizing the new Albanian regime.* Meanwhile, an unofficial, civil mission sent by the United States in the spring of 1945 was subjected to increasing harassment and hostility. Hoxha himself made deprecating noises, wondering what purpose

---

* Britain demanded compensation for the loss of life and damage to the ships concerned and when this was refused impounded Albanian gold reserves which had been in Rome and which had fallen into allied hands when the city was captured. Not until the early 1990s was the dispute settled; the Albanians conceded that, in collusion with the Yugoslavs, they had been responsible for floating the mines into the Corfu Channel, and some of the gold was then returned to the Albanians.

the mission was serving, and in the autumn it withdrew, taking with it any chance that full, official relations between Washington and Tirana would be established.

In November the Albanian authorities staged a large show-trial intended to discredit the US and Britain together with their supporters in Albania. On the bench were five Albanians who had been arrested and tortured in October. They were charged with having sabotaged the project to drain Lake Maliq, a grotesque scheme which had defied engineering reality and had certainly had no chance of being completed by the stipulated date of 28 November 1946.

In 1947 Yugoslav influence in Albania increased rapidly. In accordance with the terms of the 1946 treaty Yugoslav economic assistance was offered and a series of joint-stock enterprises created. Belgrade also provided a financial subsidy worth about 10 per cent of all Albanian government revenue, and annoyed the western powers by allocating ten thousand tons of grain to Albania when Yugoslavia itself was in receipt of foreign cereals as part of western aid. So completely did the Yugoslavs dominate Albania that the latter was not invited to the founding meeting of Cominform in Poland in September 1947. Beneath the surface, however, there were tensions. On his visit to Yugoslavia in June 1946 Hoxha had been shocked by Tito's indulgent lifestyle and discomforted by his flatulent dog, 'Lux'. More seriously, the Yugoslavs refused to aid the development of manufacturing industries in Albania. For their part many Albanians found complete reliance on Yugoslavia demeaning, and there were some who argued that if the country had to rely on patronage it would be better to seek that of a large power rather than a medium-sized one, that is of the Soviet Union rather than Yugoslavia. This became a real choice as strains developed between those two states, some of those strains being evident in Albania itself. Even in the summer of 1947 Soviet and Yugoslav advisors in the country were falling out; the Soviets behaved in their customary high-handed manner which the Yugoslavs resented all the more because, in equally haughty fashion, they regarded Albania as exclusively their patch. The Yugoslavs were all the more alarmed when they learned that one of the most influential of high-ranking Albanian communists, Naku Spiru, had direct and secret links with the Soviet representative in Tirana. In November 1947 the Yugoslavs accused him of sabotaging Yugoslav-Albanian economic cooperation. Spiru committed suicide and his demise seemed to put the pro-Yugoslav faction within the Albanian leadership firmly in the driving seat.

By early 1948 Tito was anxious to implement his plans for union with Albania before the west, or more probably Stalin, vetoed the project. The Yugoslavs encouraged their main protagonist in Albania, Koçi Xoxe, to press ahead with the plans for unification. Xoxe, as secretary of the ACP and minister of the interior, was powerfully placed to do so and in February 1948 he called a meeting of the central committee. It seemed that the moderate faction, led by Hoxha, had been defeated because the latter, as the price of retaining the party leadership, was forced to confess his failings and agree to the idea of union with Yugoslavia. The February 1948 plenum also brought about the removal of the former partisan leader Mehmet Shehu from his post as army chief of staff. After this Xoxe set about purging the doubters from the civil service and the police. In April he put before the politburo a formal proposal to ask Belgrade for the incorporation of Albania into the Yugoslav federation. But by now the tide had turned. Hoxha, sensing how matters stood between Belgrade and Moscow, dug in his heels and defeated the unification proposal. In June the open breach between Stalin and Tito offered the nationalist communists of Albania a welcome escape hatch and the idea of joining the Yugoslav federation was abandoned. Albania would seek a new patron; and the protagonists of a pro-Yugoslav line would suffer.

Notes

1. Jon Halliday (ed.), *The Artful Albanian: the Memoirs of Enver Hoxha*, London: Chatto & Windus, 1986, p.3.
2. Its Albanian initials were LNC.
3. Quoted in David Smiley, *Albanian Assignment*, with a foreword by Patrick Leigh Fermor, London/Sydney: Sphere Books, 1984, pp.91–2.
4. Stavro Skendi, *Albania*, East Central Europe under the Communists, series editor Robert F. Byrnes, published for the Mid-European Studies Center of the Free Europe Committee Inc., New York: Praeger, 1956, p.98. Despite their obvious cold war origins the books in this series frequently contain useful detail.
5. Vladimir Gsovski and Kazimierz Grzybowski, *Government, Law and Courts in the Soviet Union and eastern Europe*, London: Stevens & Sons, 2 vols, 1959, i, p.636.
6. Representative Jacobs to Secretary of State, Tirana, 1 July 1945, *Foreign Relations of the United States* (hereafter cited as FRUS) 1945, vol. iv, note p.398. That exposure to western culture was beneficial was not universally agreed. A British officer parachuted into Albania recorded meeting an Albanian who had emigrated to the USA, worked there and saved enough money to return to his native land. 'He could barely understand English, and what little he spoke was with such a broad American accent that it was often unintelligible. We later met many men of this type, and they produced American passports with great pride; sadly their stay in America had improved neither their characters nor their morals, and we found that their contact with the West had made the majority both avaricious and dishonest.' Smiley, op.cit., p.27.
7. Albania had written to the three great powers requesting recognition when those powers assembled for the Potsdam conference in July. The Americans wished to discuss the question with the British and it was never put before the conference. See Paskal Milo, 'Albania in East–West Relations, 1944–1945', a paper delivered to the conference, 'The Establishment of Communist Regimes in Eastern Europe, 1945–1950: A Reassessment', Moscow, 29–31 March 1994. Milo's paper was printed separately, Tirana: Tirana University Press, no date. See pp.20–5.

Chapter 4

BULGARIA, 1944–1948

The ethnic origin of the Bulgars is a matter of controversy, most contemporary Bulgarian scholars rejecting the idea advanced by others, that they were a Turkic race. Whatever their origin they crossed the Danube in the seventh century to settle among local Slavs into whom they were eventually assimilated. The Bulgarian state, established in the late seventh century, became Christian in the ninth century and until the early eleventh century was a major political, military and cultural power in the Balkans. In 1018 it was conquered by the Byzantines. A second Bulgarian empire emerged in 1185. It was never the equal of its predecessor and in the late fourteenth century was smashed by the Ottoman forces.

The Bulgarian state and its ruling caste were dismantled by the Ottomans but the Bulgarian language and Bulgarian customs survived under the protection of the Bulgarian Church, and more particularly its monasteries and convents. Bulgarian culture became in the process a predominantly rural phenomenon, the towns being dominated for much of Ottoman rule by Turks and Greeks. When Bulgarian national consciousness was reborn it was through the Church, the Bulgarians becoming increasingly irked by the hellenization of the Church after the suppression of the patriarchate of Ohrid in 1765. In the second quarter of the nineteenth century a growing class of Bulgarian manufacturers and merchants, many of them made wealthy by providing cloth for uniforms for the Ottoman army, funded a cultural revival which culminated in the establishment of a separate Bulgarian Orthodox Church in 1870. The revival had also produced an educational renaissance.

In 1876 a failed nationalist revolt provoked retaliation by the Ottomans and their local auxiliaries, as a result of which Russia declared war on the Ottoman empire. Russia's eventual victory brought about the creation of the modern Bulgarian state in 1878 but that state, defined in the treaty of Berlin in July 1878, was much smaller than the one originally envisaged in the peace of San Stefano at the end of the Russo-Turkish war in March of that year. The major loss was Macedonia.

The desire to retrieve Macedonia could not be acted upon effectively except in times of major European conflagration, that is the Balkan wars of

1912–13 and the two world wars, in both of which Bulgaria aligned with Germany because it alone was willing to offer Bulgaria possession of Macedonia.

In domestic affairs Bulgaria in 1879 adopted the liberal Tŭrnovo constitution which gave the country a unicameral legislature and a foreign monarch. The first monarch, Alexander of Battenberg, displeased the Russians who ejected him in 1886. In the following year Ferdinand of Saxe-Coburg-Gotha replaced him; he was succeeded by his son, Boris III, in 1918, who, after his death in August 1943, was in turn succeeded by King Simeon II.

Under Ferdinand the party political process in Bulgaria became dominated by clientalism and was subjected to occasional outbursts of violence and assassination. Partly in protest against the sterility of national party politics, and even more so because of the social pressures created by the decline in agricultural incomes in the late nineteenth century, a new political force emerged in the Bulgarian Agrarian National Union (BANU) which was dominated by the charismatic Aleksandŭr Stamboliiski. After the First World War he became prime minister but was murdered in a violent coup in June 1923. Further violence was visited upon the country in 1925 when the communists detonated a bomb in the roof of a Sofia church during a state funeral service. Official retaliation was swift, widespread and horrible. A further destabilizing and violent threat came from the various Macedonian groups whose internecine feuds were as dangerous to Bulgaria as their excursions into neighbouring Yugoslavia and Greece. The Macedonian question was to a large extent solved by a military junta which took over in Sofia in a coup on 19 May 1934; the military cleared most of the Macedonians out of enclaves they had established in south-western Bulgaria.

The military regime had few other successes and within two years had been outmanoeuvred by King Boris whose main preoccupations were to keep Bulgaria out of the looming European conflict and to try and find some constitutional midway point between the parliamentary anarchy of Bulgaria's past and the totalitarian present of much of contemporary Europe.

BULGARIA DURING THE SECOND WORLD WAR

King Boris was unable to succeed in either quest. The constitutional riddle remained unsolved while after much prevarication Boris finally committed Bulgaria to the Axis cause, signing the tripartite pact in March 1941. German troops passed through Bulgaria en route to Yugoslavia and Greece and Bulgaria's reward was the occupation of most of Macedonia and western Thrace. Bulgaria did not declare war on the Soviet Union or commit its forces to the Eastern front nor would it allow the deportation of Jews from the pre-1941 kingdom to the death camps.

Resistance in Bulgaria was weak compared to that in Albania, Greece and Yugoslavia. This was primarily because Bulgaria had not been occupied and had made territorial gains from the war.

Resistance began in a faltering fashion in 1941 with the formation of the Fatherland Front (FF). The FF was reconstituted in 1942 and consisted of four political groups opposed to the government's pro-Axis policy. They were the communists, known since 1929 as the Bulgarian Workers' Party; the more radical sections of the Bulgarian Agrarian National Union; the Social Democrats; and Zveno (link or group), an organization whose origins lay in the anti-royalist intelligentsia and officer corps and which had played a prominent part in the administration formed after the military coup of 1934. Resistance remained relatively weak. The parties were still suspicious of one another, most were heavily penetrated by the political police, and the military tactics, which were copied from the Yugoslav partisans and which involved attempts to set up liberated zones under resistance control, were inappropriate.

As the military situation deteriorated early in 1944 the Bulgarian government had put out feelers to the allies for peace talks but Sofia was unwilling to contemplate the loss of all its occupied territory and the negotiations made no progress. Changes of government took place as the military situation worsened and in August all anti-Jewish legislation and much of the apparatus of authoritarian rule were abolished. On 25 August the government ordered that all German troops in Bulgaria be disarmed. When Romania quit the Axis after a coup in Bucharest on 23 August the fear was that the Red Army would move across the Danube and occupy Bulgaria. In desperation yet another new administration was formed on 3 September which invited the FF to enter a coalition. The FF was no longer interested in coalitions. It wanted power for itself. The situation became desperate on 5 September when the Soviet Union declared war on Bulgaria. This was the worst nightmare of the Sofia administration. It meant that it would be Moscow rather than London and Washington which had the major voice in the future of the country. In a desperate attempt to retrieve the situation the cabinet declared war on Germany on 8 September, but it was of no use. The FF, and primarily the communists, had mobilized their supporters who staged strikes and demonstrations to demand the appointment of an FF government while Soviet troops crossed the Danube into north-eastern Bulgaria. In the early hours of 9 September pro-FF troops, aided and abetted by the minister of war who was in Soviet pay, occupied key points in Sofia, deposed the disintegrating government and installed an FF administration.

FACTORS IN BULGARIAN POLITICS, 1944–8

To a large extent the FF government had been placed in power by the Red Army but after 9 September 1944 domestic political factors were directly involved in Bulgaria's evolution. The sudden death of King Boris at the age of 49 in August 1943 had all but eliminated the monarchy as an active force. Boris's successor, King Simeon II, was a minor and a three-man regency was therefore established. The new Regency appointed after 9 September exercised virtually no independent political power.

The army, on the other hand, was by no means a negligible quantity. It had a history of intervention in politics. Furthermore, unlike most armies in Europe in 1944 it had not been bloodied by conflict or bruised by defeat; its prestige and its power alike were intact and considerable. It had a reputation for efficiency in the service of the national interest and its historic failures on the battlefield were generally regarded as the fault not of the military commanders but of spineless and self-serving politicians. It was a conscript force whose officer corps was open to the talents without regard to social origins; Bulgaria had no aristocracy and its army had no caste which regarded command as its natural privilege. It was therefore a popular national force, in which the vast majority of townsmen and peasants placed their trust and confidence. The political history of Bulgaria and the state of the country in 1944 suggested that no one could be secure in office if the army were against them.

The traditional political parties were weak. Those associated with the Bulgarian commercial and industrial bourgeoisie had been discredited by the failure of their policies in previous wars and after 1934 they, together with all other political parties, had been disbanded. Reconstruction in the post-war, left-dominated world was very difficult for all but a handful of such parties. The literary and cultural segment of the bourgeoisie had never been strongly committed to them; it had leaned to the left and in the inter-war period some of it had been sympathetic towards Zveno with its call for a cleansing, rationalizing and modernizing of the state and the political system on a national, non-party basis. The professional elements had a traditional leaning towards the moderate socialists of the Social Democratic Party (SDP).

If the traditional or bourgeois parties were weak in Bulgaria the radical ones were strong. And the strongest were the Agrarians who retained the loyalty of most of the peasants who still formed almost four fifths of the population. This was despite the fact that after the violent coup of 1923 and the elimination of the charismatic Stamboliiski, the Agrarian movement had divided into a number of factions, the most prominent of which were the radical *Pladne* (noon) group led by G. M. Dimitrov or 'Gemeto' as he was known to distinguish him from the communist leader of the same name, and Nikola Petkov, and the *Vrabcha* (sparrow) faction led by Dimitûr Gichev. The division was mainly personal and historic but *Vrabcha* tended to be more willing than *Pladne* to compromise with the urban left. The divisions weakened agrarianism, as did the fact that it had no foreign sponsor or supporter who could provide funding or backing in its domestic battles. Furthermore, cooperation with the bourgeois parties was difficult because the Agrarians resented the latter's role in the 1923 coup, while the traditional parties had been so appalled by Agrarian rule that a number of them regarded BANU as a greater threat than the communists. Nevertheless, their historical record and their well-entrenched network of local associations gave the Agrarians immense potential political power.

The other main radical force was the communists. The socialist movement in Bulgaria had become organized in the early 1890s but in 1903 had split between those willing to work with left-wing bourgeois parties within the existing political structures and trade unions and those who opposed any such dilution of Marxist orthodoxy. After the Russian revolution the latter became the Bulgarian Communist Party (BCP) and the former the SDP. In the early 1920s the BCP had considerable backing among the urban poor. It had been banned in 1923 but in 1927 reappeared as the Bulgarian Workers' Party (BWP). With other parties it suffered from the disbanding of all political organizations after 1934 but unlike most other parties it was steeped in the traditions and practices of underground organization and conspiracy. In addition the communists enjoyed considerable prestige in left-wing circles because a Bulgarian communist, Georgi Dimitrov, had bettered Göring at the Reichstag fire trial in Leipzig in 1934 and had subsequently been appointed head of Comintern.

Dimitrov did not return to Bulgaria with the Red Army, the party at home being led by the able Traicho Kostov who had escaped the gallows in 1942 thanks to the intervention of King Boris. Party membership had begun to expand before 9 September and did so even more rapidly thereafter. From around six thousand at the end of 1943 the BWP grew to over thirteen thousand by 9 September 1944. In January 1945 there were a quarter of a million party members. The BWP had advantages other than its size. It benefited from the remaining suspicion between bourgeois and agrarian; it was the only political group with an armed force, the partisans; and many non-communists hoped that its, and especially Dimitrov's, close connections with the Soviets would soften the peace terms to be imposed on Bulgaria.

The communists' real strength lay less in the country at large than within the FF where representation in the vital posts was skewed to favour the BWP, the most important being the chair of the national council of the FF which was occupied by Tsola Dragoicheva, a formidable communist who had withstood torture in the 1920s and who after 9 September 1944 showed little mercy to her opponents. After, and in some cases immediately before, the coup, the FF set up local committees, just over half of whose members were communists and without whose approval no decision of any importance could be taken.

The final and most decisive factor in Bulgarian politics was the Soviet Union. Britain and the USA agreed that the Soviet representative was to have charge of the Allied Control Commission in Bulgaria until the end of hostilities in Europe after which the two western powers would join the ACC which, however, would remain under Soviet chairmanship. Stalin regarded Bulgaria as part of the Soviet sphere of interest, as the percentage agreements had encouraged him to do, but as in other areas Stalin was frequently at pains to ensure that the western powers were not needlessly provoked. Until 1947 therefore his interventions in Bulgaria were not always in favour of radical action by the communists.

FROM THE COUP OF 9 SEPTEMBER 1944 TO THE POSTPONEMENT OF THE ELECTIONS IN AUGUST 1945

Between September 1944 and August 1945 Bulgaria experienced an initial, violent and at times uncontrolled purge which was followed in 1945 by the calculated and orchestrated elimination of the remainder of the pre-1944 political establishment. At the same time, the potential political influence of the military was limited, after which the BWP addressed itself to its main task, the destruction of its political opponents, and above all the Agrarians.

The new council of ministers or cabinet was formed by the four FF parties. The prime minister was Kimon Georgiev, a leading Zvenar and architect of the 1934 coup. His fellow coupster of 1934, Damian Velchev, was made minister of war while the all-important post of minister of the interior went to the communist, Anton Yugov. Another communist, Mincho Neichev, served as minister of justice. The most prominent of the four Agrarians was Petkov, Gemeto not joining the government as he was still outside the country. There were three Social Democrats.

In the early days of the new regime local government was as important as the central administration. The old order began to collapse at the local level even before 9 September with the police abandoning their posts and their uniforms. On 10 September the old police force was disbanded and an entirely new Soviet-style People's Militia formed. The militia was backed by the People's Guard formed soon after 9 September 1944 from partisan military units which were too disorganized to be incorporated into the regular army and whose political commitment to the FF made them useful additions to the domestic police apparatus.

A vital part of the new structure at the local level were the local FF committees which expanded greatly in number and power after 9 September. These were now founded in apartment blocks, places of work, military units and educational institutions as well as on a geographic basis. By the end of 1944 there were over seven thousand such committees. They appointed, without election, provincial governors, mayors and other officials; they chose head teachers and police officials; and they interfered in, if they did not assume complete control over, the administration of local economic enterprises. In October they were made permanent by a government decree, and on 22 January 1945 it was ordered that no one could hold public office without the prior approval of the local FF committee.

The first weeks of FF power witnessed a massive, nationwide purge, much of it coordinated or at least condoned by the local FF committees. Not having been occupied Bulgaria had retained its inter-war social and political structures together with their personnel. The victims of those structures streamed out of prisons and camps thirsty for revenge. Their victims included rich peasants, schoolmasters, priests, policemen and any other servant of the old regime who had incurred the copious enmities of one or more partisan or prisoner. How many died is impossible to calculate though in the first few weeks of FF power it was probably in the region of three thousand.[1] Many more lost their liberty, their homes and their livelihoods.

By October the elemental violence began to abate. It had not been welcome to the Soviet military authorities who were anxious to secure peace and stability behind their front line. Nor did the Soviets wish to alarm the western allies. Furthermore, on 6 October a decree was published establishing new People's Courts to try those accused of fascism or collaboration, the members of the new courts and the public prosecutors being appointed by the local FF committees. If the new courts meant that the purges were controlled rather than elemental, the latter were by no means ended; in the six months after 6 October, according to official statistics, 11,667 individuals were tried in the People's Courts; unofficial estimates of those accused ranged from thirty to one hundred thousand.

With the purges came other forms of control. On the same day that the People's Courts were created censorship was imposed. In the schools curricula were reformed to the detriment of 'old-fashioned' disciplines such as metaphysics and logic and to the benefit of more 'scientific' subjects, while the teaching of Russian was also increased. The Bulgarian Workers' Union set up after the coup of 1934 was dissolved, much of it being merged with a number of white collar unions to form the General Workers' Professional Union; the mass of the working class, as well as the press, the cultural resources and the educational system of the nation were under firm FF control by the spring of 1945.

At the national level the first priority of the new FF government had been to conclude an armistice with the Soviets. This was signed on 28 October and required the Bulgarians to withdraw their forces to the boundaries of March 1941. Before the signature of the armistice the Bulgarian government had made the momentous decision to join the war against Germany and to place the Bulgarian army at the disposal of Marshal Tolbukhin's Third Ukrainian Front. It was not a popular decision and it was one which was to cost thirty thousand Bulgarian lives but it was one which meant that the professional army was out of the country and under firm Soviet control in the first few months of FF rule.

The decision depressed military morale. This had been impaired by the army's inaction on 9 September and by the introduction of military committees to instil a new form of patriotism and to hasten the removal of untrustworthy officers. These committees operated with such vigour that even the Soviets had to remind their Bulgarian comrades that capable officers should be protected if the army was to be of any value against the Wehrmacht. With such attitudes prevailing in the Kremlin the minister of war, Velchev, thought he was safe in acting to preserve the officer corps from further depletion. On 23 November, when communist members were not present, the council of ministers approved a proposal that all soldiers accused by the People's Courts could, if they wished, be sent to active duty at the front; on 25 November Velchev ordered all officers to sleep in barracks and to defend themselves with firearms if threatened. The communists were furious and organized street demonstrations in protest at Velchev's actions but they also ordered the militia to stop arresting members of the army. The communists were saved by General Sergei Biryuzov, the senior Soviet officer in Bulgaria and the head of the ACC. In his first major intervention into internal Bulgarian affairs he forced Velchev to rescind his order and to accept as chief of staff Ivan Kinov, a Bulgarian who had long served in the Red Army. Thereafter the purge of regular officers continued and by December about a third of them had been dismissed.

While the army was being purged more definition had been given to Bulgaria's political structure. On 12 October a decree was issued stating that the only legal political parties were the four which comprised the FF. Opposition groups were in effect banned. It was soon clear that their former adherents were likely to be persecuted. In December a wave of arrests engulfed the entire pre-9 September political establishment from the Regents to members of parliament. The accused were put before a People's Court where few were given notice of the charges or allowed anything but minimal access to defence counsel. Nevertheless, the Bulgarian legal profession put up a stout performance, refusing to sacrifice its tradition of defending the accused, while the public openly disapproved of the trials. Dimitrov, however, decided to administer the smack of firm government. When the trials ended on 1 February the prosecution demanded fifty death penalties. Orders from the highest levels of the BWP doubled that number and insisted that the victims be shot in batches of twenty that very night. The old centre and right of Bulgarian politics had been destroyed.

To underline its determination to prevent opposition activity the government, in January 1945, passed a law for the defence of the people's authority which prohibited any act likely to contribute to the demoralization of the army or which might injure Bulgaria's international prestige. It was the catch-all type of legislation upon which authoritarian regimes rely and in subsequent months and years it was to be much used.

Opposition outside the FF was now almost impossible but criticism from within the coalition was still widely voiced. Gemeto made no secret of his views. Encouraged by the rapturous reception he received when he returned to Bulgaria on 23 September he emphasized the party slogan of 'Bread, Peace and Democracy'; the demand for bread contrasted sharply with the current food shortages; the call for peace highlighted the government's unpopular decision to commit the Bulgarian army to 'The Danube and Beyond'; and the call for democracy pointed to the restrictive policies of the FF and the current purges. At the October congress which reconstituted BANU Gemeto, who was appointed leader of the party, insisted that the agrarians and not the communists should dominate Bulgaria.

This pointed to the growing tension between the BWP and BANU which was to dominate Bulgarian domestic politics until the late summer of 1947.

The BWP's answer to Gemeto's popularity and self-confidence was first to attack Gemeto himself and then to undermine BANU from within, mainly through the leftist faction associated with Aleksandŭr Obbov. Gemeto was vulnerable because of his close links with the western allies and he resigned the leadership of BANU before he was expelled. He was succeeded by Petkov who was determined to show that the resignation of Gemeto had not been a capitulation.

The tension between the agrarians and the communists tightened in April 1945 when the government announced that the elections which the Yalta agreement had demanded should be held in the coming summer. At a BANU congress in Stara Zagora in April there were strong protests against communist hegemonialism and against the lack of proportionality in government departments and FF committees, while strong support was shown for Gemeto. Enraged by the continued support given to the former BANU leader by the April congress the communists placed Gemeto under house arrest. At the same time the communists, with Moscow's approval, moved away from trying to work through established BANU structures and began to prepare an internal coup against the agrarian leadership. Special meetings of 'Friends of the Agrarians' were staged by the communists in which Petkov and Gemeto were reviled for wanting to separate agrarian from communist, peasant from worker. In May these agents provocateurs demanded an immediate conference to free BANU from the Gemeto line. The conference was held on 8–9 May. The communists had been assiduous in preparing for it, suborning dissatisfied or venal agrarians, placing their own covert supporters in positions of influence, and even excluding known supporters of Gemeto and Petkov from the conference hall. As a result a new ruling council was elected of whom only Petkov had refused to condemn Gemeto and his supporters. On 11 May Petkov prepared a statement dissociating himself from the conference and blaming Obbov for its convocation. On 24 May Gemeto, warned of impending danger by a communist friend, climbed out of a rear window of his apartment and escaped to the safety of the home of a member of the British military mission in Bulgaria. The British refused him asylum and so he sought refuge in the house of the senior American representative in Sofia. That Gemeto was facing real danger was proved by the fate of his 25-year secretary, Mara Racheva. She was arrested on 24 May and died of torture four days later; outraged agrarian supporters broke into the morgue and exhibited her horribly mutilated corpse to the world. Nevertheless, the communists had succeeded in breaking the old BANU. On 12 June Petkov was replaced as leader of BANU by Obbov while the communist minister of the interior, Yugov, decreed that all the assets of BANU, including its property and its newspaper, belonged to the newly elected leadership. Petkov was soon to form a new party, the Bulgarian Agrarian National Union – Nikola Petkov (BANU-NP).

A similar fate befell the SDP. It had decided to hold a conference but had been forbidden to do so by the authorities. It disobeyed and the conference met on 10 June but the leaders were prevented from telling party members that it had taken place or what had been decided, the militia removing the SDP leader, Grigor Chesmedjiev, from his office and seizing control of the party newspaper, *Narod*, which continued publication under militia auspices. Thereafter a communist-organized coup removed Chesmedjiev from the leadership of the party, replacing him with a communist stooge, Dimitûr Neikov. Neikov's party was immediately recognized by the FF while Chesmedjiev was left to form a new, independent Workers' Social Democratic Party (WSDP).

The changes in BANU and the SDP had reorganized the internal structure of Bulgarian politics. This was also affected by the end of the war in Europe. The western representatives now began to play a more active part in the deliberations of the ACC and the number of westerners in Sofia increased. They were greatly welcomed by the western-orientated intelligentsia and by the embattled non-communist parties. The confidence with which they faced the forthcoming elections which now dominated the political scene was much increased.

Despite this increased confidence BANU and the SDP faced real problems. The decree of October 1944 insisted that only the four FF parties could exist. New electoral rules also stated that if a party put itself on the joint FF list in any constituency no other representatives of that party could stand in that constituency; the effect of this was that if an Obbov agrarian or a Neikov SDP candidate stood then Petkovists and candidates from the WSDP would be excluded. On 7 July Petkov issued a declaration to all local BANU organizations rejecting the decisions of the May conference, refusing to recognize the new leadership, and insisting that if he did not have a say in choosing BANU parliamentary candidates for the joint FF lists he would stand independently. On 26 July he and his supporters in the cabinet wrote to the prime minister and to the ACC arguing that the government's insistence on the use of a single list would not produce the proper conditions for a free and fair election, as prescribed at Yalta; Petkov therefore asked for international supervision of the elections, which he suggested should be postponed until October; if they were not, said the letter, the peasants would be too preoccupied with the harvest to give proper consideration to the vote. The communists reacted by saying that Petkov's communicating with the western representatives on the ACC was proof that he was in foreign pay. On 31 July Petkov was dismissed from the government; a new cabinet was formed on 17 August.

The dismissal of Petkov once more raised the political temperature in Sofia. This time, however, the western powers took effective measures to make it known that they shared Petkov's view on the effects of a single list and shortly before the scheduled polling day Stalin bowed to their pressure and agreed the elections should be postponed. It was the only time when the west successfully resisted Soviet and BWP designs in Bulgaria; it provided a huge fillip for the non-communists; and it meant that once again the political situation in Bulgaria had been transformed.

FROM THE POSTPONEMENT OF THE ELECTIONS
IN AUGUST 1945 TO THE GRAND NATIONAL
ASSEMBLY ELECTIONS OF OCTOBER 1946

The postponement of the elections signalled a respite in the communist drive for power, but it was a temporary one. By the summer of 1946 the engine was once again engaged in top gear, the chief objective being the complete neutralization of the army.

The postponement of the elections in August 1945 was not the only victory secured by the opposition. In the same month the FF amnestied around a thousand prisoners, amongst them Dimitŭr Gichev, the agrarian, and Nikola Mushanov who was allowed to reorganize his left-leaning bourgeois Democratic Party (DP). On 5 September Gemeto and his wife were allowed to leave for Italy. In September there was also an enactment legitimizing non-fascist parties outside the FF, the first to be recognized being the WSDP, others being BANU-NP, the DP and the small United Radical Party. These parties were also to be allowed to publish newspapers.

The relaxations of August and September greatly enhanced the confidence and the prestige of the opposition leaders, especially Petkov. Petkov was riding high, and when offered the post of minister for foreign affairs in a reconstructed cabinet refused it, arguing that as head of the most popular party he could only enter a cabinet as prime minister. He also demanded that the communists sacrifice their hold on the ministry of the interior, that the Obbov and Neikov rumps be dismissed from the FF, and that the FF must swear to restore all civil liberties. Petkov was further emboldened by the tough stance taken by the western participants in the council of foreign ministers' meeting in London in September and October, after which he and the other opposition leaders decided, against western advice, to boycott the elections, now scheduled for 18 November, on the grounds that unless the communists relinquished their hold on the ministry of the interior the vote would not be fair.

The opposition decision to boycott the elections produced new levels of indignation among the communists. Behind communist anger lay the question of international recognition. If there were no proper elections the west would argue that there could be no legitimate government and without a legitimate government there could be no recognition. The Soviets had agreed to recognize the FF government in August 1945 but western recognition was also needed and it was partly to enhance the prospects of achieving it that the relaxations of August and September had been allowed. The need for recognition was not just a matter of political vanity. Refusal of recognition meant that trade embargoes and other sanctions imposed during the war would remain in place; a government which was not recognized would not be allowed to plead its case at the peace conference; desperately needed loans would not be attainable; and the longer a regime remained unrecognized the longer its nation would have to remain under humiliating, oppressive and above all expensive occupation: by June occupation costs absorbed about half the total budget expenditure.

The west however still remained unconvinced that Bulgaria's elections would be fair and representative. Although the new electoral law gave the vote to all men and women over 19 – previously only married women were enfranchised – and to all former partisans, the opposition were denied any access to the radio and their supplies of newsprint could be interrupted while communist trade unionists frequently refused to print material critical of their party or its leaders. Furthermore, the conduct of the elections was to be in the hands of electoral bureaux selected by lot by the local FF committees.

The election campaign itself brought further cause for complaint. Opposition activists were subjected to increasing harassment, the trade unions continued with their unofficial censorship of anti-FF material, anyone accused of having 'fascist ideas' was removed from the registry of voters, prisoners were released on condition that they signed appeals to vote for the government, and militia tanks paraded around cities with pro-government slogans. After the elections there were unaccustomed delays in announcing the results and when they were published they were for constituencies as a whole; returns from individual villages and urban districts were not revealed. The outcome was predictable. A turnout of 86 per cent registered an 88 per cent poll for the FF, all of whose candidates were returned. The opposition did not believe the results and talked of villages where the non-government vote was as high as 70 per cent.

As the western powers refused to recognize them as fair the elections did nothing to solve the international aspect of the Bulgarian question. A solution to that came only with the Moscow foreign ministers' meeting at the end of the year. There it was agreed that two non-FF ministers should be added to the cabinet; when that was done the west agreed that recognition should take place. The Moscow decisions enabled the government to claim de facto recognition and the opposition to claim that its accusations of the government's unrepresentative nature had been justified. But real progress towards a settlement was no nearer. The government demanded that before the non-FF ministers enter the cabinet the opposition must recognize the legitimacy of the elections and endorse FF policies; the opposition, for its part, insisted that as the largest and most popular group the agrarians must be given the premiership and that the communists must relinquish the portfolios of the interior and justice. After a second bout of negotiations in March Georgiev was ready to concede that the latter ministry should change hands, that the opposition could nominate an assistant minister of the interior, and that all detainees would be released from detention camps. Then Georgiev announced that when he had said that the ministry of justice could go to the agrarians he meant the Obbovites and not the Petkovists. The reconstruction of the government on 31 March brought Obbov into the cabinet along with one further oppositionist from the WSDP. It was a cosmetic operation which did nothing to diminish FF or communist power.

By now Stalin, frustrated that concessions to the opposition seemed to bring nothing but the demand for more concessions, had revised his attitude to the Bulgarian opposition. Rather than trying to neutralize it by cooperation he now believed it should be destroyed by outright assault. The BWP was ready for the task. Since Dimitrov returned to Bulgaria shortly before the elections the party had become more radical but it was not confident that its hold on power would survive the departure of the Red Army which the peace treaty would bring. Then the Bulgarian army could be the ultimate decider of the nation's destiny. It was this which underlay the dramatic events of the summer of 1946.

In that summer there were a number of political trials and harassment of the opposition increased markedly. In June the Social Democrat Krûstiu Pastuhov, arrested in February for remarks critical of the army, was tried and sentenced. Gemeto was also tried *in absentia*. In July two high-ranking agrarians were arrested and in the same month harassment of Bulgarian employees of the western missions in Sofia increased sharply when a number of them were arrested. In June Petkov had been forced to suspend publication of his newspaper after a series of attacks by trade unionists who had even maltreated an aged satirical columnist.

There was also a growing confrontation with Zveno which, to judge by sales of its newspaper *Izgrev* (dawn), was becoming more and more popular. But any assault upon Zveno involved difficulties. After the purges of 1944 the minister of war, Velchev, a prominent Zvenar, had succeeded in keeping the army a largely autonomous force. The BWP therefore demanded that control of the army pass from the minister of war to the cabinet as a whole; were that to be secured Zveno's hold on the army would be broken. At the same time the Soviets presented Velchev with a list of seven hundred officers whom they wanted summarily dismissed. Velchev refused. His reward was to be subjected to villainous attacks in the communist press which accused him of being an ally of Mihailović who had just been tried and executed in Belgrade. Other Zveno leaders were subjected to similar intimidation. On 28 June they buckled and agreed to pass control of the army from the minister of war to the cabinet as a whole. Velchev then agreed to a purge, hoping that by being involved he might mitigate it. He failed. On 2 August he was sent on indefinite leave and was later posted as minister to Switzerland. The purge of the officer corps began as soon as he left office and in no more than two weeks almost two thousand officers were dismissed. The army had been emasculated as a political factor and Zveno had been all but eliminated as a political force.

The attack on the army had done something to deflect public opinion from the concessions on Macedonia which the communist leadership was making in the summer of 1946 and which were extremely unpopular among most Bulgarians.[2] A further distraction was the plebiscite on the future of the monarchy which the government announced would be held on 7 September. The timing of this had also been determined by the fact that negotiations for a peace treaty were about to begin in Paris and the Sofia government was anxious to show the allies that Bulgaria had broken with a dynasty which, said its critics, had dragged Bulgaria into an unpopular war. The referendum produced a massive majority in favour of a republic though the referendum itself was technically illegal because according to the constitution only a Grand National Assembly (GNA), a body twice the size of a normal parliament, could sanction constitutional change.

A GNA was elected on 27 October with the purpose of devising a new constitution for post-war Bulgaria. The elections to this assembly were more representative than those of November 1945. The campaign was more open and although a single list was still presented means were found to allow voters to express preferences between the FF parties. The new system was not of great benefit to the non-communist FF parties who managed only 18 per cent of the poll with Zveno suffering catastrophically as even its leader failed to secure a seat. The opposition took 30 per cent of the vote, which meant that the communists only had just over half the total. In some areas even the local FF committees deserted the government.

FROM THE ELECTIONS OF OCTOBER 1946 TO THE FIFTH PARTY CONGRESS IN DECEMBER 1948

Petkov took new encouragement from the GNA election results and expressed a readiness to discuss a BANU-NP and BWP coalition. Dimitrov would have none of it. When a new administration was formed on 23 November Dimitrov was prime minister, Georgiev minister for foreign affairs, Yugov remained minister of the interior and Obbov a deputy prime minister.

For the first few months after the formation of the Dimitrov government the Paris peace talks were at the top of the political agenda. When the treaty was signed in February 1947 Bulgaria was restored to its 1941 boundaries which meant the loss of Thrace, the Aegean coast and Macedonia, but the retention of the southern Dobrudja, gained from Romania in 1940. Reparations were to be paid to Yugoslavia and Greece and the armed forces were to be limited to 65,500 personnel and ninety aircraft. All citizens were to enjoy full and equal rights, there were to be no fascist or military regimes, and Bulgaria was not to pursue policies hostile to the Soviet Union or other United Nations member states. The Red Army was to leave the country ninety days after the treaty came into force.

When the focus returned to the domestic political scene it was to reveal widespread and deep-seated dissatisfaction. Even the Bulgarian Orthodox Church, usually a relatively pliant body and one which immediately after 9 September 1944 had welcomed closer ties with Russia and had cooperated in increasing lay influence within its own administration, rejected government proposals for further Church reform early in 1947.

The Bulgarian bourgeoisie was also becoming restive, and with good reason. In September 1944 the newly arrived Soviet troops had toured Sofia and other cities with loudspeaker vans promising that the Red Army was a liberating force, that the Soviets wanted to help the Bulgarians develop whatever form of democratic government they chose, that private property would be respected, and that there would be no collectivization of agriculture. Experience had soon belied many of these promises. The purges and the terror of 1944–5 did not encourage hopes for the development of democratic government and private property was far from secure. The increasing Soviet demands for the payment of occupation costs in 1944 and 1945 were frequently met through 'voluntary' contributions which all too often meant that a local FF committee detained wealthy citizens until they handed over a sum the committee deemed appropriate. The local committees were also responsible for housing policies and in the bombed cities this often meant the confiscation of some or all of the larger apartments or houses; it also meant the frequent expropriation of furniture, cars and other assets. Finally, in February 1948, the largest urban properties were confiscated.

The early days after 9 September 1944 also saw measures to deprive manufacturers of control over their enterprises. The impulse to do this had been strengthened by a rise in the number, and therefore in the potential political strength, of small private producers during the final stages of the war and immediately after it. The measures taken included an enactment of December 1944 which gave workers' councils the right to examine company accounts. Private manufacturers were also given delivery quotas, usually set by the local FF committees, and failure to meet such quotas could result in imprisonment, the loss of property, or both.

At the same time profits were limited to a set percentage of capital and any shares not publicly acknowledged were liable to confiscation. The assets of fascists were to be forfeited while anyone found guilty of profiteering at any time since 1935 would lose their property; it was for the local FF committees to decide who were profiteers. In 1946 new tax laws hit Bulgarian capitalists by allowing them only a very limited time in which to clear arrears outstanding since 1942, while shares in foreign companies were confiscated. In March 1947 new currency regulations blocked all private accounts with over twenty thousand leva and imposed a one-off tax on all other accounts, while a progressive tax on incomes and savings made the further accumulation of capital all but impossible.

Even the urban working class, whose interests the communists were supposedly serving, was increasingly discontented in 1947. There was far more unemployment than any government, let alone one dominated by communists, would wish to see. This was caused by the demobilization of the army and the return to Bulgaria of many workers who had gone to Germany during the war; the government's tardiness in repairing bomb-damaged industries and the exhausted transport sector were further causes for dissatisfaction, as was the dreadful winter of 1946–7. There was also concern at food shortages and the high prices which attended them. The shortages were in part attributable to natural causes, but inevitably some of the blame was laid at the government's door. To make matters worse, some workers who did have jobs, particularly those in the mining industry, reacted to the food shortages by leaving their work-places and returning to their family plots to grow their own food. The resultant coal shortage only made the transportation of available food and fuel more difficult and more costly.

As social unrest increased so did government repression. By May 1947 the last two opposition newspapers had been suppressed either by indignant trade unionists or by the invocation of the January 1945 defence of the people's power act. In May and June 1947 about twenty thousand people, most of them anti-communist and pro-opposition, had been rounded up and despatched to labour camps under legislation against loafers and idlers. There was increasing discrimination against and harassment of western institutions and the Bulgarians employed by them, and by 1947 it was almost impossible to distribute western journals and magazines. And in a further indication of the danger of western connections all Bulgarian diplomats were ordered at the end of 1946 to return to Sofia by 15 March 1947 on pain of losing their rights of citizenship. Velchev chose to remain in Switzerland.

Limitations on the freedom of the press meant that the main arena for opposition was the GNA and here Petkov excelled. He had been heartened by the knowledge that the Red Army would be leaving the country and even more by the Truman Doctrine, pronounced in March 1947 and pledging American support for any people resisting communist subversion. He taunted the communists with their own fear that their power would not survive the departure of the Soviet forces. He also derided them for their expenditure on the police which was far higher a proportion of the national budget than under the so-called 'monarcho-fascists'. On the question of the constitution Petkov called for the restoration of the pre-war system minus the monarchy, something to which the communists could not agree.

The BWP decided that Petkov had to be destroyed by a show trial. The first serious blow against him was landed with the arrest in February 1947 of Petŭr Kolev, a leading BANU-NP figure. By the late spring it had become clear that the western powers meant the Truman Doctrine to apply no further north than Greece and with the west taking the offensive against communists in the governments of France and Italy the BWP leadership felt less restrained in its dealings with Petkov. On 5 June, the day after the US Senate ratified the peace treaty, he was arrested in the GNA and on 23 July charged with a bizarre list of offences, including attempting to form a military conspiracy to overthrow the government and cooperating with 'monarcho-fascists' in Greece. He was tried without the benefit of a defence lawyer or the right to place evidence before the court, although the prosecution produced a series of carefully prepared witnesses. Despite his immensely dignified conduct the verdict was never in doubt; he was pronounced guilty on 16 August and sentenced to death. He was executed on 23 September, three days after the peace treaty came into force. BANU-NP had ceased to exist as a credible force.

The liquidation of Petkov meant the end of political opposition in Bulgaria. His party was disbanded shortly after his arrest while the Obbov Agrarians opted for self-emasculation by agreeing a common programme with the communists and, in July 1948, by recognizing the leading role of the BWP. In the same month the WSDP was brutally dispatched; six of its nine deputies were arrested while its elderly leader, Kosta Lulchev, was sentenced to fifteen years in prison. During the summer of 1948 the SDP, the coalitionist Radical Party, and Zveno all merged into the communist-dominated FF.

Before the *Gleichschaltung* of the parties Bulgaria had, in December 1947, adopted the 'Dimitrov constitution'. Despite its name it had been drawn up mainly by Soviet specialists who had modified their own constitution to suit Bulgarian needs. Bulgaria was declared a 'People's Republic' and the constitution guaranteed the full range of individual and civil rights, though it proscribed any organization whose aim was to deprive the people of the 'the rights and liberties gained with the national uprising of 9 September 1944'. Unlike the Soviet prototype the Bulgarian constitution allowed the individual to retain private property but it placed all the means of production in public ownership. The real power in the land remained the communist party whose network of local organizations and whose domination of the FF ensured that almost nothing could happen without its sanction.

In many areas the Dimitrov government and the BWP needed this authority to impose radical and frequently unpopular policies. One such area was Pirin Macedonia where Dimitrov, in his post-Bled honeymoon with Tito, was introducing measures to promote a Macedonian sense of identity, a policy deeply resented by most Bulgarians. When the news broke on 28 June 1948 of Tito's expulsion from Cominform there was widespread relief in Bulgaria, followed by outright rejoicing when the Pirin policies were reversed.

The removal of the Macedonian embarrassment left the government free to concentrate on the enormous tasks of social and economic reconstruction which were revealed in detail to the fifth congress of the BWP in December 1948. At that congress the BWP also reverted to its original name, the Bulgarian Communist Party (BCP). Bulgaria was on the road to socialism.

Notes

1. The figure is taken from Vesselin Tzvetanov Dimitrov, 'The Failure of Democracy in Eastern Europe and the Emergence of the Cold War, 1944–1948: A Bulgarian Case Study', Cambridge PhD, 1997, pp.137–42. Dimitrov's work is based on archival evidence and is by far the best study of this period.
2. See above, pp.28–30.

Chapter 5

ROMANIA, 1944–1948

The core of the modern Romanian state lay in the principalities of Moldavia and Wallachia which had fallen under Ottoman domination in the fourteenth and fifteenth centuries. They were not placed under direct rule from Constantinople and retained extensive rights of self-government under the ruling landowners, or boyars, but attempts by these groups in the late seventeenth and early eighteenth centuries to take advantage of the Ottoman empire's wars with the Habsburg empire and with Russia to secure a greater degree of self-rule persuaded the Ottomans to replace the local rulers, or hospodars, with Greek administrators whose families came from the Phanar district of Constantinople. Phanariot Greeks were valued by the Ottomans for their efficiency and reliability; they were resented by Romanians for their venality.

Revolt against Phanariot rule came in the 1820s under the leadership of Tudor Vladimirescu who was associated with the *Filiki Etairia* (Friendly Society) established by Greeks in the principalities and in what is now Greece. The boyars who supported the revolt sought not national independence but the restoration of native as opposed to Phanariot rule. The revolt did not succeed. The peasants used it as a vehicle to seek social reform, there were disagreements between the Romanian and Greek elements of the leadership, and, critically, the expected help from Russia did not materialize.

The revolt did, however, increase Russian influence in the principalities. Since the 1770s Russia had claimed treaty rights to the protection of 'Greeks', i.e. Orthodox Christians, in the Ottoman empire and in the 1820s the Tsar and his ministers established great influence in Moldavia and Wallachia. The Organic Statutes of 1832, which codified the administration of the principalities were vetted and partially drawn up by Russian officials. In addition to regularizing and reforming the administration the Statutes also extended the power of the boyar over his peasants, a condition the landowners exploited all the more when further reform opened the western European markets to Romanian cereal exporters; to enhance their profits the boyars required cheap labour.

Russian interference in the political affairs of the principalities was constant and increasingly resented by the boyars. In 1848 the latter, especially in

Wallachia, attempted to take advantage of the revolutionary upheavals in Europe to restore native rule, but once again they were defeated and once again their defeat led to an increase in Russian influence. As in previous years, Russian domination was made easier by the constant intriguing amongst the Romanian, boyar political élite. This convinced the reformists that true liberation could be achieved only by a union of the two principalities and by the installation of a foreign prince.

Russia's defeat in the Crimean war (1853–6) helped to achieve these goals. In 1858 an international conference in Paris agreed to the abolition of the Organic Statutes and in elections shortly thereafter the two principalities elected the same man, Alexander Cuza, as their prince. The great powers accepted this for the duration of Cuza's reign. By 1861 the powers had also acquiesced in the amalgamation of many of the principalities' institutions, not least their assemblies; this in effect created a unified Romanian political entity, though as yet it was known as the United Principalities rather than Romania.

Cuza faced tougher opposition from the boyars of the domestic political establishment, no more so than when he tried to introduce agrarian reform to ease the lot of the peasantry. To circumvent opposition in the assembly Cuza staged a *coup d'état* in 1864 and then passed an agrarian law which abolished peasant labour obligations and the tithe. Having accomplished this Cuza had no great wish to remain in power. Like many of his fellow Liberals he believed a foreign prince was necessary if local intrigues were to cease and full security from foreign interference were to be guaranteed, and he therefore scarcely resisted soldiers who demanded his abdication in February 1866. Later in the year a foreign prince was found in the person of Prince Charles of Hohenzollern-Sigmaringen, a member of the Catholic branch of the Prussian ruling dynasty who was also a cousin of the French emperor.

In the Russo-Turkish war of 1877–8 Romania gave valuable assistance to the Russian armies. In the treaty of Berlin it was given full independence but little in the way of territorial satisfaction. It lost Bessarabia to Russia and in compensation was given the northern Dobrudja, which had a mixed population. The retrieval of Bessarabia became a long-term objective, though, as with Bulgaria's aspiration towards Macedonia, this objective could only be achieved in the context of a major European upheaval. The same applied to Romania's aspiration towards Transylvania, which was an integral part of the Habsburg Kingdom of Hungary but in which the Romanians formed the largest ethnic group.

The evolution of Romania from the 1820s to the 1870s had marked that area out as distinct from the rest of the Balkans in two ways. It had created a deep suspicion of Russia, and thus in Romania it was Russia rather than the Ottoman empire which was the hostile, defining 'other'. Political events in these years had also shown that the question of the land and the peasantry would lie at the heart of Romanian affairs whatever system of government might be in place: the domination of the peasantry by large landowners was unequalled anywhere else in the Balkans with the possible exception of Slovenia, Croatia and Transylvania, but in none of these regions did so many of the landowners hand over the running of their estates to bailiffs. Class divisions in the Romanian countryside were deeper than anywhere else in the region.

The agrarian law of 1864 did not end the political domination of the landowning aristocracy whose loyalties lay either with the pro-German conservatives or with the Liberal Party which tended to be pro-French and which championed some extension of the franchise, though it departed from classic liberalism by advocating the state development and protection of industry, including in later years the valuable oil reserves found near Ploeşti. Social discontent among the peasant masses, however, could not be avoided and in 1907, following upon the convulsions in Russia, a massive peasant *émeute* broke out. Manor houses were looted, manorial records burned, and landlords and even more so their hated bailiffs, many of them Jewish, were killed. In the military operations required to contain the revolt some ten thousand peasants lost their lives.

In the second Balkan war in 1913 Romania seized the southern Dobrudja and then, despite a secret commitment to the Austro-German alliance, kept out of the First World War until 1916 when it joined the allies. It was immediately invaded and defeated by Germany but by quick footwork managed to join the victorious powers just before the end of the fighting. Under the peace settlement Romania received huge territorial gains in Transylvania, the Banat, Bukovina and Bessarabia. The allies believed these territories were better entrusted to Romania than to Hungary or Russia both of which were then under Bolshevik domination. It was also fear of Bolshevism, together with memories of 1907, which led the government, immediately after the war, to enact measures of land reform which redistributed considerable areas of boyar properties to the peasantry.

In the inter-war years Romania attempted to integrate its new territories and one notable example of the fusion of the new lands with the Regat, or old kingdom, was the combining of the Transylvanian National Party with the Peasant Party to form the National Peasant Party (NPP). The NPP was the one party which broke the convention of elections being fixed from above when, in 1928, it secured enough seats to enable its leader, Iuliu Maniu, to form a government. However, the depression and the machinations of the King Carol II ruined Maniu's administration.

In the 1930s Romania fell increasingly under the domination of King Carol and then of the fascist Iron Guard. The king was fatally compromised in 1940 when cooperation between Hitler and Stalin forced him to relinquish Bessarabia and northern Bukovina to the USSR, northern Transylvania to Hungary, and southern Dobrudja to Bulgaria. Carol left in a train together with his mistress, works of art, and van loads of other valuables. His departure left the field open to the Iron Guard, an odd assortment of racial fanatics and religious eccentrics, who rapidly reduced Romania to anarchy. But it was a violent and vicious anarchy in which many Jews were subjected to horrible indignities and deaths.

The disorders in Romania worried Berlin where Hitler was preparing his invasion of the Soviet Union, for which he would need reliable supplies of Romanian oil. He therefore gave his approval for the suppression of the fascist Iron Guard by General, later Marshal, Ion Antonescu who was to dominate Romanian affairs until August 1944. He was an enthusiastic collaborator in Hitler's assault on the Soviet Union, as a result of which Romania received back the territories it had been forced to hand over to Russia in 1940. It also received Transnistria, the area between the Dniestr and the Bug, where many thousands, especially Jews, perished.

It was not long before the relationship with Germany began to exact a high price. Stalingrad cost the lives of a quarter of all Romanian troops on the eastern front and further blood-letting was to follow as the Red Army began its westward advance. As the military situation deteriorated, so did relations between Antonescu and Romania's young king, Michael. In February 1944 a Romanian delegation was sent to Cairo to explore the possibility of extricating Romania from the war before Soviet forces reached its borders. The delegation had no luck and in April the Red Army entered the country.

FACTORS IN ROMANIAN POLITICS, 1944–8

The arrival of the Red Army reinvigorated Romanian domestic politics, the first significant response coming when the communist Lucreţiu Pătrăşcanu negotiated with the Social Democratic Party to establish a United Workers' Front (UWF). It was the first of the many shifting blocs and fronts which were to characterize Romanian politics from the spring of 1944 until the imposition of full communist rule in 1948. Until the end of the war in Europe, however, Romania's destiny was to be determined not by the kaleidoscope of blocs and alliances but by events on the battlefield. The D Day landings had put paid to lingering hopes that the Balkans might be liberated by the western allies rather than the Soviet Union and the prospect of eventual Soviet occupation became reality on 20 August when over ninety Soviet divisions crashed through the German lines on a four-hundred mile front between the Carpathians and the Black Sea and headed for Bucharest. The king ordered Antonescu to seek an armistice and when the Marshal refused King Michael staged an audacious coup on 23 August, locking the Marshal in a safe-room reserved for the royal stamp collection. In September an armistice was signed in Moscow, which required Romania to join the allies in their war against Germany. Romanian forces therefore fought alongside the Red Army in central Europe.

This prevented the army forming a close association with the king, to whom it was loyal, and whose actions on 23 August had made him a major factor in domestic affairs. The Soviets also neutralized those elements of the army which remained in the country by bringing into Romania two pro-communist divisions recruited from among Romanian prisoners of war taken between 1941 and 1944.

If the army had been removed from the political arena the 'historic' parties remained. The two major ones were the National Peasant Party (NPP) still under the leadership of Maniu, one of the few Romanian politicians to enjoy a reputation for honesty, and the Liberal Party (LP) which was traditionally dominated by the Brătianu family. The NPP retained a large following among the peasantry while the LP was supported by prominent industrialists, business, the large landowners and the hierarchy of the Romanian Orthodox Church. Both parties were stronger in the capital than in the provinces and both suffered from internal divisions. In the NPP there was still some tension between the Transylvanian nationalists and the agrarians from the Regat. In the LP the most serious division was between the 'old' faction under Constantin Brătianu and the 'young' group under Gheorghe Tătărescu, which arose mainly from Tătărescu's insatiable ambition and limitless opportunism. In December he left the party and set up his own National Liberal Party (NLP). The Social Democratic Party (SDP) was an established party, if not a 'historic' one. It had the support of many skilled workers in the Regat but these were not a large proportion of the population, and the party's organization never fully recovered from the restrictions imposed on it by the right-wing regimes of the 1930s. It too was divided, the main question at issue being the question of relations with the Romanian Communist Party (RCP), the majority faction led by Dumitru Petrescu wishing to maintain a separate party organization and an individual SDP policy.

There were two powerful political organizations which were neither established nor historic. The first was the Ploughmen's Front (PF). Formed in Transylvania in 1933 the PF's original purpose had been to champion the rural poor who, it said, had been neglected by the NPP. The PF had considerable support among the poorer peasants in Transylvania and among the Magyars of that area. Its support widened considerably after August 1944. From its foundation the PF had been led by Petru Groza, a priest's son who had made a fortune as a lawyer, but who was known less as a politician than as 'a lover, tennis player and master of the sordid joke'.[1] He was, however, so utterly compromised that even the Soviet deputy commissar for external affairs, Andrei Vyshinski, said that should Groza step out of line the Soviets would simply 'uncover the record and act accordingly'.[2] Groza's rural radicalism, his closeness to the communists and his dependence upon the Soviets made him ideal for the task he was soon to perform, that of splitting the left from the bourgeois camp.

The other non-historic force was the Romanian Communist Party. It was almost non-existent, and in August 1944, with only 844 members, was the weakest communist party in the Balkans, not excluding Albania; it had virtually no record of resistance and most of its miniscule membership were from the ethnic minorities.* After August 1944 membership expanded exponentially. By February 1945 it stood at 16,000; in October it had leapt to 257,000 and in June 1946 was 720,000. In February 1948 it topped three quarters of a million. This expansion was helped by relaxing entrance requirements and by the admission of whole groups, for example the Tudor Vladimirescu Division, one of the two formed in the Soviet Union from Romanian prisoners of war. Nor did the RCP turn its back on former members of the Iron Guard. The ex-Guardists were particularly useful. The RCP did not have a disciplined and dedicated core to dominate and lead local party members. The ex-Guardists in many instances filled the gap. They were toughened fighters, they had pasts which would not allow them to step out of line, and they were also anxious to show how loyal they were to their new master.

> In this initial period, when the communists had insufficient time to train needed cadres, these self-seekers provided a more reliable base than the members recruited from among the working class and peasantry on the basis of ideological commitment and socio-economic considerations.[3]

They could if necessary be purged later. The RCP also rapidly expanded its influence and membership via subordinate organizations such as the trade unions and the movements for youth and women. The RCP had support among the proletariat, especially in Bucharest; in June 1945 the proportion of party members who were workers was said to be 55 per cent but with rapid expansion this was diluted to 39 per cent in February 1948.

In the early summer of 1944 it was not entirely clear who was the dominating personality, if any, in the RCP. Emil Bodnăraş, parachuted into the country during the war, had impressed the king and others with his ability, and his knowledge of German and Russian, gained during his childhood in the Bukovina, was useful. Ana Pauker had spent most of the war in Moscow and had proved her Stalinist pedigree by denouncing her husband; with her in the Soviet Union had been Vasile Luca but he was an ethnic Hungarian and therefore not a serious contender for the leadership. In the event it was none of these prominenti who came out on top but Gheorghe Gheorghiu-Dej, the only senior Romanian communist who had received no schooling at all in the Soviet Union. Of genuine working-class origin Gheorghiu-Dej had organized strikes among the railway workers in the 1930s and had remained in Romania during the war. In April 1944 he had removed a potential rival in Ştefan Foriş and when the Red Army arrived he had impressed even some

---

* The largest of these were the Magyars (Hungarians) of Transylvania. The second largest was that of the Germans who consisted of the Tranyslvanian Saxons and the 'Swabians' who were found primarily in the Banat; there were also Germans in the Bukovina. In Bessarabia there were Ukrainians, Bulgarians, Tatars and Turks. The Jews of the pre-1941 kingdom largely survived the war but most of them emigrated. Given the upheavals of the war and of the ethnic transplantations that followed it, precise figures on the ethnic composition of Romania in this period are difficult to come by.

non-communists by showing in discussions with the Soviets that he was not entirely putty in their hands. This did not seem to deter Stalin who, according to one leading Romanian communist, decided that Gheorghiu-Dej should lead the party because 'the party in Romania needs a leader from the ranks of the working class, a true-born Romanian'.[4]

Like all communist parties the RCP benefited from the general leftward drift of the post-war period and, of course, the presence of the Red Army was a huge boost to its morale and its power, if only because the Soviets could supply massive logistical support in the form of vehicles, petrol, paper, offices etc. The RCP was also helped by the fact that the Soviet representative was totally dominant in the ACC where he could be relied upon to neutralize any effort by the western powers to give aid and succour to the communists' domestic political enemies.

Immediately after August 1944, however, Moscow was not prepared to push for a greater degree of communist authority within Romania. Moscow's priority was to ensure peace and stability in the rear of the Red Army and the Soviet commissar for external affairs, Vyacheslav Molotov, therefore told King Michael soon after the coup that the Soviet Union did not want Romania to become a communist state but rather a 'friendly neighbour'.[5] But events on the battlefield were soon to dictate another twist in Romania's affairs.

FROM THE COUP OF AUGUST 1944 TO THE INSTALLATION OF THE GROZA GOVERNMENT IN MARCH 1945

The first post-coup government had been established under General Constantin Sănătescu and included four representatives of the NPP, three of the SDP and one communist. Its most pressing task had been to conclude the armistice which was eventually signed on 12 September. The agreement allowed the Soviet Union to intervene in Romanian domestic affairs if it believed its security were threatened, a clause which was to be exploited fully in the coming months. Under the terms of the armistice the Romanians agreed to join the allied war effort and to place their army under the Soviet High Command, hoping that this would earn them co-belligerency status and thus avoid being punished as a defeated enemy state. This the Soviets refused, nor would they accept Romanian requests that all of Transylvania be returned to Romanian rule, even though the armistice did declare null and void the Vienna agreement of 1940 by which northern Transylvania had been ceded to Hungary. On the basis of the latter clause Romanian administrators returned to Transylvania as it was liberated in September and October but in November, claiming the Romanians were indulging in anti-Hungarian excesses, the Soviets ejected the Romanian administrators and returned northern Transylvania to Hungarian officials. This was done not for any love for the Magyars but because the restitution of Romanian authority was causing instability in the Red Army's rear.

In the face of this national humiliation Sănătescu resigned on 2 December and was replaced by a popular, non-party soldier, General Nicolae Rădescu. Neither the policies nor the problems of the Rădescu administration differed much from those of its predecessor. It carried on Sănătescu's purge of ministers and senior officials from the pre-1940 era, it intensified legal measures already initiated against war criminals and war profiteers, and it continued the action begun by the Sănătescu regime against the German minority in Transylvania: all Germans who had belonged to any paramilitary German organization or who had held a privileged position during the war were deprived of their Romanian citizenship, and all German ethnic organizations were dissolved.

Rădescu, like Sănătescu, had to contend with constant Soviet interference. The confiscation of industrial goods and equipment, not least that for the oil industry, continued, as did the expropriation of food, an increasingly painful process as winter approached after what had been one of the worst harvests for generations. Of even greater concern was the fact that the Soviets seemed ready to deport whole populations en masse. They had already transported to the Soviet Union a number of Romanians who had fled from Bukovina and Bessarabia, claiming that they were Soviet citizens. In January it was declared that all German men between 17 and 45 and women between 18 and 30 were to be taken to the Soviet Union to help rebuild Stalingrad and other ruined cities. Many of those affected were assimilated Romanians who had not spoken German for two or three generations; only after American intervention were the deportations limited.

While Sănătescu and then Rădescu attempted to cope with the pressures exerted by the Soviets the RCP was expanding its power. By exploiting their ties with the Soviets and by creative interpretation of certain clauses of the armistice agreement, they packed the higher ranks of the police with pliable officers. The prime minister had attempted to thwart communist machinations by becoming minister of the interior, but the ministry's under-secretary was a communist who simply told his officials to ignore instructions from Rădescu. Local government too fell to increasing communist encroachment. Riots were fomented in many towns and the local authorities declared incapable of maintaining order, thus giving the communists the excuse to take over themselves.

Part of the process of destabilizing local government had been to incite peasants to seize land, a policy which also had the additional advantage of dislodging some of the peasantry from its traditional loyalty to the NPP. The communists also assumed direct control of some unions, including those of the metal workers, printers, journalists and writers, while in others they exercised indirect rule via stooge parties or secret sympathizers in other parties. Union elections, almost always by open voting, were easily rigged and attempts by other parties to establish their own trade unions were frustrated. In

January 1945 a trade union congress in Bucharest established the General Labour Confederation with Gheorghe Apostol as its general secretary; it was entirely under the control of the RCP. It was also in January 1945 that Ana Pauker and Gheorghiu-Dej visited Moscow. This visit sealed the fate of Rădescu.

THE CRISIS OF FEBRUARY–MARCH 1945

In the early months of 1945 the communists, with Soviet complicity if not at Soviet instigation, plotted to show that Rădescu's government was incapable of preserving order and must be replaced by one which was. This they did both by fomenting disorders and at the same time reducing the effectiveness of the Romanian army and police. On 5 March the Soviets imposed a new government. They, like the British in Greece, were making full use of the free hands offered to them under the percentage agreements.

The first signs of real crisis appeared when Gheorghiu-Dej and Pauker returned from Moscow in January. The National Democratic Front (NDF), a bloc of leftist parties formed in October 1944 around the RCP, the PF and the SDP, issued a list of demands which included: a truly democratic government; the purging of all fascists from the civil service; the reorganization of the army on a democratic basis; and the immediate confiscation of all estates over 50 ha, those of the Church, the monasteries and the dynasty excepted. During the first half of February the NDF increased its call for agrarian reform while a number of arms caches were reported to have been discovered, the communists insisting that they were for use in a fascist counter-coup. Rădescu responded with savage criticism of the communists during a speech in the Aro Theatre on 11 February and a week later he made an unsuccessful attempt to dismiss Groza and a number of other NDF figures from the government. The communists replied by putting greater pressure on non-communist newspapers and on 14 February the Soviets reported to the ACC that the Romanian army had far too many officers in the rear: 'Such forces could only be used', asserted one of the Soviet delegates, 'against the Romanian people themselves, or against the allied nations.'[6]

The first major storm broke on 19–20 February at the Malaxa metallurgical plant in Bucharest. On 19 February communist supervisors in the plant staged an election to secure control of the works committee. It was one of the rare union elections where voting was by secret ballot and the four thousand men of the day shift voted overwhelmingly against the communist candidates. There were still three thousand night shift workers to cast their votes and the organizers of the election ordered that voting for them should be by an open show of hands. When, on the morning of 20 February, the day and night shifts overlapped, the workers angrily rejected this proposal and drove the communist organizers into the administrative offices from where they telephoned for help. This arrived in mid-morning in the shape of four hundred burly and armed 'shock troops' under the command of Gheorghiu-Dej himself. Firing soon broke out with fatalities on both sides.[7] Once more the Soviets responded to increased tension by demanding a further reduction in Romanian military and police personnel in the capital.

The Malaxa confrontation proved to be the overture to the main drama which played from 24 February to 5 March. In the afternoon of 24 February a crowd of up to fifty thousand assembled outside the Royal Palace to declare solidarity with the king. A counter-demonstration appeared in the shape of a column of communist enthusiasts marching behind the Red Flag. Whether by accident or design firing began during which one man died, apparently from a heart attack. The senior Soviet officer in Bucharest insisted the Romanian city commander restore order or the Soviets would do it for him. The Romanian promised to do his best. His best was not good enough. In the mid-evening a small crowd of NPP supporters marching towards the Palace was fired at from a passing car; two marchers were killed and eleven injured. The communists later tried to argue that those killed had been fired on by the Romanian army but forensic evidence showed that the bullets used were not of a type issued to Romanian soldiers. It was without much doubt a crude communist provocation. Rădescu knew this and said so when he spoke on the radio at ten that evening. He also said that a small band of extremists who were 'without nation or God'★ and who were headed by two foreigners, 'Ana Pauker and Luca the Hungarian', were attempting to subdue the nation through terror. It was the last uncensored broadcast made in Romania for forty-five years. The Soviets were enraged and Rădescu was summoned to the ACC headquarters at 11 p.m. where he was roundly abused for two hours.

More brutal Soviet intervention began on the evening of 27 February when deputy commissar Vyshinski arrived unexpectedly in Bucharest and demanded an immediate audience with the king. The Soviet commissar insisted that Rădescu could not maintain order, had no mass support and was not only dragging his feet on reforms but even introducing reactionary measures. Vyshinski saw the king again the following day and this time issued an ultimatum: within two hours the king was to announce the dismissal of Rădescu and by eight that evening must nominate his successor. Vyshinski's arrival in the Romanian capital coincided with the replacement of the chief Soviet delegate to the ACC, General Vinogradov, by General Susaikov, a far more political soldier than Vinogradov. He was also more ruthless. On 28 February 6,000 new Soviet troops were moved into Bucharest and were soon

---

★ The 'Without Nation or God' phrase became notorious. It was in fact part word play. Rădescu had said that FND, the Romanian initials of the NDF, should stand for 'Fără de Newam şi Dumnezeu' – Without Nation or God. Arthur G. Lee, *Crown against Sickle*, London: Hutchinson, 1950, p.104.

followed by 4,000 NKVD men. On 1 March the Soviets issued a string of new orders: 20,000 men in the air force were to be demobilized; the infantry guard regiment in Bucharest was to be sent to the front; and reserve battalions of all regiments at the front were to be disbanded and their personnel sent into battle. The Romanian army was to be kept busy away from home. At home the gendarmerie was to be reduced from 31,000 to 14,500 and there was to be a 50 per cent reduction in the country's police force, bringing it down to about 7,500, of whom 1,500 would be in Bucharest, a city of one million. The Soviets also took over most transmission facilities of the Romanian air force and all flights of Romanian personnel inside the country were banned. The Soviets had in effect disabled the Romanian authorities' internal security apparatuses; the king and Rădescu were therefore defenceless against the Soviets and their Romanian lackeys.

Vyshinski had made it plain to King Michael that the Soviet preference for Rădescu's successor was the leader of the Ploughmen's Front, Petru Groza. This was certainly not the king's first choice but he had no option; were he to refuse the nomination, he was told, the Soviet Union would regard this as a hostile act. The Soviets, however, did sweeten the Groza pill by promising that once he were installed as prime minister the armistice terms would be applied with less rigour, a number of prisoners of war would be released, and, most importantly, northern Transylvania would be returned to Romanian rule. When the king consulted the leaders of the historic parties these concessions, more especially the last, persuaded them to accept Groza, though they insisted that the historic parties be represented equally with the NDF in the new cabinet. The king therefore agreed to Groza becoming prime minister on 5 March. When the new cabinet was announced the following day fourteen of its eighteen members were from the NDF and the communists held the ministries of justice, the interior, war and communications. Rădescu fled to refuge in the British legation. The king even considered abdication, an option favoured by his mother, but the Orthodox Patriarch, senior courtiers and the LP leader, Brătianu, persuaded him to stay at his post on the grounds that this might enable him to do something to soften Soviet and communist pressures on his country.

Soviet intervention in Romania had been swift, brutal and decisive. It, like the return of northern Transylvania to Hungarian administration in late 1944, was largely a function of the military campaign against Germany. In the second week of February 1945 the Germans had launched an unexpected counter-offensive around Lake Balaton in Hungary. Were the Wehrmacht to break through the Red Army and reach the line of the Dniestr they might organize resistance movements among the anti-communist elements in Romania and thereby disrupt the Red Army's rear. This accounted for the Soviet emphasis on Rădescu's alleged inability to maintain order and for Soviet determination to render the Romanian army and police ineffective as agents in domestic affairs. The Soviets in fact were convinced that a conspiracy was afoot, or at least this is what the chief agent of Soviet intervention, Susaikov, was led to believe. At a long-drawn out and extremely bibulous dinner he told his British colleague, Stevenson, in strict confidence that the Groza government was in fact established in Romania by force.

> He said to me 'What would you have done?' At the beginning of March Malinovski was engaged in a stern struggle against heavy German resistance and reinforcement in front of Budapest. Malinovski had reliable information that a rising had been planned in Romania. According to his reports a force of 550,000 men would take part in the rising timed to take place at a critical moment in the battle for Budapest. 'I was' said Susaikov 'at once despatched to Bucharest to deal with this situation. There was no time to be lost. I disarmed the army in the interior. I reduced Romanian garrisons and I brought about [a] change of government.'[8]

As a British historian has recently observed, 'the Red Army, as any army, while fighting was still in progress, required order behind the front, but in Romania the only order acceptable to the Russians was that guaranteed by the RCP'.[9]

FROM THE INSTALLATION OF THE GROZA GOVERNMENT TO THE ELECTIONS OF NOVEMBER 1946

From March to August 1945 the Groza government faced little or no internal opposition, especially while the war in Europe continued and Soviet military and security considerations were unchallengeable. The communists used this time to introduce further land reform, to increase the government's control over the economy, to weaken its bourgeois enemies, and to extend the power of the RCP at the local and national levels. After the end of the war in Europe the king began to resist but he was not backed by those outside Romania to whom he looked for support. In 1946 the political confrontations were concentrated on the general elections to be held in November.

The Groza government was a motley crew. It included a number of renegade NPP and LP men one of whom, an Orthodox priest, had been prominent in the Iron Guard. Its first major enactment was the bill on land reform of 22 March. Having described land reform as 'a national, economic and social necessity' the act went on to confiscate without compensation all holdings over 50 ha even if they were in dispersed strips. Also confiscated was the land of: Germans and Romanian citizens of German ethnic origin who had collaborated with the Germans; war criminals and those responsible for 'the disasters of the country'; those who had fled; absentee landowners; those who had not cultivated the land themselves during the last seven years; and those who had volunteered to fight against the allies. The only properties exempt from confiscation were rice fields, Church and monastic lands, crown property, the land of certain cultural and philanthropic institutions, urban communes and cooperatives. Also confiscated were all draught animals, tractors, threshing machines, sowing machines and combines on expropriated land which were to be used as the basis for new Machine Tractor Stations (MTSs). Priority in the distribution of land was to be given to: cultivators mobilized in the anti-Hitler war; widows, orphans and invalids of that and other wars; landless peasants; labourers and peasants who worked on expropriated land; and peasants with less than five hectares. No one who already had 5 ha could receive land.

The stated purpose of the act was to create an agriculture based on farms which were the property of those who cultivated them. This involved the elimination of holdings of less than five hectares. Other objectives were: to create vegetable gardens near cities for workers, civil servants and artisans; to give landless labourers farms; and to create model farms and experimental stations run by the state. In fact, of the 1.47 million ha of confiscated land only 1.11 million ha were given to peasants, and as there were 0.92 million recipients the amount given to individual families was seldom sufficient to change their economic or social status. There were also some three million eligible peasants who did not receive land. Furthermore, the reform caused such chaos in the countryside that even in January 1946 half the tractors were lying idle because people did not know to whom the machines or even the land belonged. Nevertheless, the act finally spelled the end of the estate-owning class in Romania and, because of its anti-German clauses, destroyed a number of Saxon and Swabian communities in Transylvania and the Banat.

Another measure taken by the Groza government soon after it achieved power was the signing of a trade agreement with the Soviet Union in May 1945. The agreement provided for the setting up of joint Soviet and Romanian enterprises (sovroms) in oil, agriculture and navigation. These in turn enabled the USSR to buy up virtually all Romania's production of oil, agricultural goods and industrial items. For their part, the Soviets provided war material, machinery and technical assistance. So great was the Soviet demand for Romanian fuel, food and machinery that Romanian trade was steered away from its traditional, pre-war directions. This meant that Romania was cut off from its former sources of hard currency. It was proof that the Romanian economy was being shackled to that of the Soviet Union, something which almost all Romanians found distasteful. Their national sensitivities were further offended by the fact that the reparations their country was required to pay in kind to the USSR were assessed at pre- rather than post-war values. As the former were much lower more goods had to be handed over than would have been the case had the assessment been at post-war values. In effect, the Romanian economy was being exploited by the Soviet Union. It was something which the Romanians, the communists included, were not to forget.

The Groza government went much further than any of its predecessors in imposing state control over such vital sectors as the railways and oil extraction. It also went much further in the regulation of prices and wages, all of which diminished the freedom of manoeuvre of employers and frequently imposed on them crippling obligations which weakened and depressed Romania's industrial and commercial bourgeoisie, the strongest in the pre-war Balkans. As early as April 1945 the Groza government had demanded that the king sign a decree amending the 1923 constitution to allow the confiscation of property without compensation as a complementary punishment for 'crimes' to be determined by new laws. In the same month new people's tribunals were established which could override or ignore the usual legal procedures.

The latter was only one of the methods the communists used to extend their power base at the ground level. In May 1945 they appointed communist prefects and communist-dominated councils with extensive powers in every county. The police and gendarmerie, meanwhile, were coming under the domination of the so-called 'vigilance committees' originally sponsored by the Rădescu government. The depletion, at Soviet insistence, of the numbers in the old police and gendarmerie meant that the vigilance committees could establish virtual mastery of the local forces of public control.

Communist power was built from above as well as below. Groza with his peasantist radicalism, his dependence on the Soviets, and his uncouth behaviour, was the ideal instrument to drive a wedge between the socialist and the bourgeois camps. His position weakened somewhat, however, with the end of the war in Europe in May 1945. No longer did the Soviets have to consider the stability or otherwise of the Red Army's rear, the Romanian army could not be kept indefinitely outside the country, and now the western powers could be expected to play a fuller part in the deliberations of the ACC. These considerations gave some solace to Groza's enemies, not least the king. The second half of 1945 in Romania, in fact, was to be dominated by a vital struggle between the king and his government.

The king was greatly encouraged by the Potsdam declaration of August 1945 which stated that before a peace treaty could be concluded and before Romania could be admitted to the UN it must have a genuinely democratic government. The fact that both Britain and the United States refused to grant recognition to a government which they did not consider democratic was grist to the king's mill. In the middle of August, invoking the regal prerogative enshrined in the 1923 constitution to appoint and dismiss ministers, he ordered Groza to resign. Groza refused whereupon the king appealed to the British and Americans for help. They, however, did not wish to become embroiled in Romanian domestic affairs and declined his appeal. The king therefore went on strike. He refused to receive Groza or to sign bills into law. This caused a constitutional crisis but it also earned the king a great deal of popularity. Proof of this was seen on the king's name day, 8 November, when thousands came, as was the national tradition, to demonstrate their loyalty in front of the Royal Palace. But this time they were attacked by armed police, thugs and troops from the Tudor Vladimirescu division, all of whom arrived in lorries obviously provided by the local communists. Eleven people were killed, 85 injured and over 400 carted off by the police.

The crisis was not to be solved in Romania but at the Moscow conference of foreign ministers in December where it was decided, as in the case of Bulgaria, that the government in Romania should be widened by the addition of two non-communist ministers, one from the NPP and one from the LP. As a result Britain and the USA promised to recognize the Groza government, which they did on 4 February 1946, after which King Michael had no choice but to receive his prime minister again and to resume his constitutional duties of signing bills.

After the defeat of the king the communists turned more pressure on the historic parties. The latter were blamed for the disorders of 8 November and a new and more sinister twist came when many of those who were carted away from the demonstration were forced to sign confessions implicating Maniu and other opponents of the government.

Fire was also directed against the opposition press. Those newspapers which had not been suspended or closed during the crisis of early 1945 were subject to constant harassment, suffering temporary suspensions for misdemeanours as trivial as criticizing a rise in tram fares. Another ruse was to confiscate copies of independent newspapers when they reached the provinces, and it was not unknown for communists to be ordered to purchase all copies of a particular paper if it managed to print something which was not to the liking of the authorities. By 1946 there was blatant discrimination in the supplies of vital newsprint; in March, for example, the NPP *Dreptatea* received two rolls per day whereas the communist *Scînteia* had twenty. The opposition parties were also denied access to the radio, an entirely state-controlled medium.

In common with communist parties throughout Europe the RCP assiduously fostered or created divisions among its opponents. The friction in the NPP between the Transylvanians and the *Regateani*, that is those from the pre-1918 Romanian kingdom, was exploited. The SDP was even more a target. Petrescu had been confident in 1945 that he could keep the party united behind him if he chose to take it out of the NDF, as he promised Maniu and others he would do. But he reckoned without the dedication of the communists. They created within the SDP a faction which wanted to collaborate closely with the RCP and, when the party had to decide in March 1946 whether to join an electoral pact with the communists or to campaign alone, it was the collaborationist wing which carried the day. Petrescu therefore formed his own Independent Social Democratic Party (ISDP).

When the SDP split in March 1946 the forthcoming elections had become the dominating theme of political debate for all parties in Romania. The free and fair elections called for in the Yalta declaration could not be held before the end of the war in Europe and even after May 1945 some non-communist parties wanted them delayed until after the peace treaty and the withdrawal of the Red Army. Nor were the communists against delay which would give them time to deepen the rifts in the opposing parties. Not surprisingly in

January 1946 Groza postponed the elections which had been promised for May of that year. He also later admitted that the current food crisis, a product of Soviet requisitioning, administrative dislocation caused by the land reforms, and a severe drought, would be at its worst in May and he had not wished to face a hungry electorate.

If May 1946 did not witness elections it did see the publication of a draft electoral law which was endorsed by the cabinet in a nine-minute session on 10 July. The law also abolished the Senate and deprived the king of the prerogative of appointing or dismissing a government, this right to rest in future with the parliament. The law gave women the vote for the first time in Romania. A more controversial innovation was that voting was to take place in factories, offices, enterprises and military units. There was also intense opposition from the non-government parties to the fact that only a limited time was to be allowed to prepare electoral lists, and for the setting up of new local and central electoral commissions to verify voting procedures; all the new commissions were controlled by the NDF. The date for the elections was fixed for 19 November 1946.

The publication of the draft law marked the beginning of the electoral campaign. In May the communists formed an electoral alliance, the Bloc of Democratic Parties (BDP), with the collaborationist SDP, the Tătărescu Liberals and the PF. Throughout the campaign the BDP, directed by the communists, showed absolute ruthlessness but also enviable skill. Leading party figures were despatched to vital areas of the country as electoral managers, Bodnăraş in Moldavia, Luca in Transylvania and Pauker in the oilfields. Even the poor king was tricked and bludgeoned into giving unwilling help to the communists. He was forced to bestow a high Romanian decoration on Groza who had copies of the citation posted all over the country thus simultaneously increasing his own and diminishing the king's prestige.

More serious was the government's exploitation of political and other trials for electoral gain. The most prominent trial of 1946 was that of Antonescu which began on 4 May. It ended with the conviction of the wartime leader who was executed on 1 June. The communists and their allies did all they could to smear their electoral opponents by linking them to the accused, in which they were much helped by Maniu himself who, after giving his evidence, paused to shake hands with the prisoner telling the court that Antonescu was not an enemy but an adversary. On 11 November the first of Romania's show trials began. It was to last until the very eve of the elections and in it 91 individuals were charged with war crimes or subversion.

In addition to intimidation the government, like most in Romania's history, also used its influence over the electorate. Electoral cheating took a variety of forms. In some counties the communist-appointed electoral commissions kept two separate registers, one for all those eligible to vote and another for those who could be expected to vote for the government; the latter could then be given multiple voting slips and the ballots of those not on the second list destroyed. In some constituencies, especially rural ones, known opponents of the government were not even put on the first list; the LP leader Brătianu was one of them. At the same time many judges whose job it would normally have been to preside over district electoral commissions were temporarily transferred to other areas and other duties. In some areas the normal place of voting was changed at the last minute so that peasants might have to travel up to thirty miles or more to vote with no transportation other than oxen or horse-drawn carts. Some who did make the journey were then chased away from the polling booths. Where they did gain entry voters were required to mark a ballot paper, fold it over and pass it to an electoral official; there were no envelopes and the officials were invariably reliable BDP personnel so that a secret ballot hardly existed. Opposition votes were often destroyed or ballot boxes replaced with ones filled before the poll with pro-government votes and in some cases the stuffed ballot boxes were in place from the beginning; a lawyer in Bucharest reported arriving at the polling booth when it opened at 8 a.m. to find the urns already full. In factories workers had to vote under the gaze of trade union officials.

Despite all these precautions the government vote was embarrassingly low. Some exit polls indicated that the BDP would be lucky to achieve 10 per cent of the total; the NPP, it was estimated, took 70 per cent of the votes cast despite all the obstacles put in the way of its supporters. Not even close supervision of the voting could guarantee success for the BDP. The three thousand members of the Bucharest gendarmerie were subjected to a pre-electoral harangue by their commanding officer and were then required to vote in police headquarters. Not a single vote was cast for the BDP, though the result was doctored according to government requirements. Not even amongst Gheorghiu-Dej's own railway workers or in the communist-controlled ministries of finance and war could government majorities be produced. It made no difference. The communists and their allies simply manufactured the election 'result' which gave the BDP 84.5 per cent of the vote and 348 seats in the assembly. The NPP was said to have taken 7.75 per cent of the vote and was given 33 seats; the BDP allowed itself to be defeated in six counties in three of which an ethnic Hungarian party was declared the winner and given 29 seats. That wholesale fabrication had taken place was confirmed by archives opened after the Romanian revolution of 1989.

At the end of 1945 the communists and their allies, with the assistance of the great powers, had defeated the king. At the end of 1946 they had used electoral fraud to disable the historic parties. Now they faced no real obstacle.

THE COMPLETION OF THE COMMUNIST TAKEOVER, NOVEMBER 1946 TO MARCH 1948

After the November 1946 elections the communists had a virtual free hand. They used it immediately and energetically, imposing further economic reforms and moving in for the kill, sometimes literally, on their domestic enemies.

Their electoral 'victory' was not the only development which strengthened the communists in Romania. In February 1947 the peace treaty was signed in Paris. This meant the end of the ACC and of whatever influence the western powers had chosen or had been allowed to exercise within it. The intensification of the cold war in 1947 meant an even further increase in Soviet power. In the summer there was a massive influx of Soviet citizens who arrived as advisors, officials of the sovroms, civilian auxiliaries working for the Red Army or as secret police and security personnel.

The NDF government increased yet further its control over the economy. On 4 April and 24 May laws were enacted giving the ministry of economy and commerce 'full powers over all industrial processes, foreign capital and commercial enterprises for a period of five years'.[10] In the summer of 1948 the Romanian parliament, without debate, passed a bill nationalizing industrial, banking, insurance, mining and transport enterprises. A law of 6 June 1947 imposed strict control on the sale of land and priority in purchasing it was given to the state; the reason for this, it was said, was to prevent fragmentation but it also served to prevent the re-emergence of the entrepreneurial peasant, or, in communist demonology, the 'kulak'. In the following month the peasants' right to sell their produce privately was limited by the introduction of a tax in kind which was 'in effect, a forced delivery of crops to the state'.[11] The government rapidly extended the powers of REAZIM, an organization set up in November 1946 to develop agriculture, animal husbandry and the use of agricultural machinery. It assumed responsibility for rationalizing cultivation, supplying seeds and agricultural machinery and managing the MTSs. It was the arm of the state in the countryside.

That essential requisite of any dictatorship, a dependable judiciary, was soon in place. In the summer of 1947 Pătrăşcanu, now minister of justice, told parliament that the primary task of the judicial system at a time of revolutionary change was to provide the government with the help necessary for the implementation of its economic and social programme. Soon thereafter new people's judges were introduced who would serve three-month terms alongside career judges; mixed tribunals, introduced in October 1947, were to consist of two people's judges and one professional. The former would be elected by the workers and peasants and would serve their interests rather than rely on abstract concepts of law or accumulated legal knowledge and expertise; the election of the people's judges would be organized by the NDF or one of its subsidiary bodies. The legal profession itself was effectively purged by the neat device of replacing all previous professional organizations with new lawyers' trade unions; applications for membership of such bodies had to be presented to officials appointed directly by the minister of justice and there was no appeal against their decision; only 2,100 of the 12,000 lawyers who had belonged to the previous organizations were admitted to the new ones.

The historic parties were finally destroyed in 1947. In March thousands of supporters of the NPP, the LP and the ISDP were arrested and a second wave of arrests followed in May. On 26 July several senior figures in the NPP attempted to flee Romania by plane; they were arrested while trying to do so. Five days later Maniu himself was taken into custody and at the same time the parliamentary immunity of NPP deputies was lifted; on 30 July parliament dissolved the NPP. Maniu and his colleagues appeared before a court on 29 October and were rapidly found guilty of treason by conspiring with the British and US secret services. The trial took place a month after the founding of Cominform and was meant both to assure the Soviets of the RCP's willingness to engage in the class struggle, and to discredit the western powers. Maniu was sentenced to life imprisonment. He endured harsh conditions, including almost continuous solitary confinement, and died in prison in 1953.

The ISDP also came under sustained attack in the autumn of 1947 but its fate was sealed in February 1948 when the collaborationist SDP fused with the RCP to form the Romanian Workers' Party (RWP) under the leadership of Gheorghiu-Dej. The RWP could not tolerate any alternative source of affiliation for the working class so the ISDP was dispersed through intimidation and Petrescu arrested in May 1948. He was imprisoned without trial.

Tătărescu had signed his political death warrant by criticizing government economic and political policies in May 1947 but had been retained as long as the fiction of a coalition was needed and it was necessary to talk politely to the western powers. Neither of these conditions applied by November 1947 when Tătărescu was replaced as minister for foreign affairs by Ana Pauker. In February 1948 the remaining Tătărescu Liberals made an accommodation with the communists and ceased to have any independent existence. By then a similar fate had befallen the LP.

The RCP onslaught affected not only the historic parties. In 1947 non-communist parties within the NDF were also being subjected to pressure. On 9 January 1947 the central committee of the RCP decided that the social composition of the PF should be 'improved'. It was to lose its bourgeois elements and become a truly revolutionary body representing the poorer sections of the peasantry and cooperating with the communists. By the summer this task had been completed. The other major non-communist party inside the NDF, the collaborationist SDP, ceded real power to the RCP with fusion in February 1948. In the new RWP only one of the five senior secretaries was from the SDP and only three of the thirteen members of the new politburo were not from the RCP.

At the end of 1947 the king was removed entirely from Romanian politics. In November he had been in London to attend the royal wedding and shortly thereafter had announced his own engagement to Princess Anne of Bourbon-Parma. Ana Pauker declared that a royal wedding was too expensive an extravaganza for impoverished Romania. This was merely an excuse. Moscow was now demanding an abdication and Gheorghiu-Dej was threatening force if it were not granted. King Michael could not allow his country to be plunged into civil war and therefore bowed to necessity and signed an act of abdication on 30 December. The royal family left Romania early in January 1948.

After fusion the communists remodelled the NDF, transforming it into the People's Democratic Front (PDF). In March 1948 new elections were held which returned 405 deputies for the PDF and nine for two small opposition groups. In April the assembly rapidly drew up a new constitution, based on that of the Soviet Union, and declared Romania a People's Democracy. Romania was soundly locked into the Soviet bloc.

Notes

1. P. D. Quinlan, *Clash over Romania. British and American Policies towards Romania, 1938–1947*, Los Angeles: American Romanian Academy of Arts and Sciences, vol. 2, 1977, p.113. The prowess as a lover was all the more surprising in that an influential American journalist who visited Romania at a critical juncture in 1945 found Groza 'a singularly stupid, incoherent and brutal-looking man'. British representative in Bucharest, Le Rougetel tel.1228 22 Nov. 1945, quoting Air Commodore Stevenson, British representative on the Allied Control Commission for Romania. H. J. Yasamee and K. A. Hamilton (eds), *Documents on British Policy Overseas*, series I, volume VI, *Eastern Europe August 1945 – April 1946*, London: HMSO, 1992, microfiche 25, frames 78–9 see frame 78.
2. FRUS 1945 v, 515. Vyshinski said the same about Tătărescu, ibid.
3. Robert R. King, *History of the Romanian Communist Party*, Histories of the Ruling Communist Parties, general editor Richard F. Starr, Stanford, California: Hoover Press Publication 233, Hoover Institution Press, 1980, p.66.
4. Silviu Brucan, *The Wasted Generation: Memoirs of the Romanian Journey from Capitalism to Socialism and Back*, San Francisco and London: Westview Press, Boulder, Colorado, 1993, p.42. Of Pauker Stalin said, 'Ana is a good, reliable comrade, but you see, she is a Jewess of bourgeois origin . . .' Ibid.
5. Liliana Saiu, *The Great Powers and Romania, 1944–1946. A Study of the Early Cold War Era*, Boulder, CO: East European Monographs, no. 335, distributed by Columbia University Press, New York, 1992, p.70.
6. D. G. Giurescu, *Romania's Communist Takeover: the Radescu Government*, Boulder, CO/ New York: East European Monographs, no. 388, Distributed by Columbia University Press, 1994, p.77.
7. This account relies heavily on that given in Arthur G. Lee, *Crown against Sickle*, London: Hutchinson, 1950, pp.100–3. Lee was a member of the British delegation to the ACC.
8. Yasamee and Hamilton, microfiches, sheet 15, frame 34.
9. Dennis Deletant, *Communist Terror in Romania: Gheorghiu-Dej and the Police State, 1948–1965*, London: Hurst & Company, 1999, p.55.
10. David Turnock, *The Romanian Economy in the Twentieth Century*, London and Sydney: Croom Helm, 1966, p.51 note 2.
11. Keith Hitchins, *Rumania 1866–1947*, Oxford History of Modern Europe, Oxford: Oxford University Press, 1994, p.543.

Chapter 6

GREECE, 1944–1949

The origins of the modern Greek state lay in the revolt of 1821 in the Danubian principalities. The revolution had not prospered there but it had inspired some Greeks to take independent action; that action, sporadic and dispersed as it was, was confined to the Peloponnese where the thinly spread Ottoman troops were soon confined to their coastal fortresses. Neither side could gain the upper hand, and both indulged in acts of primitive savagery. The Greeks, however, had the advantage of their classical past. West Europeans steeped in classical education and mythology rushed to the rescue and, though they were far fewer in number than volunteers from other Balkan ethnic groups, they created strong pressures on their own governments. When Egyptian forces were sent to bolster the Ottoman cause in Greece the European powers reacted; British and French ships destroyed the Egyptian fleet in Navarino Bay in 1827 and in the following year the Russians sent their armies into the Balkans. In the final settlement in 1832 the three powers guaranteed the independence of the new state which they also required to accept a foreign king.

The war of independence had shown a steady commitment to the cause of national liberation but it had also shown a propensity for violent disagreement on internal issues; even before independence liberated areas in Greece had experimented with three constitutions and had seen the assassination of one president. This pattern of constitutional instability was to be repeated a century later.

The Greek state created in 1832 contained less than a third of the Greeks living under Ottoman rule in 1821. The expansion of the kingdom to embrace all Hellenes – the 'Great Idea' – was to remain a constant aspiration until the final quarter of the twentieth century. The first acquisition came in 1863 when Britain handed over the seven Ionian islands it had been administering since 1815. The Balkan crises of the late 1870s brought further gain, this time with the incorporation of Thessaly in 1881. This was the end of the process of peaceful expansion, and further accretion was to be achieved only by the spilling of blood. In 1897 the long-standing desire to secure Crete for the Hellenic kingdom was thwarted by defeat at the hands of the Ottoman army, though in the peace settlement the island was given autonomy and a Greek prince was made high commissioner. The Young Turk revolution of 1908 seemed to offer another chance to seize Crete and the Greek government's failure to do so led in 1909 to a military coup in Athens. There was, for Greece, a happier outcome to the Balkan wars of 1912–13 which secured full possession of Crete and brought massive gains in Macedonia, Thrace and in the Aegean islands.

In Greece party politics had always been lively but had to a large extent revolved around personalities rather than deep-rooted political issues. This changed in the First World War. Differing views on the policies which should be adopted led to a fundamental rift between the king and his supporters who favoured neutrality, and the followers of Eleftherios Venizelos and his Liberal Party which advocated alliance with France, Britain and Russia.

After the First World War the divisions were compounded by the doleful experience of the Greek campaign in Asia Minor. Encouraged by British prime minister Lloyd George, Venizelos committed Greece to a campaign to incorporate western Anatolia which had a large number of Greeks. The Greek forces became over-extended and were pushed back by a new nationalist army formed under Mustapha Kemal, or Kemal Atatürk. The campaign ended with the burning of the port of Smyrna (Izmir) in which tens of thousands of Greeks had taken refuge. The peace of Lausanne which concluded the war provided for a massive population exchange. The remaining Greeks of Asia Minor were to be moved to Greece, while the Muslims of Greece were to go to Turkey. The programme involved hundreds of thousands of families, though the Greeks of Istanbul and the Muslims of Thrace were excluded from it and remained in their original homes.

The Asia Minor campaign produced deep recriminations between the Venizelists and their opponents and these were never far below the surface of Greek politics in the inter-war years. The population exchanges also restructured the political geography of Greece in that the incomers, who were settled mainly in the north, soon found cause to complain and added a significant new element to the forces of the left. This trend was intensified by the great depression which hit agricultural prices and further impoverished the already disadvantaged immigrants.

Greece was therefore divided into royalists and Venizelists, and also into advocates of military rule and parliamentarians. These squabbles created such instability that between June 1917 and the end of 1935 there were five changes of monarch, only one of which was due to natural causes, five coups or thwarted coups, a number of assassination attempts, including one against Venizelos, and three plebiscites on the monarchy. Finally, in August 1936 the monarch, who had returned to Greece after a rigged referendum in November 1935, installed a tough-minded army officer, General Ioannis Metaxas, as prime minister. Metaxas achieved stability, but only at the price of imposing a dictatorship.

Metaxas's policies were nationalist as well as authoritarian. His great achievement came with the Italian invasion of Greece launched from Albania in
October 1940. Presented with an ultimatum in the middle of the night,
Metaxas returned to it a simple 'no', and in a few months had driven back
the much better-equipped Italian forces. Metaxas died in January 1941 but he
had lived long enough to see a triumph which was proof that whatever its
previous divisions the Greek nation had not lost its fundamental cohesion or
dedication to the preservation of its independence. But no nation as small as
Greece, no matter how determined, could have successfully resisted the invasion by the massive, modern armies of the German Reich in April 1941, after
which Greece was partitioned into areas of German, Italian and Bulgarian
occupation. The occupation, and particularly its first winter, brought appalling shortages and privations, with deaths from starvation being commonplace
in the larger cities.

During the months of its heroic resistance Greece had, with Britain, been
the only state actively resisting Axis aggression in Europe. Britain, despite its
association with Venizelos during the First World War, had been the most
influential power in Greece during the 1930s, its influence being exercised
through political tradition, through economic links and, not least, through
cooperation on security matters.

British interest in Greece did not cease with the Axis occupation. The
Greek king was given sanctuary and, when threatened by a mutiny amongst
his forces in Egypt, military help. Help was also given to the resistance in
Greece itself. This was not easy. The occupation had not meant the end of
Greek determination to fight, this time to regain rather than safeguard independence, but the unity of the struggle against the Italians could not be
preserved.

INTERNAL CONFLICTS IN GREECE DURING THE SECOND WORLD WAR

There were a number of resistance groups which took to the hills to fight
the occupying Italian, German and Bulgarian forces, but two main elements
had emerged by the summer of 1943. One was the republican but anti-
communist National Democratic Greek League (EDES). A much larger and
more powerful force emerged in the shape of the National Popular Liberation Army (ELAS), an acronym which was also a homonym for the Greek
word for Greece. The political representation of ELAS was the communist-
dominated National Liberation Front (EAM), which bore strong resemblances
to similar front organizations in Yugoslavia and other states. Like the Yugoslav
Peoples' Front EAM subjugated its long-term socialist aspirations to the short-
term objective of fighting the occupiers; its appeal was therefore primarily
patriotic though, as in Yugoslavia, in those areas under its control it initiated a
number of social and political reforms. To EDES the socialists of EAM/ELAS

seemed every bit as dangerous as the occupiers, whose star was waning by the spring of 1943.

The British recognized the socialist nature of EAM/ELAS and tried to bolster EDES as a counter to it. ELAS was convinced that the British were determined to restore the monarchy and the old order, popular opinion not-withstanding, and assumed that EDES was to be the mechanism for enforcing this; these convictions were reinforced when ELAS delegates returned empty-handed from talks with the British and the government in exile in Cairo in August 1943. On 1 October the politburo of the Communist Party of Greece (KKE), the leading force in EAM, decided to appeal to the democratic elements in EDES for common action. The response was lukewarm and ELAS there-fore took to arms against EDES, informing the allies on 12 October that it had been forced to do this by EDES's provocations and by its collaboration with the enemy. In what some observers were later to regard as the first round in the Greek civil war the fighting lasted for four months until British mediation and a German offensive against ELAS forced the latter to disengage and return to its previous tactic of trying to win EDES over by negotiation.

There was little progress. New fuel was added to EDES suspicions that EAM was attempting a takeover in Greece in March when the latter set up the Political Committee of National Liberation (PEEA). EAM insisted that this was not a provisional government but it had all the hallmarks of one and seemed very much a Greek equivalent of AVNOJ in Yugoslavia. What was more, the PEEA proved attractive to a number of Greek troops in Egypt who declared their sympathy with the EAM-sponsored group. This mutiny among the forces of the government in exile was put down with the help of British troops. The emergency enabled the British to engineer the appoint-ment of a new and much more vigorous prime minister in the shape of Georgios Papandreou. It also enabled the government in exile, with British help, to organize a new and entirely loyal military unit, the Third, or Moun-tain Brigade. Meanwhile, in Greece itself hostilities between the two main resistance groups recommenced and in April National and Social Liberation (EKKA), a small republican group, was forcibly disbanded and its military leader, Colonel Psarros, killed by an ELAS band. In May Papandreou sought to mend his political fences and convened a meeting of all major groups involved in Greek politics. At the meeting in the Lebanon Papandreou used the Psarros incident as an indication of EAM's intention to eliminate its potential political opponents and called for unity in the face of the occupy-ing enemies and in view of the tasks of reconstruction which would face the country after liberation. The KKE delegation was isolated and despite its undoubted numerical supremacy in occupied Greece agreed to join a national government with the old parties. Papandreou's seeming success in placing himself in the driving seat belied his weakness vis-à-vis the commun-ists and their resistance forces in Greece.

The KKE in Greece knew this and initially refused to accept the terms to which its delegation had agreed in the Lebanon. By the end of the summer, however, it had changed its mind and on 3 September six EAM ministers, two of them communists, joined the government in exile which had now moved to Italy in preparation for its return to the homeland. The reasons for this reversal of attitude were to be found in the interplay of global forces. In May 1944 the British foreign secretary, Sir Anthony Eden, had had conversations with the Soviet ambassador in London; they were the first steps along the path which was to lead in October to the percentages agreement. At the end of July the first Soviet mission to EAM/ELAS arrived in Greece and it is inconceivable that its chief, Colonel Popov, did not tell the Greek comrades of what was afoot.

The inclusion of EAM ministers in the national government did not prevent violence. As the Germans retreated in September 1944 they entrusted considerable supplies of food and ammunition to the Security Battalions in a number of towns. The Security Battalions had been set up during the occupation by the Quisling government as an anti-communist, anti-ELAS force, and by entrusting them with food and arms the Germans hoped to divide the Greeks and complicate the situation for the British. They succeeded. In the Peloponnese ELAS units surrounded a number of towns, demanding the surrender of the Security Battalions. ELAS hoped to seize control of the towns, together with the Security Battalions' arms and food supplies, before the British arrived. Some towns did fall to ELAS forces and in them fierce slaughter ensued.

The violence ceased, temporarily, when British forces landed. They reached Athens on 14 October, Papandreou arriving four days later. From then until the beginning of December an uneasy, and not entirely unfractured calm prevailed. Papandreou faced formidable problems. His writ only ran in the larger urban areas, and in some of these he had to share power with EAM. The country was in ruins, its economy at a virtual standstill, unemployment widespread, and the currency worthless. On the political front Papandreou had to find some way of satisfying the left's demands for revenge against the collaborators without alienating the right which was deeply suspicious of any demands put forward by EAM and the left.

LEFT AND RIGHT IN GREECE, 1944–9

EAM's programme had been formulated during the war and again it resembled what was being implemented by the victorious partisans in Yugoslavia. Its numerous demands included: mass participation in and therefore the democratization of local government; more accessible local justice with elected judges; a social welfare programme to be paid for by progressive taxation; the development of heavy industry and agriculture so as to create full employment; the reduction of Greece's dependence on foreign capital and external economic aid; the nationalization of major industries and the chief public utilities; the confiscation of some foreign concerns; worker participation in factory management; more rights for women, a demand which recognized the role they had played in the resistance; and friendly relations with the Soviet Union as well as with the western allies. There was also to be a thorough purge of all those associated with the dictatorial regimes which had ruled Greece between 1936 and 1944.

The left drew its strength from a number of quarters. Its record of resistance in the war had earned it the respect, sometimes grudging, of many patriots. The left had strong support among the former Asia Minor refugees in the north. In the towns the manual workers were regarded as natural allies but in fact the clerical workers and junior civil servants were at least as enthusiastic in their endorsement of the left; they too were suffering from massive inflation, shortages and the black market, and their disappointment at the lack of democratic liberties was greater than that of the manual workers who had never expected much from the bourgeois system anyway. The KKE could also muster strong support from the young, and especially the educated among them. Naturally idealistic, they had experienced no political freedom since 1936 and were still naive enough to believe that a communist-dominated system might give it to them. In the rural areas KKE could count on the backing of the poorer peasants who were forced to rely on partial wage labour to make ends meet, though the party's call for land redistribution had little impact as 96 per cent of holdings in Greece were already less than ten hectares. A number of the poorer rural clergy aligned with the KKE, as did two bishops, though these were exceptions to the general episcopal rule. The communists also found significant support amongst the Slav minority.

Terrified by the left's radicalism, the right insisted on respect for private property and for the traditional, patriarchal family. It also defended the privileges of the Orthodox Church, though there was as yet no indication that these might be under threat, together with the rights of those other established instruments of state power: the police, the army, the judiciary, the civil service and the state-controlled banks, all of which it wanted restored to their pre-war positions of dominance in society. The right was the champion of the wealthy businessman and the middle man in the countryside rather than the worker, the small employer, the peasant or the consumer. The right also rejected the left's demand that demotic, spoken Greek should become the official language in place of the *katharevousa*, the old, stilted and stylized version of Greek which all had to learn at school but which few could use as a functioning medium of exchange. Above all, the right trumpeted its determination to defend Greece against communism and to preserve its territorial integrity in the face of what it saw as Slav- or Albanian-communist attempts to seize parts of Macedonia or Epirus. The fear of communism was such that in many cases it overrode the old division between the Liberals (Venizelists) and the royalists; both were now so afeared of militant, international communism backed by the Soviet Union and its Balkan allies that they saw the return of the king as their best defence. The nationalism of the right found some support in all sectors of society but the right's active enthusiasts were drawn mainly from the privileged segments of the old establishment: the judiciary, the police, the army, the higher civil service, senior academics, the majority of the ecclesiastical hierarchy, the directors and owners of larger banks and industrial enterprises, and also from many of the leading figures in the old trade unions.

These huge divides in attitude and policies which had emerged during the war were to remain unchanged until the end of the civil war in 1949, if not until 1974.

THE DECEMBER EVENTS, 1944

Despite the deep divisions between left and right there was in November 1944 some indication that the Papandreou government might have found a solution to one at least of the most pressing of its immediate problems: that of dissolving the existing military formations and creating a new, national army. It proved a false dawn. By the end of the month the talks had collapsed, Papandreou and the British refusing to bow to ELAS's insistence that in the new army its units should be the equal in strength to all the other groups combined. On 2 December the EAM ministers resigned and demonstrations were called for in Athens on the following day.

That day, 3 December 1944, saw the beginning of what many later re-garded as the second round of the Greek civil war. For weeks Athens had been plastered with EAM and KKE posters and graffiti; there was no mistak-ing the largely pro-KKE mood of the capital, just as there was no doubt that the police, whose personnel was virtually unchanged, were anti–communist. Fears that the demonstrations might end in violence proved fully justified when the police fired into the crowds in Constitution Square, though had there been any substance to KKE assertions that the police deliberately fired to kill the number of dead would have been far greater. The following day a general strike was declared throughout the country while the commander of the British forces, Lieutenant-General Ronald Scobie, ordered that ELAS reinforcements must be kept out of Athens. This proved impossible. Within a few days there were over twelve thousand ELAS soldiers in the city and serious fighting had begun. By this time the British cabinet had decided that the communist threat had to be contained by all possible means and troops were rushed to Greece from the Italian front. The fighting intensified and was not confined to clashes between the British and ELAS. Units of a right-wing organization, 'Chi' (X), led by a Colonel Grivas, had also attacked ELAS forces; such units were soon to become much more prominent.

The upheavals of December, or the *Dekemvriana* as it is known in Greek, virtually killed all hope of a peaceful evolution away from Greece's post-war tensions. Papandreou, who believed his credibility depended on his ability to lead the country back to peace and away from civil strife, felt he had failed and resigned, blaming the communists for his defeat. Nor did the communists themselves emerge from the *Dekemvriana* unscathed. In refusing to compromise on the question of the army and in breaking with the national government EAM had taken a huge gamble and lost. It had underestimated the willingness of the British to intervene. Furthermore, the *Dekemvriana* exposed a basic weakness in EAM's position in the immediate post-liberation period. It had garnered much of its very considerable support − it estimated its followers at around 400,000 in the autumn − on its entirely justified claim that it had been the major force opposing the occupiers during the war. Its patriotic credentials were unimpeachable. However, to oppose the occupiers meant, by implication, to support the occupiers' enemies, which in the Greek context was at this stage primarily the British. Many who had supported EAM because of its anti-German record abandoned it when it turned against the British; its support fell to around 200,000 in April 1945.

With the fall of Papandreou the British turned to Archbishop Damaskinos of Athens. At Christmas 1944 Winston Churchill and Antony Eden flew to Athens to try and find a political solution to the crisis in Greece. The mission failed to prevent the continuation of the fighting but when the British prime minister returned to London he did manage to resolve one political difficulty by persuading King George not to return to Greece for the time being; in his absence Archbishop Damaskinos was to act as regent. Damaskinos appointed a veteran republican general, Nikolaos Plastiras, to replace Papandreou as prime minister and a few days later, on the night of 4–5 January 1945, ELAS forces slipped quietly out of Athens. An armistice was signed on 11 January. On 12 February the Varkiza agreement was signed, providing for an amnesty for those involved in the recent fighting, for a purge of those guilty of collaboration during the war, and for a plebiscite on the future of the monarchy which was to be followed by Greece's first post-war parliamentary elections. The agreement enabled EAM to save some face. Its demand for the punishment of collaborators had been met, and ELAS fighters were not to be persecuted. This enraged the right, as did the decision not actively to disarm ELAS but merely to supervise the handing in of its weapons.

'ANARCHIC BANDITRY':[1] FROM THE VARKIZA AGREEMENT TO THE ELECTIONS OF MARCH 1946

In the thirteen months between the formal end of the *Dekemvriana* and the first post-war elections the British continued with their attempts to stabilize the currency and revivify the economy but any progress made in the economic sector was more than offset by the failure of Greek political factions to repair the breach between left and right, a breach which widened as the right took to the offensive in what its opponents called 'the white terror'.

Plastiras proved a failure from the British point of view in that, like Papandreou before him, he could not construct a government of the centre, and in April 1945 the British minister intervened to secure his dismissal. He was replaced by Admiral Petros Voulgaris, a non-party figure whose main function was to guide the country through the plebiscite and the elections. His appointment made little difference and in September the regent persuaded the British that were a plebiscite to be held it would result in the immediate return of the king which in all probability would precipitate a revolt by the left and civil war; much better, Damaskinos argued, to reverse the order agreed at Varkiza and stage elections first to test the political mood, and hold the plebiscite when sufficient calm had returned to the country. London agreed to this once Washington had acknowledged that it had no objections. The order in which the votes were taken in fact made little difference and the elections brought about the very disorders which Damaskinos had feared would result from the plebiscite.

The fundamental problem remained the gulf between communism and anti-communism, a gulf which widened during the Plastiras and Voulgaris administrations. After Varkiza EAM and ELAS had been officially disbanded leaving the KKE as overtly dominant on the left. A number of high-ranking party officials had questioned the wisdom of the Varkiza settlement and many others openly rejected it, taking to the hills and reconstituting their wartime guerrilla units. As pressure from the government increased others who felt threatened followed them and though they never received official backing from the KKE they were able to rely on the remnants of EAM organizations in the hills and villages.

The right began its offensive immediately after Varkiza. In part this was because the British were now less concerned with restraining it. Britain had intervened in Greece primarily in service of the traditional British objective of keeping the Russians out of the eastern Mediterranean and away from the Aegean littoral. By early 1945 it was clear this objective had been achieved and, though the Labour government in London had no love of right-wing extremism, it did not now see any need to regulate the day-to-day affairs of Greece. It disliked, but did not prevent, Plastiras's packing of the officer corps of the reconstituted Greek army with his own political supporters.

At this stage the army was less prominent in the campaign against the left than the police and the National Guard. The police, still largely unchanged since the occupation but now demoralized and insecure, had always been the prime target of wartime guerrilla activity and had therefore taken heavy casualties both during the occupation and the *Dekemvriana*. Police action, how-ever, was confined in the main to the larger urban centres. In the rural areas the most aggressive element of 'the white terror' was the National Guard which, unlike the army, was prepared to pursue leftist bands into the country-side. The National Guard had been greatly expanded during the *Dekemvriana* and usually operated in the area where its personnel had been recruited; this being so those recruits lost few chances to take personal vengeance on their enemies. In addition to these official arms of government there were also the irregular right-wing organizations, the most prominent among them still being Grivas's Chi, which were very active in the campaign against the left. These various agencies of the right, official and unofficial, were, according to US and British observers, responsible for the majority of the 1,289 murders committed in Greece between the Varkiza agreement and the elections of March 1946. Only in a very few northern areas with a relatively large Slav population was the majority of the violence the work of the left rather than the right.

The white terror was the major preoccupation of the KKE-dominated left but it was not their only cause for opposition to the government. There was great resentment at the failure of the authorities even to begin seriously to address the social problems of the country, most of which predated the war but had been greatly exacerbated by it. Unemployment, the disruption of international trade on which many peasants relied to sell their produce and the increase in disease, predominantly TB, caused by prolonged malnutrition, were only three of the difficulties facing the country. Some relief was provided by international aid, primarily through UNRRA and the USA, but this gave rise to further complaints. The aid was for the most part distributed by the government and more often than not in a corrupt and partisan fashion with communities with strong EAM/ELAS affiliations almost certain to fare worse than those without them. This problem was intensified by the growing centralization of the post-war years. There were no local elections in Greece between 1935 and 1951. If there were a vacancy for the powerful position of prefect, or nomarch, it was filled by the government nominating one of its own flock who could be relied upon to follow the official line. A further consequence of this practice was that the nomarchs themselves tended to spend more time in Athens where power and their political patrons resided; the provinces began to feel neglected or even abandoned and increasingly resentful of the remote and seemingly unaccountable central government. This created more support for the left.

The few who were rich in post-war Greece were either members of established industrial or commercial families or war profiteers. The line between war profiteering and collaboration was a fine one and the left complained bitterly that so few economic collaborators had been brought to trial and that even if they were they were given very light sentences, particularly when compared to those handed down to the many EAM supporters brought before the courts. The situation was made worse by the fact that many war profiteers, far from being prosecuted, were allowed to grow even richer by manipulating the flourishing post-war black market. Even more scandalous in the eyes of the left was the indulgence shown to political collaborators. While leftists were being hounded in the courts or driven into the hills, many whose wartime records were dubious remained unharmed. So great had the rulers' fear of communism become that it seemed patriotic communists were regarded as much more dangerous than fiercely anti-communist collaborators.

The reaction of the KKE leadership to this deepening tension was cautious. After the *Dekemvriana* it had lost support and was anxious not to provoke the right any further. So great was its fear of provocation that it expelled one of its leading members, Aris Velouchiotis, for his outspoken opposition to the Varkiza agreement; he was to commit suicide in June when surrounded by a right-wing band. After Varkiza the party in fact trod water, leaving the settlement of major problems until the meeting of the seventh congress in October. It was also awaiting the return of its most influential pre-war figure, Nikos Zachariadis, who had been imprisoned in Dachau. He arrived in Greece in May. Zachariadis endorsed the policies adopted during his absence, including the Lebanon and the Varkiza agreements, and in a policy statement in July the party called for the application within four months of the Yalta accords with their promise of free elections for all non-fascist parties. The KKE also called for the formation of a government of all non-collaborationist forces; if, in the interim, the right resorted to force the people should adopt measures for 'mass self-defence'. It also put forward a programme for economic and social renewal. In external affairs Zachariadis had a realistic concept of Greece's geographical position and its isolation from the Soviet Union and therefore propounded the 'two poles' concept which meant cooperation with both the USSR and Britain, though this did not prevent the party from blaming the British for the majority of Greece's contemporary problems and arguing that most of these would be solved within two weeks if the British left.

The KKE seems to have remained convinced throughout 1945 that the struggle with the right was primarily political. The party had reason to be confident of the outcome of that struggle. The credibility lost by the *Dekemvriana* was steadily recouped, mainly because of the excesses of the right. The KKE was particularly successful in rebuilding its support in the larger cities, in the trade unions and in the agricultural cooperatives. By the beginning of 1946, however, attitudes were hardening. The release of three thousand leftist detainees in December 1945 had injected a greater degree of venom into the party's veins, and with no sign that the right was prepared to relax its repressive policies the party decided in February 1946 to give some support to the guerrilla units in the mountains. One result of this was an attack on the village of Litochoro on 30 March 1946. The banditry was becoming less anarchic.

THE DRIFT TO CIVIL WAR: FROM THE ELECTIONS TO THE DECLARATION OF THE PROVISIONAL GOVERNMENT, MARCH 1946 TO DECEMBER 1947

In addition to deciding to move closer to the guerrilla units the KKE had also resolved to boycott the elections which the government had finally called for March 1946. The other parties, with the exception of those on the right, would have preferred to see a further postponement of the vote. The KKE boycott meant that a quarter of the electorate voluntarily absented themselves from the polling booths, but more seriously it also marked another step away from consensus, meaning that the left would not be involved in any post-election coalition, and that any such coalition would not be able to call upon the considerable reserves of talent tied up in the left-wing parties, including the KKE. Both the KKE and Greece's already slender hopes for political stability suffered from the KKE's decision to boycott the elections.

With the KKE standing aside the election became a contest between the centre, represented by the National Political Union and the right which was organized into the United Nationalist Alliance. The National Political Union included parties led by Papandreou, Sophocles Venizelos, the son of the founder of the Venizelist tendency, and Panayotis Kanellopoulos. The right was dominated by the People's Party (PP). The elections were dominated by anti-communist hysteria and marred by considerable intimidation from the right. The right emerged the victor with 236 of the 354 seats in the national assembly.

The PP formed a government under the premiership of Konstantinos Tsaldaris who also became leader of the ruling party. Given the nature of the PP's electoral rhetoric and Tsaldaris's past record as an anti-leftist, any hope of mending the great divide in Greece had gone.

The Tsaldaris cabinet, like its predecessor, filled as many administrative posts as it could with its own nominees. This process affected not only the civil service but more importantly the agencies for maintaining public order, with senior police officers being replaced if they were not considered polit-ically trustworthy. The same happened in the army where senior posts and the general staff were packed with PP trustees. The new government also estab-lished close links with 'The Sacred Bond of Greek Officers' (IDEA), a semi-secret, anti-liberal, monarchist, conservative and partially anti-parliamentary military conspiratorial group formed in the winter of 1944/45. Both the police and the army therefore became even more right-wing than before, and both were increased in size by the new government.

It was not long before the new administration was putting its anti-leftist rhetoric into effect. Not only were the army and the police expanded but in May 1946 the pre-war Security Commissions were re-established. They could deport anyone, without the right of self-defence, who was suspected of left-wing activities. In June Resolution Three introduced special military courts in Thessaly and Epirus; these courts could try anyone accused of a number of activities which the government declared as subversive. The ruling also gave the police the right to search domestic premises for arms, to impose curfews and to demand advance notice of strikes and demonstrations. In July the first large-scale and systematic military operations were launched against leftist bands; these operations continued, without much real effect, into the autumn.

In September 1946 the Tsaldaris government implemented one of its elec-tion pledges by holding a referendum on the monarchy. Once again there were irregularities in the voting but they alone were not responsible for the victory of the pro-monarchists; even anti-monarchists voted for restoration as the best guarantee against a communist takeover. King George II returned in the same month. He reigned only until April 1947 when his death brought to the throne King Paul and his energetic wife, Frederika.

The intensification of action against the left brought about reactions which by the summer of 1946 had made open civil war all but inevitable. Ever since the second plenum of the KKE early in 1946 the party had sent former ELAS officers into the hills to help organize the leftist bands. In July the KKE took the first steps towards the formation of a new partisan army when Zachariadis ordered Markos Vaphiadis, a prominent wartime commander of ELAS and current leader of the party in Macedonia and western Thrace, to go to Belgrade to discuss this issue with other Greek politburo members then in the Yugoslav capital. By September, in response to the government offensive launched in July, the communist guerrilla units were operating on a widespread scale in Macedonia, Thessaly and Epirus; in northern Thessaly and western Macedonia they established what they referred to as 'Free Greece'. On 28 October, the anniversary of Greece's rejection of Mussolini's ultimatum in 1940, Markos established a united military command for all mainland Greece, and in December this became the Democratic Army of Greece (DAG). It claimed at that time to have ten thousand members and its numbers were growing. In early 1947 a number of former ELAS fighters moved back into Greece from Yugoslavia where they had taken refuge at the end of the war. All that remained was for the Greek communists to receive the imprimatur from the giants of the European socialist camp, Stalin and Tito. In April and May Zachariadis travelled to Moscow and Belgrade where, he believed, no objections were raised against an offensive and the KKE therefore opted for war against the nationalist government.

The KKE's decision for all-out war was brought about in part by the belief that the British, battered by economic storms and fully occupied with the problems of India and Palestine, would soon leave Greece. They did. But they were replaced by the Americans. The British departure gave occasion to President Truman's declaration in March 1947 that the United States would support any people fighting to defend itself against communist subversion. The KKE nevertheless pressed ahead with its plans for conflict, clearly believing that American intervention would have little impact. When Zachariadis visited Belgrade and Moscow in the spring neither Tito nor Stalin disabused him of this view. Tito was enthusiastic but Stalin calculating; he had always been determined to abide by the percentages agreement, and as early as January 1945 had told Dimitrov, 'I advised the Greeks not to undertake this struggle. The ELAS people should not have left the Papandreou government . . . Evidently they thought the Red Army would move down to the Aegean Sea . . . We cannot send our troops into Greece.'[2]

While the KKE moved towards outright war the government continued to pressurize the left and its supporters. In 1947 law 509 allowed the police almost a free hand in the harassment of those whom it suspected of left-wing activities, and in October the KKE press in Athens was liquidated; that in the provinces had suffered a similar fate some months earlier. The left, meanwhile, continued on a larger scale its previous tactics of sabotaging government installations, attacking individual government supporters and their homes, and conducting recruiting and foraging raids on villages and small towns. On 2 December the KKE politburo decided to break entirely with the existing political structures and formed a Provisional Democratic Government (PDG) on 25 December. The government in Athens responded by proscribing the KKE. What had been apparent for months was now acknowledged. Greece was in a state of civil war. The final round in this protracted conflict was to be the longest and the bloodiest.

THE GREEK CIVIL WAR, DECEMBER 1947 TO AUGUST 1949

The final round of the Greek conflict can be divided into two phases. In the first, from December 1947 to January 1949, the initiative was held by the communists; thereafter the long-term strengths of the government forces became more and more apparent and decisive.

From December 1947 the DAG intensified its organization and built up stores of arms and matériel. In June 1948 the force's resilience was proved when 15,000 of its troops were attacked by a government force of 50,000 in the Grammos mountains. The latter suffered heavy casualties and though the communists were driven out of the area it was not long before they re-infiltrated and they were again in command by midwinter. In January 1949 the DAG seized three small towns in western Macedonia and Roumeli. The towns did not have large or high-quality garrisons but the attackers had shown an impressive degree of organization and discipline. If the communists were to take other and larger urban centres their chances of victory would be greatly increased, command of the towns and cities being essential to control of the country as a whole. In reality the odds on a communist victory were lengthening, and had been for some time.

The first reason for this was a slow and initially scarcely perceptible improvement in the quality of the national army. At the time of liberation this had been in a state of almost total disarray. Much of its old professional officer corps had been discredited by collaboration or lack of resistance, while too many of those who escaped to exile had become mired in political intrigues. Others had been seconded to the National Guard. The mass of the army consisted of conscripts who resented the political background of their officers, and who frequently sympathized with the left. They saw little reason to fight what seemed like an unwinnable war against their fellow Greeks. These deficiencies were gradually addressed and a major advance had been achieved by the creation of mobile commando units which by the beginning of the civil war had become a small but tough and reliable élite of crack troops.

A critical move in strengthening the government's forces was the appointment in January 1949 of General Alexander Papagos as commander in chief. A hero of the war against the Italians he had resisted the occupation, had been captured and sent to a POW camp where he spent most of the war. Papagos was given wide powers and, with American backing, was able to conduct his military affairs without political interference. He made few changes in the leading ranks of the army but he let it be known that incompetence would be punished and that merit alone would determine promotion; political influence or connections would count for nothing. Surprisingly, by and large this happened and by the summer of 1949 the Greek army was a far more effective fighting force than at any time since its defeat at the hands of the Germans in 1941.

A second basic communist weakness lay in the nature of the foreign backing given to both sides in the war. The morale of the government and its supporters had been boosted by the Truman Doctrine in March 1947 and later by a US presidential warning to all and sundry against recognizing the PDG. Support from Britain and even more so the USA showed that Greece had not been abandoned by two of the most powerful, and democratic, states in the world.

The American presence also helped the government by forcing it to abandon some of its own worst practices. In September 1947 the army, wanting stable right-wing government, had become uneasy when a Liberal, Themistoclis Sophoulis, was nominated as prime minister in place of Tsaldaris. The Chief of the general staff virtually forced the king to reappoint Tsaldaris, only to find the Americans intervening equally energetically on behalf of Sophoulis. The Americans won. They were anxious to limit the interference of the military in the political sphere and to encourage acts of conciliation such as that whereby Sophoulis proclaimed an amnesty which led to four thousand left-wing activists turning in their weapons. The Americans continued along this path, insisting that more Liberals be brought into the cabinet until by 1949 the People's Party had lost all the important portfolios except that of foreign affairs, and, equally importantly, the Liberals had the same number of regional prefects as the PP. This did much to enhance the government's image.

Overt American involvement was military as well as political. In October 1947 US military liaison officers arrived in Greece and in December they established the Joint US Military Advisory and Planning Group (JUSMAPG). American and British officers took an active part in planning and in some cases carrying out military operations, and they encouraged the national army to take the battle to the enemy rather than waiting for him to attack.

The volume and nature of western help to the government contrasted sharply with the external support given to the communists. The KKE in fact miscalculated badly. Cut off from the sea and without any air capabilities, the Greek communists were entirely dependent on the land routes from Albania, Yugoslavia and Bulgaria for arms and ammunition – food they usually requisitioned from the local peasantry which was another cause of their increasing unpopularity. The requisite arms, ammunition and medical supplies never arrived in sufficient quantities. Stalin had been unwilling to provoke the Americans by giving aid and succour to the Greek communists in 1945 and was hardly likely to do so after the Truman Declaration, and the DGA therefore received virtually no material aid from the USSR. Matters became much worse after the Tito–Stalin split when the Bulgarians and Albanians, following pressure from Moscow, cut off their supplies, making Yugoslavia the only source of help. The KKE hardly furthered its own cause by siding with Moscow in the Soviet-Yugoslav dispute and in 1949 the Yugoslavs too closed their borders. KKE leaders later declared this 'stab in the back' to be the main reason for their defeat in the civil war. It was not true. The Yugoslav action made relatively little difference; the KKE goose was already cooked when the border was closed.

Even if the communists had received large quantities of supplies from the north this would not have strengthened their political position in Greece. Even left-leaning non-communists disliked the prospect of very close association with the Slav and Albanian states on the northern border, and when those states instituted increasingly rigorous social reforms and tightened political controls the dislike intensified.

The communists were also weakened by the fact that though many Greeks may not have liked their government they needed it. The state played a huge role in the everyday life of Greece. It was the state, especially in a time when local government had ceased to be elected and had become a matter of nomination from the centre, which gave jobs, concluded contracts, doled out relief aid, issued licences for all forms of economic activity from banking to running a café, and granted loans from state-owned banks, especially the Agricultural Bank. The government's power of patronage was therefore enormous and it did much to ensure that the urban population, whatever its political inclinations, remained obedient and therefore beyond the reach of the KKE and the DAG.

Finally, and most importantly, the communists were critically weakened by the fact that they never became anything more than a guerrilla force. The lack of heavy weapons meant that they could not sustain the sort of military campaign which the capture and retention of urban centres required. The government meanwhile kept a tight rein on the urban population thus depriving the DGA of volunteers from its supporters among the city workers, and forcing it to rely more and more on conscription to fill its ranks. This seriously diluted the ideological commitment with which the DAG forces had begun the civil war. It had a further and even more deleterious consequence. As many of the areas under DAG control had large Slav populations by the spring of 1949 a considerable proportion of the insurgent army's conscript ranks was Slavophone. This the government propagandists seized upon with alacrity, charging that the communists intended to dismember northern Greece and hand large chunks of Greek territory to the northern neighbours. The KKE consistently denied the charge but decisions such as that of the KKE fifth plenum in January 1949 to commit the party to 'full national restoration' for the Slav Macedonians was grist to the government's propaganda mill. In fact, the Greek communists had never fully recognized, or admitted, the importance of the Macedonian factor. Many Macedonian Slavs had played important roles in EAM/ELAS, but to admit this would be to alarm or alienate ethnic Greeks, especially when there seemed to be moves in the communist states to incorporate all ethnic Macedonians in one Macedonian, communist state. Not to admit the importance of the Macedonian Slavs in the communist movement would be to disappoint the Macedonians themselves which, when the DAG forces were confined to areas with relatively large ethnic Macedonian populations, was a further cause of weakness.

By the summer of 1949 the many weaknesses of the communist position combined to bring defeat to their army. In August it was encircled once more in the Grammos mountains. It fought ferociously despite being out-numbered and plastered with bombs and napalm. If the resistance was heroic it was also hopeless. The last action was on Mount Vitsi in August after which the remnants of the DAG struggled over the borders to the north. Apart from some mopping up operations and the occasional outburst of communist-inspired violence, the last being in Chalkidiki in January 1950, the civil war was over.

The costs of the civil war were enormous. It delayed the reconstruction of the country after the ravages of the Second World War. It produced large-scale internal displacement and mass emigration. Tens of thousands of KKE sympathizers went into exile, the total number of refugees being in the region of 136,000. Many of these were non-Greeks. A comparison of the 1940 and 1950 censuses shows that the Slavophones fell from 86,000 to 41,000, the Kutsovlachs, a semi-nomadic people who spoke a Romance language, from 54,000 to 40,000, and Albanian-speakers from 50,000 to 23,000. Most of the decline took place after October 1944. Most tragic of all was the fate of the lost children. In many areas the communists, fearing attack from their enemies, sent local children into neighbouring communist states. The KKE insisted that this was done to keep them safe; the communists' opponents denounced the policy as hostage-taking or kidnapping.

And like all civil wars that in Greece left behind a legacy of bitterness which was to poison much of public and private life for at least a generation.

Notes

1. The phrase is used by David H. Close and Thanos Veremis in David H. Close (ed.), *The Greek Civil War, 1943–1950. Studies of Polarization*, London: Routledge, 1993, pp.97–100.
2. Yordan Baev, *Voennopoliticheskite konflikti sled vtorata svetovna voina i Bŭlgariya*, Sofia: Izdatelstvo na Ministerstvoto na Otbranata 'Sv Georgi Pobedonosets', 1995, p.87.

Part II

THE BALKANS DURING THE COLD WAR, 1949–1989

Chapter 7

INTRODUCTION

The political configuration of the Balkans attained by the end of the Greek civil war in 1949 was to last for forty years; it was the longest period in the modern history of the peninsula without war or any change of frontier on the mainland. The absence of military conflict and territorial change did not mean a lack of division. Greece's continuing status as a pro-western state separated it from the rest of the region; in the socialist camp Yugoslavia had already become a pariah and by the end of the 1960s each Balkan socialist state had assumed an individual position within the socialist community.

Before then, however, the ruling communist parties, that of Yugoslavia included, had to apply themselves to the task of economic and social reconstruction; they were to impose revolution from above. That revolution involved the creation of the basic infrastructure of a modern industrial economy. The labour force for the new industry would be created by driving the surplus peasantry off the land by collectivizing agriculture, a development which would also break the back of the only social class still potentially strong enough to pose a real threat to communist domination: the peasantry. Both the development of industry and the agrarian revolution would be coordinated within a highly detailed, centrally determined economic plan, usually designed, on the Soviet pattern, to cover a five-year period. Links to the Soviet Union were strengthened by the creation of the Council for Economic Cooperation (Comecon) in 1949 which fostered trade between the socialist states, Yugoslavia excepted. A Soviet-bloc military alliance came into being in 1955 with the formation of the Warsaw Treaty Organization (WTO). Soviet influence was also exercised through the many Soviet advisors attached to ministries and other institutions in the client states. In Greece, which was bound into the western military alliance, US advisors played a similar role.

In Yugoslavia the original plans for economic development were thrown into confusion by the break with the Soviet Union and the other members of the socialist bloc, and in the 1950s the country was to establish its own mechanisms for advancing towards socialism. The Yugoslav communists faced many difficulties in doing this but they had one advantage not enjoyed by the other socialist states: Soviet hostility towards Yugoslavia helped to consolidate support behind Tito and his regime.

Elsewhere in the socialist camp Tito was also a factor in the economic revolution, but here he was a bogey man not a hero, and if Tito had not existed the Stalinists would have had to invent him. A Polish communist once remarked, 'The Party always has to have an enemy',[1] and in the late 1940s and early 1950s it was in particular need of one for two main reasons. The first was Stalin's paranoid fear that the west with its superior nuclear capability would destroy the Soviet Union and therefore that unity and obedience to Moscow were essential for the survival of the socialist camp; Titoist 'nationalist deviation' and 'revisionism' threatened unity and therefore had to be eradicated wherever it reared its ugly head. The second reason was internal. The communists' drive towards collectivization and rapid industrial-ization was creating massive social dislocation; discontent was widespread and all states experienced some armed resistance by peasants opposed to collectivization. There was therefore need for extra vigilance to contain this discontent. And if anti-communists believed, as they usually did, that these new, disruptive polices were imposed by the Soviet Union then the need to be on guard against nationalism was increased. This accounted for the inten-sification of party control over all branches of society during the latter years of Stalin's rule. But there was another facet to the purges.

A major victim of the purges in all socialist states was the communist party itself. In part this was explained by the rapid growth in party membership since the end of the war and in most countries by the fusion of various left-wing parties in the last stages of the communist drive for power. But there was a further reason for the purging of the party. During their drive for power the communist parties destroyed or emasculated all alternative mech-anisms for the lawful expression of political opinion or social discontent. If its own policies were creating such discontent the most logical, indeed the only vehicle for the expression of such discontent would be the party itself. The older members of the party showed a particular sympathy to social discon-tent; it had been concern for the underprivileged and the dispossessed which had originally led them to join the party. Many of these older comrades were to be replaced by sterner minds captured by the implacable logic of Marxism-Leninism-Stalinism and steeled by a rigorous training in the Soviet Union. The purges were therefore necessary to contain the unrest the revolution from above was causing and to steel the body of the party to what could be a distasteful task. At the same time, doubters and dissenters could be shown to be lackeys of the heretic in Belgrade and therefore subversive to the general good of socialism; for this reason the first and most prominent communist victims of the purges, in the Balkans and elsewhere in Eastern Europe, were leading figures who had been critical of Moscow and who were therefore smeared by accusations of Titoism.

The breach between Moscow and Belgrade made Yugoslavia a free operator on the international scene. Initially Tito's socialism determined his alignment and prevented any closer association with the west but with the dangers of the Korean war he sought, for a while, greater security in a closer association with Greece and Turkey which hinted at a possible division of the Balkans into a pro-Soviet north and east and a pro-western west and south, especially if the west's secret subversion of Albania succeeded. Stalin's death in March 1953 ended this danger.

Stalin's successors initiated the 'New Course' which all pro-Moscow states were required to adopt. It meant greater separation of party and state, especially at the highest level where, the Kremlin now insisted, the leader of the party must not also be the head of government; at the same time there was emphasis on collective leadership as opposed to the 'cult of personality'. The New Course also meant a welcome slackening of the drive towards the creation of heavy industry and, in theory at least, a shift towards investment in agriculture and light, or consumer industries, and, most welcome of all, a relaxation of the terror. The New Course was applied with differing speeds and differing intensity in the Soviet camp but all Balkan states in that camp made some adjustment to the new spirit emanating from Moscow.

Accommodation to that new spirit became more difficult in the mid- and late 1950s. A major problem, once again, was Tito. This time the difficulty was caused not by hostility towards him, but the reverse. By 1955 Nikita Khrushchev was emerging as the most prominent figure in the new Soviet leadership and in June that year he made a colourful visit to Belgrade. In February 1956 he delivered his famous speech to the twentieth congress of the Communist Party of the Soviet Union (CPSU) in which he listed as one of Stalin's many 'mistakes' the breach with Tito.

This was difficult for all East European leaders, not least those in the Balkans. If, after all, Tito was not a renegade, then what did that say for the legitimacy of communist rulers who since 1949 had based their authority on the violent suppression of Titoist heresies? The salvation for these discomforted rulers was the doctrine of 'polycentrism' which emerged from the upheavals of 1956 in Poland and in Hungary, a doctrine which admitted that there could be more than one locus of legitimate socialism, and that the socialist states could find varying paths to their common goal of full socialism and then the evolution into communism.

Albania and Romania were to make full use of the opportunities offered by polycentrism. For Albania the rehabilitation of Tito had awkward and frightening implications because if that process were completed it might mean the revival of the plans hatched in the immediate post-war years for incorporating Albania into the Yugoslav federation. Albania therefore began looking for an alternative sponsor in the socialist world and was to find one in the late 1950s in the People's Republic of China (PRC).

Albania became concerned at emerging Soviet plans for economic specialization in the Balkans, plans which would leave it as primarily an agrarian society; this, Tirana believed, was no way to build socialism. Much the same view was held in Bucharest. The Romanian communists had pursued a somewhat idiosyncratic line in the purges, their main victim going to the gallows after Stalin's death. They had adopted the New Course without great enthusiasm but their passions were most definitely aroused by the Kremlin's plans for economic specialization put forward in the early 1960s. Romania rejected them. Unlike Albania it did not break from the common institutions of the Soviet bloc, Comecon and the Warsaw pact, but it pursued distinctly individual policies wherever possible both in party and state affairs. By the mid-1960s only Bulgaria remained completely faithful to the Moscow line. This was to give the Bulgarians considerable economic advantage as the socialist bloc, and above all the Soviet Union, provided a secure market for its exports and a cheap source of raw materials and energy.

By the end of the 1960s Albania was a maverick cooperating closely with China, Bulgaria was an obedient Soviet satrapy, Romania was semi-aligned, and Yugoslavia allegedly non-aligned, while Greece was pro-western and, when its internal condition allowed, sought inclusion in the European Economic Community (EEC). This tessellation of the Balkans was not contested by the Soviet Union because the area lacked the strategic significance of the Warsaw pact's northern or central tiers; it is however interesting to note that the one state which stayed completely loyal to the USSR, Bulgaria, was the only one in the Balkans, and indeed the only one in the entire Warsaw pact, apart from the Soviet Union itself, which had two NATO states among its neighbours.

If in the 1960s the Balkan states assumed differing attitudes in foreign affairs they also, with the exception of Greece, enjoyed relative political stability. In fact in the fifteen years between 1965 and 1980 no Balkan communist leader was changed, and in the two cases where there was change between 1980 and 1989 this came about through the death of the incumbent.

In the 1960s all Balkan states, Greece included, expanded their industries, though in Greece there was more emphasis on secondary industry and the service sector. In all states urbanization and the growth of manufacturing proceeded at a rapid pace, usually with appalling consequences for the environment (see tables 7.1 and 7.2).

Not all economic development was rational. The socialist states, and inside Yugoslavia the individual republics, each wished to create their own heavy

Table 7.1 Percentage of population living in towns, 1950–71

	1950	1971
Bulgaria	27.5	54.7
Greece	36.3	53.2
Romania	24.7	41.1
Yugoslavia	25.9	35.3

There are no figures for Albania.

Source: John R. Lampe and Marvin R. Jackson, *Balkan Economic History, 1555–1950: From Imperial Borderlands to Developing Nations*, Bloomington, IN: Indiana University Press, 1982, p.597

Table 7.2   Industrial labour force as percentage of total labour force, 1952–70

	1952	1970
Bulgaria	14.0	38.8
Greece	19.4	25.6
Romania	14.2	35.8
Yugoslavia	7.5	18.5

Figures for Greece are for 1951 and 1971, and for Yugoslavia for 1953 and 1971. There are no figures for Albania.

Source: John R. Lampe and Marvin R. Jackson, *Balkan Economic History, 1555–1950: From Imperial Borderlands to Developing Nations*, Bloomington, IN: Indiana University Press, 1982, p.597

industrial base. This meant the construction of many manufacturing plants for which no local ores or sources of energy were available. It also meant massive duplication. To make matters worse many of the industries built in the 1960s and to a lesser extent the 1970s were hopelessly unprofitable. But in the communist context this did not much matter as the state was always there to subsidize loss-making enterprises; those chickens would come home to roost only after the collapse of the communist system.

In general the communist states, excluding Yugoslavia, considered that by the late 1960s or early 1970s they had constructed a socialist society. They adopted new constitutions and new party programmes to take account of this achievement and committed themselves to the next stage of evolution: the move towards mature socialism and the creation of a unified, classless society from which communism would emerge. Mature socialism would be a product of material abundance which would be achieved by greater productivity and efficiency; and greater productivity was to be achieved by applying 'the scientific–technological revolution' and shifting from extensive to intensive development.

The communists had proved their ability to create an industrial infrastructure and a heavy industrial base but the shift to intensive development was to prove beyond their capabilities. The scientific–technological revolution proved not to be their salvation but, in part at least, their damnation. The pace of change became so rapid that no system in which planning played a decisive part could keep up with it. Furthermore, there was not the middle-management cadre needed to apply the new technologies; managers were trained to apply centrally determined policies, not to take the initiative, and all decisions still had political overtones; factory managers, even if they had the necessary hard currency, were often frightened to order superior western machines if inferior Soviet or East European ones were available. And if a factory manager did take his courage into his hands and place an order in the west it was as likely as not that someone in the party would overrule him.

The scientific–technological revolution exacerbated another problem. The major technological advances, particularly in computers and fibre optics, were made in the west. Some of this technology was stolen but the majority had to be purchased. Many East European states borrowed heavily in the west to make such purchases. This was not dangerous as long as those states could export to the west enough to service the debts. After the oil price rise of 1979 and the subsequent contraction of western spending this became more difficult. In order to find more products for export the regimes therefore restricted domestic consumption thus forcing down living standards, with this process being taken to grotesque extremes in Romania.

The debt problem was one which faced most Balkan states, including Greece, in the 1980s. There were others. In some there had been a distinct decline in urban birth rates. A disparity between urban and rural birth rates is a general phenomenon but in the Balkans it could also mean, or could be believed to mean, a disparity in ethnic birth rates. This was a problem which affected Kosovo, Bulgaria and Romania. The growing problem of environmental pollution affected every state, whether it be in the fume-infested environs of the Parthenon, in the diseased forests of Romania, or in the dying waters of the Black Sea. The Chernobyl disaster of April 1986 heightened environmental awareness and in the final days of more than one Balkan communist regime the environmental factor was to play an important part in mobilizing the public against the party.

The Balkans were also inevitably affected by the changes in the international climate in the 1980s, especially after the advent of an entirely new form of leadership in Moscow in 1985. Gorbachev's eagerness for disengagement from the cold war meant that neither semi-alignment nor non-alignment any longer had any value as an international bargaining counter; they could no longer be used to secure preferential economic treatment or political favours from the west. Yugoslavia and Romania suffered as a result.

By the mid-1980s it was clear that the Balkans, with the exception of Greece which had found political stability and economic support within the European Community (EC) in 1981, were facing severe problems. The ruling ideology in the socialist states was bankrupt; far from producing the abundance mature socialism required it was producing the increasing impoverishment which, according to that ideology, should have been the lot of the capitalist world. As the established ideology collapsed the ruling parties intensified their appeals to nationalism which had seldom been far beneath the surface since the 1960s. At the same time many of the regimes' opponents called for much greater doses of nationalism as the only way to restructure society. It was a potent and in many cases disastrous combination as the post-communist Balkans were to show.

Note

1. Stefan Staszewski, in Teresa Toranska, *Oni: Stalin's Polish Puppets*, translated from the Polish by Agnieszka Kolakowska with an introduction by Harry Willets, London: Collins Harvill, 1987, p.194.

Chapter 8

YUGOSLAVIA, 1948–1989

FINDING 'TITO'S WAY': YUGOSLAVIA IN THE 1950S

YUGOSLAVIA ISOLATED

The break with the Soviet Union in 1948 severely dislocated and disorientated the Yugoslav leadership. They had intended to build socialism on the Soviet model and with Soviet help. Now the first priority of Tito and his colleagues had to be to protect their party and their country against Soviet subversion and the intrigues of the pro-Moscow cominformists at home. Of the latter there were an estimated ten thousand, eight and a half thousand of whom were interned on Goli Otok by the UDBa, the successor to OZNa, but still under the leadership of Ranković. More dangerous than the rank and file cominformists were the few in the upper echelons of the party and the military who could have provided an alternative leadership had the Soviets decided upon drastic action. General Branko Petričević, deputy head of the political administration of the Yugoslav army, was captured trying to escape while General Arso Jovanović, Tito's wartime chief of staff, was reportedly shot on the Romanian border. The major political casualty, however, was the former Croat communist leader, Andrija Hebrang who was arrested and never seen again in public, the likelihood being that he was murdered in prison.

The Soviets did not unleash their armies but they made threatening gestures. There were fifty flights per day over Yugoslav territory by Soviet military aircraft based in Albania or Bulgaria, and at times Red Army or satellite troops were massed on Yugoslavia's borders. Yugoslavia was also subjected to a propaganda barrage; Moscow's broadcasts per day in the Yugoslav languages were two and a half times as long as its English-language output. But most damaging of all was economic retaliation. In 1949 Yugoslavia was excluded from the newly established Comecon and placed under a virtual economic blockade, its goods being denied use both of the East European rail networks and the vital Danube shipping route. The Soviet actions caused immediate and direct losses to the Yugoslav economy of $429 million and by 1950 external trade was down to 35 per cent of its 1948 level.

Tito's government may have lost its friends but it had not lost its faith. Initially, it responded to Soviet criticisms by intensifying rather than abandoning its drive for socialism. When the Kremlin denounced the Yugoslavs for being soft on kulaks, the CPY's response at a plenum in 1949 was to step up the drive towards collectivization, the number of collective farms (SRZs) increasing fivefold by the end of the year; in 1950 the collectives covered about a fifth of the total agricultural land.

The determination to continue its pursuit of socialist objectives meant that the Yugoslav regime did not turn immediately and openly to the west for protection and help. Tito in fact was internationally isolated. In those circumstances he had only one possible pillar of support: the Yugoslav peoples themselves. They in general admired, some of them reluctantly, Tito's willingness to stand up to Soviet bullying but many of them still had grave reservations about the regime's domestic policies. To ensure popular backing some concessions had to be made, particularly in view of the severe economic crisis brought about by the Soviet blockade and the near collapse of the agricultural sector due to collectivization. In the need to end international isolation and to make his policies more acceptable at home lay the basis of the two main features of what in Yugoslavia became known as 'Tito's Way': self-management and non-alignment.

THE BEGINNINGS OF SELF-MANAGEMENT

In the second half of 1949 the Tito government at last began to strike back at Soviet criticism. This was followed by a series of measures which began to differentiate the Yugoslav from the Soviet variant of socialism. In 1949 local government reform increased the responsibilities of the district as opposed to the republican or federal authorities, and the local peoples' committees were to be required to report on their doings every two months to meetings of electors. In the autumn of 1950 Tito reduced the privileges enjoyed by party members, especially in the provision of food, a very significant development given the dreadful shortages which the country faced at the time. A year later the political commissars were removed from the army. In January 1950 the list system for elections was abolished; public meetings were now to adopt candidates, though all those nominated had been approved by the local branch of the Peoples' Front (PF). There were also attempts to soften attitudes towards other major groups. In 1950 a number of major properties were returned to the Serbian Orthodox Church and the first offer was made to release Cardinal Stepinac if he would go into exile. He refused. The most dramatic of these conciliatory gestures, however, concerned the police. In its attempts to contain the cominformists the Yugoslav government had never imposed a reign of terror similar to those inflicted on the Soviet Union in the 1930s and the satellite states in the late 1940s and early 1950s but the authorities did admit that they had used a heavier hand than had been necessary and promised that in future they would relax their grip.

Since the summer of 1949 Yugoslav propaganda had pointed consistently and regularly to what it denounced as 'deformations' in socialism as practised in the USSR. The Yugoslavs now argued that the problem was not, as previous Yugoslav statements had said, that Stalin had deformed the system, but that the Russian revolution itself had been incomplete and had allowed a new bureaucracy to entrench itself in power. The new socialism to be constructed in Yugoslavia would avoid this error; here the controlling force in the economy and society would not be the bureaucracy but the workers who would exercise their authority through worker self-management.

The ideology of self-management was the work of two of Tito's closest collaborators, the Montenegrin Milovan Djilas and the Slovene Edvard Kardelj, but it was Tito, a late and reluctant convert to this ideology, who launched the self-management revolution when he proclaimed 'The Factories to the Workers' and enacted the basic law on the management of state economic enterprises and higher economic associations by the work collectives on 27 June 1950. In introducing the law on workers' self-management Tito also stressed the fact that the law would differentiate Yugoslav from Soviet socialism; self-management, said Tito, was a higher form of socialism than that of nationalized and state-owned industries and was therefore a return to Leninism from its Stalinist deformations. It would, he said, mark the beginning of the 'withering away of the state', this being a rejection of the Stalinist concept that the power of the state had to increase during the transition from a bourgeois to a socialist society. The law proclaimed that the means of production were no longer owned by the state but were 'social property'. The management of this social property was to be left to working collectives. In practice this was to mean that in enterprises with fewer than thirty workers all were to be members of the managerial councils, while in larger concerns workers' councils of between fifteen and a hundred and twenty members were to be elected in secret every year to appoint management boards of less than two dozen members with the director of the enterprise being an ex officio but non-voting member of the management board.

If the economy was to be run mainly by the workers there was less room in it for the state. The state therefore began a phased, if partial, withdrawal. A number of federal economic ministries, and with them a hundred thousand party and state jobs, were already marked for the scrap heap as a result of the 1949 local government reforms, and at the end of 1950 the current five-year plan was extended for one year and, it was announced, in future plans would be for one rather than five years. In December 1951 the law on the planned management of the economy replaced the old planning system with one in which the enterprises were given targets which were indicative rather than prescriptive, that is they suggested production goals rather than dictated them. The state would retain its right to set the general parameters of economic growth and it would also supervise investment strategy. Central power was further decreased by a reform of 1954 which enabled local workers' councils to supervise how enterprises disposed of their profits. In 1958 personal incomes were theoretically abolished and replaced by a share of enterprise profits; in theory the workers' councils were to decide how the income or profit of their enterprise was to be distributed between wages, investment and savings. But if these laws stripped the state of much of its power in the economic sector, later amendments were to do much to restore it, and throughout the 1950s the state retained its control over most prices.

The partial withdrawal of the state from the economy had been forced on the Yugoslav authorities because the breaking of economic ties with the rest of the Soviet bloc had ruined the basis on which the state plans had been made. Necessity also drove the government to its most obvious break with Soviet practices, the dilution of the state and collective system on the land. Marx's writings on the idiocy of rural life had been superseded by the lunacy of collectivization. Huge pressures, fiscal and physical, had been brought to bear to enforce the hated *otkup*, the compulsory deliveries of agricultural produce to the state purchasing authorities at fixed prices, the eventual objective being to drive the reluctant peasant into the collective farms. The peasant had resisted and his obstructionism, plus a withering drought in 1950, had all but wrecked agricultural production, raising the nightmarish prospect of starvation in the cities and the barracks. A central committee plenum in December 1949 had seen the dangers of collectivization and warned against proceeding too rapidly; at the same time it urged more concentration on the traditional forms of credit and marketing cooperatives. By September 1950 there was need for urgent action and in that month the MTSs, in many ways the symbols of collectivized farming, were disbanded. In the following year the compulsory deliveries were abolished and finally on 30 March 1953 came an announcement that the peasants were free to leave the collectives and take with them their land, equipment and animals. By 1957 only 9 per cent of arable land was in the collectivized sector, compared to a quarter in 1952. An upper limit of ten hectares per individual farm was introduced in May 1953 and remained in force, notwithstanding some concessions to mountain farmers in 1970, until the end of the 1980s. It did restrict the development of the most profitable forms of private farming but despite this the end of collectivization brought about a dramatic improvement in agricultural production in the second half of the 1950s.

THE REFORM OF PARTY AND STATE INSTITUTIONS, 1950–3

The process of redesigning Yugoslavia could not be complete if the state's political institutions remained unchanged. The most powerful of all such institutions, the CPY, underwent considerable restructuring at its sixth congress held in Zagreb in November 1952. Its most obvious reform was to change its name to the League of Communists of Yugoslavia (LCY) in order to mark its separation from the cominformist parties. Again to differentiate itself from the Soviet parties the LCY talked of its playing a 'conscious' rather than a 'leading' role in the state and society. Party cells in the work-place were abolished and the meetings of basic party organizations were to be opened to the public with non-party members being encouraged to attend. At the peak of the party, again to distance the LCY from the Soviet-style parties, the politburo was renamed the executive committee. The republican and provincial party organizations underwent similar changes and in February 1953, at its fourth congress, the Peoples' Front changed its name to the Socialist Alliance of the Working People of Yugoslavia (SAWPY).

There were major changes in state as well as party and social structures when a new constitution was introduced in January 1953. It was intended further to differentiate Yugoslavia from the Soviet bloc and to bind into the political fabric the new concept of self-management. The 'basic organs of state authority' were declared to be the peoples' councils of the municipalities and districts, while at the other end of the scale the head of state, formerly the praesidium of the peoples' assembly, was henceforth to be a president, with Tito stepping into that position. The federal government ceased to be a traditional style council of ministers, becoming instead a Federal Executive Council (FEC) which was to be a collective with no individual ministerial responsibilities or administrative functions. Similarly, the separate departments of state ceased to have ministerial chiefs but, to give the appearance of self-management, were to be headed by councils. All republics and provinces were to be represented in the FEC. The parliament was also reorganized. The Chamber of Nationalities was absorbed into the Federal Chamber which was now to consist of seventy deputies delegated by the republican and provincial assemblies together with representatives from single-member territorial constituencies.

The most striking innovations came in the second chamber. This was to be a chamber of producers chosen via the workers' councils. Once again these changes were replicated in the republican and provincial constitutions. Producers' councils were also part of the local government structure and thus at every level workers' collectives had been built into the institutions of Yugoslavia. The new constitution was the institutional expression of the intention expounded in the June 1950 act that the workers' councils were to manage social property on behalf of the social community. The constitutional changes enabled Yugoslav theorists such as Kardelj to argue that their variant of socialism had passed power and responsibility to the workers and was therefore a different animal to the state or police socialism constructed in the Soviet Union and its satellites.

Self-managing, workers' democracy did not mean immediate and full freedom of speech as the case of Milovan Djilas was soon to prove. A hero of the partisan war, an intellectual and one of the inner circle of Tito's advisers, Djilas had become concerned at the repressive nature of the regime in the early 1950s. Initially Tito and Kardelj rebuffed Djilas's calls for a slackening of the police regime but the sixth congress in 1952 encouraged Djilas who was soon arguing that if its goals were to be achieved the party as well as the state must begin to wither away. He also implied that Stalinism was not the result solely of the Soviet system but of one-party rule in general. Towards the end of 1953 he published articles in which he castigated the partisan establishment for its decline into a new privileged self-indulgent caste, his most withering scorn being reserved for the wives of many party prominenti who had distinguished themselves by their crass and vulgar materialism. He was denounced at a central committee plenum in January 1954 and then expelled from the party. In late 1954 he requested permission to form a social democratic party. Two years later he compounded his errors by publishing in the west articles which approved of the Hungarian revolution. For this he was imprisoned.

Djilas had very rapidly delineated the limits of Yugoslav political tolerance but his persecution was the result of external as well as internal factors.

FOREIGN POLICY AND 'NON-ALIGNMENT'

In the immediate aftermath of Yugoslavia's expulsion from Cominform Tito had not wished to turn to the west, hoping initially at least that the Chinese communists might provide an ally. The west, on the other hand, knew a political opportunity when it saw one. Within weeks of the expulsion Washington had removed the bloc on $30 million worth of gold deposited in the United States by the royal Yugoslav government during the Second World War. Yet it was not until September 1949 that Belgrade accepted its first loan from the west. The sum was not large, $20 million, and it was described as a 'normal business transaction', but no one could be blind to its political implications. In the following year came agricultural aid which ameliorated the effects of the drought and made it easier to move towards the decollectivization of agriculture. In the summer of 1950 military aid was also accepted. The Yugoslav government feared that the outbreak of the Korean war might unleash general world instability in which Stalin would launch an attack on the disobedient Balkan communists. Although no such attack materialized the intensity of the cold war nevertheless forced Yugoslavia towards the west just as it made the west ready to accept a non-conformist socialist state as an ally in the confrontation with Stalin. A conference in London in the summer of 1951 produced an agreement that Yugoslavia should be given further aid to help it overcome the effects of collectivization and the drought and was then to receive a variable annual grant to which the USA, Britain and France would contribute. In November of the same year the United States agreed to re-equip the Yugoslav army. There were also moves to bring Yugoslavia closer to the NATO alliance and in February 1953 a treaty of friendship and cooperation with Greece and Turkey was signed in Ankara. In August it was supplemented by a military agreement signed in Bled, Slovenia.

Yugoslavia made a number of concessions to the west during this period of increasing cooperation. In the summer of 1950 Belgrade and Skopje ceased its propaganda on behalf of the Slav minority in northern Greece, and the Yugoslav line on the Slovenes of Carinthia softened. The major concession, however, was over Trieste. In October 1954 the Yugoslavs signed the London agreement by which Zone A of Trieste was absorbed into Italy and Zone B, mainly the area around the city, was handed to Yugoslavia. It was a major concession by the Yugoslavs but the pill was sugared by a western promise to provide aid to build a Yugoslav port at Koper in Slovenia.

That dependence on the west was ideologically uncongenial was proved by the fact that Tito distanced himself from it as soon as conditions allowed. He was never in danger from the west; the real peril came from the east and no movement away from dependence on the former was possible without changes in the latter. The first major change was the death of Stalin on 5 March 1953. As soon as Nikita Khrushchev was secure at home he moved to ensure that neither of the two non-Soviet giants of international communism, Tito and Mao, should establish themselves as the new leaders of the world movement. He visited both leaders. Arriving in Belgrade at the head of a state delegation in May 1955 he immediately apologized at the airport for the Soviet Union's having caused the quarrel of 1948. One reason why Khrushchev felt able to go to Yugoslavia was that the disciplining of Djilas had reassured him that the Yugoslav party had not given up its willingness to impose its will. Khrushchev and the head of the Soviet government, Bulganin, stayed in the Yugoslav capital for eight bibulous days at the end of which they were just about sober enough to sign the 'Belgrade Declaration' which confirmed Yugoslavia's right to pursue its own road to socialism and pledged the two governments to respect one another's sovereignty and territorial integrity. Khrushchev, it seemed, had been to Canossa but Tito had proved an unforgiving pope. He received Khrushchev's airport apologies in stony silence and was adamant that the time had not yet come for reconciliation between the two parties. What made that possible was Khrushchev's speech to the twentieth congress of the CPSU in February 1956 in which he criticized Stalin and his role in the events of 1948; even more important for Tito was the dissolution of Cominform in April 1956. Tito repaid Khrushchev's state visit in May–June of that year. The main objective of the visit was to bring about an improvement in relations between the two parties and that this had been achieved was announced in the 'Moscow Declaration' at the end of the visit.

In late 1956 Hungary inevitably dominated Yugoslav–Soviet relations. Tito had hoped that the regime of Imre Nagy might survive as a neutral but communist state, the alternatives being a pro-western and capitalist or a Soviet-dominated Hungary, both of which could threaten Yugoslav security. However, when renewed Soviet military intervention brought about the second of these possibilities Tito accepted it as the lesser of the two evils. He had intense talks with Khrushchev on the island of Brioni on the night of 2 November, two days before the Soviet tanks went into action for the second time, and became convinced that such action was necessary to save socialism. He made this public in a speech at Pula on 11 November. At the end of the Hungarian revolt some forty-two Hungarian public figures, led by Imre Nagy, the head of the revolutionary government, took refuge in the Yugoslav embassy in Budapest. The Yugoslavs secured verbal and then written assurances of safety for the refugees before the latter left the embassy on 22 November. Despite the promises they were immediately arrested.

If Tito thought, which is unlikely, that the Soviet regime would be overcome with gratitude for Yugoslav policies during 1956 he was to be disappointed. In the communist world Soviet foreign policy now allocated its highest priority not to Yugoslavia but to China. Yugoslavia would always be sacrificed if Moscow thought it could increase its standing in or improve its relations with China by doing so. It was the need to please Mao and to prove his virility in the fight against so-called revisionism which led Khrushchev in 1957 to delay and then freeze for five years credits agreed for Yugoslavia. At the same time he said that he thought that fundamentally the Cominform decision of 1948 had been correct. Tito was not unduly perturbed. He had enough experience of the international communist movement to know what was going on and therefore waited unobtrusively for another change in circumstances. It came in 1961 when relations between China and the Soviet Union broke almost irretrievably. After that, and following Khrushchev's excoriation of Stalin at the twenty-second congress of the CPSU in 1961, there was the base on which to build a more secure and lasting accommodation with Moscow. As a symbol of this in August 1963 Khrushchev visited Yugoslavia once more and admitted that workers' councils had certain advantages. Yugoslavia was also accorded observer status in Comecon.

By the early 1960s Tito's Yugoslavia could maintain that it no longer needed close ties with or dependence on either the east or the west. It could rely instead on 'non-alignment'. Evolved as relations with the Soviet Union began to improve and those with the west became less intense, non-alignment pretended to neutralism in the cold war. In 1955 Tito visited premier Nehru of India and on the return journey his yacht stopped in Suez so that the Yugoslav leader could meet president Nasser of Egypt. In 1956 Nehru, Nasser and president Sukarno of Indonesia visited Yugoslavia. After a meeting on Brioni they issued a declaration in favour of 'positive neutralism', a message which had both a powerful general appeal after the international crises of 1956 and a particular attraction to states emerging from colonialism. The non-aligned states supported a number of organizations hostile to the west, including the Palestine Liberation Organization, and they held periodic summits but they had little economic, military or political clout. Non-alignment was good for local, Yugoslav consumption in that it gave Yugoslavia a distinctive role in world affairs and further differentiated Yugoslavia from the Soviet Union and the satellite states. Non-alignment no doubt flattered Tito's considerable vanity and it was also well received by the more gullible of western liberals.

DOMESTIC AFFAIRS IN THE LATE 1950S

The normalization of relations with the Soviet Union and the Hungarian crisis of 1956 caused some regression from the relaxations of the early 1950s, Djilas being the most notable victim. Even before the Hungarian crisis assumed serious dimensions the LCY had gone back on some of the reforms introduced by the sixth congress. In March 1956 party cells on the factory shop floor and in other basic work organizations were reinstated, the party schools closed by Djilas a few years earlier were reopened, and a number of party administrative posts were reintroduced. In the economic sector it seemed there had been a shift back to orthodoxy in 1957 when a second five-year plan was introduced.

One question which did not much preoccupy Yugoslavia's rulers in the 1950s was that of internal nationalism. The tensions created by the Soviet threat of the early 1950s and, to a lesser degree, by the Hungarian crisis of 1956, did something to bring the peoples of Yugoslavia closer together, or at least persuaded the nationalist zealots among them that this was not the time to pursue separate, to say nothing of separatist agendas. The LCY championed the idea of Yugoslavism and its official ideology followed Marx in believing that nationalism would wither away once the working class was established in power; until it did the safest policy was to say little about it. To say nothing was certainly more intelligible than to issue statements such as that from the LCY's seventh congress which met in Ljubljana in April 1958 and was the highpoint of 'Yugoslavism'. It stated that the future of national relations was to lie in the development of socialist relations and of a 'socialist Yugoslav consciousness, in the conditions of a socialist community of peoples'.[1] The most positive indication of Yugoslavism in action had come in the Novi Sad agreement of 1954 when the writers' unions of Serbia and Croatia agreed to cooperate in linguistic and literary matters.

Yugoslavism did not preclude decentralization. The economic reforms had decreased the influence of the federal authorities to the benefit of those at republican level and most important of all had been the decision of the sixth congress in 1952 that in future the party bosses of Bosnia, Croatia, Macedonia and Slovenia would be resident in their own republics rather than in the federal capital.

During the 1950s five important features of Yugoslav development had become clear. The first was that Tito remained the undisputed master of the Yugoslav political machine. He was confirmed as a leader in peace as well as war; it was his voice which was decisive on such sensitive matters as how to deal with Djilas who was, after all, a hero of the partisan war, just as it was Tito who dominated Yugoslavia's foreign policy. The second was that the Yugoslav communists had successfully plotted their own road to socialism. The local, communal and working-class democracy created in the early 1950s, it was argued, would provide the vehicle in which Yugoslav society would

travel the road through socialism to a classless society and eventual communism. They had created a system which was different from and more successful than the Soviet. Worker self-management was added to the myth of the
partisan war and the notion of 'brotherhood and unity' as a source of legitimacy for the Yugoslav regime. The third feature was that the real power of
the party had not been sacrificed. Worker self-management was diluted very
considerably by the fact that it was the party, frequently acting through the
SAWPY, which controlled the elections to the workers' councils and all
other elected bodies, its vital power being that to vet the list of nominated
candidates. Fourthly, the economy had been decentralized but not effectively
de-bureaucratized; too often reform meant little more than passing responsibility and power from a higher to a lower and frequently less experienced
and less capable officialdom. At the same time many in the partisan establishment resented the devolution of power to nominally non-party bodies. The
fifth was that the leadership was prepared to tinker with the machinery it had
created as economic and political conditions, at home and abroad, changed.
This was to become a permanent feature of Yugoslav life where frequent
institutional reform, combined with the inherent complexity of the state, as
often as not compounded rather than diminished the problems which that
state faced.

THE SEARCH FOR STABILITY: YUGOSLAVIA
1960–76

THE EMPOWERMENT OF THE REPUBLICS, 1960–5

The 1960s in Yugoslavia were dominated by domestic affairs. There were
major and inextricably linked changes in the political and economic structures, and for the first time since the end of the Second World War ethnic
questions resurfaced to cause serious problems.

The 1960s began on a reasonably optimistic note with the regime mending
fences with some of its former enemies. In the vital, if low-key religious
sector there were considerable reductions in tension. A new Patriarch, German, had been elected head of the Serbian Orthodox Church in 1958 and he
adopted a less confrontational stance than his predecessor vis-à-vis the communist authorities. In 1960 Cardinal Stepinac died and this, together with the
appointment of a liberal pope in 1963, helped to diffuse tensions with the
Roman Catholic Church, as did a brave gesture on the part of the Catholic
bishop of Banja Luka in Bosnia who, knowing that the Orthodox bishop in
the city had been tortured to death by the Ustaše in 1941, acknowledged the
terrible crimes of the past and asked for forgiveness from his Orthodox
brothers in Christ; many of his flock resented the statement but it was a
notable attempt to mend the wounds of the recent past. At the same time,
non-alignment meant that Yugoslavia wished to present a respectable profile

among the non-committed Muslim states. From 1948 to 1953 Muslims who did not wish to register themselves as one of the recognized 'narodi', or major ethnic groups, had to define themselves as 'indeterminate Muslims'; after 1953 this category would have been 'indeterminate Yugoslav' but in 1961 they were allowed to describe themselves as 'Muslims in the ethnic sense'. A decade later they were accorded the category of 'Muslim in the sense of nationality', though it was to be a further decade before 'Muslim' without qualification was accepted as a national identity.

Another important stabilizing factor was the 'ethnic key'. Introduced in the early days of communist rule this was a system under which important posts in the federal apparatus, including the Yugoslav National Army (JNA), were allocated to the different nations roughly in proportion to their numerical strength. It was not a precise mechanism, nor was it a regulation, but it was a guiding principle which people knew was operating and which was generally accepted as fair.

In the economic sector the 1950s had ended on a high note with encouraging increases in agrarian production and an overall growth rate between 1957 and 1960 which was not only greater than the five-year plan had foreseen but was also the second highest in the world. This did not last. By 1961 over-investment, wage hikes without concomitant rises in productivity, a shrinking in the supply of agricultural produce without any accompanying fall in demand for them, and an increase in imports on short-term credits had produced inflation and the need rapidly to pay off foreign debts. The economic downturn produced predictable social dissatisfaction some of which was expressed in strikes. In 1961 the current five-year plan was abandoned. Inflation brought about efforts in 1961 to move towards some form of diluted monetarism by gradually dismantling the system of price fixing, and in the same year the foreign trading regulations were reformed so that Yugoslavia was able to join the GATT in the following year. But these measures were palliatives and few serious observers believed there could be any solution other than a radical restructuring of Yugoslavia's economic and political systems.

Some saw the answer in a move back towards socialist orthodoxy as expressed in centralization and planning, while others could see salvation only by moving further away from that orthodoxy towards the free market. In the Yugoslav context the debate became one in which conservatism was seen as centralist while reformism, or liberalism, was decentralist and, to an increasing degree, de-étatist.

The liberal, decentralist faction was considerably strengthened by the controversy over the Belgrade to Bar railway which in many ways was an exemplar of the complexity and sensitivity of the Yugoslav system. In December 1963 the Serbian and Montenegrin party leaderships, and not the governments, signed an agreement to complete a railway line from the Serbian capital to Bar on the Adriatic coast of Montenegro. The line had been mentioned in all strategic plans since the communists came to power but only short sections at either end had been constructed. The remaining *tracé* would take the line through difficult and therefore expensive terrain, terrain which was also inhabited almost entirely by Orthodox Serbs. Agreement to complete the project was secured because the Macedonian and Kosovan parties supported the scheme. It was not completed until 1976; the construction of the harbour at Bar proved the most expensive marine project undertaken by Yugoslavia and to the costs of that had to be added those of blasting over fifty miles of tunnels. To the Slovenes, Croats and, to a lesser degree the Bosnians, the railway seemed to be an example of Serbian, or Orthodox hegemonism hiding behind the doctrine of Yugoslavism, or *Jugoslavenstvo*, which was used to justify it.

The Bar railway controversy helped to strengthen a new alliance of liberals and decentralizers which was already emerging and was increasing its influence in the political sphere, a fact seen in the new constitution which had been adopted in April 1963.

The new constitution changed the title of the state to the Socialist Federative Republic of Yugoslavia but its basic idea was that the state would wither away as its functions were assumed by the organs of self-management. The constitution also encouraged the further separation of party and state by enacting that no one, Tito excepted, could hold office in both. There was also a new emphasis on the rule of law. The state was no longer to nominate judges and a new constitutional court was introduced. But what the constitution achieved was less the withering away of the state machine than the weakening of the federal as opposed to the republican state apparatuses.

The most original feature of the constitution was to be found in the arrangements for the federal assemblies. The basic federal political body was to be the Federal Chamber which was to have 120 members and which was to contain within it the Chamber of Nationalities which had ten representatives from each republic and five from each of the two autonomous provinces, Vojvodina and Kosovo. The Chamber of Nationalities was to sit separately only on rare occasions and in specific circumstances. In addition to the Federal Chamber there were four chambers whose members were nominated by and chosen from work organizations and elected communal councils. The four were: the Economic Chamber; the Chamber of Education and Culture; the Chamber of Welfare and Health; and the Organizational-Political Chamber. The Federal Chamber had to agree legislation with one of the four other chambers thus making the legislature in effect bicameral. The system was replicated in the individual republics and provinces, and even communal assemblies were now to have at least one corporate chamber. The number of elected representatives was therefore huge; in the elections of April and May 1963 620 federal deputies, 2,779 republican and provincial deputies, and 40,279 communal councillors were elected.

The constitution was to go through a number of amendments before it was replaced in 1974 but neither the original document nor the changes made to it did much to alter one basic condition: no matter how many offices or posts were made open to election the power of the LCY was little if at all diminished. It continued to exercise full control over the SAWPY which remained responsible for vetting the nominations of all candidates who were put forward for election at any level.

The party met for its eighth congress in Belgrade in December 1964. In the aftermath of controversies such as that over the Bar railway Tito called for the linking of self-management to rational investment decisions, criticized those who thought only in terms of their own republics and condemned republican nationalism as a bourgeois, bureaucratic or managerial phenomenon. Nevertheless, despite Tito's words the mood of the congress seemed to be that 'unitarism', a code word for Serbian hegemonism and centralism, was a greater danger than republican nationalism. Therefore, the congress decided that in future republican and provincial party congresses should precede the federal, which meant that delegates to the latter would arrive not so much as representatives but as mandated delegates with their own republican interests already fully articulated. Inevitably the party congresses became more subject to individual republican pressures and united federal policies became more difficult to achieve. The power of the republican and provincial parties had been significantly increased at the cost of the LCY.

The greater consciousness of local, republican interests was also seen in the debates of the federal chambers after the elections of April and May 1963. The wide dissemination of these debates by both the press and radio, together with the decision of the LCY to allow the economic debate to become public, added new vigour to that already intense discussion. And as it became more intense the debate became more political: the control of investment strategy and national income distribution became a critical issue, as did the relationship between the political and economic systems the country was to follow. In Croatia a powerful reformist lobby argued that central planning had been an appropriate mechanism for mobilizing labour and allocating resources in the early days after the socialist revolution but now that the economic system had become more complex centralism was dysfunctional. The reformists also argued that Yugoslavia must move closer to the western and world economies, a precondition for which was the abandonment of a one-party, centralized political system and the adoption of social democracy.

THE ECONOMIC REFORMS OF THE MID-1960S

The liberals had been considerably helped by the fact that although the weak monetarist reforms of 1961 had produced no noticeable improvement, a subsequent retreat towards more conservative practices in 1962 and 1963 had been even less effective. The liberals exploited this to argue that the problem was not too much but too little reform. By 1964 liberal policies were back on the agenda. In July price increases were announced for a number of staple commodities including milk, flour, bread and fuel; these changes would increase the cost of living and were a firm answer to the question which some critics of the liberals had posed: could the government afford to raise prices at a time of increasing income differentials and when the poor were already suffering from an increasing cost of living? In February 1965 the government investment schemes at federal and republican level were scrapped and a new Fund for the Development of Underdeveloped Republics and Regions (FADURK) was established. These were the prelude to the major changes which came in the summer of 1965.

The main reform legislation was enacted in some thirty separate laws. Their stated purpose was to increase the role of market forces, to reduce the power of the state and to rationalize foreign trade. They were also intended to enhance the role in decision-making of ordinary citizens acting through the self-managing institutions. The law on banks and credit transactions in March restructured the financial system and the foreign trade regime. The role of the state in investment was drastically reduced; in 1961 it had been responsible for over 60 per cent of investment but by 1968 this figure had fallen to 15.7 per cent. The banks replaced the state, their share of investment rising from almost nothing at the beginning of the decade to 47 per cent in 1968. The power of the state over the banks was also reduced by making them responsible not to government departments but to their institutional depositors. The banks were thus simultaneously decentralized and de-étatized. Further powers were given to them in 1967 by the introduction of retention quotas under which enterprises were allowed to keep only a set portion, on average 7 per cent, of their foreign currency earnings, the remainder being deposited with the banks. To increase the amount of hard-currency earnings from foreign trade the dinar was devalued twice in 1965, depriving it of almost three quarters of its previous value against the US dollar.

In July 1965 a major item of reform legislation redesigned the tax system with the result that the state took only 29 per cent rather than the previous 49 per cent of the net income of enterprises; the tax cuts were made possible by the virtual abolition of state subsidies to enterprises and by handing the state's role in investment to the banks. Most price controls were abolished and there was a further 30 per cent hike in those which were retained. Against Tito's wishes it was decided to sanction the employment of wage earners, catering establishments being allowed to take on three and workshops five. Private farmers were now to be allowed access to bank credits on equal terms with those in the socialist sector. In November personal taxes and health service contributions were reduced to compensate for the price increases.

The Reform, as the July 1965 legislation was known, increased private activity in the economy. In 1965 and 1966 some twelve thousand new small workshops were opened in Serbia while in Croatia the number of private road hauliers doubled to seventeen thousand and accounted for four fifths of the goods carried on the republic's roads. Croatia's already healthy tourist industry also benefited considerably from the relaxation of economic regulation and from the devaluation of the dinar. The changes moved Yugoslavia towards a more modern economy and society, but as with any process of modernization it also created economic dislocation and social tensions.

From 1965 Yugoslavia was persistently at or near the top of the European inflation league and internally the banking reforms had a distorting effect. The decentralized banks usually had close links with local large enterprises, both being controlled ultimately by the same party clique. The banks which should have played, especially in an inflationary environment, a prudent, restraining role instead colluded with local enterprise managers to procure yet more funding, not all of which was rationally deployed. Nor was the National Bank able to exercise sufficient restraint. Its directors were nominees of the republican national banks and were allies and dependents of the local, republican political and economic bosses.

With the Reform centralism had been smashed. It had to be. Yugoslavia's economy had been in desperate need of restructuring. But in many respects there was no Yugoslav economy, rather a series of economies at different stages of development. Given such diversity reform could not be universally applied. The only alternative was to allow the republics more power to mould the reforms to suit their particular economic needs. In 1967 six constitutional amendments further increased the power of the republics against the centre, and further amendments in December 1968 had the same effect by abolishing the Federal Chamber of the Federal Assembly and by making the Chamber of Nationalities a fully separate assembly. It was now to consist of twenty members from each republic and ten from each province and it soon became the most influential body in the federal parliament. At the same time the power of the provinces was increased.

THE FALL OF RANKOVIĆ AND THE BEGINNINGS OF UNREST, 1966–8

The reforms inevitably produced political casualties. In 1963 one of the few victories of the conservatives had been the creation of the post of vice president for when Tito was absent. It was a post created for the chief of the secret police, Ranković who, in addition to being chief of police, was generally regarded as the stoutest of centralizers and conservatives. His star seemed to be falling with the general relaxation which came with the reforms and when Vladimir Bakarić, the leader of the League of Communists of Croatia (LCC), who enjoyed considerable popularity and respect outside as well as within his native republic, called for a reorganization of the party to take account of the changes recently introduced, this was recognized as a thinly veiled attack on Ranković who was responsible for organizational questions within the LCY. Here was the reformist versus conservative battle in gladiatorial form. Bakarić and his allies then had a huge slice of luck. The military intelligence organization, which was controlled by Croats and over which Ranković and the Serb-dominated political police had little influence, reported that Ranković's agents had bugged the houses of all top party officials, including even Tito himself. A commission under the Macedonian communist leader, Krste Tsrvenkovski, was established to enquire into the activities of Ranković's UDBa. Tsrvenkovski presented his findings to the fourth plenum of the seventh congress of the LCY held on Brioni at the beginning of July 1966. They were dynamite. They showed widespread UDBa interference in appointments and policy-making, the foreign service, for example, being completely under its control. Some of the police actions were to protect Tito and/or Ranković but many others were simply to return political favours or secure jobs for the boys of the old partisan network. The details of UDBa action in Kosovo were also revealed, showing that the area had been treated to the sort of police terror which had been abandoned in the rest of the country after 1948. Even more damaging were revelations of police corruption which ranged from the relatively harmless provision of prison labour for the building of villas for party bosses to direct involvement in crimes such as smuggling. By the end of 1966 Ranković had been sacked from all his posts, removed from the Federal Assembly and expelled from the LCY. But to the anger of Montenegrin, Bosnian, Kosovan and Macedonian party groups he was not arrested. Djilas, however, was released from gaol after serving half his sentence.

The fall of Ranković was welcomed by the liberals and by most Yugoslavs outside Serbia. But this political gain could not disguise unpleasant economic realities. The Reform was producing many of the disadvantages of modernization but few of its benefits. A survey in October 1965 showed that 455 enterprises had laid off some 12,500 workers and were planning to discharge 20,000 more. Inflation, too, was increasing. In February 1966 a special LCY plenum was called to bolster support for the new system but this failed to improve results which for the next three years remained depressing. It was not long before discontent was manifested.

The first major outbreak occurred in the universities. In 1966 students in Zagreb and Skopje protested at poor living conditions but the major outburst was to come in Belgrade, not surprisingly in the summer of 1968. Dismal living conditions, rising prices, poor job prospects and the heady example of the west were the ingredients which produced the outburst. The trigger was a clash between students and youth brigade workers over admission to a satirical review. The police over-reacted and were even more tough when students marched in protest on the following day; 169 students were injured, some from gunshot wounds. The protests spread to Ljubljana, Sarajevo and Zagreb and were typical of 1968. The students were offended by the inequalities produced and encouraged by the reforms and demanded greater freedom, less opulence and more equality. They carried portraits of Marx and Tito and their slogans included 'Workers – We Are With You', 'More Schools – Fewer Cars', and 'There is No Socialism without Freedom, and No Freedom without Socialism'. The students abandoned their action after Tito had appeared on television and seemed to support many of their demands. Significantly the protests had been non-violent and without any ethnic or nationalist content.

This was not the case with the other major outbreak of unrest in 1968, that in Kosovo. The break with Stalin had brought no relaxation of UDBa's grip on the region. The police were of course under the command of Ranković and nowhere was his ouster more warmly greeted than in Kosovo, though that joy was tempered by the leniency with which he was treated. In Kosovo, as in Serbia, it was the students who first took to the streets, this time on 28 November, Albania's national day. Prishtina college was at that time an affiliate of the University of Belgrade and teaching was therefore in Serbian rather than Albanian, as was all education in Kosovo above the primary level. This was one of the issues over which the students protested, demanding that they receive education in their native Albanian. Other demands were soon added as the protest spread to Albanian communities in Macedonia and Montenegro. Now there were calls for Kosovo to be given full republican status; why, it was asked, were over a million Albanians in Yugoslavia refused republican status when it was accorded to 370,000 Montenegrins? The answer, of course, was that were an Albanian-based republic to be created in Kosovo there would be irresistible pressure from the Albanians of Macedonia and Montenegro to be included in it, and, further-more, it might wish to secede from the federation. Such a republic would gravely weaken Macedonia and Montenegro and thereby disrupt what was left of the balance between Yugoslavia's constituent republics. It would also mean a complete redesigning of investment strategies which was unthinkable so soon after the introduction of a new constitution and the reforms of 1965. In February 1969 the federal leadership ruled out any change in Yugoslavia's internal boundaries. Nor would it accept Kosovan Albanian demands to be recognized as a nation in Yugoslavia rather than a nationality. Nations were only those which were the majority in a constituent republic, in addition to which no nation had a nation-state beyond Yugoslavia's borders; were the Albanians given that status, it was argued, they might try and join the Alba-nian state. The Kosovan Albanian riposte that the Montenegrins, who were ethnic Serbs, had not wished to abandon their republican status to join Serbia, so why should Yugoslav Albanians want to abandon theirs to join Hoxha's Albanian reign of terror, fell on deaf ears.

Nevertheless, the Albanians could not be left without concessions once the unrest had been contained. Some had already been made. It had been announced that Prishtina college was to become an independent, Albanian-language university and secondary education in Albanian was to be made available. The constitutional amendments of 1968 had given Kosovo equality of status with Vojvodina as 'constitutive federal elements', and the Albanians had been allowed to display their own national symbol, the double-headed eagle and red and black flag of Albania. Also, the name 'Kosovo-Metohija', or 'Kosmet', was dropped; these terms had been used since 1945 and had always offended Albanians because the word Metohija was purely Serbian. Kosovo was now to be given priority over Bosnia, Montenegro and Macedo-nia in the allocation of aid from central funds, and in 1971 credits extended via FADURK between 1966 and 1970 were written off as grants. In January 1969 the Serbian parliament enacted a new constitution for Kosovo which was now to have its own supreme court and to be able to pass its own constitutional laws. In the early 1970s it was enacted that all official pronouncements in Kosovo were to be published in Serbo-Croat, Albanian and Turkish, the language still used by many urban Albanians in Kosovo who wished to distinguish themselves from the unsophisticated Albanians moving from the countryside to the cities. Although denied their ultimate objective of separate republican status the Albanians of Kosovo derived considerable advantage from the fall of Ranković and the disturbances of 1968.

Events in Kosovo had shown that the national or ethnic issue was still a major factor in Yugoslavia. This had been recognized from the beginning of the debate on economic reform, notwithstanding Tito's confident statement in 1962 that 'We have solved the national question.'[2] The problem was at this stage not so much ethnic incompatibility as structural disparity. Slovenia was approaching the economic level of Italy, Kosovo that of Thailand and, if Slovenia's average per capita income in 1963 was 95 per cent above the federal average, that of Macedonia was 36 per cent below it. The poorer south, particularly Kosovo, Macedonia and Montenegro, demanded a greater share of central investment. The northern republics, on the other hand, argued that investment in the north would yield greater dividends because their industries were more efficient than those in the south where investment had to be defrayed to build up the infrastructure. The reformers of the early 1960s had argued that more rational investment would raise living standards generally and increase the funds available for capital expenditure everywhere. They also argued that enterprises freed from bureaucratic control would be successful and would expand into other republics in search of cheaper labour and/or wider markets. Thus industry would spread naturally, bringing modernization and increasing wealth with it. Reform and the market would solve the disparity problem.

They did not. Federal investment could not be cut off immediately and therefore projects under way continued to receive money from federal funds which were administered primarily by bureaucrats based in Belgrade. This was resented by the Croats and Slovenes. The Slovenes also found particular cause for complaint over road building. In 1965 the World Bank agreed to fund three road-building projects in Yugoslavia, one of which was for a highway linking Slovenia with Austria and parts of northern Italy. When the money arrived, however, the federal government diverted that earmarked for the Slovene project to the two other schemes; Slovene demands for a return to the previous allocations were blocked by an alliance of the poorer republics, and although the World Bank made a further loan in 1971 to finance the Slovene road the controversy had caused great tension and left a bitter legacy; it was the first time that a republican government or party had contested a decision of the centre in this way, and when the argument was at its height the Slovenes had muttered darkly about secession, a word previously unmentioned and unmentionable.

That the northern republics were discontented did not mean that their southern counterparts were happy. Before the ninth congress of the LCY met in March 1969 both the Bosnian and the Montenegrin party congresses had passed resolutions demanding compensation for the damage done to their economies by the reforms. The Bosnian representatives complained that they received per capita only a third of that invested in Kosovo, while the Serbs also expressed resentment at the amount of money given to Kosovo. The loudest complaints, however, came from Croatia.

THE CROATIAN SPRING, 1968–71

Croat national sensitivities were profound. There was a widespread underlying feeling that for a thousand years other and usually less advanced nations had deprived the Croats of their independence. In the 1960s there were more precise anxieties, not least that over demography, ever a sensitive issue. The natural population growth of the Croats was being nullified by emigration, mainly of young men of child-rearing age who were going abroad to work. What was worse was that their place was being taken by incoming Serbs. There were economic as well as demographic concerns. Croats had taken a prominent part in the campaigns for economic and political reform in the 1960s not least because Croatians generally favoured an economy focused on the Adriatic and linked to western markets, and feared that the Serbs leaned rather towards a Danubian orientation which would lock Yugoslavia into the closed economies of the socialist and Black Sea states. This concern had been intensified by economic developments since 1948. Immediately after the Second World War Croatian acceptance of Belgrade's political dominance in Yugoslavia had been made easier by the knowledge that Croatia was economically stronger than both Serbia and the federation as a whole. By the mid-1960s that had changed. Almost two thirds of Yugoslav bank assets were now in Serbia, Croatia having only 17 per cent, the three largest banks, whose powers were considerably increased by the reforms, had their headquarters in Belgrade, and Belgrade firms controlled two thirds of Yugoslavia's foreign trade.

The political atmosphere changed rapidly after the fall of Ranković, an indication of this being a best-selling record of carols issued by the Catholic Church in Christmas 1966, something which would have been unthinkable even a few years previously. In 1967 the nineteenth-century cultural organization, Matica Hrvatska,★ began a spectacular revival. It was among the eighteen societies and a hundred and forty prominent men and women of letters who put their names to the Declaration on the Name and Position of the Croatian Literary Language signed on 17 March and published on 7 April

---

★ Similar organizations existed for a number of other Slav nations, Matica Srpska for the Serbs and Matica Slovenská for the Slovaks for example. Matica means a queen bee but also has connotations of home and 'motherland'. One function of the organizations in the nineteenth century had been to keep émigrés in the new world in contact with their native languages and cultures.

1967. The language issue had been brought to the forefront of cultural debate by the publication of the first two volumes of what was supposed to be a dictionary of standard Serbo-Croat, the origins of this project going back to the Novi Sad agreement of 1954. The dictionary had been prepared by the Matica Srpska and in all cases where Serbian and Croatian usage differed the Croatian version was presented as a dialectal variation of the standard, Serbian form. The Declaration condemned the dictionary and renounced the Novi Sad agreement. It also demanded that Croatian be taught in all schools in Croatia, and that it be recognized as the fourth official language of the federation, the existing three being Slovene, Macedonian and Serbo-Croat. This demand was in effect an affirmation that Croatian was an entirely separate language. The pent-up national frustrations crystallized around the language issue because the Declaration provoked a massive outburst of national emotion, so much so that the LCC had to launch a campaign against nationalism, expelling a number of party members in the process.

The Croatian national movement subsided for a short period when the Soviet invasion of Czechoslovakia in August 1968 forced Yugoslavs of all groups to concentrate upon a possible threat from outside and to consider the defence of Yugoslavia as a whole. The all-national defence law of 1969 based national defence on the concept of a nation in arms; it institutionalized partisan warfare, merged the regular and irregular forces, and called for the mobilization of the entire population in time of war. All Yugoslavs were to keep weapons at home and defence was to be prepared on a local as well as a federal basis with each republic establishing its own territorial defence force. In the long run this meant that even some military capability was devolved from the centre to the republics.

When the fears generated by Soviet action in Czechoslovakia receded the nationalist movement in Croatia resumed its forward march. By 1970 three elements had come together to produce what became known as the 'maspok', from *masovni pokret* or mass movement. These were: Matica Hrvatska; the students who, led by Dražen Budiša, formed the first independent students' movement in Yugoslavia; and reformist elements in the LCC. The last were led by a triumvirate of Savka Dabčević-Kučar, who had become leader of the party in 1968, Miko Tripalo and Pero Pirker. Concerned elements in the party fought back, Miloš Žanko using the LCY mouthpiece *Borba* to attack Croat nationalism in general and Matica Hrvatska in particular. At the LCC's tenth plenum in January 1970 Žanko continued his assault, denouncing the increase in nationalism as a plot to destabilize Yugoslavia and destroy socialism. The plenum did not agree; Žanko's arguments were rejected by the central committee, which called for a united front, the cleansing of the party and the 'homogenization of Croatia'. The attack on Žanko was led by Dabčević-Kučar herself, after she had phoned Tito to get approval from the federal boss for her action.

The plenum's defeat of Žanko, together with a LCY decision in April 1970 which recognized the sovereignty of the republics and provinces in all affairs not specifically reserved to the federal institutions, seemed to give the green light to Croat nationalism. What became known as 'The Croatian Spring' had begun. Matica Hrvatska expanded even more rapidly than before. Its journal, *Kniževni list*, which had begun publication in 1969, became more outspoken; when it was suppressed in April 1971 it was replaced by the even more outspoken *Hrvatski tjednik*. National exuberance spilled over at times into hostility to others. There were a series of minor actions against Serbs in Croatia with cyrillic signs being defaced or destroyed. There were also some outbreaks of violence, particularly at soccer matches. Serbian anxieties were natural and were increased by fears of the Ustaša which had been active in the 1960s, especially in Australia, and which by the early 1970s had intensified its activity in Europe, assassinating the Yugoslav ambassador in Stockholm in April 1971.

There were growing concerns in the federal party leadership which early in 1971 had appointed a party commission to investigate the problem of growing nationalism. By July Tito was sufficiently concerned to pay a visit to Croatia, making a speech in which he said that Serbian peasants were arming and drilling in Croatian villages; do you really wish, he asked his audience, to return to 1941? The Croatian leadership managed to persuade Tito that they had the situation under control and did so again when he paid another visit to Croatia; on this occasion he stood grim-faced at the airport when the Croatian national anthem was played after the Yugoslav one. When Tito returned from a visit to the United States in November he was no longer to be reassured; he had determined that the maspok must be brought to an end. Prominent among the developments which had produced this change in attitude was the decision by Matica Hrvatska to set up branches in other republics, particularly Bosnia and Hercegovina where, the organization claimed, Croats were being denied their rights. This posed the danger of destabilizing another republic and therefore infringed one of communist Yugoslavia's sacred but unwritten rules: that one republic must not interfere in the domestic affairs of another. Matica Hrvatska went further in November when it published a new programme, claiming a voice in political and economic as well as cultural affairs. Croatia, it demanded, should be declared the sovereign state of the Croat nation; it should have a seat in the United Nations; it should also have its own bank of issue, that is its own currency; it should retain all its foreign currency earnings; Croatian should be used as a language of command in the JNA; and Croat conscripts should not be compelled to serve outside their own republic. It was in effect a demand for the independence of Croatia.

In this atmosphere of mounting crisis the Croat central committee met on 5 November. Dabčević-Kučar insisted that the maspok was still a socialist movement and did not threaten the stability of the federation. In fact the Croat triumvirate, having decided to ride the nationalist tiger could not now get off it: if they did they would be jettisoned by the nationalists who would find alternative leaders. Action by the students confirmed this. They took up the demands put forward by Matica Hrvatska and at a meeting in Zagreb university on 17 November agreed on a strike over the issue of the retention of foreign currency. They hoped that the workers would join them and thus force Dabčević-Kučar and the leadership to follow them and commit themselves irrevocably to the anti-federalist side. The workers, however, showed little interest in supporting the students and on 29 November Dabčević-Kučar appealed on television for an end to the student strike.

By the time she appeared on television Dabčević-Kučar had already received from Tito a summons to a crisis meeting at the former royal hunting lodge at Karadjordjevo in Vojvodina. By this time Tito's decision to take stern measures had been confirmed by calls for action from the long-serving Croat liberal Bakarić, from Kardelj and from the minister of defence, General Nikola Ljubičić. At the Karadjordjevo meeting, which began on 1 December and lasted some twenty hours, Tito accused the Croats of degenerate liberalism and of failing to contain counter-revolution. He saw the root of the problem in the party's ideological failings and weaknesses, not the least of which was the laxity of Marxist education and the prevalence of western ideas in the universities. The pressure on the Croatian triumvirate was intense and all three of them agreed to resign, though the public announcement of this was delayed until after it could be reported to a meeting of the Croatian central committee on 12 December. The crack-down also involved the closure of Matica Hrvatska and the arrest of the student leader Budiša. Despite fears of a strong public reaction against these measures Zagreb remained calm and, observers generally agreed, this was not solely because of the heavy police and army presence in the city.

The resignations were the beginning of an extensive purge. By mid-January 1972 four hundred nationalists had been arrested while around 50,000 Croats were expelled from the LCC and 50,000 students denounced publicly as 'class enemies'. In an attempt to sugar the pill retention quotas were increased from 7–12 per cent to 20 per cent and from 12 per cent to 45 per cent in the tourist industry which was a vital part of the Croatian economy.

THE PURGES AND INSTITUTIONAL RECONSTRUCTION, 1971–6

With the clampdown on the nationalists a new economic and political era dawned for Croatia and for all Yugoslavia. The small, private firms were relegated and the large-scale, and frequently loss-making industrial combines, so beloved of socialists everywhere, were restored to official favour.

In the political arena the changes were more immediate and more striking. After the Karadjordjevo meeting Tito issued a number of statements which made clear his inclination towards authoritarianism. He had never, he said, much liked the decisions of the sixth congress in 1952 and what was needed, he continued, was a reunited, recentralized and redisciplined party. The liberals were blamed for permitting the rise of hegemonic nationalism and for allowing a technocratic-managerial élite to control the economy and much of the political system, especially at the republican level. There was action as well as words. After the LCC had been brought to order Tito and his colleagues turned their attention to the other republics. The Serbian party leaders, Marko Nikezić and Latinka Perović, were attacked for liberalism and although they and their allies put up a stout fight they were forced from office in October 1972. The same fate befell the rulers of Macedonia, Vojvodina and Slovenia. Nor was it the party apparatuses alone which were purged. The editors of the influential Belgrade newspaper, *Politika*, and the news agency NIN were both removed and replaced by less adventurous souls. The tightening of the political reins continued throughout the early and mid-1970s; in 1977 Djilas maintained that per head of population Yugoslavia had more political prisoners than the Soviet Union, though it has to be said that the Tito regime was not a rule of terror and its citizens enjoyed greater freedom to travel and to read western literature than did the subjects of any of the Soviet satellite states.

Nationalism was not the only sin for which the victims of the purge were condemned. In Croatia 12,000 technicians and managers lost their jobs; 'technocratism' had become a deformation as horrible as 'nationalism' and 'liberalism'. Leading positions in the economy, in the professions and in the cultural organizations were now available only to those on whom the party could rely, even if that meant sacrificing technical expertise. Yet if the purges pulled Yugoslavia away from liberalism they did not mean a break with Titoist federalism or with self-management. For Tito unitarism remained as great, if not a greater danger than particularism. The latter could be tolerated as long as the devolved governments of the republics remained in conservative rather than liberal hands. Tito even wanted to retain the liberals' economic reforms; it was the liberal political agenda he could no longer tolerate. Nor was self-management to be abandoned; rather it was to be strengthened. The problem, argued Tito and Kardelj, was not that there had been too much worker self-management but too little. What was needed was to oust the managerial-technocratic élite and put the working class back in command.

This was to be achieved institutionally through the introduction of a new constitution in 1974 and the passing of the law on associated labour in 1976. Constitutional revision had been almost constant since 1963. The status of the provinces had been enhanced in 1968 and in April 1970 the provinces and the republics had been granted sovereignty in all internal affairs. In September 1970 Tito, conscious of his age (he was then 78), suggested that he be replaced as president not by an individual but by a collective or collegiate presidency in which all republics and provinces would be represented; the post of chairman or president of the federal presidency was to rotate among the representatives of the republics and provinces. His proposal was accepted and at the same time an LCY commission was set up to study possible further constitutional changes which would ensure inter-republican consensus. In 1971 party activists, concerned at the rising tensions in Croatia and by apparently uncontrolled inflation, exercised such pressure that the commission was confined to the island of Brioni until it had reached its conclusions. This being hardly the most arduous of impositions, the proposals were soon completed and most of the suggested changes, many of them the work of Kardelj, were then incorporated into the new constitution enacted in February 1974.

The February 1974 constitution, communist Yugoslavia's fourth, was a device of the most extraordinary complexity, containing no fewer than 406 clauses, a world record.

The most important change was the raising of the status of the two provinces which were now to enjoy the same rights as the republics. The provinces were to have one representative each in the new nine-person presidency, they were to enjoy the same right of veto as the other members and Serbia was forbidden to interfere in the internal affairs of either province. Most civic rights were guaranteed in the constitution but they were frequently qualified; the freedom of speech, for example, was allowed but no one was to utter 'inimical propaganda'. Some entirely new rights were created, including those allowing parents to determine the number and timing of their children, and that guaranteeing everyone the right to live in a healthy environment. On the other hand, there was no guarantee of freedom of conscience, and there was no right to form political parties.

The bewildering complexity of the constitution was to be found in the representative system it created. Every commune, republic and province was to have, in addition to its executive organs, an assembly consisting of three chambers: associated labour; citizens; and the five socio-political organizations: the League of Communists; the SAWPY; the Trade Union Federation; the Veterans' Federation; and the League of Socialist Youth. The chambers of associated labour were to consist of representatives chosen by and from within the workers' councils which, in 1971, had been reorganized into smaller units known as basic organizations of associated labour (BOALs). The two houses of the new federal parliament were to be the Federal Chamber and the Chamber of Republics and Provinces. The Federal Chamber was to consist of thirty delegates from each republic and twenty from each province. The Chamber of Republics and Provinces was to have twelve delegates from each republic and eight from each province, chosen *inter se* by the provincial and republican assemblies. This chamber was to have jurisdiction over all economic matters and delegates were to vote as republican or provincial blocs on instructions from their home republic or province. Except in very rare circumstances all republican and provincial blocs had to approve a bill before it could become law which meant in effect that each republic and province had a veto on federal legislation. The economy had been republicanized, or in the eyes of some commentators, feudalized into eight small units, each one jealously guarding its own powers.

The other major institutional change which was meant to restore the working class to power was the law on associated labour of 1976. Again this owed much to the thinking of Kardelj. The new law had 671 clauses. It completed the process, begun in 1971, by which the four thousand or so workers' councils became nineteen thousand BOALs. The BOAL, in addition to being the basic economic unit, was also to become the mechanism through which the individual secured access to basic rights and to participation in social organizations. The reform brought massive dislocation and huge inefficiencies. Established enterprises were split up into smaller, less efficient parts, one in Slovenia dissolving into no less than thirty-one such minor units. This multiplied bureaucracy and involved managers in endless hours of unnecessary negotiations. The dislocation of management was intentional. The purpose was to dislodge the technocratic-managerial élite from its positions of dominance: worker self-management would be able to play a larger role in a smaller unit. In fact, many experienced managers were dismissed as a result of the new law. At the same time the proliferation of BOALs likewise increased the amount of working time which employees spent in nonproductive meetings.

Kardelj had believed that workers had become alienated because they did not have full control over the production process and this belief, plus his fear of the technocratic élite, underlay the legislation of 1976. The problem was that the reform did not put the working class in the driving seat. As had always been the case, the communists could never allow power to slip from their hands and therefore, almost by instinct, they continued to dominate all electoral procedures through the control which the SAWPY exercised over the nomination of candidates. And the further up the system one went the greater that control became. Furthermore, the republicanization of the economy turned all economic debate into nationalist discourse because the republics themselves were essentially nationalist constructions. From the mid-1970s Yugoslavia seemed increasingly to become a system based upon its dominant nations not, as its founders had hoped, one based upon a dominant class.

YUGOSLAV FOREIGN POLICY IN THE 1960S AND 1970S

Given its internal problems it was hardly surprising that foreign affairs played a relatively minor role in Yugoslav politics in the 1960s and 1970s. Non-alignment remained the official stance in the cold war, with Belgrade hosting the non-aligned summit of 1961 when Yugoslavia was the only European state to be represented.

After the Sino-Soviet rift relations between Yugoslavia and the Soviet Union stabilized. Tito was initially disturbed by the fall of Khrushchev in October 1964 but a trip to Moscow in 1965 and Brezhnev's return visit the following year showed that relations between Belgrade and Moscow had been unaffected by the changes in the Kremlin. The Yugoslavs condemned the Soviet invasion of Czechoslovakia in 1968 but the effects of this on Soviet-Yugoslav relations were neither profound nor protracted. The new defence strategy meant that Tito could threaten the Soviets with Vietnamese-style resistance should they be unwise enough to invade Yugoslavia, but such an eventuality became ever less likely as the 1970s moved towards a lessening of tension between east and west and the Helsinki agreements of 1975. With the Soviet Union posing no real threat, Tito's dependence on the west decreased still further and he could be outspoken in his commitment to socialism. His statement in December 1975 in the theoretical journal, *Komunist*, that Yugoslavia stood for socialism and that non-alignment was an anti-imperialist movement, was the foreign-policy equivalent of the domestic repressions and restructurings which followed the suppression of the Croatian Spring.

Tito paid his first visit to the United States in 1963. He was the last foreign head of state to be received by President Kennedy and Tito was visibly moved by the latter's assassination, being in tears when he signed the book of condolences in the United States embassy in Belgrade. Thereafter relations with Washington were untroubled but without any real warmth.

The major foreign policy development in this period was in fact with Romania which had distanced itself from Soviet foreign-policy orthodoxy in a number of ways. A fellow Balkan, socialist rebel was a natural partner for Tito's Yugoslavia. In June 1963 the Romanian and Yugoslav governments announced that they were to cooperate on a scheme to harness the Iron Gates on the Danube for the generation of electricity; it was the greatest hydro-electric scheme seen in Europe and was to be financed by the two governments alone. In April 1966 Tito travelled to Bucharest for the first of what was to become a series of visits. Further economic cooperation came with the agreement in 1968 to build a joint Yugoslav-Romanian jet fighter, the twin-engined IAR-93. The plane went into production in 1979 with Romania having ordered 185 of them, but economic difficulties and problems with the aircraft itself soon removed it from the headlines.

Though not a conventional diplomatic development, the migration of huge numbers of Yugoslav workers to the west was probably in the long run the most important of all developments in Yugoslavia's external relations. By 1969 some 22 per cent of the entire domestic workforce, in all 800,000 persons, had left the country to work in Germany, Sweden, Austria, Switzerland and elsewhere. Their remittances played an important part in the domestic economy, as did the fact that they were out of the country and therefore placed no strain on Yugoslavia's meagre social services. When the western economies went into recession remittances dwindled and many *Gastarbeiter* returned home.

This was not the only way in which Yugoslavia's domestic situation had become dependent on the economic vagaries of the west, as the 1980s was soon to show.

YUGOSLAVIA IN DECLINE, 1980–9

When the LCY central committee met in Belgrade in July 1987 the building was surrounded by hostile demonstrators and had to be protected by the police. Such a thing had never happened before but it was not the only pointer to a decline in the popularity of Yugoslavia's long-ruling party. In a 1983 opinion poll 36 per cent of those polled had expressed satisfaction with the federal government; in 1985 the figure was 20 per cent, and in 1987 only 10 per cent. In a different poll in 1986 none of those questioned expressed faith in the party and 73 per cent thought it incapable of finding solutions to the country's problems. In the same year, young people were asked to choose their preferences as role models from a given list of twenty-four. The winning three were Pope John Paul II, Mother Theresa and President Reagan; the last-but-one was Princess Caroline of Monaco with only Lenin trailing behind her; tactfully Tito was not among the twenty-four.

There were signs that not only were the country's young people losing faith in previous generations' idols, but that some institutional decay was also taking place. In June 1987 the Yugoslav Writers' Union, the only federal cultural organization, dissolved after the Slovene delegation broke with tradition and voted against the choice of the Writers' Union of Serbia whose turn it was to nominate a candidate for the presidency of the federal body. More serious was the fact that in the first six months of 1986 all federal units except Bosnia and Slovenia failed to pay their obligatory portion of the federal budget; in November of that year it was agreed that in future the federal government would rely on federal revenues only for its income. Fiscal sovereignty had in effect been removed from the central authorities and handed to the republics, a lesson driven home in 1987 by the Slovenes when they refused to impose the wage restraint required by a federal incomes policy. By the end of the 1980s the federal government was so enfeebled that, for the first time in over forty years, the demise of Yugoslavia had become a real possibility.

The decline of the Titoist system had three basic causes: the deaths of its founding fathers and the subsequent questioning of their sustaining myths; a continuing and intensifying economic crisis which discredited self-management; and nationalism which not only grew in strength but also changed in nature, thus precipitating a fatal constitutional conflict between Serbia and Slovenia.

THE DEMISE OF THE OLD GUARD AND THEIR SUSTAINING MYTHS

Of the four main founding fathers of post-war Yugoslavia Djilas had been dismissed in the 1950s and Ranković disgraced in the 1960s. Kardelj remained in office until his death in 1979 and then, on 4 May 1980, Tito breathed his last. Even to their final days Kardelj and Tito had dominated Yugoslav affairs and it was they who had taken the important decisions, the official machinery of the state remaining for most of the time little more than a theoretical construct. Their deaths meant that the system created in 1974 now had to be made to work. Here there were two entwined difficulties. First, the system itself was incredibly complex. Second, the system had to be made to work by men and women whose capabilities did not measure up to those of the founding fathers. The slogan 'After Tito, Tito', coined in 1982 at the LCY's twelfth congress, was meant to indicate continuity with the policies of the great man, but it can equally be seen as recognition that there was no one of any stature to succeed him; Yugoslavia had no Wałęsa or Havel. In part this was a product of the long domination exercised by Kardelj and Tito and their lesser partisan colleagues in the federal party and state apparatuses. Most of these men and women had been young when they took office with the result that successive generations, finding the road to higher posts blocked, gravitated more to the republican administrations. In the 1980s therefore more talent and ability was to be found in the republican and provincial structures than in the federal system. Moreover, the members of the presidency were not federal politicians but persons seconded from their republican posts; for many the latter remained the main focus of loyalty and this was one of the many factors which strengthened the republics vis-à-vis the federal centre.

Titoism had been, when necessary, an authoritarian doctrine. After Tito there were efforts to retain the authority of the police. In 1984 twenty-eight dissidents were interned for a short period for meeting Djilas and in July of that year a young academic, Vojislav Šešelj, was sentenced to eight years for endangering the socialist order in his writings. Yet however aggressive the authorities became they did not have the gravitas of the former leaders and were not able to stem a gradually swelling tide of critical new thinking. The cumulative effect of this tide was to erode the foundations of all the arguments, concepts and myths previously used to legitimize the system.

The intellectuals were in the first wave. In 1981 Vladimir Dedijer, who had been close to Tito and a vigorous upholder of the Tito legend, published *New Contributions to the Biography of Josip Broz Tito* in which he made no secret of the great man's lascivious nature; many people protested but more read the book. In the first half of the decade there was a series of novels by writers such as Dobrica Ćosić, Antonije Isaković and Vuk Drašković which presented previously unpublished interpretations of such subjects as the Second World War, Mihailović and the chetniks, and Goli Otok. The historians were hard on the heels of the novelists. In 1985 Veselin Djuretić published a book on the extent of Ustaša violence against the Serbs. The book was neither well-written nor well-researched but it treated a subject which had had public airing only briefly during the Croatian Spring, and it provoked further and more scholarly treatments, primarily that by Bogoljub Kočović who applied sophisticated methods of mathematical analysis to neutral sources such as successive census records. His research destroyed the establishment myth that 1.7 million Yugoslavs had died during the Second World War, though the true figure of one million was still appalling. In December 1985 Mišo Leković published on a subject previously under total ban: the negotiations between Tito's partisans and the Germans in March 1943. If Leković questioned the official presentation of the partisan war, Vojislav Koštunica and Kosta Čavoški undermined the established version of the communist takeover in Yugoslavia. Their book[3] showed how the Yugoslav communists had pretended to be in favour of an open system but had skilfully and cynically moved towards a one-party regime. The book caused a sensation and was seen by many as an implicit call for multi-party democracy in Yugoslavia.

Central to the concept of Titoism had been the slogan 'Brotherhood and Unity'. That too lost its lustre in the 1980s. In the first place no amount of sloganizing could end the vast economic and social disparities of the country. The poorer regions resented the wealth of the richer, while the richer questioned not only the amount of money given to the poorer areas but the way in which that money was spent, particularly when it was used for the construction of sports stadia and prestige public buildings. Nor was the rich–poor divide purely regional. In 1984 there were one and a half million hard-currency accounts in Yugoslav banks; holders of such accounts could live comfortably but their comfort was resented by those who did not have access to such funds and who had to live on a dinar in precipitate decline. To the old-fashioned ideologue the existence of such accounts was an affront to socialist sensitivities; to the account holders the persistence of socialist sensitivities was often seen as the reason why wealth was not more widely enjoyed.

'Brotherhood and Unity' was of course an ethnic rather than an economic concept, but here too it decayed in the 1980s. The key system and the proportional allocation of office was no longer so widely applied or respected. The decay had begun in Croatia after 1972 when the LCY leadership, anxious to prevent another Croatian Spring, had increased the number of Serbs holding high office in the LCC. A further blow to brotherhood came in 1988 when it was decided to adopt as the federal anthem a nineteenth-century pan-Slav song; it was not a move which could make Albanians, Hungarians or Turks feel more content. Also in 1988 came a proposal from the Serbs that the anniversary of the foundation of the first Yugoslav state in 1918 should be celebrated. This offended the notion of brotherhood in that large groups within Yugoslavia, including the Croats and Macedonians, saw the first Yugoslav state as a device created by Serbian hegemonists. But the proposal also questioned the foundations of the second Yugoslav state whose creators and defenders had always represented it as a revolution against the first Yugoslavia.

Another plank of Titoism, non-alignment, lost its relevance during the 1980s. The advent of more hardline leaders in the west in 1979 and 1980 in the personages of Mrs Thatcher and President Reagan made London and Washington less indulgent to those who were not specifically with them in the confrontation with 'the evil empire'. This wounded and weakened non-alignment but the *coup de grâce* was delivered in 1985 when Mikhail Gorbachev assumed power in the Soviet Union. His rapid disengagement from the cold war meant that non-alignment no longer had any meaning or validity. It continued as a concept and in September 1988 at its meeting in Nicosia the non-aligned movement elected Yugoslavia as its next chairman, but the organization no longer gave Yugoslavia the standing in the world which it had previously endowed, and the country's leaders could no longer evoke it as a legitimizing factor.

The main feature of Titoism, however, had been self-management. By the end of the 1980s that too had been seriously disabled if not destroyed by the economic problems endured by Yugoslavia during that decade.

ECONOMIC CRISIS AND THE DISCREDITING OF SELF-MANAGEMENT

The roots of economic crisis of the 1980s were to be found in the great oil price hike of 1973. Between June and December of that year crude oil prices increased fourfold, disrupting world trade patterns and shattering the balance of payments of Yugoslavia and other states which had little or nothing in the way of native resources of oil. Dour counsel in the west advised retrenchment and a cut in living standards for the affected economies but socialist governments were not in business for that; such policies would prevent the construction of mature socialism and would negate their incessant success propaganda. Along with Poland and a number of other states Yugoslavia chose not to retrench but to borrow, mainly from private banks in the west. It was easily done. The banks were flush with petro-dollars and the Yugoslavs had an excellent record in debt servicing. Although the loans gave some industries a breathing space in which to adjust to new price levels for energy and primary products, the borrowings were a palliative rather than a panacea. In cushioning some of the effects of the increase in oil prices they diminished the incentive to reform; borrowed money was poured into, for example, the hopelessly inefficient Smederevo steel works in Serbia, or was used to build unneeded, duplicate production facilities to assuage republican pressures when the funds would have been much better deployed in financing new plants or industries with much higher levels of productivity.

In 1979 the second great oil price rise produced similar but more profound effects. The doubling of the dollar price for oil was 'the final blow'[4] to Yugoslavia's balance of payments and this time the west was more deeply affected. For Yugoslavia this meant that there were fewer hard-currency purchasers for its exporters and fewer western tourists for its resorts. Furthermore, the recession in the west, combined with the effects of the post-Second World War baby boom meant that western labour markets were satiated; there was a greatly reduced demand for the Yugoslav *Gastarbeiter* and therefore hard-currency remittances fell sharply. The fall in convertible currency income meant that it was more difficult to service the mounting foreign debt and maintain domestic expenditure at its existing levels. Interest on the loans had to be paid but at the same time, for political reasons, the government could not suspend or decrease the vast sums it expended on the army, on pensions for the large numbers of partisan veterans, and on social security benefits for the thousands of workers who in previous years would have been able to find jobs abroad. At the same time, despite the promises of self-management theory, the central government still had to maintain a significant number of bureaucrats. It could meet these domestic obligations only by printing more money, the natural consequence of which was inflation.

In 1983 the International Monetary Fund (IMF) decided it was time to call the Yugoslav government to heel. It did so ruthlessly. When the Belgrade authorities asked for further credits and for a rescheduling of existing debts the IMF laid down strict conditions. It demanded the removal of price controls from more goods and a cutback in government expenditure. This, together with the removal of subsidies on petrol, food, heating and transportation costs in 1982, meant further sharp rises which were seldom matched by wage increases. Furthermore, the government's efforts to squeeze hard-currency imports out of the domestic market meant, for the first time in twenty years, that Yugoslavs faced shortages of and queues for items such as coffee, meat, detergents, sugar and petrol. In 1987 there were further price increases together with the introduction of a federal value added tax and two devaluations in two months.

Despite the intervention of the IMF inflation could not be contained. By 1984 Yugoslavia had the highest inflation rate in Europe, 62 per cent, and by the middle of the decade foreign currencies were being preferred to the dinar in domestic exchanges; by the beginning of 1989 the inflation rate was 2,500 per cent. At the same time the government was finding it increasingly difficult to service its foreign debt and was forced into the dangerous practice of trying to borrow to meet existing debt obligations. In 1984 the external debt had been officially put at $21 billion, but was probably considerably more than that because official estimates did not include all the hard-currency loans taken out by individual banks.

The social effects of the economic crisis were soon visible. With austerity and shortages inevitably came the black market and corruption. Unemployment too increased markedly as disposable incomes shrank and less government money was available for supporting manufacturing. In 1985 unemployment passed the one million mark. In Serbia in 1990 it stood at 16.4 per cent. In Kosovo it was 38.4 per cent and even in Slovenia in 1991 it had reached 8.2 per cent.

Protests over the deteriorating standard of living took various forms. Workers at a textile plant in Bosnia, angry at their union's apparent lack of concern with their plight, voted to withhold their union dues. In Belgrade and other large towns thousands of citizens stopped paying their rents and their utility bills, while strikes, almost all of them for economic objectives and of short duration, became more widespread and more frequent, the longest being at Labin in Croatia in April and May 1987. The most dramatic act of protest came in July 1988 when workers invaded the federal assembly in Belgrade.

By 1988 a further grievance had been added to that of falling standards of living. In 1987 a fire in a warehouse led to the discovery of records which showed that the Agrokomerc enterprise, a huge business conglomerate based in north-west Bosnia and run by Fikret Abdić, had drawn credits of around $865 million which was ultimately guaranteed, without their knowledge, by around sixty Yugoslav banks. These revelations led to the collapse of the conglomerate. In north-west Bosnia this produced almost total economic breakdown. The social banks, through which social benefits were paid, had no cash; the shops closed because they had no money to buy stocks; and on poultry farms run by the conglomerate there was no money to buy feed – some birds survived through cannibalism but so many did not that the army had to be called in to plough their carcasses into the ground. The Agrokomerc affair had a profound effect on the whole of Yugoslavia. The scandal had showed that a few very highly placed officials in and close to the conglomer-ate had grown exceedingly rich, much in contrast to the vast majority of the working population who had recently become much poorer. Official calls for more self-sacrifice and belt-tightening fell on less receptive ears after the Agrokomerc revelations. For many the scandal dealt the final blow to an already declining confidence in the probity and efficacy of the nation's insti-tutions, political as well as financial. It also called into question the national economic and political strategy pursued since 1974; some argued that Agrokomerc proved that there had been too much decentralization and therefore called for more central control, others were convinced of the oppo-site, that such disasters would not occur if the centre was no longer allowed to meddle in local affairs.

Perhaps the most damaging aspect of the Agrokomerc scandal was that what had been done was in itself normal practice in much of Yugoslavia: Abdić's mistakes were that he had been found out, and that he had gone too far; it was a quantitive rather than a qualitative sin.

The whole economic crisis of the 1980s in fact revealed in sharp focus many of the structural errors of Yugoslavia, not least of its banking system where the domination of republican interests in the National Bank prevented tight money control.

The growing pressure on public funds made many question how such monies had been spent in the past. It was clear even from cursory examina-tion that investment policy had been flawed, a particular failing being the notion that each republic should have its own prestige industrial plants. This meant both that there was massive over-capacity in the federation and that many of the plants built essentially for political reasons lacked any economic rationale and were hopelessly unprofitable.

Examination of the economic record highlighted the many shortcomings of the self-management system. In 1982 *Komunist* carried an article which claimed that each day an average of one out of eleven workers was absent in Yugoslav factories. Two years later *Borba*[5] estimated the effective working day in the socialized sector of the economy to be four hours and nine minutes.

One reason for this was that work finished at 2 p.m. in order to give women time to shop, but another explanation was the fact that the self-management system involved 'endless time spent on interminable discussions at perpetual meetings of innumerable institutions producing an inexhaustible number of decisions . . . [sic] but little effective action'.[6]

Many of those decisions were inappropriate in the strained economic circumstances of the 1980s. There had always been a tendency in self-managing enterprises for the workers to decide to use profits to enhance wages rather than invest in improved productivity, not least because the latter usually meant shedding jobs. In the 1980s when jobs did have to be shed for financial reasons, workers' councils tended to sack a few much needed technicians and engineers rather than a larger number of supernumerary unskilled hands.

Economic faults, however, were not the main cause for the steady disintegration of Yugoslavia in the second half of the 1980s. In fact, as the decade drew to its close it seemed that these economic faults had been repaired. In July 1988 the federal assembly adopted the 'intervention programme' drawn up by federal prime minister Branko Mikulić which involved the partial liberalization of prices and wages frozen since November 1987. In November 1988 the assembly agreed to thirty-nine constitutional amendments intended to pave the way for further market reforms and to speed up the revitalization of the economy. A standby credit of $1.4 billion from the IMF and loans of half a billion dollars from western banks enabled the government to institute some reforms but in December 1988 the assembly balked at further changes demanded by the IMF and Mikulić resigned.

In March 1989 Ante Marković became federal prime minister determined to succeed where Mikulić had failed. Marković was a Croat who in addition to having experience in industrial management, was blessed with unbounded energy and unlimited self-confidence. He set out with the object of reforming and improving socialism but like so many others in that climacteric year he soon realized that that was not enough; socialism needed not reforming but replacing with market-style capitalism. His tactics were bold. On coming to office he tied the dinar to the Deutschemark and announced that come what may Yugoslavia's currency would become convertible on 1 January 1990. He set out to restore the three free markets – in commodities, labour and capital – which the communists had abolished after the Second World War. His law on enterprises freed public-sector concerns from political control and allowed them to establish joint ventures with foreign firms, and later legislation even allowed foreigners to have a majority holding in Yugoslav companies. He vigorously attacked inflation, cutting government subsidies to industry and pegging wages but allowing prices to move upwards; by the middle of 1990 he had brought inflation down to zero from a high barely a year before of 2,714 per cent. For a short while he was one of the most popular figures in the country.

But if he enjoyed the support of individuals he faced a great deal of institutional suspicion and hostility, above all because his centralizing programme threatened the powers of the republican governments and the privileges of their dominant oligarchies. They used the federal parliament to frustrate him. This did not necessarily deter Marković. He drew the conclusion that it was not his policies but the parliament which needed changing. He called therefore for a modernized assembly directly elected by the citizens of the federation, not indirectly chosen through the republics. All the republics but Serbia opposed this and when he tried to establish a federal TV channel to publicize his ideas some republican networks relayed it only in the middle of the night, and he was even refused radio time for his state of the federation message. Undaunted he set up his own federal political party, the Alliance of Reform Forces (ARF), which would argue his case for direct, federal-wide elections to the federal assembly, but Marković's expertise was economic rather than political and the party failed, not least because it was established too late, in July 1990, after elections had taken place in Slovenia and Croatia.

Marković was to remain in office until the middle of 1991. He had always known that his policies would meet strong opposition but had hoped that in the last resort the majority of his fellow Yugoslavs would see reason and the west would be willing to support him in his struggle with the reactionaries. He was wrong on both accounts. The hoped-for help from the west did not arrive and when he left office it was mainly because Yugoslavia had to all intents and purposes ceased to exist. It was his tragedy, and that of Yugoslavia, that his policies came too late. Had he been able to tackle inflation in the first rather than the second half of the 1980s his reformist ideas for the economy and for the federation's political structures would have been given a longer and, one suspects, a more sympathetic hearing. As it is he is remembered by many supporters of the Yugoslav ideal as a *deus contra machinam*. To those who have no views on Yugoslavia, its viability and its desirability, he appears more as a Don Quixote tilting at the windmill of republican privilege and ethnic nationalism.

ETHNIC NATIONALISM AND THE END OF 'BROTHERHOOD AND UNITY'

One might argue that after so many years of a comfortably collective identity within the system, the common man was simply unprepared to take on the responsibility to exercise his individual freedom. The easiest option therefore was to seek another form of collective identity, another protective shield against the confusion. This was nationalism.[7]

Nationalism was certainly not a new phenomenon in Yugoslavia. What was different in the 1980s was that it operated domestically in a system whose coercive and anti-nationalist wills were in decline while the international context was simultaneously being transformed so that there was no longer even one world power which might feel its interests seriously affected were Yugoslavia to disintegrate.

The 1980s began and ended with crises in and over Kosovo. The first began on 11 March 1981 when students protested at standards in a canteen in Prishtina university. These complaints rapidly developed into protests against those who ran the university and assumed a political complexion on 25 March. On that day the 'Youth relay-race', an event started under Tito to mark his birthday and to emphasize brotherhood and unity, was due to reach Kosovo's capital. Demonstrators took to the streets with calls for a separate republic for Kosovo and, in a few isolated instances, even for union with Albania. In the next two months the unrest spread not only throughout Kosovo but also to Albanian communities in Macedonia and Montenegro. The authorities reacted harshly. Troops, mainly from Croatia and Slovenia, were rushed into the province but full order was not restored in the Albanian areas until 1983. Meanwhile the Kosovan party and state apparatuses were thoroughly purged. Official accounts acknowledge 10 fatalities, one of them a policeman, but unofficial estimates have put the number of dead in the first half of 1981 at over 1,000, with more than that number being imprisoned. The unrest was contained but it was not completely stifled. In 1984 the Yugoslav news agency, Tanjug, reported that seventy-two illegal organizations had been uncovered in the province, and in 1985 it was alleged that an Albanian conspiracy, which included a number of army officers, had been broken up.

The 1981 Kosovo crisis had many causes. Despite the post-1968 reforms Kosovan Albanians still felt themselves to be a colonial and exploited people, a feeling reinforced by the continuing and growing disparities of wealth: in 1954 per capita income in Kosovo had been 48 per cent of the federal average, in 1980 it was only 27.8 per cent of the average. This sense of colonial status might also have been sharpened by the success of the Islamic revolution in Iran in 1979 and there were complaints from the Serbs of increased attacks on Orthodox religious buildings, but the dedication of the Kosovan Albanians, especially the young, to a strict religious faith, particularly one which banned the consumption of alcohol, was limited. More influential than Islam had been the writings of Albania's communist boss, Enver Hoxha, one of whose volumes of memoirs had asserted that at the end of the war Tito had told him that Kosovo should remain in Albania. Hoxha's memoirs had been among the many Albanian-produced books imported into Kosovo after the introduction of teaching in Albanian in secondary and tertiary education after 1968, such imports being necessary because there were not enough Yugoslav-printed books in Albanian. The most serious problem created by the Albanianization of Prishtina university however was the over-production of graduates. The university grew rapidly after 1968 and by 1980 had 51,000 students, a third of the adult population of Prishtina. The university did not enjoy a high reputation in Yugoslavia, and this, together with the fact that most of them had poor Serbo-Croat, made it difficult for its graduates to find jobs. An unemployed and to a large extent unemployable graduate mass is a dangerous phenomenon.

Whatever their causes the Kosovo disorders of 1981 were the worst outbreak of unrest in Yugoslavia since 1944. Also the open use of military force against the demonstrators was seen as a new departure. Tito had tried to remain impartial in internal disputes and strove to create a system in which all peoples were treated equally: the bullets fired at protesters in Prishtina damaged that image of the impartial, paternalist state. After Tito Yugoslavia had two roads before it: democratization or repression. Kosovo 1981 indicated that the second had been chosen.

Nowhere was the impact of the 1981 Kosovo revolt greater than among the Serbs. A decade earlier the Croats had been alienated from the system, now it was the turn of the Serbs. In the first place after 1981 a number of concessions were made to Kosovo which reinforced the growing conviction among many Serbs in the province that they had no future there. Serbian emigration had been in progress since 1968; in 1961 the Serbs had formed 23.5 per cent of Kosovo's population but in 1981 the figure was down to 13.2 per cent. After 1981 the pace of emigration accelerated; by 1991 the Serbs formed only 9.9 per cent of the Kosovan population. After 1968 the egress had been mainly of professional people who feared for their positions in view of the increasing Albanianization of the province; after 1981 all sections of the Serbian population streamed out of the area. Many feared being swamped under what they feared was an Albanian demographic explosion. In 1986 the average Yugoslav birth rate was 6.4 per thousand; in 'inner' Serbia, i.e. Serbia without the provinces, it was 2.7 per thousand; in Kosovo it was 24.5 per thousand. In fact, the discrepancy was as much social as ethnic. It represented not so much the fact that Albanians bred more rapidly than anyone else as that Kosovo was a deeply backward, highly rural region, and in the remoter communities Serbian birth rates were as high as the Albanian with, conversely, Albanian birth rates in the towns being almost as low as the Serbian. But the fears of the emigrating Serbs were based on emotion not on dispassionate analysis. Rumours soon began circulating that the Serbs were being victimized by the Albanians and, in particular, that Serbian women were being systematically raped by Albanians. So intense did these rumours become that in 1987 the Serbian republic, in the face of vehement opposition from women's organizations, passed a special law doubling the sentence for rape if it were committed by a man of a different ethnic group to the victim. The Albanians rejected such charges out of hand and sober analysis revealed that the incidence of rape was lower in Kosovo than in any other part of Yugoslavia. The Albanians also rejected Serbian claims that the Serbs were being driven out; they were, said the Albanians, selling their homes and farms of their own free will for the very favourable prices which a number of returning Albanian migrant workers were ready to pay.

The realities of the situation scarcely mattered because the vital point was that Kosovo was the raw nerve of Serbian nationalism; anything which touched it produced a reflex howl of anguish. Kosovo was believed by Serbs to be the heartland of mediaeval Serbia, the birthplace of Serbian nationhood, and it was in Kosovo that mediaeval Serbia went to its doom on 28 June 1389 in the battle of Kosovo Polje against the invading Ottoman armies. It was in effect the Serbian Jerusalem. It was part of the myth which enabled the Serbs, particularly religious ones, to think of themselves as a victim nation.

The sufferings of the Kosovan Serbs, real and imagined, injected a new element into Serbian nationalism and brought it to critical mass. A revival had been under way since at least the beginning of the decade. Its component elements were the former members of the security apparatus whose status had declined since the disgrace of Ranković, some elements in the Orthodox Church hierarchy, and a small number of ambitious politicians who were looking for a vehicle on which to ride to power. Many Serbs believed that communist Yugoslavia, a creation of Tito, a Croat, and Kardelj, a Slovene, had been rigged against their republic. Vojvodina, Kosovo, Montenegro, parts of Croatia's eastern Slavonia and most of Bosnia were all regarded as historically Serbian lands. They had been taken away from Serbia to placate the other nations and to weaken Serbia against the other republics. It followed therefore, the extremists argued, that Serbia's ills could be cured only if the unnatural creation of Tito and Kardelj were restructured to give Serbia its historic rights and influence.

Outward expression of such frustrations was first seen in 1983 at the funeral of Ranković who died on 20 August. Ranković had in fact been a unitarist but he was a Serb and the Serb nationalists regarded him as one of their own who had been removed from power not because of any wrongdoings but because he was a Serb. Thousands lined the streets as his cortège passed, many shouting slogans about the status of the Serbs in Kosovo and elsewhere or chanting 'Serbia is Rising'.

The growing anger and frustration of the Serbs were codified in January 1986 by some two hundred prominent intellectuals who signed a petition to the Serbian and federal assemblies protesting at the 'genocide' being committed against the Serbian nation in Kosovo. The petition demanded that the two provinces be placed once again under the authority of the Republic of Serbia, that Serbo-Croat be made the official language in the provinces, and that the alleged 200,000 migrant workers from Albania be expelled. Almost contemporaneous with the petition was a draft memorandum drawn up by the Serbian Academy of Sciences. The memorandum repeated many of the complaints voiced in the petition, particularly with reference to the 'genocide' in Kosovo and also, it said, in Croatia. It stated three main objections to Tito's Yugoslavia: it discriminated economically against Serbia; it had partitioned Serbia into three in 1974 by making the provinces autonomous; and it had condoned the anti-Serbian and separatist policies pursued in Kosovo. The implication was that because of the conspiracy hatched against them the Serbs had the right to defend their own national interests. Parts of the memorandum were published in *Večernje Novosti* on 24 and 25 September

1986. They had a sensational effect, rallying the Serbs to their own defence and putting many non-Serbs on their guard against a new and strident form of Serbian hegemonialism.

Four months before the publication of extracts from the memorandum the Serbian League of Communists acquired a new leader. Slobodan Milošević was born in August 1941 in Požarevac, central Serbia, though his family came originally from Montenegro. Both his parents had committed suicide while he was young and the mainstay of his life was Mirjana Marković, the girl he had met while still at school and whom he married when they were both students in Belgrade university. Before entering the political mainstream he was given a party appointment in a New York bank which, it was hoped, would give him experience of the outside world and of economics. His first major advance at home came in 1984 when he was appointed head of the Belgrade party committee by his personal friend Ivan Stambolić, the Serbian party leader. Milošević appeared to be a quiet, dependable and capable, if anti-bureaucratic bureaucrat who was an economic liberal but a political conservative. When Stambolić became president of Serbia in May 1986 he nominated the head of the Belgrade apparat to succeed him as Serbian party boss. It seemed a safe and uncontroversial choice.

That this was a miscalculation was shown on the night of 24 April 1987. Stambolić had been invited to speak to a meeting of workers in a suburb of Prishtina but in view of a number of recent speeches in which he had been highly critical of Serbian nationalists and nationalism in general, the party leader asked Milošević to go in his place. Most of the delegates to the meeting were in fact Albanians but around fifteen thousand Serbs turned up and demanded admission. The police refused and drove them off with some brutality. Milošević appeared and ordered the policemen to stand to, at the same time assuring the assembled Serbs that 'No one has the right to beat you.'[8] Thereafter Milošević stayed in the meeting hall all night, listening for thirteen hours as the Serbs poured out their complaints to him. Yugoslavia and the Balkans had been greatly changed.

Although he moved cautiously Milošević had now come to believe that Stambolić was taking too weak a line on Kosovo. Stambolić had condemned the Academy draft memorandum on the grounds that it would incite other nationalisms against Serbia. Serbia, he argued, needed Yugoslavia because that was the only way in which all Serbs could remain together in one state, and he sought to ease the Kosovo difficulties in cooperation with the other republics. This implied that Serbia had to tailor its policies to preserve and placate Yugoslavia. Milošević moved to the opposite pole. After April 1987 he insisted that Yugoslavia needed to be refashioned to meet Serbia's needs, and that Kosovo was a Serbian not a Yugoslav problem which should be solved by an assertive Serbian leader and not by the collective federal machinery. Stambolić took little notice of Milošević's shift in opinion and in September 1987 paid the price for his indifference. At a meeting of the Serbian party leadership Milošević managed to remove Stambolić's protégé, Dragiša Pavlović, after which Milošević purged the party apparat of opponents. It was a classic Stalinist move by which the self-effacing bureaucrat out-manoeuvred all his rivals. In a further refinement of Stalinism Milošević referred to his use of the bureaucratic machine as 'the anti-bureaucratic revolution'.

His ambition ignited by office Milošević had decided that the surest means of entrenching and extending his power was to exploit Serbian nationalism. Consequently, he endorsed growing nationalist demands for a restructuring of Yugoslavia, and more particularly for the re-incorporation of the two provinces into Serbia. He knew, however, that the federal leadership as present constituted would never agree to such constitutional reform. He therefore determined to create a more amenable federal leadership by putting his own supporters into power in the two provinces and in Montenegro. That would give him four votes in the federal presidency which would at least mean that he could not be outvoted in the eight-member body.

One of his chief instruments for packing the federal executive council was the Committee for the Protection of Kosovo Serbs and Montenegrins established in 1988 with Milošević at its head. It was a mass lobby group to voice the grievances and demands of the Serbs, the main one being the incorporation of Vojvodina and Kosovo into Serbia. Between July and November 1988 the Committee organized forty rallies, or 'Meetings of Truth', the largest being in Belgrade on 19 November when an estimated million people turned out for the 'Meeting of All Meetings'. The committee's first success came in Vojvodina. On 5 October its supporters besieged the head-quarters of the local League of Communists (LC) in Novi Sad, and later that night the embattled leaders resigned to make way for a team devoted to Milošević. A similar manoeuvre two days later in Podgorica failed but in January 1989 Milošević finally succeeded in installing his acolytes in the Montenegrin leadership.

The battle in Kosovo was more complex. On 17 November Milošević had succeeded in removing the leaders of the League of Communists of Kosovo (LCK) on the grounds that they had abetted the persecution of Serbs in Kosovo. In protest the miners of Trepča, most of them ethnic Albanians, marched to Prishtina. They were placated for the while but in February staged a much more serious protest when they stayed in the pits without food. Their anger had been stirred by Milošević's packing of the LCK with his own placemen, by his obvious intention to push through constitutional change by force if necessary and by his statement that he would impose a state of emergency in Kosovo. The miners, old-fashioned communists who carried portraits of Tito, were duped into leaving the pits by promises which were soon broken but this was not the end of resistance in Kosovo where, in the eyes of one observer, an 'Albanian intifada' had begun.[9]

Other republics and ethnic groups in Yugoslavia could not but be affected by the rise of militant nationalism in Serbia. Indeed, with Milošević's assumption of power in 1987 the history of Yugoslavia becomes ever more the history of its constituent republics and peoples, and much of that history is a reaction against Milošević and his policies.

Croatian nationalism was quiet and restrained for most of the 1980s. The clampdown of 1971–2 was still fresh in the political mind and the Catholic Church provided an alternative refuge for those disenchanted with the system. That the party still feared the Church was indicated in January 1981 when Jakov Blažević, the new president of the Croatian party praesidium but a very old style politician, unleashed a savage attack on the leader of the Croatian Church, Cardinal Kuharić. Eight hundred priests attended a congress to express support for their Cardinal and an even more impressive expression of religious solidarity came on 10 February when over seven thousand attended a mass to mark the twenty-first anniversary of Cardinal Stepinac's death. Popular religious emotions were further stirred in June when a number of children reported seeing visions of the Virgin Mary near Medjugorije in Hercegovina which soon became a place of international pilgrimage. Not until 1988, however, had the political atmosphere relaxed enough to allow Zagreb television, for the first time, to extend its good wishes to Catholics at Christmas.

By this time the Serbian press had ensured that the Croats would not remain politically dormant. There were vitriolic attacks on Croatia, past and present, some of them wild beyond any limit of reason. The LCC leader, Ivica Račan, was routinely described as Ustaša although his parents had been murdered by the Ustaše in the war, and in 1988 there were totally unfounded allegations that the lives of Serbs in Croatia were being threatened by the Croat authorities dumping radio-active waste near their villages; two years after Chernobyl such allegations, irresponsible though they were, aroused considerable anxiety. There was some quiet discussion of political change and in February 1987, for the first time in fifteen years, there was public debate on the issue of multi-party elections, but in general Croatian political opinion did not become fully mobilized until the spring of 1989.

The position was different in Slovenia. From the beginning of the 1980s Slovenia's remarkable openness and pluralism had been apparent in the cultural, social and even political fields; so relaxed had the atmosphere become by June 1988 that in Maribor Djilas was allowed to speak in public for the first time in thirty-five years. This had been made possible by a relatively free and highly courageous press and, especially after the appointment of Milan Kučan as leader in 1986, an indulgent party leadership. The League of Communists of Slovenia (LCS) was prepared to give the nation's youth, feminists, gay rights activists and ecologists such a free hand because it increased the differentials between Slovenia and the federal authorities. And the Slovene leadership was even more determined to keep its distance from Belgrade when Milošević began pressing for constitutional reforms which would increase Serbian power within the federation.

The federal conservatives, especially those in the JNA, were alarmed by developments in Slovenia and a confrontation soon emerged between them and the radical forces, especially those in *Mladina*, the outspoken youth journal. In the last years of the decade it made the JNA one of its chief targets, at the same time giving forceful backing to the students' demands for an alternative to military conscription and to the general call to make Slovene a language of command in the forces. *Mladina* also had considerable experience in investigative journalism, and this too it deployed against the JNA. A *Mladina* journalist, Janez Janša, had come into possession of a secret transcript of a federal central committee meeting on 25 March 1988 convened to discuss the imposition of military rule in Slovenia. On 13 May *Mladina* used the transcript as the basis for an article which insisted that the JNA had drawn up a list of Slovenes to be arrested. Janša and three colleagues were indeed arrested that same evening and later received sentences ranging from eight months to four years.

The contest between *Mladina* and the JNA had galvanized the normally docile Slovenes. A huge crowd besieged the courthouse and for a while prevented the four convicted men being moved to prison. More significantly, after the arrests an opposition journalist, Igor Bavčar, had set up the Committee for the Defence of Human Rights, Odbor, to rally journalists, politicians and others to the defence of the accused. Odbor bore striking resemblances to KSS/KOR in Poland and was a clear example of civil society in action. By the beginning of 1989 there were an estimated hundred organizations which could be similarly classified, in addition to which there were ten separate political parties. The Slovenes had also decided to break with established practice and choose their representative to the federal presidency through a nationwide election rather than allowing the republican LC to nominate him or her. It was the first free election in Yugoslavia since the Second World War and in it the communist candidate lost to Janez Drnovšek, a young economist.

The political atmospheres of Kučan's Slovenia and Milošević's Serbia could scarcely have been more different. *Mladina* had denounced the marriage of nationalism and neo-Stalinism consummated in the Milošević regime and Slovene opinion suspected Serbian designs for recasting the federation and the ruthlessness with which these demands were being pursued. The Albanians and the Slovenes were roughly equal in number and if Milošević could, as he threatened to do, use the JNA to force the former into his new Serbia, he could also, many Slovenes feared, use the army to discipline Slovenia and force it into a unitarist straitjacket. For this reason, and for the sake of human rights, Odbor came out in strong support of the Trepča miners in February. At the same time over a million Slovenes, more than half the total population, signed a petition against a declaration of a state of emergency in Kosovo. On 27 February 1989 a huge rally, organized by Odbor, took place in Cankarjev Dom, the cultural centre in Ljubljana. Until this point the party leadership in Slovenia had been reserved in its attitude to protests against their Serbian colleagues, but by now Kučan and his allies were convinced that they had to make a firm stand against Milošević. Kučan realized he was in danger of being left behind by public opinion, but, more importantly, he had also seen at first hand how dangerous Milošević had now become when, on 26 February, the Serbian leader had told the federal party leadership that Serbia would not abandon its proposed constitutional changes which would be imposed by any means, legal or otherwise; that, Kučan had replied, would mean the end of Yugoslavia as a consensual federation. At the Cankarjev Dom meeting Kučan therefore linked the cause of the Trepča miners – the preservation of Kosovo's separate status within the 1974 constitution – to that of the future of Yugoslavia; human rights in Kosovo and the preservation of the internal territorial settlement were, he implied, two sides of the same coin. The Ljubljana rally was broadcast live over Serbian television. It provoked uproar. Huge crowds converged on the centre of Belgrade demanding the introduction of the constitutional changes and the arrest of Kosovan Albanian leader, Azem Vllasi. The crowd remained in the centre of the city for over twenty-four hours, until Milošević appeared and in a short, stumbling speech promised them that if they dispersed he would have Vllasi arrested. They did and on 2 March Vllasi was taken into custody.

Before the end of the Belgrade rally another crisis meeting of the federal leadership was convened in which Milošević, despite Kučan's objections, secured agreement for the imposition of a state of emergency in Kosovo. On 23 March, with JNA tanks surrounding its building the Kosovo assembly agreed to the constitutional changes which stripped the province of its autonomy and put it under the authority of Belgrade. A few days later the Serbian assembly also enacted the changes which incorporated the two provinces into Serbia. Protests in Kosovo were put down with ruthless efficiency, leaving 22 demonstrators and 2 policemen dead, with many more wounded.

The dismantling of the 1974 constitution had begun and with it the process of Yugoslavia's reconstruction. That process was soon to become one of destruction.

Notes

1. Quoted in Dennison Rusinow, *The Yugoslav Experiment, 1948–1974*, London: C. Hurst for The Royal Institute for International Affairs, 1977, p.106.
2. Quoted in Sir Duncan Wilson, *Tito's Yugoslavia*, Cambridge: Cambridge University Press, 1979, p.14.
3. It was later published in English: Vojislav Koštunica and Kosta Čavoški, *From Pluralism to Monism: Social Movements and the Political System in Yugoslavia 1944–1949*, Boulder, CO/New York: East European Monographs no.189, distributed by Columbia University Press, 1985.
4. Harold Lydall, *Yugoslavia in Crisis*, Oxford: the Clarendon Press, 1989, p.50.
5. On 19 March 1984.
6. Rusinow (1977), p.270.
7. Zoran Pajić, 'Bosnia-Herzegovina: from Multiethnic Coexistence to "Apartheid"', in Payam Akhavan and Robert Howse (eds), *Yugoslavia the Former and the Future: Reflections*

by Scholars from the Region, Washington: the Brookings Institution; Geneva: the United Nations Research Institute for Social Development, 1995, pp.152–63, see p.153.

8. The precise form of words used varies from source to source, but there is no disagreement as to their effect.

9. Tim Judah, *Kosovo: War and Revenge*, New Haven, CT/London: Yale University Press, 2000, p.55.

Chapter 9

ALBANIA, 1948–1991

Under communist rule Albania was to attempt a transition from being Europe's most backward state to one which was in the vanguard of social and political progress. Success in this gargantuan task could not be achieved, Albania's rulers believed, without strict internal controls and substantial external help, at least in the initial stages of the process. The belief in the necessity of strict discipline at home made the Albanian regime the most vicious and vindictive in Europe. Its dependence on help from without produced abrupt changes in external orientation but did not moderate its intense nationalism.

THE SOVIET PERIOD, 1948–61

In the first few years in power the Albanian communists had assumed that their main external sponsor would be Yugoslavia but when Tito was expelled from the Cominform all help from that quarter ceased and Albania was forced to reconsider its strategy. The obvious new sponsor was the Soviet Union which was able as well as willing to step into the breach, Moscow not wishing Albania to remain dependent upon the revisionists in Belgrade. Albania for its part welcomed a great power as a sponsor in the hope that it would provide not only economic assistance but also military security.

Before either economic assistance or military security could be secured internal discipline and unity had to be ensured. In September 1948 therefore Koçi Xoxe, who had been the most prominent proponent of the pro-Yugoslav line, was dismissed as first secretary of the party and minister of the interior and expelled from the party in November; in May 1949 he was secretly tried and executed; according to Tito[1] he was personally throttled by Mehmet Shehu who had replaced him as minister of the interior and boss of the secret police, the Sigurimi.

Xoxe's expulsion from the Albanian Communist Party had taken place when it met for its first congress, the main function of which had been to reassess the party's position and its strategy in the light of the breach with Yugoslavia. The congress, at Stalin's suggestion, changed the name of the party to the Albanian Party of Labour (APL) to reflect its predominantly peasant origin and composition. It then ascribed all the failings of the 1944–8 period to malign Yugoslav influence before expelling Xoxe and his associates. This was followed by a widespread purge of pro-Yugoslav 'revisionists' within the party and state apparatuses. The Albanian purge was the first of those which were to sweep through the ruling parties of the Soviet bloc with charges of pro-Titoist deviation being levied against the major victims. In Albania the reign of terror unleashed in 1948–9 continued until almost the middle of the 1950s and was intensified in February 1951 after a bomb exploded outside the Soviet embassy in Tirana killing a number of Soviet diplomats.

Xoxe's fall and the subsequent blood-letting left Enver Hoxha, who was also prime minister, as unchallenged leader of the Albanian party; it was a position he was to retain until his death in 1985. He was a fierce nationalist and a dedicated admirer of Stalin. He was also an educated man who in the exacting conditions of wartime had proved himself to be a tough, able and ruthless leader.

The first congress in September 1948 had absorbed the shock of the breach with Yugoslavia and endorsed close cooperation with Stalin's Soviet Union. The Soviets were now to provide the capital and expertise Albania needed to begin building socialism. They continued to finance the creation of a modern infrastructure which had begun after the war; the few existing roads were repaired and new ones built while the country's first railway lines were laid to serve new industrial complexes and later to link the major towns with the capital. There was also considerable Soviet assistance in social reform. The health system remained rudimentary by western standards but it improved appreciably with the training of rural doctors and nurses and with the draining of malarial swamps. In education there was more spectacular progress. Even during the war the partisans had been keen to improve education and in Muslim areas under their control one of their first acts had been to set up schools for girls and women. After the war bright Albanian students had gone to Yugoslav universities for their training. After 1948 they went to the Soviet Union or the other bloc states. In Albania itself Soviet advisors helped to remodel the education system on the Soviet pattern. In 1949 a law required all adults to attend literacy classes in the evening; the results were dramatic, illiteracy among adults under forty fell from 80 per cent in 1946 to 30 per cent in 1950 and by 1955 had been eliminated altogether. In 1957 Albania's first university was opened in Tirana and a Pedagogical Institute, later to be made a university, was established in Shkoder.

Albania did not introduce its first five-year plan until the ALP held its second congress in March 1952 which proudly proclaimed that socialism would be built 'With a pickaxe in one hand, and a rifle in the other'. The plan concentrated on developing Albania's considerable reserves of chrome, copper, nickel, oil and lignite, but the intention was to make these the basis of secondary, manufacturing industries; Albania would not be satisfied with primary, extractive operations alone. While keen to develop modern industry the communists were still reluctant to grasp the nettle of radical agricultural reform. Some moves towards collectivization had been made in 1951 but, as in the late 1940s, the reaction had been so sharp that the idea was dropped. Not until 1955 did systematic collectivization begin.

A major reason for the relatively slow adoption of a fully planned economy and for the reluctance to introduce collectivization was that the Albanian leadership still did not feel free from foreign pressures. The split with Tito had raised fears that Yugoslavia might attempt to incorporate all or part of Albania into the FRY. There was also danger to the south. Technically Albania and Greece were still at war and Tirana feared that the anti-communist victory in the Greek civil war might reactivate Greek territorial claims on the south of Albania where most of the country's 5 per cent Greek minority lived. There was another fear: western subversion. This was no fantasy. In the late 1940s and early 1950s western intelligence agencies became convinced Albania was the soft underbelly of European communism which, if destabilized, could precipitate unrest in other communist states and initiate the 'roll back' of communism. Over three hundred exiled anti-communist Albanians were trained and sent back to their homeland. Almost all of them went to instant capture and probable death because the British spy Philby, and others, had betrayed the entire scheme to their Soviet masters.

The fact that Albania was attempting to create socialism from a very low level of development and at the same time feared it was surrounded by enemies bent upon its destruction had made Stalin a particularly appropriate patron and protector for the Albanians, Albania's situation in the late 1940s and early 1950s seemingly reflecting that of the infant Soviet Union in the opening years of the Stalinist dictatorship. After Stalin's death Hoxha feared the Kremlin's new masters might move away from Stalinism which could mean both a rapprochement with Belgrade and, with the heretic no longer a danger, a relaxation of domestic political controls. Albania, he believed, could afford neither and therefore he was never a dedicated disciple of the New Course. He did agree in 1954 to give up the prime ministership, which went to Shehu, but he refused to rehabilitate Xoxe.

The APL was more compliant in its response to Khrushchev's criticism of Stalin in his speech to the twentieth congress of the CPSU in February 1956. A special APL meeting was called in Tirana in April which produced a torrent of criticism of the party, of the purges and even of the leadership. When the APL's third congress met in May Hoxha adopted a suitably chastened and Khrushchevian line, though once again he resisted Soviet pressure to rehabilitate Xoxe. In reality Hoxha had no intention of following Khrushchev into a more relaxed regime, as many of those who had spoken out in April were soon to discover. When the Hungarian revolution convulsed the communist bloc Hoxha felt vindicated and preened himself on his ideological rectitude. His stern attitudes were admired by a number of East European communists and even Khrushchev's Kremlin made a number of concessions to him, cancelling some debts and increasing food deliveries in 1957. For his part, Hoxha happily tightened his internal grip and began purging those who had been unwise enough to put their heads above the parapet in April 1956. One victim was Liri Gega who, though pregnant, was shot despite pleas for moderation from Moscow.

The Soviet concessions of 1957 could not hide the fact that Hoxha could never afford Khrushchev the same respect he had shown for Stalin. This was emphasized in 1958 when an Albania delegation visited China just as the PRC was embarking on its 'great leap forward' which, if successful, would have useful lessons for any state wishing to bring about a rapid transition from an agrarian to an industrialized economy. Mao had the added attraction of being an unrepentant Stalinist, at least as far as the retention of tight party and police controls were concerned.

Partly in an attempt to deflect Albania from any move towards China Khrushchev paid a twelve-day visit to Albania in May 1959. It was a disaster from which Soviet-Albanian relations were never to recover. A number of minor frictions had already become apparent. Albanians resented the Soviet advisors and technicians who lived in separate and better accommodation and received higher wages than their Albanian equivalents. The Albanians also resented the behaviour of Soviet troops in Albania, including those at the submarine base the Red Navy had established on Sasun island outside Vlore. A more serious issue was that despite the bases established in Albania the Soviets had never signed a mutual defence treaty, something which the Albanian leadership in the embattled days of the early 1950s had desperately desired. Even though the inclusion of Albania as a founder member of the Warsaw pact in 1955 had rectified this to some extent the Albanians still felt they had been neglected.

This grievance was nothing beside the economic disagreements which increased in the second half of the 1950s and exploded during Khrushchev's visit in 1959. Albania's oil industry had been developed with Soviet help and with its exports of crude to Eastern Europe Albania had paid for imported manufactured goods and petroleum products. In the 1950s further deposits of high-grade oil were discovered in Albania and a new refinery constructed, again with Soviet help. When it came on stream in 1957, however, the Soviets announced they would not invest further in the Albanian oil industry. The Soviet Union, itself having a surplus of oil which it wished to export for hard currency, was not keen to promote potentially competitive production in a client state. Khrushchev made matters infinitely worse in May 1959. He suggested that Albania should give up growing grain; the mice of the Soviet Union, he said, ate as much as Albania consumed and the Soviets would supply all the country's needs. Instead, Khrushchev told Hoxha, the Albanians should concentrate on growing bay trees and oranges plus a few industrial crops for which the soil and climate were ideal. Anything more insulting to an intensely proud nationalist intellectual bent on industrializing his nation could scarcely be imagined; it was, said Hoxha, asking Albania to become an East European equivalent of a South American banana republic. The gloves were off and they were never replaced.

The big fight took place at the meetings of world communist parties held in Bucharest and Moscow in June and November 1960 respectively. At the Bucharest meeting the Albanian delegation sided openly with the Chinese, as a result of which the Soviets announced that they would not be able to deliver the fifty thousand tons of grain which they had promised to Albania; they could deliver only ten thousand tons which had to be paid for in gold. This was a bitter blow because Albania, having been hit by floods, droughts and earthquakes, was in desperate need of food. At the November meeting in Moscow Hoxha appeared in person. His speech was astounding for the verbal vitriol which he poured over Khrushchev; characteristically, Khrushchev had a more down-to-earth description, describing the experience as akin to having a bucket of ordure poured over him. After his outburst Hoxha left Moscow before the end of the conference, travelling by train lest an aircraft be sabotaged. He never set foot outside Albania again.

In February 1961 the APL's fourth congress confirmed the leadership's stance. It was the last APL congress in Hoxha's lifetime to be attended by representatives of the bloc states. It cocked a snook at Soviet economic advice by endorsing the third five-year plan which allocated 54 per cent of investment to industry and only 14.6 per cent to agriculture. Shortly after the congress the Soviet and East European advisors were withdrawn, Albanian students were expelled from Soviet and East European universities, the Soviet naval base at Sasun was closed and some Albanian vessels refitting in Soviet yards were seized. In December 1961 the Soviet Union broke off diplomatic relations with Albania. They were not restored until 1990.

THE CHINESE PERIOD, 1961–78

Albania was to be closely associated with China for a decade and a half. Those years included one of the most turbulent periods of the latter's recent history, the cultural revolution. The Albanians copied some but not all of the Chinese party's radical policies but in essence Albanian strategy and tactics remained unaltered: rapid industrialization coupled with rigid controls on the population.

The sudden end of Soviet aid and trade hit Albania hard, Hoxha later admitting that the years 1961 to 1965 were the most difficult he ever faced. The Chinese came to the rescue with an aid package of $132 million and some six thousand advisors who continued Soviet-backed projects such as the construction of a new steel-processing complex at Elbasan. The Chinese were different patrons to the Soviets. Chinese advisors did not enjoy or expect differential wage levels and they left many more decisions in the hands of locals. The APL, however, did not change and as after the breach with Yugoslavia a shift in external alignment once again brought savage internal repression. In 1961 ten senior party figures were arrested and, as with Xoxe in 1948, this was the prelude to a wide-ranging purge of those in both party and state machines suspected of retaining pro-Soviet sympathies.

During the pro-Chinese period Albanian agriculture was fully collectivized by linking the clannish, parochial and frequently Catholic communities of the northern hills with existing, lowland cooperatives. In the 1970s private animal rearing was banned, livestock brought into the collective system and the private plots reduced in size. In 1981, after the Chinese period, even peasant markets were banned in an attempt to eliminate private trading in food-stuffs produced on the private plots.

The extension of collectivization had also brought reforms which offered individual collective farms and industrial enterprises more responsibility and, in theory at least, greater freedom of action. This was part of the general anti-bureaucratic, decentralizing process of the cultural revolution. Albania's cultural revolution began with an 'open letter' from the central committee to all APL members in March 1966. It attacked the evils of Soviet-style bureaucracy and called for uninterrupted revolution on Maoist lines. In response the leadership reduced the number of central ministries, that of justice being among those abolished, and the staffs of the surviving departments were reduced. The remaining bureaucrats were required to spend at least one month per year doing manual labour, usually in the countryside. In reality the anti-bureaucratic campaign had no lasting effect and even by the early 1970s the number of civil servants was rising and the fact that many of them were party members meant that the gap between the population at large and the party, a gap which the cultural revolution had been meant to narrow, was widening.

Equality as well as a reduction in bureaucracy had been an objective of the cultural revolution. To this end ranks were abolished in the armed forces and in February 1967 a campaign was initiated to end the subjugation of women and extirpate traditional practices such as arranged marriages. There is little doubt that women played an increasing role in public affairs, but in the domestic context entrenched attitudes were harder to overcome, and even after the cultural revolution women still made up over half the agricultural labour force.

The most notable change brought about by the cultural revolution was the alleged abolition of religion in Albania. Hoxha considered religious belief to be a major cause of Albania's backwardness, not least because it encouraged, he said, the subjugation of women. When the campaign for liberating women was launched therefore there was a simultaneous assault on organized religion. By the end of 1967 over two thousand religious buildings had been closed and Hoxha proclaimed that Albania had become the world's first atheist state. The former religious buildings, unless they were of great historic significance, were turned into warehouses, leisure centres or cinemas. As part of the anti-religious movement parents were encouraged to give their children non-religious names and when this did not prove to be wildly popular the government resorted to force and issued a decree ordering all Albanians to assume secular names. Few seem to have bothered, especially among the 'former' Muslims who had made up 70 per cent of the population.

A notable change which occurred during rather than because of the cultural revolution was the decision in 1972 to adopt the southern Albanian, or Tosk, dialect as the language's standard literary form. Hoxha and most of the communist leadership were southerners, as had been the majority of those who had launched the Albanian national revival in the late nineteenth and early twentieth centuries.

The cultural revolution also brought increased restriction on access to western publications and media. Almost no foreign material was allowed into the country, except from China, and Albanians suspected of tuning in to western or East European radio stations could face heavy punishment.

Suspicion of external influences, the Chinese excepted, was reflected in the new constitution enacted in 1976, after a similar step had been taken in the PRC. Albania was declared a people's socialist republic rather than merely a people's republic. The workers were said to exercise control over the administration, the economy and the social organizations, that control being exercised through the workers' party, the APL, whose leading role the constitution recognized. The constitution also declared that the Albanian economy was to be based on self-reliance with aid being taken only from other socialist states, the taking of loans from capitalist or revisionist sources being explicitly forbidden. The foundations of religious belief were declared to have been abolished. For individual citizens the usual rights were guaranteed but they were restricted by clauses insisting that they could only be exercised if they did not conflict with a citizen's duty to the socialist order. The right to own personal property was limited to wages, homes and items for personal or family use, a definition which did not include personal automobiles.

There were some aspects of the Chinese cultural revolution which Hoxha did not embrace. The Albanian cultural revolution was never one from below; there were no Red Guards, the 'workers' control movement' being a sham in which party-controlled workers' units simply ensured that the party's orders were being carried out: the tide of radicalism was not allowed to flood through the sacred portals of the party. Nor was the cultural revolution popular. Bureaucrats and managers disliked it not only for its attack on them but also for the dislocation it caused in the administration and the economy. The under-30s, who made up two thirds of the population, resented the enhanced restrictions on dress or personal appearance which came with prohibitions on miniskirts for women and long hair and beards for men.

More serious was the effect of the cultural revolution on the army. Professional soldiers did not welcome the abolition of ranks and they were suspicious of Hoxha's remarks on the desirability of a 'people's army' as opposed to the existing élite, trained body responsible to the general staff. The professionals' fears were increased by the invasion of Czechoslovakia in 1968. After that Hoxha was convinced that the greatest danger facing Albania was Soviet dominance, either by invasion or subversion. To avert these dangers all Albanians were required to join local volunteer defence units, much like those being set up at the same time in Yugoslavia. To the professional soldiers such a 'nation in arms' policy meant passing control of the country's forces from the general staff to the party hierarchy. The tension reached such a level that a number of leading army officers and the minister of defence were accused of plotting to overthrow the regime. In October 1974 they were tried and executed. Shehu became minister of defence as well as prime minister, and in 1976 the new constitution decreed that the party leader was henceforth to be chief of staff and chairman of the defence committee which controlled the army.

The issue of defence was one of a number which underlay a gradual decline in the warmth of Albania's relations with China. The PRC was clearly too far distant for it to be able to offer any form of military guarantee to Albania but the Albanians were further concerned because by the early 1970s it was becoming clear their interests would count for little in the formulation of Chinese policy. The Chinese had hoped that other communist parties in Europe would join the APL in an anti-Soviet bloc, but when the most likely candidate for such action, Romania, refused to break fully with Moscow the Chinese knew that such hopes were not to be fulfilled. The Chinese also pressed on Albania the uncomfortable truth that, in view of the aggression shown by the USSR towards Czechoslovakia in 1968, Albania would be better off in cooperation rather than conflict with Yugoslavia. This unwelcome advice was followed; diplomatic relations were restored between Belgrade and Tirana in 1971 and Albania formally withdrew from the Warsaw pact. Ambassadors were also exchanged with Greece.

Most offensive of all to the Albanian leadership, however, was the apparent reconciliation between China and the USA, symbolized by President Nixon's visit to Peking in February 1972. The Albanians were soon being told by Peking that they should not rely solely upon China and, if necessary, should seek aid from the west. This the proud Hoxha would not do. Relations continued to deteriorate with the Chinese now pressing Albania to start paying the interest on its accumulated debt to the PRC, much of which derived from the huge imbalance in trade between the two states. This Hoxha could not do. The break came in the following year. When the seventh congress of the APL met in November 1976 the Chinese comrades were not invited to attend. This studied insult would have been unlikely had Mao not died in September. His dogmatism had in some ways helped the Albanians but with his more pragmatic successors in office there was little reason for the Albanians to believe the Chinese would provide any further assistance. The peculiar alliance between tiny, European Albania and the Asiatic communist giant no longer had any useful purpose for either side. In July 1978 Chinese aid was stopped altogether, Chinese advisors were recalled and Albanian students in China were sent home.

THE PERIOD OF ISOLATION, 1978-91

For a dozen years after the official break with China Albania remained in isolation. Having tried association with revisionist Yugoslavia, the orthodox

Soviet Union, and radical China, the Albanian communists had no one left in the socialist world with whom to align. Hoxha, who would never contemplate diluting socialism, had to strike out on his own. In doing so he was helped by the fact that by mid-1970s Albania had become self-sufficient in grain, oil and electricity.

Not surprisingly, a change in external alignment, or in this case the rejection of all alignments, produced the by now traditional purge. What was surprising this time was the identity of the chief victim. Mehmet Shehu had been Hoxha's right-hand man since 1948 and had accumulated great power as prime minister, minister of the interior and minister of defence. In 1980 he relinquished his post as minister of defence. In December 1981 it was announced that he had committed suicide following a nervous collapse. This seemed improbable. A veteran of the Spanish civil war and a partisan commander in the Second World War Shehu had suffered and survived many crises and seemed an unlikely candidate for suicide. Rumours were soon circulating in Tirana that in fact Shehu had been shot at a politburo meeting, possibly by Hoxha himself.★ Soon after Shehu's death his wife was put away for twenty years in a penal colony and a purge of the secret police was conducted to remove Shehu's supporters. Hoxha then announced that Shehu had been a secret agent working for an improbable if not unholy alliance of the Vatican, the British and the Americans.

If post-1978 Albania could be without a direct patron it could not remain unresponsive to the major changes then taking place in the Balkans. The improvement in relations with Yugoslavia which had followed the Soviet invasion of Czechoslovakia had progressed steadily but it was impaired by the Kosovo unrest early in 1981. There was no question of Albania incorporating Kosovo into its own borders; not only would that throw the Balkans into turmoil but it would also upset the internal Albanian balance between the northern Ghegs and the southern Tosks, the Kosovan Albanians being mainly Gheg. In fact the Kosovo question posed a dilemma for Hoxha. He did not want to incite greater Albanian feelings in Kosovo but on the other hand his party was committed to the cultural unity of the Albanian nation. At the eighth APL congress in November 1981 he therefore stated that Albania recognized the justice of Kosovo's calls for republican status within Yugoslavia but had no territorial claim on Yugoslavia and recognized the sanctity of existing borders.

★ Shehu's body was discovered on 21 July 2001 'near the Erzen River in the village of Ndroq between Tirana and the Adriatic. Shehu's wife, Fiqirete, died in a communist labour camp in 1988, and his eldest son committed suicide. Shehu's two surviving sons had looked for their father's grave since the fall of communism in 1991. They plan to rebury him in a Tirana cemetery next to his wife. Mehmet Shehu was long regarded as Hoxha's right-hand man. The circumstances of his death in December 1981 remain a mystery.' Radio Free Europe/Radio Liberty Newsline, vol. 05, no. 137, Part II, 23 July 2001.

After 1981 the Kosovo issue disappeared for the time being from the international arena. On 11 April 1985 Hoxha, who had been growing increasingly ill during the 1980s, did likewise. His successor was Ramiz Alia, a young northerner from Shkoder, who had taken over many of Shehu's responsibilities in 1980.

When Enver Hoxha was buried Albanians watching the ceremony on television witnessed an amazing sight: an old lady standing near the graveside crossing herself. It was a sign both that religious modes of thought had not been eradicated and that people were not afraid to acknowledge them. If Hoxhaism was so superficial the new regime could expect demands for change, the more so given the intensifying pressure for radical reform in other socialist states.

In many respects the new regime welcomed change, not least in escaping from isolation. Alia immediately began to seek new contacts in Europe, turning first to his Balkan neighbours. Relations with Greece were eased in 1987 when Athens decided to end the state of war between Greece and Albania, though this did not dispose of the questions of the Greek minority in Albania or of the Greek claim to southern Albania. At the same time, the Kosovo issue stood in the way of a full rapprochement with Yugoslavia. Despite these inhibiting factors Albania attended the conference of Balkan foreign ministers in Belgrade in February 1988.

By now the new regime was seeking to establish closer contact with parts of the world beyond the Balkans. Major economic gain was expected from the establishment of diplomatic relations with the FRG in 1987, after Franz Josef Strauss had paid 'private' visits to Albania in 1984, 1986 and 1987. The pace of Albania's integration into the world system quickened markedly at the turn of the decade. In May 1990 the UN Secretary General, Javier Pérez de Cuellar, visited the country; in July diplomatic relations with the Soviet Union were restored and in November friendly messages were exchanged with Peking. In September–October Alia visited the United States but diplomatic relations with Washington were not to be established until March 1991 when the Americans were satisfied that political pluralism had been introduced in the country. In May 1991 official links were restored between Britain and Albania after a settlement had been reached over the Corfu Channel incident of 1946. Albania had returned to the international community.

In internal affairs the Alia regime was less willing to abandon Hoxhaist principles, most notably the monopoly of power enjoyed by the APL. But it could not withstand the pressures of 1989 in the socialist world. Ismail Kadare, Albania's most famous novelist, and no enemy of the regime, criticized the government for interfering in literature while other voices were raised over Albania's record on civil rights. In response the government amnestied a number of political prisoners but then, early in 1991, struck back using the Sigurimi to suppress protests on the streets of Shkoder, while a party plenum in the same month insisted that though economic reform would be granted there would be no change in the leading role of the party.

This was the beginning of a process under which grudging concession alternated with attempted coercion, but it was the former which advanced the further as public pressure grew stronger, being expressed in demonstrations, strikes and attempted mass emigration. In May 1990 religious practice was allowed, and by the end of the year the ministry of justice had been restored, the penal code reformed to reduce the large number of capital offences, and the APL had finally agreed to the formation of alternative political parties and multi-party elections. New parties appeared rapidly, the most important being the Democratic Party of Albania (DPA) established on 19 December 1990.

The appearance of new parties did not end the see-sawing between coercion and concession. In December 1990 150 people were sent to gaol, some for as long as 20 years, for their part in recent disturbances, but the opposition was no longer cowed by such acts, and the government was soon forced into further concessions. In the early months of 1991 these included the right to Muslim worship, together with the right to own cars, wear beards and to run private businesses. The remaining political prisoners were released and in January strikes and demonstrations persuaded the government to bow to opposition demands and postpone the elections scheduled for February until March to give the new parties more time to prepare. In February students demonstrated vigorously against the continuation of examinations in Marxism-Leninism and in favour of renaming Tirana's 'Enver Hoxha' University. They succeeded on both accounts and also toppled the statue of the former dictator in the centre of the capital, that of Stalin having been removed some months before. The student demonstrators had been attacked by police using tanks and the military were again in action to prevent further mass escapes by sea to Italy after 20,000 had fled in March.

The oppositionists alleged that the government had encouraged the exodus in March in order to deprive them of votes in the elections which were held on 31 March and 7 and 14 April. The government won a convincing victory at the polls, the APL taking 60 per cent of the vote and 169 of the 250 seats in the assembly. The DPA had 75 seats, The National Veterans' Committee 1 and Omonia, the defender of the Greek ethnic minority, 5. The APL victory had been won not because of the exodus of March but because, like the former communist parties in Bulgaria and Romania, it commanded the loyalty, and the fear, of the rural voters. In the towns the oppositionists reigned supreme with Ramiz Alia even failing to secure his own Tirana constituency.

The Albanian communists had not been removed from power. But it was a very different Albania. It was one which had growing links to the outside world; it was one which had toppled the statues of Stalin and Hoxha; and it was one in which the communists had had to fight an election against other parties. Albania had again set out on the road to transition. The direction was different but the going was to be no easier.

Note

1. Jon Haliday (ed.), *The Artful Albanian: The Memoirs of Enver Hoxha*, London: Chatto & Windus, 1986, p.327. Haliday quotes from Nikita Khrushchev, *Khrushchev Remembers*, vol. i, translated and edited by Strobe Talbott, with an introduction, commentary and notes by Edward Crankshaw, London: André Deutsch, 1971, p.476.

Chapter 10

BULGARIA, 1948–1989

THE STALINIST PERIOD, 1948–54

Even before their fifth congress in December 1948 the Bulgarian communists had begun the socialization and even the sovietization of their country. Most branches of public life were refashioned, usually with the help of soviet advisors and nearly always on the Soviet pattern.

The chief focus of reforming activity was the economy. There had been moves towards greater government control of industry after 1944 but it was not until December 1947 that the regime felt confident enough to take into public ownership the six thousand enterprises still in private hands. At the same time Bulgaria's thirty-two banks were merged into the Central Bank and in February 1948 a government monopoly over foreign trade was established. By 1948 Dimitrov's government felt confident enough to move towards the collectivization of agriculture. Collective farms (TKZSs)★ had been introduced in April 1945 but membership was voluntary and it was only after the destruction of political agrarianism that the regime dared to take forcible measures to drive the peasants into the collectives. In February 1948 all privately owned farm machinery was confiscated and handed to the new Machine Tractor Stations (MTSs). There were also fiscal pressures to persuade peasants to join the TKZSs and by the end of the year the number of these had risen to 1,100, above the government's target of 800. The process of collectivization was to continue until full collectivization was declared in 1958.

Meanwhile, Bulgaria's economy was increasingly linked to that of the Soviet Union. By 1948 joint Soviet-Bulgarian companies had been established for civil aviation, lead and zinc processing, uranium extraction, the construction industry and shipbuilding, and in 1949 Bulgaria was a founding member of Comecon. Until the early 1950s Soviet trading practices frequently militated

---

★ Technically the Bulgarian farms were cooperative rather than collective farms until 1968. Their functioning, however, was little different from the collectives found elsewhere in the socialist bloc and the term collective has been used here to distinguish between those holdings and other forms of cooperative organization.

against Bulgarian interests because Moscow purchased goods at 1935 prices and sold them at current values usually for convertible currency; immediately after the war, for example, the Soviets were buying Bulgarian rose oil at $110 per kilo and selling it on the world market for $1,200 per kilo.

Much of the economic reform process in Bulgaria had been improvised or opportunist, the 1947 two-year plan giving little more than general guidelines to producers. This changed with the fifth congress of the BWP/BCP in December 1948. Here precise and detailed orders were drawn up which were then codified in Bulgaria's first five-year plan which was to come into effect in 1949.

Economic restructuring, and above all collectivization, caused bitter hostility to the regime. Peasants in the north-west of the country took to arms in an attempt to resist being forced into the collectives and elsewhere they protested by slaughtering livestock or damaging machines rather than allow them to pass into general ownership. A further cause of anger was that the collectivization process drove many people off the land into towns. This was intentional, collectivization being meant to create the new urban proletariat which was required to provide the workforce for the new industrial concerns. The problem was that few towns were capable of absorbing this sudden influx. In the north-eastern region of the Dobrudja, the richest agricultural area in the country, collectivization produced a mass emigration movement amongst the local population which had a high percentage of ethnic Turks. This too was intentional. In January 1950 the regime announced that a quarter of a million ethnic Turks would be allowed to emigrate; this was more than the Turkish government could cope with and in 1952 it closed its borders after 162,000 ethnic Turks had entered the country from Bulgaria.

The departure of the Turks eased but did not solve the problem of social distress which the government contained in true Stalinist fashion by purging the party and all social organizations. In the party the major victims were branded as Trotskyites and Titoists. The first among them was Traicho Kostov, a popular communist who had spent the war inside Bulgaria, most of it in prison. In March 1949 he was removed from his government and party posts and made director of the National Library. Soon he was arrested and in December put on trial, found guilty of absurd charges and executed. In the following years thousands of party members were punished by expulsion from the party, imprisonment and in some cases execution. Equal numbers of non-party members suffered similar fates.

The purges affected institutions as well as individuals. After its incumbent head, the Exarch Stefan, had been packed off to a monastery priests in the Bulgarian Orthodox Church were required to join the party-dominated Union of Bulgarian Priests; those who did not were usually sent to a labour camp. In 1951 the Church's already tenuous links with the Ecumenical Patriarchate in Istanbul were finally severed when the status of the Bulgarian Church was raised to that of a fully independent patriarchate. The Protestant and Roman

Catholic churches, which had much stronger links with the outside world, suffered much greater persecution; in 1949 the government refused permission for the newly nominated apostolic legate to take up his post in Sofia and the backbone of the Protestant churches was broken when a high-profile trial sentenced fifteen of their leading pastors to long terms of imprisonment.

The fall of Kostov had coincided with a change in the leadership of the BCP. Dimitrov, who had been ill since his return from the Soviet Union, died in July 1949 and the heir presumptive, Vasil Kolarov, was already mortally ill. Dimitrov's eventual successor was Vŭlko Chervenkov who revelled in the nickname of 'Bulgaria's Little Stalin'. It was Chervenkov who presided over the purges.

Chervenkov's position was threatened by the death of Stalin in 1953. The New Course required the satellite states to separate party and state offices and thus at the BCP's sixth congress Chervenkov, at Khrushchev's insistence, relinquished the leadership of the party which went to a young apparatchik, Todor Zhivkov. The New Course bought other changes to Bulgaria. The terror was relaxed and some prisoners were released from the gaols and the labour camps. Many of the Soviet advisors who had overseen the sovietization of Bulgaria returned home and the joint stock companies were dissolved. In external affairs the New Course brought about the restoration of diplomatic relations with Yugoslavia, a relaxation of tension with Greece, and even talk of overcoming the gulf which had opened up between Sofia and Washington.

Chervenkov's relinquishing of power had been apparent rather than real. Behind the scenes he continued to pull the strings, Zhivkov later admitting that at this time he was no more than a puppet. It was Khrushchev's rehabilitation of Tito and the speech to the twentieth congress of the CPSU in February 1956 which undermined Chervenkov whose claim to legitimacy rested largely on his extirpation of the Titoists within the BCP. A special plenum of the BCP central committee in April 1956 denounced the cult of personality and Chervenkov resigned to be replaced as prime minister by Anton Yugov. For the next three decades the 'April Line' with its rejection of the cult of personality and of 'socialist deformations' was to be regarded as the guiding principle of the BCP. It was also closely associated with the name of Todor Zhivkov.

THE RISE OF TODOR ZHIVKOV, 1954–65

It was significant that the report which Zhivkov had presented to the April plenum which formed the basis of the 'April Line' had been drawn up in close consultation with the Soviet ambassador in Sofia.* Zhivkov's total

---

* Until the end of Zhivkov's rule in November 1989 the protocols of and report to the April plenum were kept secret in a safe which needed nine separate keys to open it.

dependence on the Soviet Union was to become the main characteristic of his regime, and it was to be one of the major reasons both for his rise to power and for his descent therefrom.

In the years immediately after the April plenum Zhivkov's hold on power was far from secure. In 1961, when Khrushchev launched his second and far more vitriolic attack on Stalin and Stalinism, Chervenkov was finally removed from the arena, but this only emphasized the potential power of Yugov. Yugov had a justified reputation as a tough man. He had been minister of the interior from 1944 to 1949 and as deputy prime minister in 1953 he had dealt severely with striking tobacco workers in Plovdiv. As prime minister after 1956 he was an obvious potential alternative leader and he made political capital out of a number of Zhivkov's mistakes, particularly the latter's mishandling of agriculture which led in the early 1960s to Bulgaria having to import food from the west. Yugov's faction also criticized Zhivkov's patron, Khrushchev, for his adventurism in Cuba and for alienating the Chinese communists. This did nothing to shake Zhivkov's dependence on Moscow which in 1962 was displayed in dramatic fashion. The eighth congress of the BCP had been due to meet in August but was postponed until November because of the food crisis. Shortly before the congress a central committee plenum was called during which Zhivkov made a sudden and unannounced trip to Moscow, returning a couple of days later to inform an astounded audience that Yugov had been removed from the politburo and sacked as prime minister. Zhivkov now packed the party and state administrations with his own supporters. Two years later his hold on the party was secure enough for him to survive the fall of his sponsor in Moscow.

Musical chairs at the top of the party and the government may have given Zhivkov control of both state and party apparatuses but this did not mean that opposition was entirely eliminated. The country was suffering, not for the last time, from ill-thought out reforms foisted on the economy by Zhivkov and his supporters. In 1958, having boasted that Bulgaria had become the first country after the Soviet Union to achieve the full collectivization of agriculture, the number of collective farms was reduced by forming huge new combines. In 1960 the 'Zhivkov Theses' showed how the economy was to achieve ludicrous growth rates; the schemes were abandoned in 1963 but only after the economy had suffered considerable damage. Nor did bureaucrats take easily to the ruling that they must all spend a certain period each year working in a factory or on a collective farm to prevent them from losing touch with the proletariat.

Some of these notions gave the impression that Bulgaria was staging its own Chinese-style cultural revolution but Zhivkov, as ever, was borrowing from the Soviet rather than the Chinese example. There were, however, some Bulgarian opponents of Zhivkov who were prepared to learn at least partially from Peking. The Bulgarian army had not intervened effectively in politics since the coup of 1934 but by the mid-1960s there were some soldiers who were prepared to do so again. A conspiracy was hatched among a number of senior officers, many of whom seemed disappointed in their post-1944 careers. They were critical of the *embourgeoisement* of Bulgarian socialism and were imbued with vague and ill-formed notions of Stalinism, Maoism and a desire for greater independence from Moscow on the Romanian or even the Yugoslav pattern. Their plan was to overthrow Zhivkov at a central committee meeting but they were doomed to failure. The secret police had wind of the plot in its earliest stages and, having planted a microphone in the cap badge of one of the leading conspirators, could follow every stage of the conspiracy in minutest detail. A small number of leading plotters were executed and hundreds of officials in the ministry of the interior were sacked; thereafter Zhivkov allowed no one but his most trusted acolytes to have a dominant influence in the police or the army.

ZHIVKOV ASCENDANT, 1965–81

For a decade and a half after the military plot Zhivkov's domination of Bulgaria was absolute. The main characteristic of his rule, subservience to the Soviet Union, remained unchanged but by the end of the 1970s he was facing increasingly intractable problems in the economy.

After the fall of Khrushchev Zhivkov rapidly established good relations with Brezhnev to whom he remained as doggedly loyal as he had been to Khrushchev. In this he was helped to a considerable degree by the fact that an official in the Bulgarian embassy in Moscow showered gifts on Brezhnev's daughter and other members of the leader's circle of intimates; in return the official received valuable inside information on the latest twists and turns in Kremlin policies and personal relationships. Relations between the two party leaders were particularly close in the early 1970s, Zhivkov declaring in September 1973 that Bulgaria and the Soviet Union would 'act as a single body, breathing with the same lungs and nourished by the same bloodstream'. It was also in the early 1970s that Zhivkov proposed secretly that Bulgaria become a constituent republic of the USSR. Brezhnev rejected the idea as being diplomatically too complicated; Khrushchev had rejected a similar proposal on the more down-to-earth argument that Zhivkov just wanted to improve Bulgaria's standard of living.

Many Bulgarians, most dramatically the military conspirators of 1965, found Bulgarian subservience to the Soviet Union demeaning and distasteful. But it also paid dividends. In diplomatic terms Zhivkov persuaded Brezhnev to remain neutral in Bulgarian-Yugoslav debates over Macedonia, this being a reversal of the traditional Russian and Soviet stance in these disputes. In material terms the close links to the USSR brought considerable advantages, at least in the short term. Bulgaria, unlike Romania, did not reject Soviet plans for economic specialization within the socialist bloc and by an agreement of 1965 was allowed to assemble cars and lorries made in the Soviet

Union. Bulgaria thereafter specialized in the production of certain types of commercial vehicle, especially fork-lift trucks, and in the 1970s emerged as Comecon's main producer of certain computer components such as magnetic disks. In general, close trading associations with the Comecon states and especially the Soviet Union gave Bulgaria a secure market for its agricultural produce and for its low-quality manufactured goods. More importantly, it also provided Bulgaria with a source of cheap raw materials, especially oil and petroleum products. Bulgaria has little in the way of fossil fuels and its industry and economic growth were much helped in the short run by being able not only to buy Soviet oil and petrol at discounted prices but by being able to re-export some of what it received for hard currency. Soviet indulgence towards Bulgaria was a major reason why Bulgarian living standards were able to rise steadily in the 1960s and for most of the 1970s.

Zhivkov's subservience to Moscow was mostly in the external sector. After the slavish adoption of the Soviet system in the late 1940s and early 1950s, Bulgaria was prepared to undertake a number of internal reform, some of which did not follow the Soviet pattern. They were usually disastrous, as had been the case with the Zhivkov Theses which Khrushchev had criticized as revisionist. Zhivkov introduced further reforms in 1965, this time aiming for large-scale decentralization of the economy. These were abandoned after events in Czechoslovakia in 1968 had shown how economic reforms might get out of hand, but in 1969 a further experiment was introduced in agriculture. Once again a number of collectives were amalgamated, this time to form Agro-Industrial Complexes (AICs) which were to concentrate on a small number of crops which the local conditions favoured, and which in some cases were to undertake the industrial processing of those crops. These ideas owed something to Soviet experiments but they were taken further and lasted longer, the AICs remaining in place until the end of communist rule. They enjoyed a modicum of success, especially in the early days.

Economic reform and the rise in the standard of living did not bring political change. The Czechoslovak lesson of 1968 was quickly learned in Bulgaria where the party insisted upon 'iron discipline' within its ranks and a tightening of its hold on society as a whole. Zhivkov still kept a very close eye on his colleagues, frequently moving leading party and state officials from one post to another lest they accumulate too much power. Nor was he above the occasional dismissal. In May 1977 a leading politburo member, Boris Velchev, was sacked and in the following months 38,500 were expelled from the party in what was the largest purge conducted during Zhivkov's rule. Velchev's sin seems to have been his willingness to contemplate more liberal policies at home; his fall and the subsequent purge served to warn Bulgarians not to expect too much either from détente with the west or from the Helsinki agreements of 1975.

A more sinister warning was issued to Bulgarian exiles in September 1977 when Georgi Markov, a freelance journalist who had once been a member of Zhivkov's charmed inner circle, died after being injected with a poisoned pellet while standing at a bus stop in London; two weeks later a similar attack was made upon Vladimir Kostov in Paris, though Kostov survived. Markov's transgression had been to spill the beans on *la dolce vita* at the top of the BCP; Kostov's had been to reveal the extent to which the Soviet Union dominated every aspect of Bulgarian affairs, including the secret police for whom he had worked. These acts of vengeance, however, were taken against declared opponents and in general police activity was reactive rather than pro-active; Bulgarians under Zhivkov lived in a controlled, restrictive and authoritarian system, but they no longer had to endure a reign of terror.

The country and the party had clearly evolved from the early days of communist rule and to mark that evolution both a new constitution and a new party programme were adopted in 1971. The new constitution declared Bulgaria to be a socialist state headed by its working class. The leading role of the BCP was recognized, as was Bulgaria's membership of the socialist community. A new body was established, the state council, which was to have legislative and executive powers, and whose chairperson was to be head of state, that person being, of course, Todor Zhivkov. The party programme declared that the 'April Line' still provided its basic guidance but now that socialism had been achieved by the construction of a socially owned industrial infrastructure and the collectivization of agriculture, the party's task was to organize the construction of 'mature socialism' by applying 'the scientific-technological revolution'. Mature socialism was to evolve and develop in 'a unified socialist society'. The latter was portrayed as the bringing together of town and country and of intelligentsia and proletariat, but it was also to mean ethnic homogenization.

Before that was to become widely known a new figure flitted across Bulgaria's political stage. Zhivkov's daughter, Liudmila Zhivkova, was arguably the most extraordinary personality in the leading circles of any post-Stalinist East European state. Brought up in an intensely privileged manner she had even spent an academic year at St Antony's College, Oxford, where her arrival caused some bemusement as no one had realized who she was. She made her mark soon after she left Oxford and in 1971 was appointed as deputy chairperson of the committee for culture and art, becoming its chairperson in 1975. In the following year she was placed in charge of the media and in 1980 was made head of the politburo's commission on science, culture and art. Long before she attained such high office she had become the darling of the intelligentsia, holding regular séances each Friday evening in her apartment. Her company and her patronage exhilarated the Sofia intelligentsia. She had little interest in Marxism or the party and was anxious to stress Bulgaria's cultural individuality. In private she was prepared to admit to overt anti-Soviet feelings, telling one associate that 'We made a great historical mistake when we allied ourselves to the most uncivilized country in the world'.[1] Her own real interest was in mysticism. In the later 1970s she visited India and was rumoured to have disappeared for days to live alone in a cave and commune with the higher spirits. Some of her later pronouncements bordered on the absurd, such as her assertions that Bulgaria would become the cultural centre of the world and that by 1990 the world would be speaking Bulgarian, or her statement that she saw herself as a resurrected mediaeval Bulgarian saint or even as a reincarnation of Jesus Christ. However bizarre, such ideas were attractive because they were a world apart from the dry Marxism which was the daily bread of most of the intelligentsia. Furthermore, Zhivkova offered protection. Within two hours of informing Zhivkov that he had found compromising material concerning one of Liudmila's close associates the head of the relevant department of the secret police was clearing his desk.

In addition to providing variety and the freedom to flirt with non-Marxist lines of thought, Zhivkova also provided a sense of enhanced national pride. It was much needed. Subservience to the Soviet Union had depressed Bulgaria's stock in the socialist bloc and in the west, and to this had been added the disgrace of the Markov/Kostov allegations which, no matter how strenuously the government denied them, were widely believed to be true. There were other accusations: that Bulgaria had been producing and selling counterfeit whisky, that it had been supplying arms to terrorists and buying those arms with the proceeds of government-sponsored drug smuggling, and that Bulgarian agents had been involved in the plot to kill the pope in 1981. Bulgaria needed relief from such a relentlessly bad press, and Zhivkova provided it. In 1981 she staged an international jamboree to celebrate the 1,300[th] anniversary of the first Bulgarian state, a celebration which implicitly indicated that Bulgaria had been a state before Russia had been born; and when she marked the anniversary of Bulgaria's conversion to Christianity the Bulgarians were again conscious that they had joined Europe's dominant religious community before the Russians. When Zhivkova died in 1981 at the age of only 39 many Bulgarians assumed, wrongly, that she had been murdered by the Soviets.

THE DECLINE AND FALL OF TODOR ZHIVKOV, 1981–9

The death of Liudmila Zhivkova coincided with the beginning of a rapid decline in her father's fortunes. There were major problems in the economy which were compounded by incessant administrative reforms, and Zhivkov plunged his country into international disgrace by adopting repressive policies towards its Turkish minority.

The eighth five-year plan, introduced in 1981, marked a new note of caution, predicting a modest overall growth in the economy of 20 per cent. The seventh five-year plan had planned for growth at 45 per cent which had not been achieved. The transition from extensive to intensive development was proving much more difficult than anticipated partly because, as all East European states were learning, the pace of that revolution was outstripping the capability of a planned economy to cope with it. There were also political obstacles to rapid economic restructuring. In the 1980s the United States insisted under the Cocom (The Coordinating Committee for Multilateral Export Controls) scheme that its trading partners observe restrictions on their commerce with communist countries which were not to receive goods which might help enhance their military capability; this definition included computer hard- and software. But even if these hurdles were overcome, as they frequently were, there were still internal obstacles in an authoritarian system. An anecdotal instance of this illustrates the difficulties involved. A Bulgarian working in a state enterprise producing computer software recalled that colleagues managed to 'come by' a copy of a secret American software programme; all programmers in the enterprise were desperate to see the purloined document to advance their own programme designing. But they had to wait. The enterprise had only one photocopier and the party secretary refused to allow anyone to use that machine out of hours or when he was not there to supervise them lest they use the opportunity to copy subversive literature.[2]

Bulgaria, like other states, was also having increasing difficulties in trading with the west in non-sensitive commodities, and such trade was increasingly necessary as debt burdens and trade deficits mounted. The problem was in the first place the general one that the oil price increases of 1979 had decreased the west's ability to purchase, and in the second place the specific one that Bulgaria's industrial produce was not good enough to meet western demands while its primary and semi-manufactured exports – food, processed food and wine – were the very commodities that western Europe already had in abundance.

Radical attempts to address the economic problem began in March 1979 when a central committee plenum adopted the so-called New Economic Mechanism (NEM) which was applied to the entire economy in 1982. The NEM was to provide 'a new approach to the management of the economy in the scientific-technological revolution'. Five principles underlay this new approach. First, decentralization which would allow much greater freedom to enterprises which would henceforth receive from the central planning agencies only general guidelines rather than detailed production quotas. Second, 'mobilization from below' which decreed that officials within an enterprise were to be elected rather than nominated by local communist party officials. Third, individual enterprises were to be required to find their own investments and would if necessary have to compete with one another in that search; enterprises were also to compete for labour, adjusting wage levels in the process. Fourth, enterprises were also to be required to find their own sources of raw materials and their own markets, rather than relying on central authorities to do this for them. And fifth, plants which did not make a profit were not to be guaranteed subsidies from central government funds.

The purpose of the NEM was to raise productivity, to improve the quality of production and to increase industrial democracy. It did not enjoy conspicuous success. In 1983 Zhivkov railed on TV and radio at the appalling state of Bulgarian industrial produce, citing, among many other available examples, a baked-bean factory which produced thousands of cans full of nothing but water. In March 1984 a special party conference, an unusual event, was convened to address the problem of the quality of production.

The NEM could have had greater success had the Bulgarian economy not been so burdened by debt, but the need to service these debts meant that the first call on any hard currency earned was to service the debt rather than to buy modern machinery from the west. The economic problems were to intensify in the second half of the 1980s, as were efforts to address them. But by then other problems had also arisen to plague Bulgaria's communist rulers.

In the 1980s the country opened itself ever more to western influence. It had little choice. Western radio, television and above all audio and video cassettes could not be kept out of the country, particularly as more Bulgarians were travelling to the west and more westerners were visiting Bulgaria. These media showed the contrast between the ever-more relaxed west and the relaxing, but still conformity-ridden Bulgaria. By the end of the decade the intelligentsia and particularly the youth of Bulgaria, like those elsewhere in the Soviet imperium, had lost their parents' fear of or respect for the authorities.

There was one issue in which the regime had itself done much to fritter away its legitimacy in the eyes of its own intelligentsia and those of many external observers. The call in the 1971 BCP programme for the creation of a 'unified socialist society' could be interpreted in ethnic terms. That nationalism could be a popular rallying cry had been proved by Liudmila but her nationalism had been cultural not ethnic and it had been combined with covert anti-Sovietism and overt liberalism in ideological affairs. Her father could adopt nationalism but he could not, he believed, divorce himself from the Kremlin nor could he afford to relax his ideological controls. If Zhivkov could not break away from the Kremlin he could not express Bulgarian nationalism through an independent stance in foreign policy; nationalism therefore had to be exercised at home. That came to mean a crude and eventually disastrous campaign to force the country's ethnic Turkish minority, about a tenth of the population, to abandoned their Turkish characteristics.

Assimilationist pressures had been applied to smaller groups earlier in communist rule. Gypsy or Roma identity had been allowed, even encouraged, in the post-war years with a gypsy theatre in Sofia which was renowned throughout the Balkans. This, together with gypsy language textbooks had disappeared by the late 1960s. So too had any official recognition of a Macedonian identity in Bulgaria, the category 'Macedonian' having been excised from the census of 1965. By the end of the 1960s all but one journal and newspaper published in Turkish had also disappeared. In the early 1970s there was a sustained campaign against the Pomaks, or Bulgarian-speaking Muslims. Local authorities in some areas had become alarmed when a number of Pomaks ceased to be Bulgarian-speaking and became Turcophone; they were then put under great pressure to take Bulgarian or Slav names and to stop speaking Turkish. Many who did not were sent to labour camps.

The Pomaks were told they were regaining a Bulgarian identity lost through forced conversion in the past. Initially this 'regenerative' process was applied mostly in areas of mixed population and only to Pomaks. In the early 1980s, however, it began to be applied in purely Pomak and then Turkish communities. Misled by reports that the process was progressing in an orderly fashion Zhivkov in 1984 backed that section of the leadership which wanted to impose the regenerative programme throughout the country. The Turks resisted and the Bulgarian army, including tank units and the crack red beret paratroopers, had to be deployed to enforce the government's policy; it was the largest operation carried out by the Bulgarian army since the end of the Second World War. In addition to being forced to adopt Bulgarian or Slav names the Turks lost their radio broadcasts, their remaining newspaper and all teaching in the Turkish language. But the assault was not merely against a sense of Turkish cultural identity. It was also against Islam. The adoption of a Muslim name is an important rite of passage for the Muslim adolescent and its denial was another instance of the state banning Muslim practices; in the recent past similar prohibitions had been placed on washing the dead and circumcision, while it had become almost impossible to make the pilgrimage to Mecca and many Muslim places of worship had been allowed to fall into disrepair.

Part of the original impulse to the regenerative process had come from below and its continuance and extension was not unpopular with many Bulgarians. There were those in the middle and upper echelons of the party and government who believed Islam was incapable of accommodating itself to the mores of mature socialism and to the demands of the scientific-cultural revolution. There were more Bulgarians who feared the high birth rate of the Turks would create enclaves in Bulgaria which might one day declare autonomy and then demand incorporation into the Turkish state, citing the example of northern Cyprus to justify their fears. But among others the regenerative process did incite hostility. In 1984 bombs were detonated at places which Zhivkov was due to visit, and placards appeared threatening 'Forty years, forty bombs'. Forty bombs were not exploded but in the final days of the Zhivkov regime the regenerative process was to alienate, in addition to Bulgarian Turks themselves, much of the Bulgarian intelligentsia and a powerful section of foreign opinion.

The regenerative process was at its height when another change took place which was to have profound effects on the Zhivkov regime: Mikhail Gorbachev became leader of the Soviet Union. As long as Brezhnev was in office Zhivkov could be confident that no Bulgarian communist would find support in the Kremlin for any attempt to stab him in the back. During the gerontocracy of the early 1980s he was equally safe in that no would-be conspirator could have had enough confidence in the Soviet leader's life expectancy to involve him in any plot. With the advent of Gorbachev neither restraint applied and even if the new Soviet leader made no move to topple Zhivkov, the latter could no longer be confident of support from Moscow against his domestic opponents.

Gorbachev's advent also meant a change in Soviet policies. For the Zhivkov regime one of the most significant was the decision to end subsidized oil and petrol sales to Bulgaria. The impact of this was not only that Bulgaria would now have to pay more for the energy it used; it also meant that it would no longer be able to earn foreign currency by re-exporting cheaply purchased Soviet crude and petrol. This had a huge impact on the entire economy because between 1975 and 1985 these re-exports had earned Bulgaria in the region of four billion dollars which had been used to subsidize non-profit making Bulgarian industries. The withdrawal of the disguised Soviet subsidy pulled another plank from beneath an already failing Bulgarian economy.

By the mid-1980s it was also obvious that the Bulgarian managerial cadres could not cope with the increased responsibilities which the NEM was placing upon them. This, plus the other mounting economic problems, brought about a series of attempts to create a new mentality in the productive enterprises. Central committee plena were held in February 1985 and January 1986 which, it was announced, would chart the change from bureaucratic to economic planning. In December 1986 yet another plenum moved further, this time insisting that the answer to Bulgaria's economic woes was to be found in self-management. The greatest changes, however, were introduced after the plenum of 28–29 July 1987. The object of attack in the July plenum was the party apparatus, especially its middle ranks which were to be re-formed and made more accountable to the population at large. The party, in fact, was to be deprived of much of its former power not least in the running of the economy where competition was to be encouraged as much as possible; so profound were the changes that the April Line of 1956 was at last jettisoned and the guiding principle of the party was now to be the 'July Concept'. Legislation introduced soon after implemented many of the reforms outlined in July, reducing the number of central ministries and restructuring local government.

In his speech to the July 1987 plenum Zhivkov had quoted the words of the great nineteenth-century Bulgarian nationalist hero and martyr, Vasil Levski: 'Either we shall live up to our times, or they will destroy us'. Within the next two years it was Zhivkov who was to be destroyed as his opponents closed in on what in fact had been wounded prey since the turn of the decade.

One of the first hounds to bite was his former protector, the Kremlin. The July Concept was disliked in Moscow. The secretary of the CPSU central committee, V. Medvedev, appeared in Sofia and in a four-hour conversation let it be known that Moscow did not approve of what was going on in Bulgaria and suggested that Zhivkov go to the Soviet Union to explain things, which he did on 16 October 1987. Here Gorbachev accused Zhivkov of going too far and of wanting to make Bulgaria into a 'mini-FRG' or 'mini-Japan'; all solutions, he said, must be based on socialism, and although it was acceptable to exclude the party from areas which were not properly its own Bulgaria was trying to separate state and party and that was inadmissible.

Gorbachev also accused Zhivkov of having too much 'perestroika' and not enough 'glasnost'; Zhivkov's line was that glasnost was only needed to facilitate perestroika and because Bulgaria already had perestroika it did not need glasnost. He would have done well to follow Gorbachev's advice. Bulgarian perestroika did little more than inflict a series of dislocating changes on the administration of the economy without much affecting productivity or the quality of production. The lack of glasnost also frustrated the Bulgarian intelligentsia. In another irony, Zhivkov's traditional devotion to the Soviet Union meant Soviet literature was widely available in Bulgaria and that on Fridays one channel of Soviet TV was relayed direct to Bulgaria; from what had in the past been the source of orthodox conservatism the intelligentsia now imbibed reformist propaganda and previously banned western literature.

A frustrated intelligentsia is little threat unless it can find a common cause with the population at large. The environment provided that common cause. The Chernobyl disaster in April 1986 had spread fears that the Bulgarians were being given food contaminated by the explosion while party big-wigs lived off safe supplies brought in from Egypt and elsewhere. In 1987 the party allowed an exhibition in the northern city of Rusé in which one exhibit was a simple statement of the incidence of lung disease in the city; it had increased from 969 per 100,000 in 1975 to 17,386 per 100,000 in 1985, thanks in no small measure to periodic malfunctions in a chemical plant on the other side of the Danube in Romania. Agitation on the issue increased and a number of non-official groups were formed to press for action to clear up the environment; this in turn encouraged others to form groups with different objectives, and by early 1989 civil society was active in Bulgaria.

In the spring of 1989 sections of the intelligentsia took up the cause of the Bulgarian Turks. Shortly before a meeting of the CSCE in Paris in May active elements in the intelligentsia linked up with leaders of the Turkish community and encouraged the Turks to take action. Within days a number of leading Turks had begun a very public hunger strike and large areas of the country, especially in the compact Turkish areas of the north-east, were in a state of more or less open rebellion. That the regime knew it was facing real difficulties was revealed when Zhivkov convened a meeting of the politburo on 28 May, a Sunday. His strategy was to make a speech on TV in which he told the Turks that if they really thought life would be better in capitalist Turkey than in socialist Bulgaria they were free to leave. He did not expect many would take up his suggestion but he was wrong. By August 344,000 had abandoned their homes. Many had left crops unharvested and cattle untended; these losses plus the fact that the departure of the Turks stripped many industries, particularly in the distributive services, of much of their labour force inflicted further massive damage on the already fragile economy.

Outside Bulgaria the picture of the fleeing Turks further diminished the country's already besmirched reputation. President Bush gave very public support to Turkey while the Soviet Union let it be known that it did not wish to become involved in Bulgaria's internal affairs. The country was isolated.

It suffered further international condemnation on 26 October when, in front of foreign press- and camera-men, police manhandled a demonstration organized by one of the new ecological pressure groups. Some Bulgarians were convinced the roughing-up of the demonstrators was deliberately staged by dissident elements in the party leadership to ease the path to Zhivkov's removal. Whatever their short-term tactics, the plotters' strategy was to wait until they had Soviet blessing before taking radical action. This was secured when the minister for foreign affairs, Petûr Mladenov, returning from a visit to China, called on Gorbachev in Moscow. On 10 November, the day after the breaching of the Berlin wall, Zhivkov was forced into resignation by the party chiefs. He had been toppled by a palace coup, not people power.

Notes

1. Kostadin Chakŭrov, *Vtoriya Etazh*, Sofia: no publishing house indicated, 1990, p.160.
2. Personal information.

Chapter 11

ROMANIA, 1948–1989

ROMANIA UNDER GHEORGHIU-DEJ, 1948–65
THE STALINIST PERIOD, 1948–56

Soon after the formation of the Romanian Workers' Party in February 1948 and even before the new constitution had been enacted in April, the communist leadership under Gheorghiu-Dej moved to consolidate its power, to entrench its leader, and to refashion the country on the Soviet, or more accurately, the Stalinist pattern; Stalinism involved terror and between 1948 and 1956 Romania went through that Stalinist nightmare.

The instruments of the terror were refined as the process continued. In 1949 the old police and gendarmerie were dissolved and replaced by a militia totally under party control. The justice system was also radically redesigned, the revised penal code punishing acts 'considered dangerous to society' even if such acts were not technically crimes.

One of the first victims of the terror, as elsewhere in Eastern Europe, was the party itself. Its dizzyingly rapid growth from under nine hundred in the early summer of 1944 to over three quarters of a million in February 1948 had meant the admission of many whom in more stable times the communists would not have welcomed. In November 1948 party cards were called in for 'verification' and by December 1955 465,000, or 44 per cent of the total membership, had been expelled for careerism, previous association with the Iron Guard, or for being compromised through contacts with foreign elements. The slimmed down party, it was assumed, would be of greater ideological reliability and would be kept in line by fear. Arrest and trial were frequently formalities, if they were not dispensed with entirely, and detention usually meant despatch to a labour camp, in all probability one of those involved in the construction of the Danube–Black Sea canal. An authoritative estimate has put the number of those accused between 1949 and 1960 at 549,400; those sent to prison or labour camps in the early 1950s have been estimated at one hundred thousand.[1]

The terror was all-pervasive and affected society in general as well as party members. Those who had belonged to former opposition parties, ex-landlords and anyone known to oppose the communists were vulnerable. So too were those suspected of having loyalties to any person or institution outside Romania. Members of the old intelligentsia who had been educated abroad, anyone who had married a foreigner, or even those who had been fortunate enough in pre-war times to travel abroad were liable to arbitrary arrest.

Particularly at risk were the 1.7 million Uniate Christians, most of whom were in Transylvania. The Uniate Church had emerged at the end of the sixteenth century in the Polish and Hungarian lands, and proved attractive in Transylvania a century later when Orthodox Christians were seeking protection from Ottoman or Russian domination. Uniates were allowed to worship in their own language, they retained their Orthodox rituals, and their lower clergy could marry, but they recognized the supremacy of the pope. That condemned them in Stalin's eyes and what Stalin condemned Gheorghiu-Dej would never tolerate. In December 1948 the Uniate Church was forcibly merged with the Romanian Orthodox Church; about 1,400 priests and 5,000 lay believers were imprisoned, as were all the Uniate bishops, all but one of whom died in prison. The Roman Catholic Church also suffered persecution and by 1953, according to figures from the Vatican, 55 clergy or monks had been executed, 250 had been exiled, 200 imprisoned and a similar number sent to labour camps. The Romanian Orthodox Church did not suffer persecution similar to that of the Uniates or the Catholics. It had no loyalties outside the Soviet bloc and the Patriarch, Justinian, had once sheltered Gheorghiu-Dej in the days of the communists' illegality. Justinian developed the doctrine of 'double fidelity' which enabled the Romanian Orthodox Church to worship both God and Caesar with a clear conscience.

The terror served not merely to consolidate communist authority; it was also meant to entrench the personal power of Gheorghiu-Dej. He eliminated personal rivals at the top of the party, primarily Ana Pauker and Vasile Luca, who were arrested in 1952 and tried on charges of right-wing deviationism. Another prominent victim was Lucrețiu Pătrășcanu, scion of a prominent academic family who had studied in Leipzig and Paris as well as Bucharest. He was arrested in 1948 and executed in 1954. These purges bore similarities to the anti-Titoist terror in the rest of the Soviet bloc, but they did not have a clear 'pro-Moscow versus home-communist' aspect: Pauker and Luca, for example, were Moscow communists through and through, as was Emil Bodnaraș who survived, while the luckless Pătrășcanu was a home communist without qualification, as was the man who personally monitored his two years of interrogation, Gheorghiu-Dej himself.

Like all good Stalinists Gheorghiu-Dej packed the party with those loyal to himself. A reform of local government in September 1950 greatly helped him to do this. It abolished the traditional counties, or judeţs, and replaced them with a three-tier Soviet system of regions, districts (including towns) and communes. This involved a huge increase in local bureaucracy and a perfect prospect for patronage which the communists and Gheorghiu-Dej were not slow to exploit.

In the early years of communist rule the ethnic minorities enjoyed an unprecedented freedom from official discrimination. The Jews were offered the right to emigrate, and most of them did so, and even the Germans found that by 1948 the post-war restrictions imposed upon them were being eased, but it was the Magyars who fared best. They had their own political organization, controlled of course by the RWP, and in 1952 constitutional reform gave them the Hungarian Autonomous Region (HAR) in the heart of Transylvania. They now enjoyed extensive rights in the use of their own language in education, publication etc. The exception to the rule of ethnic well-being was the Serbs and Germans near the border with Yugoslavia who were deported inland during the confrontation with Tito in the early 1950s.

In economic policy the Gheorghiu-Dej regime followed the general pattern in satellite states. In 1948 the bulk of industry was nationalized and the first national plan introduced. This provided, as did all others in Eastern Europe, for the rapid construction of heavy industry and also for the collectivization of agriculture. The first 'agricultural production cooperatives' were set up in the summer of 1949 and although the process was supposed to be gradual and voluntary there was soon a massive wave of terror against peasants who showed any sign of reluctance. The government declared the process complete in 1962 but, as Gheorghiu-Dej later admitted, it had involved the arrest of 80,000 peasants. With collectivization came total state and party control of the agrarian sector with compulsory delivery quotas at set prices.

The early 1950s were years of such total Soviet domination that there were rumours that Romania might become a constituent republic of the Soviet Union. As elsewhere in Soviet-dominated Europe the economy, education, the military and culture were refashioned on the Soviet model; at the same time streets, parks, squares and even towns were named in honour of Soviet or Russian heroes. In 1952, the Romanian alphabet was modified to make it look closer to its Slav neighbours, and in 1954 even the name of the country itself changed to 'Romînia', the traditional 'Romania' being considered too western.

Measures such as these were extremely distasteful to most Romanians who were even more affected by Soviet economic policies in Romania. The Romanians had not forgotten either Soviet exploitation of their economy in the immediate post-war years, or the fact that even after the establishment of communist party rule Romania received much less per capita in Soviet aid than did other satellite states. The sovroms established before 1948 were not nationalized with the rest of Romanian industry and continued to be a means by which the Soviet Union extracted money from Romania. Another aspect of Soviet economic colonialism in the early 1950s was the 'agreement' to peg raw materials prices at pre-Korean war levels; this fulfilled its avowed purpose of keeping inflation at bay but it also meant that Romania could not take advantage of higher world commodity prices.

Some relaxation of the terror and of the exploitative nature of Soviet economic policies followed the death of Stalin. The New Course meant a decrease in, though not an end to arbitrary arrests. Work on the hated Danube–Black Sea canal had been abandoned in 1952 partly for economic reasons and further relaxations came with the release of thousands of political prisoners in 1954 when the Soviets and the Romanians were anxious to secure Romanian admission to the UN. In the economic sphere reparations were eased and the sovroms gradually disbanded, the last disappearing in 1955, while for the agricultural sector there was a temporary slackening of the collectivization drive and, in 1956, the virtual abolition of the compuls-ory quota system. The real turning point for Romania, however, was not the death of Stalin, nor even Khrushchev's speech to the twentieth congress of the CPSU in February 1956, but the revolution in Hungary in November of that year.

Like all communist party bosses in Europe Gheorghiu-Dej was alarmed by the outbursts of anger in Poland and then in Hungary, but the Romanian leader had more to worry about than most. The large Hungarian minority in Transylvania, the largest ethnic minority in Europe, could not but be affected by the events in Budapest and there were signs of fraternal sympathy with the revolutionaries in Hungary. Gheorghiu-Dej therefore made sure that a tight grip was maintained on Transylvania and he also cooperated in the suppres-sion of the revolution in Hungary itself. Even before the final military inter-vention by the Red Army a number of Transylvanian Magyars had been sent to join the revolutionaries as undercover agents, and when the decisive milit-ary blow fell on Budapest the Soviet forces were allowed to use Romanian territory in order to achieve a greater degree of surprise. When the revolu-tionaries in Budapest itself had been crushed it was the Romanians who offered the leader of the revolution, Imre Nagy, safe conduct and freedom from arrest if he left the Yugoslav embassy. He was immediately arrested and then incarcerated in Romania. Gheorghiu-Dej also helped establish the new Kádár regime in power and provided it with much-needed financial support and scores of Transylvanian Magyars to help build new cadres, espe-cially in the secret police.

DESATELLIZATION AND DESTALINIZATION: 1956–65

Between 1956 and the death of Gheorghiu-Dej in 1965 the major develop-ment in Romania was the withdrawal of Red Army troops in 1958. This made possible the nationally orientated policies which were adopted by the Romanian leadership in the late 1950s and which were given dramatic expression in the first half of the 1960s.

The fact that Gheorghiu-Dej had maintained such rigid control in Romania and had helped in the suppression of the Hungarian revolution strengthened his call, first voiced in 1955, for the withdrawal of the Red Army from Romania. Under the terms of the 1947 peace treaty Soviet troops had been garrisoned in Romania to help guard the supply lines to Soviet bases in eastern Austria. After the Austrian State Treaty in 1955 that excuse was no longer valid and the Romanians suggested that the Red Army might reconsider its need to maintain a presence in Romania. Khrushchev's reaction was hostile and after the Hungarian revolution it was 'agreed' that Red Army troops would have to stay in Romania to counter the threat presented by NATO and its alleged attempts to subvert the socialist order. By 1958, however, Khrushchev was looking for ways to improve his relations with the west. At a Warsaw pact meeting in May 1958 it was announced that the Red Army would leave Romania; the withdrawal began in early July and was complete by the end of that month. It was no doubt also meant to deflect attention from, and dilute Romanian disgust at the fate of Imre Nagy who in June had been flown back to Hungary in a Romanian aircraft and executed.

Romania was never really to destalinize in the way most other East European states did, but the withdrawal of the Red Army was the first major step towards desovietization and desatellization. There was to be no turning back.

With the Red Army gone there was no difficulty in moving towards greater assertion of Romanian nationality in internal affairs. During the recent emergency Gheorghiu-Dej had been concerned that the Hungarians of Transylvania clearly felt closer to their ethnic brethren in Hungary than to their co-citizens in the Romanian state. The Romanian leader concluded that the Transylvanian Magyars must be integrated into Romania and the links with Hungary reduced. Minority schools began to be amalgamated with Romanian ones and, although teaching in minority languages continued in many cases, all schools now had to teach Romanian. The most dramatic manifestation of the new policy was the merger of the Bolyai University in Cluj with its Romanian counterpart, Babeş. Thereafter Romanians dominated the administration and what was first portrayed as a merger became in fact a takeover. Secondary education was also Romanianized; parallel Romanian sections were introduced into purely Hungarian schools, the Hungarian sections in mixed schools disappeared, and only the eldest child of a family was allowed to be educated in Hungarian. In 1960 the HAR was renamed the Mureş Hungarian Autonomous Region (MHAR), to make it sound more Romanian; more significantly, its boundaries were changed, adding a region with a high percentage of Romanians and shaving off the two most Hungarian areas and adding them to Romanian regions; the percentage of Magyars in the MHAR fell from 77 to 62.

A further indication of desatellization and desovietization came in 1963 with the changing of street and other names back to their Romanian originals or, if these were no longer politically acceptable, to Romanian rather than Russian ones. The old spelling of the country's name was also restored. The Russian Institute in Bucharest was closed, and within a few years Russian had ceased to be the second language taught in Romanian schools, its place being taken by French, English or German. History books, films and novels were by now downplaying the role of the Red Army in the liberation of 1944, there was veiled criticism of the Soviets in films and even some cautious discussion of Bessarabia, the area assigned to the Soviet Union in 1940 and retained by it after the war, and until the 1960s a topic unmentionable in public.

By this time the desovietizing trends were well established in the economy. In the second half of the 1950s trade with western Europe increased markedly while that with the Soviet Union declined as a percentage of the whole. In 1959 Romania agreed to purchase a tyre-making plant from Britain and petro-chemical equipment from France and Italy. There were also shifts in economic strategy which indicated growing self-confidence and self-interest on the part of Romania's economic planners. The disruption of the East European economies caused by the upheavals of 1956 had forced the Romanian leadership to redesign their five-year plan of 1956 to 1961, and in 1960 a new six-year plan was introduced. Its basic concept was that Romania could and would become a fully developed industrial nation; the objective therefore was 'rapid and all-round industrialization', the greatest symbol of which was a massive iron and steel complex to be built at Galaţi.

This issue was soon to bring about a decisive confrontation between Romania and the Soviet Union. That confrontation was intensified by personal differences between the two leaders and by a growing independence in Romanian foreign policy, both of which were in symbiotic relationship with the major clash on economic policy.

Gheorghiu-Dej and Khrushchev had never been on good terms. When the Romanian leader was in Moscow for the twenty-second congress of the CPSU in 1961 Khrushchev upbraided him for forcing through the final stages of collectivization in Romania: collectivization, said Khrushchev, had failed everywhere so why did the Romanians persist with it when they could have followed the Polish or Yugoslav roads and abandoned it? Gheorghiu-Dej was enraged and accused the Soviet boss of abandoning Marxism. In 1962 Gheorghiu-Dej was again in Moscow at a critical juncture: the Cuban crisis. He thought Khrushchev had gone mad and was terrified lest the Soviet leader's irresponsibility drag Romania, which had not been consulted on the installation of Soviet missiles in the Caribbean, into war with NATO.

The Cuban crisis also deepened the growing rift between Moscow and Peking. This was another issue on which Romania differed from the Soviet Union. Romania avoided full commitment to either side in the ideological debate and attempted to play a mediating role between them. In 1963 the Romanians allowed publication of the anti-Soviet 'Twenty-Five Chinese Points' and in the following year Bodnăraş headed a Romanian party delegation on a visit to the PRC. Romania also refused to follow the Soviet line in condemning Albania as a communist heretic. Gheorghiu-Dej had no particular ideological predisposition to the anti-Soviet communist states but were his efforts at mediation to succeed he would establish Romania as the leader of a third bloc in the communist world and thereby greatly enhance its international prestige.

The Kremlin was never seriously threatened by Romania's ideological or diplomatic initiatives but it did have real interests at stake in the great economic confrontation of the early 1960s. The economies of Eastern Europe had hardly recovered from the disruptions of 1956 when they were destabilized by the German crisis. The flight of trained workers and professionals from the German Democratic Republic (GDR) had forced the building of the Berlin wall, an immediate consequence of which was the need to build up the GDR as a viable, socialist competitor to the Federal Republic. Investment funds and the best Comecon equipment should therefore be concentrated on the GDR, it was argued in Moscow. This did not suit the Romanians who were relying on Czechoslovak and German heavy equipment to build their own industrial system. Matters came to a head in February 1963 when the Comecon executive committee submitted to member states a Soviet proposal for the setting up of a supra-national Comecon planning authority which could issue instructions and orders to member states. The committee also put forward plans for regional, economic specialization. For Romania this was to mean concentration on agriculture and related food industries together with petroleum and petro-chemicals, but it was not to mean the heavy industry to which the party had committed itself in 1959. The proposals meant that the Romanians were no longer free to determine their own economic policy. The RWP leadership feared they would also condemn Romania to second-class status in the socialist world: they would retard Romania's historically ordained progress, because if there were no heavy industry the proletariat would be slower to emerge, and the dictatorship of the proletariat and the evolution through socialism to communism correspondingly delayed.

The crucial turning point came with a meeting of the RWP central committee (CC) in April 1964 which produced 'A Statement on the Stand of the Romanian Workers' Party concerning the Problems of the World Communist and Working-Class Movement'. The socialist state, it insisted, had to take and retain effective control of all aspects of the economy and society; 'to hand over these levers to the competence of some super-state or extra-state bodies would be to turn sovereignty into a concept without any real content'.[2] The document went on to reject all claims to hegemony, economic or otherwise, by any one party and to assert that it was 'a sovereign right of each socialist state to elaborate, choose or change the forms and methods of socialist construction. . . . No party has, or can have, a privileged place, or can impose its line and opinions on other parties.'[3]

Shortly after the CC statement the RWP allowed publication of a piece by Karl Marx, *Notes on the Romanians*, recently unearthed in Amsterdam. This condemned the Russian annexation of Bessarabia in 1812 and criticized further Russian pressure on the Romanian principalities in the mid-nineteenth century. It was political dynamite: an article by Marx himself which criticized Russia for its policy on an issue which for a decade and a half in Romania had been virtually unmentionable.

It was soon clear that the independent line taken by Bucharest enjoyed at least the tacit endorsement of other ruling communist parties, all of which sent delegations to the Romanian capital to help celebrate the twentieth anniversary of the liberation. By this time the Kremlin knew it had lost. Two days after Khrushchev was deposed in October 1964 the new Soviet leaders signed an agreement accepting Romania's industrialization plans. In December they agreed to withdraw Soviet advisors from Romania, including those in the intelligence and security services, a privilege not secured by any other Warsaw pact state.

Gheorghiu-Dej's victory had no doubt been helped by Khrushchev's weakening hold on the Soviet party. His own position strengthened as Khrushchev's declined. The early 1960s at last saw sustained economic growth and a rise in consumption sufficient to allow the end of rationing. There was political relaxation too with, according to official figures, 12,750 prisoners being released between 1962 and 1965. One of those released was the former manager at the famous Capşa's restaurant in Bucharest; he returned to work immediately and brought a little colour back to Bucharest life.

These improvements, major or minor, in the quality of life helped to legitimize communist rule. Gheorghiu-Dej's assertion of Romanian national interests vis-à-vis the mighty Soviet Union did so even more. Communist Romania was to leave neither the Warsaw pact nor Comecon but nor was it ever again to be a docile member of either. The RWP in rejecting Soviet-backed economic specialization had invalidated the old communist assumption that their policies were legitimate because they were following in the footsteps of the infallible Soviet master. A new legitimization was needed. Romanian nationalism was to provide it. It was the perfect answer because in Romania, unlike all other Balkan states, the historic national demon is not the Turk but the Russian or, to a lesser extent, the Hungarian.

When he died in March 1965 Gheorghiu-Dej was not greatly mourned by most Romanians but his last years in office had brought them a slightly better quality of life and a greatly increased sense of national self-reliance. His successor, Nicolae Ceauşescu, was to pursue the latter with demonic frenzy; in so doing he destroyed any improvements in the former.

CEAUŞESCU'S ROMANIA, 1965–89

Nicolae Ceauşescu was of peasant origin and little education. He had been active in the party before the Second World War but his knowledge of theory was limited to say the least; according to an intellectual communist, in 1951 Ceauşescu had never heard of *Das Kapital* although he could recite huge chunks of Stalin's *Problems of Leninism*.[4] He was to remain a Stalinist all his life. In 1954 he was made CC secretary in charge of cadres, always a powerful position in a ruling communist party; in 1955 he was admitted to the politburo and in 1956 was prominent in Romania's policy towards the Hungarian revolution; it was Ceauşescu who organized the spurious guarantees of safety offered to Nagy. When he assumed office in March 1965 Ceauşescu was the youngest party leader in Eastern Europe but he was also a largely unknown, colourless apparatchik who had never been out of Romania.

Ceauşescu was to rule Romania for almost a quarter of a century. His rule was based on the skilful use of the party, the relentless exploitation of nationalism, and the peculiarities of the cold war. His rule was to become a byword for the vicious, vindictive and corrupt use of power. But it was not initially so, nor did it indulge in the mass terror of the early years of Gheorghiu-Dej's regime. Its nationalism assured it some respect in the 1970s even though it was by then becoming more and more authoritarian. In the 1980s it became a travesty of its own propaganda, spouting gobbledegook about prosperity, freedom and happiness as it plunged the populace into privation and despair unparalleled in recent Romanian history.

THE HONEYMOON PERIOD, 1965–71

Ceauşescu set out to distance Romania from the Soviet Union and himself from Gheorghiu-Dej. In doing so he initially gave reason to hope that the new regime, though equally nationalist, would be more relaxed and permissive than its predecessor.

It was a matter of luck for Ceauşescu that the ninth party congress was scheduled to take place in July 1965, only four months after he became leader. This congress could endorse his accession to power, and he could use it to stamp his own image on the party. That he intended his rule not to be a copy of Gheorghiu-Dej's was underlined at the very beginning of the congress when Ceauşescu failed to ask for a minute's silence in memory of the dead leader. The congress went on to declare Romania a socialist state rather than a people's democracy. This again emphasized the transition to a new era, while also flattering Romanian nationalist vanity in placing the country at an equal stage of historical development with the Soviet Union. The congress readopted the original name of the party, the Romanian Communist Party (RCP). Gheorghiu-Dej had been regarded as the founding father of the RWP and reversion to the original nomenclature would further downgrade his memory and image.

Ceauşescu reinforced the differences between the Romanian and the Soviet parties in a speech in May 1966 to mark the 45th anniversary of the founding of the RCP. He criticized the Comintern and the Soviet Union for their interference in the affairs of the RCP in the inter-war years, and in particular for forcing it to accept non-Romanians in leading positions.

In 1968 he neutralized possible opposition in the party. At a CC plenum in April not only did he rehabilitate party members executed during the 1940s and 1950s but went on to make shocking revelations of how Pătrăşcanu had been persecuted by Gheorghiu-Dej and his colleagues, with Gheorghiu-Dej personally reading and annotating witnesses' statements and giving orders on what further statements should be extracted. The immediate political effect of this was to isolate Alexandru Drăghici, the only member of the leadership who had been one of Gheorghiu-Dej's politburo colleagues and who had been in charge of the security police and therefore had had a major role in the persecution of Pătrăşcanu. The revelations discredited Drăghici and party members were shocked by the vicious and damaging factionalism which had seemingly flourished under the previous leadership. This fear of factionalism was used thereafter to entrench Ceauşescu's authority.

Local government reform in 1968 further bolstered Ceauşescu's position. The three-tier Soviet system introduced by Gheorghiu-Dej was abandoned and the traditional judeţ restored. The reform again meant a wholesale change in leading personnel at all levels of local administration and it was accompanied by a simultaneous replacement of most senior army officers. The newcomers were all loyal Ceauşescu supporters.

In the summer of 1968 the Soviet invasion of Czechoslovakia enabled Ceauşescu to distance himself further from the Soviet Union and to strengthen the solidarity between himself and the Romanian nation. Ceauşescu addressed a huge crowd in the centre of Bucharest and for once he spoke with real passion and feeling. His audience was amazed less by the style than the substance of the speech. Ceauşescu condemned the invasion as 'a great mistake' and 'a shameful moment' in the history of the communist movement, and then stunned his audience with the words, 'Let us be ready, comrades, to defend at any moment our socialist homeland, Romania.'[5] He in turn was amazed by the electric reaction of the crowd. He discovered a rapport which was always to be remembered but seldom if ever to be recaptured; the experience enforced his conviction that his power would be most securely based on the appeal to national sentiment.

The August speech had impressed all Romanians and for the intelligentsia in particular it confirmed hopes that their new leader was a champion of a more relaxed form of socialism; if not, why had he raised his voice so loudly against the action taken against Czechoslovakia's 'socialism with a human face'? The August speech was not the first such encouraging sign. In his address to the ninth congress in 1965 Ceauşescu had put great emphasis on the need for collective leadership as opposed to the cult of personality which, he maintained, Gheorghiu-Dej had practised. The new leader even went on to promise that the excesses of the past would not be repeated and that Romanians would enjoy a new era free from the abuse of police power. In 1965 a new constitution stated that the judiciary was to be free and subject only to the law and that the right of defence was to be guaranteed to all accused. In 1968 control of the militia was removed from the ministry of the interior and passed to the State Security Council; a police under collective leadership, it was assumed, would be less of a threat to individual freedoms than one under the control of a single person.

There was one notable exception to the general pattern of relaxation. In 1966 Ceauşescu introduced measures to increase the birth rate. Abortions and other forms of birth control were banned, women of child-bearing age were required to have regular pregnancy tests and were to face severe penalties in the event of termination, a tax was imposed on childless couples and divorce was made much more difficult. The birth rate rose from 14.7 per thousand in 1966 to 27.4 per thousand in 1967, though it soon declined to close to its former level. There was no attempt to provide extra clothes, prams or baby food.

THE CEAUŞESCU DICTATORSHIP, 1971–89

The natalist law of 1965 was a straw in the wind. It indicated that personal rights were still subject to collective needs as interpreted by one individual leader. At the tenth party congress in 1969 the power of that individual was reinforced as notions of collective leadership faded into the background. In 1971 Ceauşescu paid an official visit to the People's Republic of China and to Kim Il Sung's Stalinist bastion of North Korea. He liked what he saw, particularly in the latter, and thereafter he developed the cult of personality which was to dominate the rest of his odious rule. In 1974 Ceauşescu made himself president of Romania in addition to being party boss and the attendant ceremonies bore all the characteristics of a coronation. In later years Ceauşescu was to affect the title of 'Conducator', or leader, or even Führer; the only other Romanian leader of modern times to use the title was Marshal Antonescu who had sent his legions to fight alongside the Nazis against Soviet Russia.

The trip to the Far East also had a profound effect upon Ceauşescu's wife, Elena. His lifelong partner, Elena was always his equal in ambition, but never in intelligence. She had joined the Bucharest party committee in 1968 but after 1971 her star ascended with dizzying speed. In 1972 she was elected to the CC and in the following year she became a member of the permanent executive committee, since 1965 Romania's equivalent of a politburo. In 1979 she was given the hugely powerful position of chairwoman of the CC commission for state and party cadres; she was in effect the personnel manager for the entire party and state machines, deciding even where various senior officials should reside. During the 1980s she assumed more and more control over internal affairs, her husband choosing to concentrate more upon charting Romania's course to international greatness. Elena was also a scientist of international renown. Or so it was said. The problem in Romania was that no one could ever remember seeing her as a student or a researcher; nor could she ever spare the time from her manifold duties in helping to destroy her nation to exchange with anyone a single remark indicating any knowledge in her alleged field of expertise, chemistry.

It was not just Ceauşescu's wife who was allowed access to the reins of power. In the 1970s one estimate put the number of the Ceauşescu clan in senior posts at over forty. Two of the Conducator's brothers were given senior posts in controlling security, one as minister of defence the other as minister of the interior. His son, Nicu, allegedly an expert in nuclear physics, was groomed for the succession and in the meantime enjoyed enormous powers which he abused to the furthest extent of his insatiable and depraved appetites.

Ceauşescu and his family were corrupt. Like potentates of old they treated the country as if it were their own personal and family fiefdom, the main purpose of which was to enrich its rulers. They amassed huge quantities of gifts, given ostensibly to the Romanian people; when many of them were displayed after the revolution of 1989 they presented a pathetic picture of petty-bourgeois vulgarity. The most hideous monument, literally, to their bad taste, and to their indifference to or ignorance of the human suffering involved, was the huge palace built in Bucharest. It was sited in one of the few areas of the city deemed immune from earthquakes and its construction involved the destruction, often at very short notice, of thousands of homes as well as a number of historic churches. Construction began as a result of a decree signed by both the ruling couple in the appropriately Orwellian year of 1984.

This was not the only Orwellian feature of the 1980s in Romania. In 1982 Ceauşescu announced that the dictatorship of the proletariat had ended and that Romania was now a 'workers' democracy', a change endorsed by a national party conference in December 1982. By the mid-1980s official propaganda was trumpeting the achievements of Romania's 'Golden Era', and at the fourteenth party congress in November 1989 the great leader received sixty-seven standing ovations. In reality police controls were tightened to an unprecedented degree. By the middle of the decade the Securitate, the special security forces built up by Ceauşescu, were ubiquitous, with an estimated one in ten of the population working as informers. Romanians were not allowed to consort with foreigners other than in designated places which everyone knew had been 'prepared'. In 1983 a decree on typewriters ruled that office machines had to be kept padlocked when not in official use and individuals with typewriters of their own had not only to register them with the police but also to submit each year a set text which the police could then check against any samizdat literature which might appear. The natalist policies were intensified and by the end of the decade there was a Securitate agent in every gynaecological ward and any woman brought in suffering from complications arising from an illegal abortion was refused treatment until she had revealed the name of the abortionist. Some women were reported to have chosen to die rather than talk.

The regime attempted systematically to destroy any individual autonomy or privacy. The fear of the informer atomized society, while the reopening of the Danube–Black Sea canal project reawoke memories of the ubiquity of the police and the savagery of their punishment. The canal was finished in 1984; the volume of traffic using it was one tenth of that predicted. In March 1988 Ceauşescu introduced his plan for the 'systematization' of about half Romania's thirteen thousand villages. This meant in effect their destruction. The houses were to be bulldozed and their inhabitants moved to 'agro-industrial' complexes where they would live in apartment blocks with communal facilities for eating and other social activities. The programme had a number of objectives, one of which was to destroy what was left of the autonomy of the peasant family. In fact relatively few villages were 'systematized' but the proposals provoked intense outrage in the country and widespread condemnation from abroad.

As for the 'Golden Era', which the propagandists declared Romania was enjoying, the term would have been comic had the situation not been so tragic. In 1981 bread rationing was reintroduced for the first time for twenty-seven years, and as the decade progressed prices rose and the shortages of food and fuel became worse; in 1988 the use of private cars was banned during the winter and there was also a prohibition on the use of private vacuum cleaners and refrigerators. Power was so limited that urban families were restricted to one 40-watt bulb per room with gas for heating and cooking frequently available only in the middle of the night. Queues even for staple foods were long and supplies so exiguous that not even these staples could be guaranteed. Romanian diet became unhealthy as well as unappetizing, a fact all too obvious at the end of the decade in the emaciation and skin defects which were everywhere apparent.

CEAUŞESCU'S EXPLOITATION OF ROMANIAN NATIONALISM

Ceauşescu continued Gheorghiu-Dej's use of Romanian nationalism both internally and externally. Internally this was to be seen in government policies towards the national minorities and in the continuing drive for industrialization. Externally, it meant a decrease in dependence on the Soviet Union which was to be brought about by fostering relations, economic and political, with anti-Soviet communist states, the third world and the west.

There was never any doubt but that Ceauşescu would continue the nationalist policies initiated by Gheorghiu-Dej. What had not been predictable was the extent to which he would take them. One new tactic introduced by Ceauşescu was to link himself with the great figures of Romania's past. In 1966 and 1967 he conducted a series of 'personal encounters' with actors decked out as such figures. These toe-curling episodes served to create the impression that the present leader was the equal of these great men and that there were links between the heroic times of the past and the present. By the late 1970s the urge to identify with the nationalist past had become so strong that it overcame the ideological dislike even of Antonescu, and although Ceauşescu never staged a meeting with him some of his policies, especially the winning back of Bessarabia in 1941, were reassessed in positive light in a number of historical works; in the 1980s plays, films or novels which looked favourably on the former dictator were commonplace.

A much longer historical continuity was asserted in the Dacian origins of the Romanian people which was increasingly emphasized in the 1970s. There is not a great deal of evidence for this but it was considered sufficient to 'prove' that the Romanians had always inhabited the northern bank of the lower Danube and Transylvania; to emphasize this continuity a number of Romanian towns and cities were required to add Latin suffixes to their names, and thus the Transylvanian capital became Cluj-Napoca.

Along with its longevity Ceauşescu wished to emphasize Romania's unity. The 1965 constitution declared Romania a 'unified' state and a unified state could obviously not include autonomous areas; in 1966 the MHAR was therefore abolished. In the next few years pressures on minority groups would ease if there were a perceived threat from the Soviets, as was the case in 1968 and in 1971 when Ceauşescu paid his ostentatious visit to China. But after 1971 there was no real threat from without and the pressures on the minorities increased. In 1973 the percentage of pupils required to secure education in a minority language in primary and secondary schools was raised to 25 and 35 respectively and even these rules were regularly evaded, as was that providing for university classes for a minority of 15 per cent. From the mid-1970s a policy of Romanianization was adopted in Transylvania with the settlement in the area of Romanians from Wallachia and Moldavia, a process which, according to figures unearthed after 1989, increased the Romanian population of Transylvania from 32 to 49 per cent between 1975 and 1989. The systematization policy of the late 1980s was also meant to break up Magyar communities and dissolve their culture in the new, predominantly Romanian agro-industrial complexes. The other large minority group in Transylvania and western Romania, the Germans, was depleted rather than diluted. The establishment of diplomatic relations and then important trading links with west Germany encouraged many Saxons to apply for emigration permits. Government policy varied but from 1956 to 1977 the Germans declined from 2.2 to 1.6 per cent of the total population and in the 1980s more were allowed to leave because Bonn was willing to pay a fee for each emigrant. Shortly after the 1989 revolution almost all the Germans had left and Transylvania had lost one of its most colourful and distinctive ethnic groups.

There were economic aspects to Ceauşescu's nationalist policies and, as under Gheorghiu-Dej, they frequently involved tweaking the noses of the Soviets. At the ninth congress in 1965 Ceauşescu had stressed two strands of party policy: national autonomy and industrialization. Investment in industry was to rise between 1966 and 1970 to 28.8 per cent of national income; it had been 24.3 per cent for the years 1961 to 1965. Characteristically he emphasized that this stood full square in line with national tradition, quoting nineteenth-century thinkers and twentieth-century politicians, communist and non-communist, to prove his point.

In foreign policy relations with the Soviet Union remained correct, generally cool and occasionally cold. Ceauşescu's flirtation with China was not welcome in the Kremlin but the most serious disagreements continued to be those over economic strategy. In July 1971 a Comecon summit in Bucharest agreed on greater cooperation but within days Ceauşescu had stated that he would not be bound by any supra-national planning agency. On 2 August he cut a meeting in the Crimea of East European leaders. Later in August he addressed a huge public rally in Bucharest and told the crowd that the communist movement could no longer be led from any one centre. At the end of the 1970s Ceauşescu visited Phnom Penh and became the first Soviet-bloc leader to sign an agreement with the Khmer Rouge; in 1979 he condemned both the Soviet-backed Vietnamese incursion into Cambodia and the Soviet invasion of Afghanistan. Ceauşescu also refused to join the general Warsaw pact condemnation of the American deployment of Pershing missiles in Europe and when the Soviets replied by introducing their own missiles into the GDR he castigated both sides for pushing Europe closer to war. Nor were the Soviets pleased when at this time of rising international tension the Romanians cut back on their military spending which became proportionately the lowest in the WTO. That Romania failed to observe the East European boycott of the Los Angeles Olympic Games of 1984 was in comparison only a minor annoyance to Moscow.

Ceauşescu's hopes that the Chinese might prove useful economic partners came to little. He had similar hopes of the better relations he established with the United States of America, a process which again caused concern in Moscow, as it was intended to do. The Americans had welcomed the fact that in 1967 Romania, unlike the other WTO states, did not sever diplomatic relations with Israel over the six-day war. Washington had also been pleased when, in the same year, Romania again broke ranks with her Warsaw pact partners and established full diplomatic relations with the FRG. After these acts of independence and the condemnation of the invasion of Czechoslovakia Romania's independent foreign policy line deserved recognition and bolstering. In August 1969 therefore President Nixon journeyed to Bucharest thus becoming the first US president to set foot in a communist East European capital. He was not the last. President Ford came in August 1975 and Vice-President Bush in 1983. In return the Romanian leader visited the United States in December 1970, January 1973 and April 1978, and never believed that Macy's was not a Potemkin store set up to deceive him.

Exchanges of official visits with one of the two super-powers noticeably increased Romania's international profile. So too did trips to France and the United Kingdom where the Ceauşescus were billeted in the Elysée and Buckingham Palace respectively. In the former they tore down priceless tapestries looking for hidden microphones and in the latter they infuriated Her already displeased Majesty by requesting permission for Ceauşescu's food taster to sample the fare prepared for an official banquet. But Britain needed to sell BAC 1–11 aircraft to Romania.

Some economic benefit was derived, at least initially, from these closer relations with the west. In 1971 Romania was admitted to the GATT, and in 1972 it became the first East European state to become a member of the IMF. Four years later it was included in the 'Group of 77' which enabled it to benefit from certain trading preferences, and the Americans gave more than the Soviets in aid to help overcome the floods of 1970 and 1975. An agreement was also concluded to manufacture French cars under licence, while another with a Canadian consortium provided for the construction of a nuclear power station at Černavoda. But it was not economic benefit alone which Ceauşescu sought. He wanted to make Romania a major player on the world stage and he was useful in helping to bring about the Camp David meeting in 1978.

Romania, however, was never to be anything other than a minor factor in international relations. The autonomy which Ceauşescu vaunted before his people was based not on strength but on weakness. The Soviets tolerated his impudence because he could do them no real harm, the more so in the 1980s when the appalling domestic situation in Romania advertised the dangers rather than the attractions of ploughing a non-Soviet socialist furrow. To liquidate the Genghis Khan of socialism would have caused more trouble to Moscow than it was worth. For China, Romania was a useful counterweight to the Soviet Union in the late 1960s and very early 1970s, but once Nixon had been to Peking in 1972 and the Sino-American thaw had set in, China had little need of Romania. The Americans and the west obviously welcomed a maverick in the Soviet camp but in the last resort they would not go much beyond minor economic help towards Romania; and in the long run economic assistance from the capitalist world was to create huge internal problems for the Romanian regime. Furthermore, western indulgence of Ceauşescu, shameful as it became in the late 1970s and beyond, was a factor of the cold war. Once Gorbachev made it clear that he was no longer interested in confrontation and the arms race, Ceauşescu lost what diplomatic market value he had left in the west. In Europe Ceauşescu's autonomous line produced only one lasting ally, Tito's Yugoslavia.[6]

Outside Europe and the sphere of super-power diplomacy Ceauşescu's Romania did have considerable success in establishing links with the so-called third world, links which were again seeded and nurtured by relentless exchanges of official visits. In 1976 Romania was an invited guest at the Colombo conference of the non-aligned nations and at similar meetings in Havana in 1979, New Delhi in 1983 and Harare in 1986.

CEAUŞESCU AND THE RCP

Despite his chauvinism Ceauşescu was a communist ruling through a communist party. He would have been unable to hold on to power had he not been able to control the party itself. Nor would the party have carried out his policies had it not been able to provide theoretical justification for them.

One means Ceauşescu used to entrench his power was nepotism. Another was the rotation of party and state posts the principle of which was included in an amended party statute of July 1972. This principle was never precisely defined except that it was known that only Ceauşescu and his wife were exempt from it.

Even before Ceauşescu became leader the party had differentiated itself from most of the others in the Soviet camp by once again expanding its membership. Between April 1962 and December 1964 it increased in numbers by about 50 per cent; the breach with the Soviet Union on economic policy deprived the party of the support which had placed it in office in 1944 and kept it there in the early years of communist rule. As an alternative basis for its power the party turned to the Romanian people. The party set out to become a mass party, and in 1965 it took another step in that direction by deciding that acceptable applicants could become party members without serving the probationary or 'candidate stage' of membership. By 1975 almost a quarter of the active workforce were party members, whereas when Ceauşescu came to power the figure had been only 10 per cent.

The RCP was also keen to 'reproletarianize' the party and to involve more workers in its activities. With this objective in view the ninth congress decided that national congresses of workers in various sectors of the economy should be held. The first, of those involved in agriculture, was held in March 1966. Like the many others which followed, its objective was not so much to endorse or amend policy but to bind the population in with the process of policy enactment.

In this regard the congresses were one feature of the general strategy of *impletirea* or blending. The regime wished to deepen the commitment to the party and its policies not only of the workers but also of those with the technical expertise and managerial skills upon which the successful implementation of policy would depend. The experts would become 'red'. Blending was to affect local government too as Romania decided that local party leaders should simultaneously serve as the heads of the local government apparatus of the same area. More so than anywhere else in communist Europe the party merged with administrative and social organizations. This process was part of the 'takeover from within', as opposed to that from without, i.e. from the Soviet Union. Blending, coupled with the expansion of the party into a mass organization, would integrate party, society and nation to a degree not achieved elsewhere in the socialist community.

Blending also fitted in with the new theoretical analysis of Romanian socialism put forward by the party in the 1970s. This classed the years 1948 to 1965 as those of building the base of socialist power, those from 1965 to 1969 as the period of the consolidation of socialist power; and after 1969 Romania would be constructing a 'multi-laterally developed socialist society'. In 1972 an RCP national conference decided that 'blending' was an inevitable part of social evolution and it was given a prominent place in the new RCP programme introduced in December 1974. According to the more codified expositions of the theory the party was to be the agent for blending society, the economy and the nation into a new multi-developed socialist consciousness and once that process had been completed the party, and the state with which it had become inextricably intertwined, would begin to wither away. This was the Romanian road to communism.

Ceauşescu's theoreticians had to find a place in their new ideological framework for the nationalism which underlay so many of the Conducator's policies. The line as laid down at the ninth congress was that a nation can only achieve full cohesion after the exploiting classes have been eliminated, that is in a socialist society. Socialist culture was therefore the culture of full national cohesion and was a synthesis of national tradition and socialist values; the socialist society was 'socialist in form but national in content'; Lenin had described it in precisely the opposite terms. If one element of a socialist society was national tradition and, if a socialist society could only be built, as Marx had taught, by the action of the working class, then it followed that any socialist society had to be created by the working class which had been formed within that national tradition; it could not be created by an outside or an international agency. This version of post-Marxian socialism served the Romanian autonomists well. It rejected the post-1968 Brezhnev doctrine and the Leninist notion that the emergence of the socialist state would see a decline in national identity and feeling.

THE ECONOMIC DISASTERS

Ceauşescu, who was a great believer in his own infallibility in economics, had determined that Romania should achieve a high international economic profile by becoming an exporter of machinery manufactured by its own iron and steel industry. The fact that Romania had almost no iron ore deposits did not deter him, nor was he put off by the Soviet Union's refusal to increase its exports from Krivoi Rog; instead Ceauşescu went to Brazil, Australia and India to find the necessary raw materials.

In the late 1970s the economic situation began to deteriorate markedly; in the 1980s it became calamitous. In the first place Romania was unlucky. Natural disasters had inflicted severe damage with the floods of 1970 and 1975 but their impact was insignificant compared to that of the earthquake which struck Bucharest in March 1977; apart from the terrifying impact this had on national morale it cost the country an estimated $630 million in lost exports and tourist income and in increased imports. Shortly after came severe weather in 1980 and 1981 which was one of the reasons why Romania became the second Comecon state, Poland being the first, to ask for a rescheduling of its debts. The IMF agreed on condition that the Romanians provide accurate statistics and introduce some economic reforms. These conditions were accepted but never implemented.

The problems of Romania's economy could not be ascribed entirely to natural causes. There were political problems too. After almost a decade of indecision the Romanian regime committed itself to thorough-going reforms in the New Economic and Financial Mechanism (NEFM) which was to be applied on 1 January 1979 and which was to promote efficiency through a reduction in central control and an increase in the role of 'financial levers, profitability requirements and material incentives'. But despite this rhetoric the Romanian economy remained more centralized and disciplined than any other in Europe except the Albanian; the text of the last economic plan produced under the Ceauşescu regime, for example, was forty metres long.[7] Even the private plots allowed to the peasants on collective farms were subject to state directives, and the MTSs, long abandoned in the rest of socialist Europe, were retained. The result was that Romanian industry, despite all the hurrah propaganda poured out by the regime, remained incredibly inefficient: one aluminium factory used more electricity than all 23 million Romanians. Industry was also hideously polluting.

The two greatest problems facing the Romanian economy, however, were oil and debt. In 1973 the regime decided to increase Romania's oil-refining capacity, and between 1973 and 1978 this rose from 18.5 million tons to 25.4 million tons. Much of the equipment needed to expand and modernize refining capacity had to be bought in the west for hard currency; so too, after 1976, did crude because Romania's native reserves were virtually exhausted. Romania now bought its supplies from OPEC countries, particularly Iran. The costs of buying western equipment and some of the costs of purchasing crude were covered by loans. As a member of western financial and trading institutions such as the GATT and the IMF Romania had relatively easy access to western money, but both lender and borrower operated under the illusion that the other knew what it was doing; the Romanians borrowed as much as they could on the assumption that the western bankers would not lend beyond their estimation of Romania's ability to service and repay, while the bankers lent on the assumption that the Romanians would not borrow beyond what they knew they could afford. Both assumptions were mistaken.

The problems really began with the Iranian crisis of 1979 which disrupted crude supplies, as did the protracted Iran–Iraq war which began in 1980. Unlike the rise of crude prices in 1973 the hike of 1979 was not accompanied by a sustained concomitant rise in the price of refined petrol; by 1981 Romania was receiving $25 a ton less for the refined petrol it was selling than it had paid for the crude from which it was manufactured. At the same time the recession in the west meant a decline in exports and in Romania's foreign currency earnings, and therefore in its ability to service its debts. Indeed, so scarce had hard currency become that Romania could not afford to buy enough crude to keep its refineries busy; by 1981 a third of refining capacity was idle even though not enough petrol had been produced to satisfy domestic demand. Romania's economic ills, together with a rise in interest rates in the west, meant that no more money could be borrowed and therefore the rescheduling of existing debt had to be requested.

By the early 1980s the debt had come to dominate Romanian economic strategy. It stood at over $10 billion. For a nationalist and socialist regime which had made so much of economic independence the debt enforced a humiliating dependence on foreign and capitalist creditors. From the onset of the crisis Ceauşescu had decided that the damage inflicted by the debt, and the restrictions it imposed on Romanian sovereignty, were so great that the only possible escape was to liquidate it. To this end a huge export drive was launched to earn the hard currency needed to pay off the debt. The export drive depleted the home market while imports were kept to an absolute minimum.

The economic emergency led also to a tightening of regimentation, aimed at increasing production, preventing hoarding or black-marketeering and containing possible unrest. Ceauşescu's determination and the discipline it imposed succeeded in its stated objective in that by the end of the 1980s the debt had been cleared. But the cost for the Romanian people had been appalling. It had been high too for the regime because the crisis had liquidated not only the debt but any remaining legitimacy enjoyed by Ceauşescu and his clique.

THE END OF THE CEAUŞESCU REGIME

Opposition to the Ceauşescu regime had never been absent but was always contained and perhaps the most remarkable feature of the regime was that it was able to survive so long, particularly in the late 1980s when internal conditions were at their worst and when other East European states were experiencing exhilarating liberalization. When it did come Romania's revolt began more gently and ended more violently than all the others in the Soviet bloc.

If opposition to Ceauşescu had never been absent it had always been dangerous. As early as 1969 one of his physicians decided the leader was insane and expressed his opinion in a highly secret report. This may have shown medical competence but it revealed a lack of political wisdom. A few days later the doctor was found dead on the pavement beneath his fourth-floor flat.

There were always a few courageous individuals in the party who were prepared to criticize and oppose. One was Constantin Pârvulescu. At the eleventh party congress in 1979 he accused the Conducator of putting his personal interests above those of the party and the nation, stating that he would not vote for his re-election. That evening the 84 year old communist veteran was evicted from his flat and no reference to his speech appeared in the official records of the congress. Rarely a party member might register disapproval by defection, the most prominent being Ion Pachepa, the second most senior officer of the Securitate's external espionage apparat, who fled to the west in July 1978 and provided posterity with colourful insights into the world of the Romanian security apparatus.[8]

Not until 1989 however did there appear a real indication of concerted party action against the dictator when on 10 March 1989 Romanian language radio stations in the west broadcast 'the letter of the six'. Signed by six prominent communists the letter catalogued the sufferings of the nation and then called for, in this order, an end to the systematization programme, the restoration of constitutionally guaranteed civil rights and an end to food exports which, it said, were 'threatening the biological existence of our nation'. The letter put the lie to the regime's oft-repeated assertion that it enjoyed the support of the whole party. A number of the six were immediately arrested.

The intelligentsia had always produced its crop of critics, though Ceauşescu's Romania was too restrictive to allow the development of anything which could have been described as a dissident movement. In 1970 the novelist Paul Goma attempted to publish a book critical of Elena Ceauşescu and was of course denied permission. In 1977 he circulated a letter of solidarity with Charter 77 in Prague but only a few of his fellow intellectuals signed it, all but two of them from the ethnic minority groups. Goma was forced into exile. Doina Cornea, a Uniate who had taught French in the University of Cluj, was placed under house arrest in 1982 for her constant criticism of the regime, but this did not prevent her from smuggling out further damaging details of the government's actions, particularly its systematization programme and its destruction of cultural traditions. Understandably, few could find the courage of a Cornea and instead took solace in internal migration. For some religion provided their refuge, sometimes clandestinely as with the Uniates who continued a tenuous existence underground. Others, disillusioned by the collaborationist policies of the Romanian Orthodox Church, which increased after the death of Patriarch Justinian in 1977, joined the Pentecostalists or other sects; some of these had American connections which the regime could attack only at the cost of endangering its relations with Washington. In general, however, the intelligentsia opposition was weak. In part this was because after the severe repression of the Gheorghiu-Dej era the children of political prisoners, who were denied higher education until 1963, left the country when they were free to do so in the 1960s and early 1970s; had they remained they would have provided the obvious crystallization point for intelligentsia opposition in the 1980s.

If the Ceauşescu regime was not troubled by the protests of a few intellectuals or religious observers, it was much more concerned at the possibility of organized dissent within the army. There was an attempt at a military coup in 1976 when the defence minister General Ion Ioniţa conspired with the chief of the army staff, General Ion Gheorghe, to overthrow Ceauşescu but they decided they could not be assured of popular support and abandoned the plan. They revived it in 1983 but were betrayed. Twelve officers were shot and Gheorghe died of a cancer which he was convinced had been injected into him on a crowded bus.

The ultimate threat to any regime is from the masses. The working class, in whose name he ruled, showed periodic anger towards Ceauşescu. The miners of the Jiu valley had voiced their discontents when Ceauşescu visited them during a strike in 1972 and in August 1977 they struck again. On the third day of the stoppage Ceauşescu responded to the demand that he should go and talk with the strikers but when he arrived he was booed and jeered with shouts of 'Down with the Red Bourgeoisie'. He beat a hasty retreat but soon afterwards two leaders of the strike died in mysterious accidents and over 4,000 strikers were transferred to other mines. Retribution awaited others who took direct action, including once more workers in the Jiu valley who in 1979 tried to form an independent trade union. There were occasional strikes elsewhere including protests at the workings of the NEFM in the Maramureş area and, in 1983, in the Red Star Tractor plant in Braşov. That plant was to provide the most serious of all the threats to the stability of the Ceauşescu regime. On 15 November 1987 protests over wage cuts led the workers to leave their factory and invade the town where they ransacked the party headquarters. This was an old-fashioned hunger riot but it had enormous consequences. Over two hundred workers were arrested and tortured in an attempt to discover the identity of the non-existent organizers. Even more importantly, it persuaded Ceauşescu that the existing apparatus for controlling the population was inadequate; after Braşov the main instrument for social control ceased to be the party and became the Securitate. In 1988 all judeţs and municipalities were ordered to prepare plans for suppressing disorder, in which process the anti-terrorist units of the Securitate were to play a prominent role.

Yet when the final revolt against the Ceauşescu regime began it started not with an army coup, nor with a hunger riot, but with poetry readings. Despite the crumbling of socialist power elsewhere in Eastern Europe in 1989 the fourteenth congress of the RCP in November seemed to indicate that the Ceauşescu regime was impervious to the political tides flowing around it. A confident Ceauşescu left for a visit to Iran in December. While he was away a young Magyar Protestant pastor, Lászlo Tőkés, breached regulations by allowing three students to recite poetry during one of his services in Timişoara. His bishop, feeling discretion the better part of valour, decided to transfer him to another, and much more remote, parish. Tőkés refused to go, and within days his protest had received support from local people, Hungarian and Romanian, Christian and non-Christian. When the vigil outside Tőkés's church turned into a demonstration the army intervened and blood was spilt. When Ceauşescu arrived back from Iran on 20 December he appeared on television and dismissed the protests as the work of 'a few groups of hooligan elements'.[9] But the unrest was spreading. On the day of his broadcast there were outbreaks in Arad and other cities and then on 21 December in Bucharest itself. A huge crowd had gathered outside the party headquarters in the centre of the city to hear the Conducator speak but the most important sounds came not from Ceauşescu but from two boys aged fourteen and sixteen. It was they, it seems,[10] who began the booing and the catcalls which were to disorientate Ceauşescu whose discomposure was seen throughout the nation on television. When he learned from reports from helicopters flying over the city that crowds of workers were moving towards the party headquarters, Ceauşescu and his party called down one of the helicopters and fled.

The overthrow of Ceauşescu was not accomplished without violence. Loyal units of his Securitate, supported, rumour had it, by groups of Arab terrorists, fought fiercely for his restoration. The fear that they might succeed was a major factor in persuading Romania's new rulers to execute the former ruling couple on Christmas Day; only when Romanian television had given extensive and repeated coverage of the trial and execution did the Securitate abandon the fight. Until the wars of Yugoslav succession the Romanian revolution produced the worst violence seen in the collapse of the communist system in Europe.

Notes

1. Dennis Deletant, *Communist Terror in Romania: Gheorghiu-Dej and the Police State, 1948–1965*, London: Hurst, 1999, pp.135, 196.
2. Cited in David Floyd, *Rumania: Russia's Dissident Ally*, London: Pall Mall Press, 1965, pp.viii–ix.
3. *Statement of the Rumanian Communist Party*, April 1964, quoted in Floyd, p.83.
4. Silviu Brucan, *The Wasted Generation: Memoirs of the Romanian Journey from Capitalism to Socialism and Back*, Boulder, CO; San Francisco, CA; and Oxford: Westview Press, 1993, p.101.
5. Cited in Julian Hale, *Ceauşescu's Romania: A Political Documentary*, London: Harrap, 1971, p.11.
6. See above p.138.
7. Martyn Rady, *Romania in Turmoil: A Contemporary History*, London: Taurus Books, 1992, p.63.
8. In his memoirs, *Red Horizons: the Extraordinary Memoirs of a Communist Spy Chief*, London: Heinemann, 1988.
9. Quoted in Robert Cullen, *Twilight of Empire: Inside the Crumbling Soviet Bloc*, London: The Bodley Head, 1991, p.84.
10. See Brucan (1993), p.1.

Chapter 12

GREECE, 1949–1990

When the civil war ended Greece had endured a period of occupation and war longer than that experienced anywhere else in Europe, in addition to which it had also had to suffer authoritarian or semi-authoritarian government since 1936. That representative institutions and parliamentary democracy were to be reborn was testimony to Greece's dedication to the open society, but the evolution towards that society was gradual and it was not entirely the work of the Greeks or their leaders; other vital factors were the cold war, American aid and the impact of the Cyprus problem.

THE BEGINNINGS OF POLITICAL RELAXATION, 1949–52

After such a long and bitter civil war the Athens government, even in victory, could scarcely feel secure and many of the restrictions imposed during the emergency remained in force for years to come. Throughout the 1950s tens of thousands of communist sympathizers remained in exile while many more, some of them under sentence of death, still languished in gaols or camps in Greece itself. For all Greek citizens law 509 of 1947 remained in force enabling the police to take action against anyone suspected of left-wing activities, and a certificate of social beliefs still had to be produced by anyone wishing to secure a post in the civil service or even to acquire a passport or driving licence. Nor had the police relinquished the voluminous files they kept on almost every inhabitant of the country. Many of these restrictions were to remain in place until the mid-1970s.

Some progress to relaxation was, however, made. In February 1950 the end of martial law was proclaimed and in the following month the first elections since 1946 were held. They were conducted under the same system of proportional representation as the immediate post-war election and produced a narrow victory for Tsaldaris's People's Party (PP) which gained the largest number of seats in parliament although most votes went to the three centre parties, the Liberals under Sophocles Venizelos, Nikolaos Plastiras's National Progressive Union (EPEK), and the eponymous Georgios Papandreou

Party. This did not make for stable government and after a succession of five feeble ministries further elections were held in September 1951. The most notable feature of this poll was the appearance of new formations on the right with Greek Rally, created and led by civil war commander Alexander Papagos in imitation of de Gaulle's movement in France, and on the left the United Democratic Left (EDA) which was a cover for the still-banned KKE. Papagos's Rally replaced the PP which secured only two seats in the new parliament compared to the Rally's 114. The EDA had 10 seats leaving the majority with EPEK and the Liberals whose combined tally was 131. On the basis of their support a new government was formed under Plastiras.

The Plastiras cabinet managed to enact a new constitution in January 1952. It left in place many of the restrictions imposed in the civil war and even introduced further limitations, such as the denial of the right to strike to civil servants, but it also enacted the basic democratic freedoms. In April Plastiras felt confident enough to introduce the first measures of conciliation towards the defeated of the civil war; most death sentences were commuted to prison terms, existing prison sentences were reduced and many, but by no means all, detainees were released.

If Plastiras could make conciliatory gestures he could not secure the holy grail of Greek parliamentary politics, stable government. In November 1952 yet another general election was held. This time the Rally won an outright majority in the chamber because this election had been held under the majoritarian system. Tinkering with the system of voting was to become customary in Greek politics and was usually carried out in order to enhance an incumbent ministry's electoral prospects. In this instance, however, the main proponent of change was neither the ruling government nor the chief opposition faction, but the United States ambassador who had publicly threatened an end to American aid if such a change were not made.

This was by no means the first time that the embassy had involved itself in Greek affairs. After the March 1950 elections there had been frequent attempts by the United States' representative to bring the centre parties together in some form of workable alliance. The American government was acting within the context of the cold war. Although the Tito–Stalin split had fractured communist unity in the Balkans and made a Soviet-Bulgarian descent upon the Aegean coast more difficult it had not rendered it impossible, and after communist aggression in Korea in the summer of 1950 there was no guarantee that forward policies would not be pursued elsewhere. While this accounted for American willingness to involve itself in Greece, Greek willingness to tolerate that involvement was encouraged by communist rule in Albania, Bulgaria, Romania and elsewhere, where the purges were in full spate and where forced economic change was producing massive social dislocation with little material betterment. American intervention in Greece, on the other hand, was bringing massive economic benefit. Nevertheless, when the communist bogey became less threatening Greek tolerance of American interference would diminish.

YEARS OF STABILITY, 1952–61

The primary objective of the new electoral system was achieved in that the elections of November 1952 ushered in almost a decade of stable government. It was a decade in which Greece made enormous economic progress and in which the Cyprus problem threw its long shadow over Greek affairs.

The economic revival of Greece owed much to aid from the United States which between 1947 and 1966 amounted to $3.75 billion, around half of it in military supplies. The non-military funds helped Greece to improve its communications system, especially its roads, and to create a national electricity grid. But it was not American aid alone which ensured Greece's economic progress. In 1953 the drachma was devalued by a drastic 50 per cent which, when coupled with the subsequent monetarist policies, gave Greece a stable currency, a blessing unknown for a generation. At the same time, some state control of industry was removed, while agricultural reform and investment were encouraged by both American advisors and government officials. An energetic programme of irrigation, drainage, the rationalization of holdings and the introduction of new seed varieties helped Greece to become self-sufficient in food, a great psychological boost in view of the horrendous famine of the early war years. The economy was helped further by the beginnings of a tourist industry and even more so by remittances from the growing number of Greeks who had gone abroad to work; between 1951 and 1970, it has been estimated, about one in eight of the population emigrated. Remittances helped to strengthen the currency but the fact that many Greeks were now going to western Germany rather than Australia or the United States also meant that they retained closer links to their homeland, to which many of them soon returned to establish their own small enterprises in manufacturing or the service sector. Some enterprises were far from small. A few Greek ship owners, some of whom had wisely bought up American liberty boats at the end of the Second World War, made healthy fortunes and contributed significantly to the country's economic revival.

The increase in national wealth was not spread equally among the various social groups but it was experienced to some degree by almost all of them. In 1951 the average per capita income was $112, by 1956 it had risen to $270 and by 1964 it had reached $500, an increase of almost 350 per cent in a period when prices had risen much more slowly. The ravages of war and inflation meant that most Greeks had little faith in investment or savings and they therefore poured their wealth into property and construction. This meant the disfiguration of many Greek towns and villages, a process by no means confined to that country, and Athens grew disproportionately, partly because agricultural reform and high birth rates produced rural population displacement.

The American sponsorship which did much to create economic growth naturally determined Greece's foreign policy alignment. In 1952 Greece had become a member of NATO and in 1953 it had moved closer to Yugoslavia, which was regarded as natural and acceptable by most Greeks, and to Turkey, which they found more problematical. Relations with Yugoslavia soon became more distant, the partial reconciliation between Belgrade and Moscow making Yugoslavia's need for friends in the west less pressing. Good relations with Turkey remained a necessity as far as NATO strategists were concerned but were made difficult by the tensions arising over Cyprus.

The island had been occupied by Great Britain in 1878 and annexed in 1914 when the suzerain power, the Ottoman empire, joined Germany in the First World War. In 1925 it had become a crown colony. Agitation for *enosis*, or union with Greece, had broken out in the early 1930s but had achieved little. During the Second World War the British Foreign Secretary, Sir Anthony Eden, had publicly suggested that union with Greece might take place after the war on condition that Britain retained bases on the island, but his remarks had been made chiefly to forestall any German move to make the same offer. After the war Greece's initial dependence on the British and then its preoccupation with its own civil war meant that the Cyprus issue was not in the forefront of discussion. This changed with the end of the civil war and with the replacement of Britain by the United States as the chief patron of Greece; it was rightly assumed that Washington would be more willing than London to contemplate changes in the status of Cyprus, where 18 per cent of the population were Turkish and 80 per cent Greek. In January 1950 the Orthodox Church in Cyprus conducted a poll among the Greeks, 96 per cent of whom declared in favour of *enosis*. In March of that year a new archbishop of Cyprus, Makarios, was elected. Now the Greek Cypriots had a leader as well as a cause.

Pressure for *enosis* grew steadily but not dramatically. The issue was discussed in London where Greek suggestions of a move in that direction were brusquely rejected. By the middle of the decade the Greeks had turned to the United Nations, hoping that the growing anti-colonialism of world opinion would help them. It did not, and in April 1955 serious rioting broke out in the Cypriot capital, Nicosia. This prompted the British to enlist the Turkish government, which had previously remained outside the fray, as a counterbalance to the Greek lobby. It did not help. In September 1955 an arson attack on the Salonika house in which the founder of the modern Turkish republic, Kemal Atatürk, had been born provoked a pogrom against the Greek populations of Istanbul and Izmir. One hundred thousand Greeks had been allowed to remain in Istanbul under the terms of the treaty of Lausanne in 1923; after 1955 most of them left, their homes and shops plundered and burnt, their churches desecrated. In 1955 the Greek population of the city was around 80,000; by 1980 it had fallen to about 6,000.

In Cyprus itself tensions rose when Britain increased coercion and exiled Makarios to the Seychelles in March 1956. The removal of Makarios increased the influence of the National Organization of Cypriot Fighters (EOKA), led by Colonel Grivas, the former head of the post-war right-wing organization Chi, whose men now took to attacking Turkish policemen and British soldiers in addition to the non-compliant members of the Greek community who had previously been their main targets. In 1957 British attitudes softened with Makarios being allowed to leave the Seychelles for Athens, but efforts to reach a constitutional settlement were blocked by Greece which still hoped to secure *enosis* via the UN. By now the United States was becoming increasingly frustrated. The dispute was endangering NATO's south-eastern flank and was also encouraging what was to Washington a disturbing revival of the left in Greece. A further change came about when Makarios let it be known that he would consider Cypriot independence as an alternative to *enosis*, and the British for their part said they would be satisfied with such a settlement as long as the United Kingdom retained sovereignty over the island's two main airbases.

This provided the basis for a settlement reached between the Greek and Turkish prime ministers in Zürich in February 1959. In 1960 Cyprus became an independent member of the British commonwealth, its independence being guaranteed by Britain, Greece and Turkey, each of which had the right to act unilaterally to defend the settlement. The island's complicated constitution attempted to create a working, bi-communal system. The president was to be a Greek Cypriot and the vice president was to be chosen from the Turkish community, while its House of Representatives was to have 35 Greek and 15 Turkish deputies. In the administration posts were to be divided between the two communities with the Turks being allocated very generous proportions; 40 per cent of the police, for example, were to be drawn from the Turkish population. Also Greece was to be allowed to keep 950 troops on the island, and the Turks 650.

The settlement enraged Grivas and gave the Greek left much ammunition to use against the government. Since the beginning of the Cyprus emergency in 1955 the Athens government had changed in personnel but not in direction. Papagos had died in October 1955, shortly after the Istanbul pogrom, his successor being Konstantinos Karamanlis. Karamanlis, of relatively poor, provincial origin, had been a surprise nomination made by the king, but if he were humble in origin he was to prove long in duration. His nomination caused some disgruntled members of the Rally to leave the party, whereupon Karamanlis refashioned it into a new organization, the National Radical Union (ERE). In February 1956 a general election was held. A new and complicated franchise was introduced which included women for the first time in Greek history. The main opposing force was the Democratic Union, a catch-all organization which stretched from the remnants of the PP on the right to the EDA on the left and which fell apart immediately after the election. The Democratic Union in fact polled more votes than the ERE, 48 per cent as opposed to 47 per cent, but the vagaries of the electoral system gave the ERE 165 seats in parliament and the Democratic Union 132.

When the next elections were held, in May 1958, the electoral system was again changed, a new form of 'reinforced PR' being introduced to limit the prospects of electoral coalitions. The elections were the first crack in the post-1953 edifice of stability and solidity. The centre parties could not cohere and therefore the main opposition came from the EDA which took almost a quarter of the votes and 79 seats in the assembly. The ERE's share of the vote fell from the 48 per cent of 1956 to 41 per cent but, again thanks to the peculiarities of the system, their number of seats actually rose from 165 to 171.

The 1958 elections had shown the inadequacies of the voting system and the growing power of the left. The latter had several causes. Anger at the semi-fixing of the elections was one. Another was growing frustration over the Cyprus issue. A third was increasing anti-Americanism, with the left castigating NATO and the USA for their failure to help over Cyprus. But there was more to the growing antipathy to Uncle Sam than his failure to help Greece over Cyprus. American penetration of Greece had been deep and in many cases insensitive. American advisors were attached not only to the Greek armed forces but, under the terms of an agreement of October 1953, to civilian ministries too; the American supervising the ministry of national economy, for example, not only signed all outgoing documents but also carefully checked the carbon copies. Ministries, nationalized industries and private concerns which were in receipt of American aid were expected to accept American supervisors and advisors whose jobs were to ensure that corruption did not squander or sully US investment. The rise of the left also had sociological causes, most notably the appearance in the cities of a new stratum of incoming poor whose lack of wealth or welfare contrasted sharply, as they could daily see, with the lifestyle of the few urban rich.

The sudden rise of the left was one of the reasons why Karamanlis, with full American backing, approached the European Economic Community (EEC) in June 1959. In July 1961 Greece became the first state to sign an association agreement with that organization, the agreement holding out the prospect of full membership of the EEC in 1984. The intention on both sides was to anchor Greece firmly in the western camp and to make it more difficult for any subsequent leftist administration to move the country out of that camp.

THE RETURN OF POLITICAL INSTABILITY, 1961–7

Between 1961 and 1967 Greece became increasingly unstable. Public faith in the electoral system was shaken and the established political order was compromised by proven associations with non-official and violent elements and by clientalism, especially in the army. In addition to these problems the Cyprus question became ever more intractable and destabilizing.

In many ways the elections of 1958 were re-fought in October 1961. Anger and resentment over Cyprus were even greater after the granting of independence in the previous year. The international situation and the role of the United States in Greek affairs were again very much at issue. Karamanlis believed that the Soviet Union had once more bared its teeth in building the Berlin wall in August and that the Greek electorate would react against this, which to some extent it did. On the other hand, many Greeks were alarmed at the prospect of the installation of nuclear weapons in US bases in Greece, Khrushchev having threatened to disintegrate the Acropolis in retaliation to such a deployment. Furthermore, reaction against communist aggression bene-fited the centre as well as the right. Papandreou, who had proved his anti-communist credentials when in office in 1944–5, had been as alarmed as Karamanlis at the growth of the EDA in 1958 and had therefore taken great pains to construct the Centre Union to fence off the left, and communist aggression in Europe helped him to do this. He could legitimately present himself to the electorate as a proven, dedicated anti-communist alternative to Karamanlis. In addition he could offer some minimal degree of social welfare, which was not part of the ERE's legislative agenda.

According to the official results of the October 1961 poll 51 per cent of the electorate had voted for the ERE, 34 per cent for the Centre Union and its ally the Progressive Alliance, and 15 per cent for the EDA. The ERE had 176 seats in the new assembly, the Centre Union/Progressive Alliance 100 and the EDA 24. The opposition refused to accept the results as a true reflection of political opinion. In the first place, the voting lists had been based on the census of 1951 which meant very considerable under-representation of the cities which had grown so rapidly in the intervening decade. More serious was the widely voiced suspicion that the government vote had been augmented by pressure exercised unfairly and unlawfully by the police, the army and other 'dark forces'; the army, for example, was rumoured to have implemented an 'Operation Pericles' to prevent the defeat of the government.

The October 1961 election was the end of political stability in Greece for a decade and a half. Papandreou denounced the results as an 'electoral fraud' and devoted much of his considerable campaigning skills to demanding a fresh poll. This constant onslaught weakened the Karamanlis administration. So too did the murder in May 1963 of Grigoris Lambrakis, a popular left-wing deputy who was killed after a peace rally in Salonika. The Greek political mind, quick as ever to suspect conspiracy and intrigue, assumed there had been collusion between Lambrakis's murderers and the authorities; for once the Greek political mind was correct, an official investigation estab-lishing links between the killers and senior policemen. Public fears that the Karamanlis government was covertly working with sinister, right-wing 'parastate' elements were confirmed. In such circumstances the prime minis-ter could scarcely afford to lose the support of the king and queen. Yet this he did when in the summer of 1963 he advised against proceeding with a visit to London on the justifiable grounds that the royal couple would be met with large demonstrations demanding the release of the communist and other leftist prisoners still held in Greek jails. When this advice was disregarded Karamanlis resigned.

It was the end of an era, an era dominated in many ways by the fall-out from the civil war, but nevertheless an era of increasing stability and prosperity. The subsequent era was to be very different.

From the elections called for November 1963 the Centre Union emerged with the most seats. Papandreou formed an administration but his majority in parliament was not absolute and he was forced to rely on the EDA. This he could not stomach and on 24 December resigned, gambling that fresh elections would give him the total control of parliament he needed to modernize Greece without pushing the country too far to the left. His gamble paid off. In February 1964 fresh elections gave him 53 per cent of the poll and 171 seats in parliament; the ERE had 35 per cent and 107 seats and were therefore the main opposition force, the EDA being reduced to 12 per cent of the vote and 22 deputies. In the following month King Paul died. He was succeeded by his son who came to the throne as King Constantine II.

The political scene in Greece appeared secure. The prime minister had a dependable majority. A new king had come to the throne when, for the first time since the Second World War, Greece had a loyalist opposition as well as a loyalist government. And even the Americans now seemed to believe that a reformist left of centre administration was as good a bulwark against communism as rule by the right. Within eighteen months any optimism created by this favourable conjunction had evaporated.

On taking office Papandreou was faced with problems over Cyprus. In November 1963 Archbishop Makarios had demanded a reduction in the rights afforded to the Turkish minority under the 1960 constitution, a demand which had been rejected by the Turkish government in Ankara speaking on behalf of the Turkish Cypriots. Tensions rose rapidly and in December furious fighting broke out on the island, raising the threat of Turkish military intervention. Papandreou sent Greek troops to reinforce the Cypriot National Guard but the dangers did not subside until the summer of 1964 when United Nations forces were deployed to maintain order. By this time a sizeable proportion of the Turks on the island had congregated in enclaves while both the resident Greeks and Papandreou had turned down an American peace proposal under which Cyprus, with Turkish self-governing cantons and military bases established to protect the minority population, would have become part of Greece. Makarios, meanwhile, had completely forsaken *enosis* in favour of independence and neutrality; and he now looked to the Soviet bloc for help in achieving this aim.

The Cypriot emergency embarrassed Papandreou. He had failed to advance the Greek cause and at the same time Makarios's turn towards the socialist bloc won the warm approval of Papandreou's leftist domestic opponents and enabled them to pose as the best defenders of the Greek Cypriot cause. The Cyprus question also deflected Papandreou from his main purpose: the modernization of Greece. Nevertheless he was able to make some progress in this direction. He arranged for the release of many, though not all, of the political prisoners, but his main achievement was educational reform. The school leaving age was raised from twelve to fifteen, and in primary schools instruction was henceforth to be in demotic Greek rather than in the *katharevousa*, while the time given to classical Greek studies was to be decreased to make way for more mathematics and science and for modern subjects such as law, economics and sociology.

When he turned his reforming attention to the army, however, Papandreou ran into very stormy waters. After the civil war Greek political parties had relied less on ideology than on personalities for their cohesion and this had meant that followers frequently joined parties not because they believed in their programmes – frequently they did not have one – but in the hope of advancement through personal connections with the leadership who, once in power, would have huge numbers of government jobs and contracts at their disposal. Because the right had been in office for eleven years before Papandreou became prime minister it had built up a huge body of support in all branches of the state apparatus, including, Papandreou feared, the armed forces. His anxieties were not diminished by the conspiratorial activities of the right-wing Sacred Bond of Greek Officers. The army and the right were, in turn, wary of and worried by Papandreou's reforming intentions; in their eyes the release of political prisoners and the downgrading of the cherished *katharevousa* had been bad enough, but the introduction of reformist officers into the forces was a good deal worse. And from May 1965 they too had a conspiracy to fear. The left-leaning 'Aspida' (Shield) group had emerged among officers, particularly in Cyprus, who felt their promotion prospects and conditions of service had been blighted because they did not share the political affiliations of their right-wing seniors. It was widely rumoured that they looked for political support and leadership to Andreas Papandreou, the prime minister's son. 'Aspida's' Nasserite tendencies, the right alleged, posed a threat to the military establishment and to the foreign policy orientation of post-civil war Greece.

The prime minister was not unduly concerned at the activities of the 'Aspida' group but he was determined to weaken what he saw as the right's entrenched position in the army, and especially in the military intelligence service. In 1965 he therefore set about replacing overtly hostile officers and produced plans for a thorough reform of the military establishment. When his minister of defence refused to obey him, Papandreou sacked him and announced that he was taking temporary charge of the ministry. The minister, however, declined to leave office. In July 1965 Papandreou asked the king to dismiss the disobliging minister but this the king refused to do, insisting that it would be inappropriate for Papandreou to become minister for defence when his own son was under investigation in connection with the 'Aspida' affair. The king had not gone beyond the letter of his constitutional rights, but his conduct was scarcely conducive to political stability, as was proved when Papandreou submitted his resignation. He had not expected that it would be accepted but when it was tens of thousands of his supporters poured onto the streets of Athens, denouncing the whole affair as a royal putsch. Greece was not to enjoy political repose for nine years.

THE RULE OF THE COLONELS, 1967–74

In the summer of 1965 the king had wanted to split the Centre Union but it was to be three months before he could find enough 'apostates' within it to form a government, and when it was formed it had a majority of only two in parliament. Faced by implacable Papandreou supporters within the assembly and frequent, massive but overwhelmingly peaceful demonstrations on the streets the new administration was virtually impotent. In December 1966 its death sentence was pronounced when Papandreou and the ERE leader, Panayiotis Kanellopoulos, agreed that elections should be held in May 1967 and that a caretaker government should be formed to supervise them.

The election campaign was intense with the left within the Centre Union aligning behind Andreas Papandreou on the assumption that his father had done an electoral deal with the right not to make the monarchy or the army an election issue. The latter inevitably became one in March 1967 when fifteen officers were convicted in the 'Aspida' trial, after which the public prosecutor demanded that Andreas Papandreou's parliamentary immunity be lifted so that he too might stand trial. The Centre Union's response was to table a bill prolonging the immunity of incumbent deputies throughout the electoral campaign. This was too much for the ERE; the December 1966 agreement collapsed and the caretaker administration resigned. Greece it seemed was drifting towards chaos and in the light of this the king and a number of senior officers met to consider a military takeover should order collapse or if, *horribile dictu*, the Centre Union won a thumping majority in the elections. These deliberations were otiose. On the morning of 21 April 1967 a group of middle-ranking officers acted and in a well-organized and effective coup placed the country under military rule. Greece had become the first 'western' European state to fall to dictatorship since the Second World War, and the regime of 'the colonels', as they became known, was to be the longest period of military rule in the history of modern Greece.

After the swift action of 21 April the king agreed to recognize what was in effect a shadow civilian government, though the real authority lay with a triumvirate of Colonel Georgios Papadopoulos, Colonel Nikolaos Makarezos and Brigadier Stylianos Pattakos. The colonels set up a 'Revolutionary Council' of twelve officers and for a few months ruled with the king. The king had little power, however, and on 13 December attempted to remove the usurpers, but his efforts were amateurish almost to the point of ridicule and his attempted counter-coup failed utterly. He went into exile. A regency was established but the shadow civilian administration was disbanded, Papadopoulos becoming prime minister.

The departure of the king made it easier for the colonels to restructure Greece. In 1968 they introduced a new constitution which was endorsed in an entirely fraudulent plebiscite. The constitution placed power effectively in the hands of the military. Parliament, if and when it were reinstated, was not to be allowed to investigate issues of foreign policy or defence, and the military was to have absolute control over appointments, promotions and postings in its own ranks. The electorate was to be slimmed down, if not explicitly then through the regulation that anyone convicted of an act 'directed against the existing political or social order' was to be denied the right to vote; those wishing to stand for election had to be of Greek citizenship, a clause which made impossible the election of anyone who had gone into exile and had then been arbitrarily deprived of their citizenship. Any party wishing to contest an election had to be approved by the constitutional court, and there was an explicit prohibition on any party which endangered public security or advocated changes in the form of government, the social order or the territorial integrity of Greece. The constitution also revoked most of Papandreou's educational reforms.

For a while the regime still maintained, mostly for the sake of world opinion, that it intended to return the country to democracy but in August 1969 the minister for foreign affairs indiscreetly admitted to journalists in Switzerland that there was no such intention. In fact, rather than moving towards democracy Greece was coming closer to personal dictatorship under Papadopoulos. By 1970 he had emerged as the major power holder in the junta and he completed his internal takeover in the following year. Tensions within the Revolutionary Council had grown since 1969 and in 1971 Papadopoulos used a reform in local government to appoint potential rivals as district governors and thus put them a safe distance both from the capital and from others of like mind with whom they might conspire. Papadopoulos was to remain the dominant figure in Greece for the next two years.

The colonels' regime is sometimes remembered for its absurdities. It was a regime which, until the tourist trade suffered too much, banned foreigners with miniskirts, beards or long hair; it was a government which insisted everyone stand for the national anthem and that all schoolchildren must carry satchels; and all schoolchildren and their teachers were required by another decree to attend church every Sunday. But it was also a vicious regime. It imprisoned and deported to camps thousands of its opponents, actual or assumed, and it inflicted savage, mediaeval forms of torture on many of them.

Initially it claimed that it had seized power to save Greece from communism or from a left-wing coup. Both claims were absurd. The colonels failed to produce any real evidence of a communist plot, and the fact that they bowed to American pressure and allowed Andreas Papandreou to go into exile, even though he had been indicted, indicates that there was little proof of intended left-wing subversion. After the departure of the king the colonels said less about communist or left-wing plots and justified their 'revolution' more on the grounds that a new brush had been needed to sweep away the corruption of parliamentary and party politics.

The 'revolution', as its architects liked to call the 21 April putsch, had little in the way of ideology. Its propaganda included slogans such as 'Greece of the Christian Greeks' and 'Helleno-Christian civilization'. The regime stressed Greek traditions against the liberalism and decadence of the west, and it emphasized Greek national interests as against any form of internationalism, especially of the socialist variety. The latter was inseparable from Russia and the Slav world and therefore the colonels' propaganda contained a high degree of anti-Slav sentiment. The regime was also populist and paternalist, the colonels being fond of pointing out their own overwhelmingly peasant or lower-middle-class origins.

In actual policies the regime was first and foremost a military-police dictatorship. The military police assumed wide responsibilities for the maintenance of law and order, and in this it was helped by newly created military units which specialized in neutralizing political opposition. In the powerful Greek civil service most senior civilian officials, if they were lucky enough to keep their jobs, found they had to work alongside military men, many of them friends or relations of leading junta figures.

In the universities the student movement was controlled by the insertion of secret police agents into all committees; in fact most of them made no effort to disguise their identity or function, finding that such overt intimidation was as effective as surreptitious surveillance. Teaching staff who were not reliable were persecuted and all educational institutions, even private ones, were subjected to the authorities. From September 1970 deans and other senior officials were no longer to be elected by their faculties but appointed by the ministry from a list of three submitted by the relevant senate.

Other non-governmental bodies had to submit to similar controls. Leaders of left-wing trade unions, especially those allied to EDA, were arrested immediately after the coup and sent to prison camps, and on 4 May 1968 158 unions were dissolved. So strong was the international reaction that a new policy was adopted: rather than being abolished unions were to be restructured, their elected councils dissolved and anti-junta elements neutralized. In May 1969 the General Confederation of Greek Workers, until then untouched, saw its leaders dismissed although they were right-wing and had cooperated willingly with the employers. Thereafter the government changed the confederation's leadership frequently in order to keep it weak and ineffective. As a further, and characteristically paternalist blow to working-class organizations, the 1968 constitution banned any strikes which the government or the security forces chose to declare was against the 'material or moral interests of the workers'. The extensive cooperative movement which had been a feature of Greek peasant life for generations was also neutered; as with the trade unions recalcitrant leaders were arrested and elected councils replaced by appointed officials.

The press came under rigid control. Immediately after the coup pre-publication censorship was imposed on all newspapers and an index of banned publications was introduced. The latter was meant to include any work connected to the dreaded world of Slav-communism, and thus *Teach Yourself Russian* and a *Greek-Bulgarian Dictionary* became proscribed works. Pre-censorship was abolished in October 1969 as was the index of banned books in the following year, but an extremely tough press law held out condign punishment for anyone whose works offended the regime and this acted as an effective mechanism of censorship. Newspapers were also subjected to a sliding-scale import duty on newsprint; newspapers with a circulation of over 25,000, which included almost all publications considered anti-junta, paid an increasing scale of duty. But the urban Greek was, as ever, addicted to his newspaper and despite the sliding scale, and the censorship regulations notwithstanding, newspapers continued both to appear and to find ways around the regulations.

The judiciary in Greece technically enjoyed security of tenure. This inconvenience the colonels circumvented by suspending security of tenure for three days, during which they dismissed thirty senior judges. Not even the Orthodox Church was exempt from government interference. Shortly after coming to power the colonels dismissed the Archbishop of Athens and All Greece and went on to alter the composition of the Holy Synod and to sack a number of leading clerics who had showed signs of dissent, the Metropolitan of Salonika among them.

The restrictions the regime placed on so many institutions and professions illustrated above all its fear of opposition. Its support came from three quarters. First, the army generally welcomed the suppression of civilian political strife. Second, big business was won over by a series of concessions, especially to the wealthy Greek ship-owning fraternity who were offered favourable terms to register their vessels in Greece. And third, the regime received the tacit support of the United States not least because Greek ports were the only ones available to the US Sixth Fleet.

When they first assumed power the colonels were grudgingly given the benefit of the doubt by many Greeks. But there were also sections of the Greek people who never condoned the regime, and there were many others who soon came to loathe it. There were some acts of violent protest. In 1968 there was an attempt to assassinate Papadopoulos; there was a spate of bomb-throwing in Athens in the summer of 1971, and in Crete in October of the same year when US vice-president Spiro Agnew, himself of Greek descent, visited the island bombs were thrown and leaflets distributed, but by and large protest was non-violent, its most impressive manifestation being the funeral of Georgios Papandreou on 3 November 1968 when an estimated half million Athenians, about a fifth of the capital's population, spontaneously took to the streets to honour the enemy of the colonels. Less obtrusive, but much more widespread acts of disobedience were listening to the Greek-language broadcasts of foreign radio stations, while any film, play or novel which contained even the slightest hint of anti-authoritarian sentiment was rapturously received. Overall, however, the resistance to the regime was limited. The few activists did not find mass support and if the majority of the population disapproved of the regime they registered that disapproval not in overt opposition but in apathy and passive resistance.

The actual achievements of the colonels were few. The peasantry, which formed so important a part of the sentimental propaganda of the regime, received little benefit. Reforms in agriculture were introduced in 1968 but these had been drafted by previous administrations. They provided for the withdrawal of price support for wheat, dried fruits and tobacco, Greece's main agricultural exports, the support being replaced by government intervention if prices fell below fixed levels. The peasants were also guaranteed minimum incomes and, to great government fanfares, all agricultural debts were cancelled. In reality, most peasants had already paid off their debts and the real beneficiaries of government policies in the countryside were not the small producer but the middleman and the large landowners and cooperatives. Other government enactments, such as the abolition of free school meals and the closure of many village schools, increased the financial burden on the small peasants many of whom decided they could no longer bear the strain and left their smallholdings for the factories of Germany.

In economic terms the colonels had a relatively easy ride. Until 1973 the European and world economies were expanding and Greece's economic growth, which had been strong in the 1960s, continued after April 1967, albeit at a reduced rate. It was in foreign policy that the regime came unstuck. Ironically for a government dedicated to the defence of national interests the foreign policy of the colonels brought about defeat on some of the most important and cherished aspects of Greek national interests.

In the first place the EEC turned a cold shoulder, suspending the Association Agreement concluded in 1961; the European Investment Bank did the same, refusing to issue any further instalments of long-term loans already agreed. In NATO the Scandinavian nations and Canada pressed for Greece's expulsion and were frustrated primarily by the United States and Britain; even so, Greece was not allowed to take its due turn as president of the NATO council. In the summer of 1969, shortly after the minister for foreign affairs had made his gaffe in Switzerland, the colonels suffered further embarrassment when details were leaked of a supposedly secret Report of the Human Rights Commission of the Council of Europe which revealed a catalogue of bestiality and brutality towards political detainees in Greece. After that came the bizarre revelation that the colonels had thought of trying to precipitate a coup in Italy. In December 1969 Greece withdrew from the Council of Europe before it could be expelled.

The despised states of communist Eastern Europe were far less censorious, and much more accommodating. Papadopoulos's first trip abroad was to Romania and by 1971 the ministers for foreign affairs of Romania, Bulgaria and Yugoslavia had come to Athens. They saw their new ties with the Greek colonels as an embarrassment for NATO which was enough to justify closer association with a right-wing dictatorship.

By tradition Greece also had relatively close ties with the Arab world, not least because of the Greek diaspora in cities such as Alexandria which had existed until recent times; also Greece, with Spain, had been the only Mediterranean country not to recognize Israel *de jure*. These links were maintained under the colonels and new ones were established with a number of ex-colonial African states.

With two states, Albania and Turkey, the foreign policy of the colonels proved of crucial importance. Greece had remained technically at war with Albania because Tirana would not heed Greek pleas on behalf of the Greek minority in Albania, nor would it entertain Greek claims to northern Epirus. Yet in 1971 the colonels concluded an agreement with Albania which established diplomatic relations between the two countries and opened up the possibility of trade between them. But it made no mention of the Greek minority in Albania and this for many nationalist-minded Greeks, the very element from which the regime drew the majority of what support it had, was a cause of great puzzlement, if not distress.

Difficulties over Turkey and Cyprus were even more distressing. In September 1967 Papadopoulos and his stooge civilian prime minister held negotiations with the Turks at Keşan and Alexandroupolis in Thrace. The Greeks demanded *enosis*, a demand which the Turks contemptuously dismissed. The Turks then exploited Papadopoulos's diplomatic inexperience and naivety to extract concessions favourable to the Turkish side over the Turkish minority in western Thrace and over the status of the Greeks and their patriarch in Istanbul. After these negotiations the Turks also squeezed most of the Greeks out of Imbros and Tenedos, two islands near the mouth of the Straits, by populating them with the inmates of Turkish gaols. In November 1967 there were more violent clashes between the Turkish and Greek populations on Cyprus and only American intervention prevented military action by Greece and/or Turkey. The Americans secured an agreement whereby both states would withdraw their forces from Cyprus, but the agreement contained no measures for monitoring the withdrawal and while most Greek soldiers left most Turkish troops remained. Once again nationalist Greek opinion was outraged. Then in May 1971 Papadopoulos told a Turkish paper that the two governments should persuade the two communities on Cyprus to come to their senses. Now it was Cypriot Greek opinion which was outraged; many Greek Cypriots who until then had supported *enosis* now switched to backing Makarios and his efforts to keep Cyprus independent.

The growing complexity of the Cyprus problem was one reason why the colonels needed to re-establish what little legitimacy they enjoyed in Greece. Another arose in 1973 when the world oil crisis put an end to the long era of steady economic growth. In that year, for the first time in two decades, inflation reached double figures. As the economic clouds gathered frustrated elements in Greek society began to shed their fears and inhibitions. The most important of these, and the first to act, was the students. In May they occupied the law faculty in the University of Athens; later that month there was a mutiny in the navy. Papadopoulos accused the exiled king of meddling in the navy and used the mutiny as an excuse to depose Constantine and make Greece a 'presidential parliamentary republic'. Papadopoulos was then 'elected' president – there was only one candidate – for eight years and a minor civilian politician was brought in to supervise elections in what was to be a 'guided' democracy. The elections never took place. In November students occupied Athens Polytechnic from which they were ejected with such extraordinary brutality that over 40 people were killed. Papadopoulos was also a casualty. Unable to tolerate such anarchy extreme hard-right elements in the junta, led by Brigadier Dimitrios Ioannidis, the head of the hated military police, deposed him, accusing him of 'weakness' and dragging the country towards 'an electoral adventure'. Lieutenant-General Phaidon Gizikis was made president.

While Athens was in turmoil relations with Turkey suddenly deteriorated yet further. In 1973 oil, albeit in small quantities, had been discovered beneath the Aegean Sea which immediately raised conflicting claims. To make matters more complicated, the Ioannidis regime insisted that Makarios accept that Greece was the 'national centre' of Hellenism. Makarios was by now no more disposed to subjugate Cyprus to a military dictatorship based in Athens than he had previously been prepared to accept rule from an imperial author-ity in London, and in July 1974 he demanded that Greece withdraw all its officers from the Cyprus National Guard. Ioannidis launched a coup against him and Makarios fled. The government in Athens had intended to secure a massive nationalist triumph by bringing about *enosis* although this was in flat contravention of the 1960 agreement on Cyprus. What they brought about instead was a Turkish invasion of the island, Turkish troops landing in the north of Cyprus on 20 July 1974 to prevent *enosis*. Both sides mobilized but in Greece the process was a shambles with military commanders refusing Ioannidis's orders to attack the Turks.

A military dictatorship which cannot enforce discipline in its own officer corps is not destined to live long. Within days members of the old political establishment met with a number of officers and agreed to ask Karamanlis to return from exile to supervise the dismantling of the dictatorship and a return to democracy. He arrived early in the morning of 24 July 1974.

STABLE DEMOCRACY AND THE ROAD TO THE EEC, 1974–90

After his return to Greece Karamanlis rapidly created the national consensus essential for the return of political stability. His task was made easier by the removal of the monarchy and the army from the political arena. In external affairs his supreme achievement was to set Greece on the road to full mem-bership of the European community.

In the 1970s Greece was a mirror image of itself in the 1950s. In the 1950s the centre-right had enlisted the help of the extreme right to contain the extreme left. From 1967 to 1974 the threat to Greek democracy had come from the right rather than the left, and therefore the new centre rulers were more willing to work with the left to contain the extreme right. Other features of Greek political life, however, did not change, and one was con-tinuing tension with Turkey.

In August 1974 Turkish troops in Cyprus moved forward to what became known as the 'Attila Line'. Two-fifths of the island were now under Turkish control and 180,000 Greek refugees fled into the southern, Greek section.

There was little Karamanlis could do to help them. His immediate priority had been to create and preserve a coalition which would command the loyalty of a majority of Greeks. In this he succeeded, not least because he recognized the general shift to the left which had taken place in public feeling. The KKE was granted legal recognition, though this was not so bold a step as it would have been before the party had split in 1968 into pro-Moscow and Euro-communist wings. Karamanlis also had to acknowledge the intense anti-American sentiment which was rife in the country. The United States had never disowned the colonels, but even worse in Greek eyes was the fact that the Americans had not only failed to back the Greek cause in Cyprus but had also done nothing to prevent or reverse the Turkish invasion. For most Greeks loyalty to the United States and membership of NATO seemed to have brought little tangible reward. Karamanlis acknowledged this by withdrawing Greece from the military command structure of NATO and by admitting that the future of the four US bases in Greece should be debated. Another immediate concession which the new government had to make was to go some way towards slaking the national thirst for revenge against the military junta and to redressing as many of its wrongs as possible. The three main leaders of the coup, Papadopoulos, Makarezos and Pattakos, were therefore detained on an island, while those interned under the military regime were released, and those sacked restored where possible to their previous jobs.

Within less than four months of returning to Greece Karamanlis thought he had soothed enough ruffled feathers to risk a general election which was to be followed by a referendum on the monarchy. The first vote was held on 17 November 1974. It was the first general election in post-war Greece which saw participation by parties from right across the political spectrum. On the far left the two communist parties and the EDA joined to campaign for nationalization of the economy and neutrality in foreign policy. A new party appeared in the centre left, the Panhellenic Socialist Movement (PASOK) led by Andreas Papandreou. It called for the punishment of those responsible for the 1967 coup and military rule; it was republican and also suspicious of the USA, NATO and the EEC. In the centre the old Centre Union, now led by a former minister for foreign affairs, Georgios Mavros, was also republican but it supported membership of the European Community. Another new group was to be found on the centre right, New Democracy. This was Karamanlis's party and was a revitalized version of ERE. It stood for free enterprise, integration into the EEC and, notwithstanding Karamanlis's strictures on NATO, a pro-western foreign policy; it was, in theory at least, neutral with regard to the future of the monarchy. To its right was the National Democratic Union which was monarchist and had leanings towards authoritarian rule.

New Democracy emerged an easy winner from the electoral contest with 54 per cent of the vote. The workings of reinforced PR gave it 219 of the 300 seats in the assembly. New Democracy's victory surprised no one. Karamanlis was presented by the party, with considerable justification, as the saviour of the nation, New Democracy's main election slogan having been 'Karamanlis or the tanks'. The Centre Union was the second largest party, its 21 per cent of the poll giving it 60 seats in parliament. PASOK performed surprisingly well with 14 per cent of the vote and 13 seats. The EDA had 9 per cent of the vote and 8 seats.

On 8 December the second major vote, the referendum on the future of the monarchy, was held. It showed 69 per cent of Greeks in favour of a republic. The referendum was the sixth vote in the twentieth century on the issue and the fact that a clear decision had been arrived at in what was universally acknowledged as a free and fair poll removed from politics an issue which had bedevilled the country since the First World War. It was a welcome sign, at last, that Greeks could solve major domestic questions in an orderly, non-violent fashion.

If the question of the monarchy had been removed from the agenda, there remained that of the army. It was the army which had brought the civilians back to office, and the soldiers therefore could not be alienated: they may have refused to turn their guns on the Turkish army but there was no guarantee that they would not meddle once again in Greek politics. The reality of this danger became apparent in February 1975 with the discovery of a military conspiracy against both the Greek prime minister and Archbishop Makarios who had returned as president of Cyprus in December 1974. The plot was not the first to be hatched by the military since July 1974 but it was the most widespread and the most dangerous. Its containment and then its political exploitation had to be carefully managed. This Karamanlis did. Sixty officers involved in the plot were tried, most being found guilty, but the conspiracy, by opening up the question of military accountability before the law, allowed Karamanlis to go further and arraign the leading figures involved in the coup of 1967 and the military regime which followed it. Papadopoulos, Makarezos and Pattakos were sentenced to death, though this was rapidly commuted to life imprisonment, the new government not wishing to create military martyrs. Other prominent figures were given long gaol terms. Equally gratifying to the Greek public was the trial of thirty-one members of the former military police who had been responsible for some of the worst tortures inflicted upon political and other prisoners. These wretches were given the punishment they deserved, as were a small number of men responsible for the killings in Athens Polytechnic in November 1973. The trials had been televised and provided a form of catharsis for the much-troubled Greek political soul. They also removed the army from the forefront of the political scene so that within a matter of months two of the issues which had plagued public life for almost a century, the monarchy and the political role of the army, seemed to have been solved.

Karamanlis, with the support of the vast majority of the Greek people, had created a new political environment. He took advantage of this to introduce a new constitution, the removal of the monarchy having already made this necessary. The constitution of 9 June 1975 had a number of Gaullist features as it increased the powers of the president vis-à-vis those of parliament and the prime minister; the president was to have the right, for example, to dissolve the assembly if he believed it no longer enjoyed the confidence of the nation or if it had proved incapable of ensuring stable government, a provision which was clearly meant to prevent the instability of the mid-1960s. Yet Karamanlis was no de Gaulle. He did not himself yet seek the new office of president which went instead to an academic philosopher of conservative inclinations, Konstantinos Tsatsos.

With the questions of the monarchy and the army removed from centre stage and a new constitution and president installed, Karamanlis was free to concentrate more on the day-to-day affairs which dominate stable, working political systems. There were two major areas in which he was engaged: the economy and foreign policy.

The mid-1970s were a tough time economically for all western governments. They had to adjust to the great oil-price shock of 1973 but in Greece the situation was complicated by three factors. The colonels had over-borrowed and had made too many concessions to foreign investors which meant that Greece's overseas debt was larger and more difficult to pay back than it need have been; secondly, the recession in western Europe meant a fall in tourist revenues and, even more so, in remittances from Greek workers, income from this source falling by 13 per cent in a year; and finally, as the economy contracted, mounting tension with Turkey forced Greece to increase its military spending until it absorbed around a fifth of government income. There was little Karamanlis could do other than attempt to secure a larger take from wealthy shipping interests.

Deteriorating relations with Turkey resulted in part from the Cyprus problem, but not from that alone. There was a constant, low-level war of words on the question of the respective minorities, the Turkish in Thrace and the smaller Greek one in Istanbul and on islands near the mouth of the Dardanelles. There were mutual complaints over military measures which only increased the wariness of each side and made them more prone to increase defence spending. The Greeks took fright when the Turks created a new army group, 'the Army of the Aegean' based in Izmir: what function could it have, the Greeks asked, other than to attack the Greek islands, islands which the Turks refused to call Greek and referred to only as 'Aegean'? The Turks, meanwhile, insisted they had to create such an army because the Greeks, contrary to treaty agreements, had fortified islands such as Rhodes, Samos, Mytilini and Chios near the Turkish coast: why was this being done, the Turks asked, if Greece intended to remain at peace with Turkey just as Turkey intended to remain at peace with Greece? There were also disagreements over flight control operations in the Aegean area, which often meant that international airliners had to make long detours to avoid the area. The most serious disagreement, however, was on the continental shelf.

Greece and Turkey had long disagreed over this but until the discovery of oil in 1973 these had been largely academic or legal differences. Now the question had a hard political edge which was made harder in 1976 when a Turkish survey vessel, *Sismik I*, began prospecting in disputed waters between Limnos and Mytilini. This inflamed Greek suspicions and tempers, Andreas Papandreou even calling for the sinking of the offending vessel. This dangerous escalation of tension was contained only by shunting the multitudinous Graeco-Turkish disputes and disagreements into the siding of the UN.

The deterioration in relations with Ankara forced Athens to look for new foreign policy orientations. Popular anti-American feeling did not recede after the restoration of civilian rule while Athens' politicians believed that the USA would not back Greece against Turkey which was larger, and, more importantly, was limitrophe with the Soviet Union and therefore in the front line of the defence against communism. Alternative balances against Turkey were needed. There were two on offer. Greece's northern neighbours shared a sentimental antipathy to the successor state of the Ottoman empire, but with communist regimes in power this antipathy was political as well as sentimental. Furthermore, the Helsinki accords and the atmosphere of détente meant that anti-Turkish considerations carried at least as much weight as anti-communist fears; anti-communist and anti-Turkish Greece could therefore cooperate with communist but anti-Turkish regimes to the north. In the first half of 1975, even before tension with Ankara had reached its height, Karamanlis had visited Romania, Yugoslavia and Bulgaria, and his visits were reciprocated in the next few years. In 1976 a Balkan summit was held in Athens, which was significant not so much for what it did, which was little or nothing, but for the fact that it existed. In January 1981 a British expert on Greece could write that 'On Greece's northern frontier the Iron Curtain is almost ceasing to exist'.[1]

The other alternative to American patronage was Europe. Karamanlis made it a major platform of his policy to reactivate and develop the association agreement which the EEC has suspended during military rule. This was, he insisted, the way in which Greece could escape from its 'age-long isolation'. He found sympathetic listeners in Brussels and wherever there was a strong desire to preserve political stability in Greece. In July 1976 substantive negotiations on Greece's entry into the EEC were resumed.

Karamanlis decided in 1977 that any government taking the momentous step of bringing Greece into the EEC needed a fresh endorsement from the population. He therefore called a general election in November, a year before the expiry of the existing parliament's mandate. There was some regrouping of forces before the vote. On the far right National Rally attempted to revitalize what had seemed in 1974 a lost cause, while in the centre a rightist alignment calling itself the New Liberals appeared under the leadership of Konstantinos Mitsotakis. The former Centre Union joined with another group to form the Union of the Democratic Centre (EDIK), a social democratic party which was pro-EEC but anti-NATO. The pro-Moscow KKE (external) fought on its own.

There was little likelihood that New Democracy would be defeated. Karamanlis was still enjoying credit for the return to civilian rule while EEC membership, many believed, promised greater stability and increased material well-being. Nevertheless, New Democracy's share of the vote declined from the 54 per cent of 1975 to 42 per cent, giving it 172 seats in parliament. The old centre, now represented by EDIK, took only 12 per cent of the poll and had 15 seats, the KKE (external) 9 per cent and 11 seats, National Rally 7 per cent and 5 seats, and assorted leftist parties 3 per cent of the votes and 2 seats. The surprise of the election was the performance of PASOK. Its share of the vote went up from 14 per cent to 25 per cent giving it 93 seats in the assembly. It was now the major opposition force. The centre left had replaced the centre as the locus of opposition; fear of the extreme right remained at least as strong as fear of the extreme left. Greece was once more polarized and lacking a centre, but with the extreme left enfeebled, the monarchy removed and the army subjected to the law, there was no malign internal force to exploit this polarization for its own sectional interests.

If Karamanlis had hoped that the elections would give his government a renewed and reinforced mandate to take Greece into the EEC he was disappointed in that 39 per cent of the electorate voted for parties which were lukewarm or hostile in their attitudes to Brussels. It did not deter him. Negotiations continued until May 1979 when a treaty providing for Greece's accession to the European Community was signed in Athens. Instead of an entry date of 1984, which the original agreement of 1961 had contained, the 1979 treaty provided for Greek entry on 1 January 1981.

Karamanlis had achieved a huge amount in his five years in office and to him must go much of the credit for restoring Greece to peaceful, democratic government, and to putting it on the road towards an economic growth far beyond the reach of any other Balkan state. He chose to quit while he was winning. In May 1980 president Tsatsos's second term of office came to an end. The constitution prohibited a further term and Karamanlis therefore stepped into his place, leaving the premiership and the leadership of New Democracy in the hands of Georgios Rallis. Rallis's major act as head of government was to take Greece back into the military arm of NATO in October 1980. Greece was more firmly embedded than ever in the liberal, western, camp.

PASOK IN POWER, 1981–90

The election of October 1981 was a contest primarily between PASOK and New Democracy. After six years in office the latter was jaded and tired, and its new leader had nothing of the charisma or distinction of his predecessor.

Meanwhile, PASOK's appetite for power had grown sharply after the 1977 elections. To enhance yet further its electoral prospects it embarked on an extensive make-over. The 1960s student attire favoured by many leaders, not excluding Papandreou, was discarded for the suit, collar and tie; like the German SPD in the 1950s, PASOK ditched Marxism and presented itself as the party of small-property owning democracy. Its former suspicion of the EEC was muted, not least because it saw the economic benefits membership would bring to the small-property owner, especially in the countryside, and at the same time its anti-NATO rhetoric was played down, as was its previous trumpeting of the virtues of association with the third world. To all this was added a fashionable, and very understandable, drop of greenery with a call, welcomed by all, for action to disperse the appalling smog which descended all too frequently on Athens. Despite its greater sobriety PASOK remained a socialist–populist movement. Its appeal was most successful among the young, among the many poor immigrants into the cities and among women. It called for change; it represented a generational shift; its energetic leader contrasted powerfully with Rallis's tired image; and to elect a socialist government would prove to Greece, to Europe and to the world, that Greek democracy functioned and that the traumas of the civil war and military rule had been finally put aside.

The make-over succeeded completely. PASOK emerged with 48 per cent of the vote and 172 seats in parliament, an absolute majority. Papandreou formed Greece's first socialist government and set out to implement his populist programme. Like all such programmes it proved stronger on promise than delivery, but it did bring significant changes and did its country an admirable service by forcing it to come to terms with and overcome some uncomfortable aspects of the past. It recognized the resistance record of ELAS and allowed the return of ethnic Greek exiles who had fled after the civil war; Slavophone exiles who had made up a large proportion of the refugees, however, were not allowed to return. The new government also ended the ceremonies celebrating the defeat of the DAG.

In its efforts to modernize Greece the PASOK government simplified the system of accents in the written language and brought about some reform in the universities. It angered the Orthodox Church by allowing civil marriage and divorce by consent, and by decriminalizing adultery; it even legislated to outlaw the giving of dowries at marriage though this regulation proved impossible to enforce. The first steps were taken to introduce a national health service, though few wealthy or influential Greeks were prepared to entrust themselves or their families to its care. The promise to give Greece a fully developed welfare system proved even more difficult to fulfil; the economy was simply not developed or efficient enough to generate the necessary funds. Plans to decentralize the country were equally unsuccessful, mainly because the central government was not willing or able to find the cash necessary to give local authorities the degree of financial independence necessary to develop regional autonomy. Similarly, the talk of delivering Athens from the curse of atmospheric pollution remained empty words. The populist promises to index salaries and wages to inflation also had to be abandoned; rather the government moved in the opposite direction as economic pressures forced it into retrenchment. Nor did the promised worker socialization or self-management become a reality, the former seemingly becoming a means for extending government patronage by expanding yet again the number of appointments in the government's gift.

PASOK had promised it would pursue a foreign policy of which Greece could be 'nationally proud', but such pre-election rhetoric was soon tempered by the realities of office. Talk of a referendum on membership of the EEC, which had been toned down during the election campaign, was now dropped. Nor was there any move to withdraw from NATO or to close the US bases, and the demands for a guarantee of the Greek-Turkish border which had formed a part of the electoral promises were stilled. If it did not break away from western alliances and institutions the PASOK administration did follow individual, and frequently embarrassing policies within them. It gave energetic support to the notion of a nuclear-free zone in the Balkans, an idea put forward at times by both Ceauşescu and Zhivkov. The Greek socialist government also refused to join its western partners in imposing sanctions on Poland after the military coup of 1981. When the Soviet defences blasted a Korean airliner out of the Pacific skies in September 1983 Greece, then occupying the presidency of the EEC, stifled protests from the European states. At the same time it gave at least verbal support to anti-western movements such as the Sandinistas in Nicaragua and the Palestine Liberation Organization, while at home it infuriated the Americans by apparently doing nothing to suppress a highly secret and dauntingly successful terrorist organization, 'November 17', which killed a number of American officials as well as Greek businessmen.

Given the extreme stance Papandreou had taken against the *Sismik I* in 1976 it was not surprising that relations with Turkey did not improve when he became prime minister. They became much worse in 1984 when two Turkish warships were alleged to have fired at Greek vessels in Greek territorial waters. By the end of the year the Greek government had officially acknowledged that it regarded Turkey rather than the communist regimes to the north as its main potential enemy. The incident in the Aegean had mercifully not resulted in any casualties but this was not the case when Greek and Turkish troops were involved in a frontier incident on the river Evros in December 1986, one Greek and two Turkish soldiers being killed. This was the prelude to even greater tension in the Aegean in 1987 over exploration rights and the possible extension of territorial waters. The worst of consequences were avoided when both governments drew back from the brink and agreed to operate only in territorial waters and in January 1988 the Greek and Turkish premiers, meeting in Davos, agreed to take steps to decrease the tension and prevent a recurrence of the recent crisis. To this end a hot line was installed between Ankara and Athens and restrictions on travel between the two states were greatly eased. Relations thereafter improved markedly though by the end of the year there were signs that the spirit of Davos was not to be long-lived.

By the second half of the 1980s PASOK's popularity was in decline. Elections to the European parliament in 1984 had seen a rise of 7 per cent in New Democracy's share of the vote compared to the 1981 poll; PASOK's vote fell by a similar percentage. After this Mitsotakis moved from the now virtually defunct New Liberals to take over the leadership of New Democracy from Rallis. This added a bitter personal edge to the political rivalry between the two main factions; Mitsotakis had been one of the Centre Union 'apostates' whose defection in 1965 had precipitated the departure of Papandreou's father from office and this Papandreou *fils* could never forgive. The forthcoming elections of 1985 promised to be as bitter as any in recent Greek history. Before they took place, however, another political bombshell exploded.

In March 1985 Karamanlis's term of office as president came to an end. There was a general expectation that the grand old man of Greek politics would be unopposed if he sought, as he showed every sign of doing, a second term. Papandreou then astounded the political world by nominating an alternative candidate, Christos Sartzetakis, a lawyer who had exposed the murderers of Lambrakis, the left-wing politician slain in Salonika in 1963. Papandreou also announced that he intended to introduce constitutional changes which would reduce the president's powers. Neither Tsatsos nor Karamanlis had, as Papandreou acknowledged, attempted to use these powers to the full but this did not mean, he said, that a future incumbent would be so restrained. Even though Karamanlis now stepped aside Sartzetakis was only elected on the vote of the PASOK president of the assembly. It had not been a dignified transfer of office.

The promised constitutional changes were enacted, and before the general election was held in June the PR system was again modified to discriminate against the smaller parties. To this New Democracy could have no objection but to outside observers it seemed that some of the more regrettable features of previous Greek political behaviour were reappearing. The changes in the electoral system had little effect on the two main parties, PASOK losing 2 per cent of its 1981 share of the vote, and New Democracy gaining 5 per cent.

Papandreou had been given the second term in office which he had always said he would need to implement his full programme of reconstruction and modernization. In fact during his second term he was even less free to develop a reform programme. Greece was facing a mounting debt problem which forced the government to decrease imports, cut government spending and increase taxes. Had Greece not received substantial loans from the EEC and the European Investment Bank the situation would have been considerably worse. The growing economic difficulties did have one positive result, however. As the economy contracted and as European policies and investment worked to the benefit of rural areas the drift to the cities slowed. This eased the pressure on the urban areas but it also contributed further to the slow revival of the rural sector.

The economic difficulties facing the government brought the opposition some increased support and New Democracy took control of Athens, Piraeus and Salonika in the local elections of October 1986. The growing tensions with Turkey also harmed PASOK which was further weakened in August 1988 when Papandreou, who had long been suffering from heart disease, had to undergo major surgery, performed not in the Greek national health service but at Harefield Hospital in the UK. Shortly after his operation he announced that he was to forsake his wife of thirty-seven years and marry Dimitra Liana, a former air hostess thirty-five years his junior.

A much more serious scandal broke shortly after Papandreou's return to Greece when financial irregularities in the affairs of a Greek-American businessman, George Koskotas, were disclosed: a sum equivalent to $132 million had disappeared from the Bank of Crete which Koskotas owned. Revelation followed revelation, each one seemingly more damaging than the last. The tide of scandal lapped close to the threshold of senior PASOK figures, one of whom was said to have carried off a diaper box stuffed with five thousand drachma notes. It was also alleged that there had been widespread misappropriation of European grants, loans and the sums advanced for the purchase of arms.

Papandreou was unbowed. He continued in office until his full term had run; then he changed the electoral system once more, this time switching to unalloyed PR, and went to the country in June 1989. It was the beginning of a period of renewed instability in Greek politics, but one from which the democratic system emerged more or less unscathed. Once more Karamanlis's settling of the monarchist question and his taming of the army paid dividends.

The June 1989 elections made New Democracy the largest party in the assembly with 144 seats to PASOK's 135; the only other significant group was the Alliance of the Left and of Progress, a combination of the two communist parties, which had 28 seats. Horse trading on a massive scale ensued before a new, albeit temporary, administration emerged. It was one of the oddest in modern Greek history, a coalition of New Democracy and the Alliance of the Left, and not only were the communists included in the government but they were given the ministry of the interior, something which a generation before would have been a death sentence for democracy. They performed one major act in that ministry when, with the approval of their coalition partners, they burnt the masses of police files which had accumulated since the days of the civil war.

The main function of the temporary administration was to establish parliamentary procedures to investigate the Bank of Crete scandal and to prepare for another general election. By late 1989 both had been accomplished and on 5 November the Greeks once again trooped into the polling booths. The results were little different from those of June and so in April 1990 the exercise was repeated once more. This time New Democracy secured precisely half the assembly, 150 seats, and with the support of one independent deputy who later joined the party, had enough support to form a government under the leadership of Mitsotakis. A month after the general election Sartzetakis's presidency came to an end; the new parliament elected as his successor the veteran Karamanlis, now aged 83.

Not only in the communist Balkans was the left in retreat.

Note

1. C. M. Woodhouse, 'Greece and Europe', in Richard Clogg (ed.), *Greece in the 1980s*, London and Basingstoke: Macmillan, 1983, pp.1–8, see p.8.

Part III

THE POST-COMMUNIST BALKANS

Chapter 13

INTRODUCTION

The collapse of the bi-polar world and the Soviet Union transformed the Balkans as it did the rest of the planet. The most dramatic development was obviously the implosion of Yugoslavia.

All the Balkan states studied in this book have borders with the former Yugoslavia. All of them were therefore affected by the crisis in that state. None of them took action to exploit the crisis for their own ends, least of all to seize territory. This was due to the international community's insistence that borders could not be changed by force. But, even if there had been any popular disposition to embark on adventurous policies, the Balkan states were hardly in a condition to pursue them. Their economies were in desperate straits and any attempt to repair them would, in the new international configuration of forces, depend on loans and grants from the west. These would not be forthcoming if the Balkan states, individually or collectively, made the region even more unstable by attempting to exploit its existing difficulties for territorial gain.

While the Balkan states stood aside from the Yugoslav crisis the international community became involved, thus placing the Balkans more at the focus of world attention than at any time since, arguably, before the First World War.

A number of international bodies became involved. The first was the EC. In 1991 it sent a three-person delegation to Yugoslavia in what appeared initially to be a successful attempt to contain the Slovene and Croatian crises. Success went to its head. Thereafter EC and EU ministers produced a series of fatuously vainglorious claims to the effect that because Yugoslavia was a European state it would be the EC which would settle this problem; Yugoslavia was to be the first triumph of Europe's new common foreign and defence policies. The nonsense of this Maastrichtian 'Europhoria' became apparent when one major European power adopted an entirely individual policy towards the disintegrating federation, the others following grumpily behind.

More sensible and effective were the joint EC and UN peace efforts under Lord Owen and Cyrus Vance, initiated after an international conference in London in the summer of 1992. As the EC had no military command structure the first external forces to be deployed in the Balkans came under the flag of the UN; these troops became an essential ingredient in the cease-fire eventually agreed in Croatia. The UN was then dragged into the conflict in Bosnia. Here local antipathies proved too much for it, though its humanitarian efforts were prodigious and without them many thousands of Bosnians would have died of hunger, disease or cold. The UN's structure had been too complex, however, to allow it to deploy military force rapidly and in strength. That was eventually done by NATO, the most powerful military alliance in the world which in April 1994, in the Balkans, fired its first shots in anger. The diplomacy of NATO was for much of the time dominated by its most powerful member, the USA, and it was on American territory, at Dayton, Ohio, that the peace settlement for Bosnia was decided at the end of 1995. Thereafter, NATO went on to undertake much more extensive operations to impose the western powers' will over Kosovo in 1999, this time without specific endorsement from the UN.

A basic rule laid down by all the international bodies which became engaged in the Yugoslav crisis was that boundaries could not be changed by force. This was to apply to Yugoslavia's internal as well as its external boundaries. Herein lay many difficulties. The internal boundaries, drawn up by the communists soon after the Second World War, had many anomalies. Also, many within Yugoslavia did not consider the post-1945 settlement fair or just, and they were therefore prepared to disregard international warnings and attempt to change it by force. The outside world's insistence, though made with the best of motives, greatly complicated the search for a solution to the problem of the Serbs living outside Serbia. It also led to the farcical pretence after the end of the Kosovo emergency that Kosovo was still part of Serbia; no Serb writ ran in the area and any attempt by Serbia to give substance to its sovereignty brought howls of anguish or rage from the international community. Meanwhile, all Albanians in Kosovo, including the moderates, insisted they could accept no long-term settlement which did not provide for the separation of Kosovo from Serbia.

Macedonia, the only state whose separation from Yugoslavia had been achieved without violence, faced difficulties on its southern border because Greece could not accept any international entity which had the same name as one of Greece's provinces. There was also international concern that Macedonia, an impoverished state with serious internal ethnic divisions, might become prey to neighbours who had historical claims upon the region, and the UN therefore sent troops to guard the new state's borders. On the north-eastern perimeter of the Balkans another new state, Moldova, posed the danger that Romania might stake a claim to an area which had once been Romanian territory and in which the largest ethnic group was Romanian; so far, however, neither Romania nor Moldova has shown any great interest in a closer relationship.

Other potential flash points also remained quiet. Croatia and Slovenia disputed a number of small villages on the Gulf of Piran while there was a more complex issue at stake over the Prevlaka peninsula. Technically Croatian territory, this small area controls access to Yugoslavia's only deep-water naval base, in the Bay of Kotor. A small contingent of UN peacekeepers ensured that this dispute did not burst into flames.

A major reason why the Balkan states remained outside the Yugoslav conflict was their preoccupation with internal reconstruction and international realignment, the ultimate goals usually being admission to NATO and the EU.

In political terms internal reconstruction did not prove too difficult. The objectives were clear. With the exception of Greece and until 2000 Serbia, all states were reacting against their communist past and seeking an end to the one-party state, the establishment of representative democracy, the guarantee of individual rights and the rule of law.

The political process of dismembering the one-party system was relatively simple. Constitutional guarantees that the communist party had a leading role in the state and in society were soon abolished, as were those twin pillars of communist control, the secret police and the party cell in the work-place. Links between the former ruling party and social organizations such as the trade unions, youth movements and women's groups were equally easily dissolved. New rights such as those to form political parties, to publish without censorship, to form independent civil societies and to travel were rapidly enacted, though some of the states involved in the wars of Yugoslav succession were slower than others to move along this path. By the time the Dayton accords had brought the fighting in Bosnia and Hercegovina to an end, however, all the states of south-eastern Europe, old and new, had, at least in theory, multi-party systems with assemblies elected by universal suffrage. All states with the exception of Bosnia have also seen governments changed as a result of popular elections, though in Serbia it took forceful popular action on the streets to secure recognition of the results in October 2000. There was less official willingness to accept the results of local elections which turned out not to favour the ruling parties. Changes of government also came about as a result of street pressure, as in Bulgaria in 1990 and 1997, and in Albania in 1997.

Despite these protests the transition to a new political system was relatively peaceful, the violence in the former Yugoslavia arising from questions of borders and the ethnic composition of society, not from disagreements over political structures. A peaceful transition was possible because for the most part the victors of the revolution were not doctrinaire ideologues with an already defined political system they were determined to impose whatever the cost; they merely wanted to construct a functioning, open, democratic system. Former communists were for the most part not purged but were allowed to find their own role in the new system. The exceptions to this rule were Romania, where the former dictatorial ruling couple were executed, and Albania where there was for a time systematic persecution, though not execution, of former leading communists. In Bulgaria the former party boss was tried and convicted on a number of criminal charges, and a handful of other leading party activists were also imprisoned. In other states there was a remarkable continuity between the old élites and the new ruling groups. This applied not only to Serbia, which for a decade was hardly touched by the revolutions of 1989, but also to Macedonia, Slovenia and Croatia.

The parties which emerged in the years following the collapse of communism covered the entire political spectrum. They were of four types: the former ruling communist parties; anti-communist electoral alliances; resurrected parties; and new parties.

The former communist parties changed their names and liberalized their structures. The strongest among them were those of Serbia, Montenegro, Romania, Bulgaria and Albania, all of which remained united and most of which continued the close association with nationalism established before 1989. Cohesion and continuity among the anti-communist electoral alliances was rare, though not unknown. Generally, these were loose associations which fell apart once their one unifying demand, the removal of the communists from office, had been achieved. The third group of parties, those resurrected from the past, played very little part in the evolution of the area since 1989. Most of them had little in the way of infrastructure or funds and their leadership, though venerated, was old and had been too long in exile to be in touch with contemporary affairs. In general newly formed parties were much more important than resurrected ones. But they too faced considerable difficulties. The social and political purges of communist rule had meant the elimination of former distinctions of class, status and wealth upon which old party divisions were based, and there had not been time for market forces to create or recreate the social bases for bourgeois parties. Some new parties were founded on issues such as the environment and most countries soon had their Green party or its equivalent. But despite the obviously pressing nature of environmental problems serious green politics with their implicit renunciation of material improvement and consumerism proved too demanding for most people who were already economically disadvantaged and for whom the easiest form of political allegiance was ethnic identity. Parties representing ethnic majorities and minorities appeared in all states.

In most states a multitude of parties appeared which together with proportional representation, one variant or another of which was adopted in all states except Serbia and Macedonia, meant that coalition governments were the norm. The major exceptions to this rule were, until 2000, Croatia and Serbia. There were also occasions on which states entrusted power to non-party administrations which were usually intentionally of limited duration.

One of the most surprising features of the 1990s in the Balkans was that the military played so little part in domestic politics. This was despite the long tradition of military coups in the region and notwithstanding the fact that in a number of states the military became increasingly discontented as they were forced to rethink their strategies after the end of the cold war and, much worse, to endure severe cuts in their budgets and reductions in their numbers.

In addition, the peninsula was subject to extraordinary tensions generated by the collapse of Yugoslavia, and domestically the economic transition was causing enormous privation.

A greater hidden threat than the army to political and social stability appeared in the shape of organized crime. The end of authoritarian rule meant that many more freedoms were available and that respect for and fear of the forces of law and order decreased. A rapid increase in mugging, petty theft, prostitution, the abuse of recreational drugs and a series of other relatively minor crimes was common throughout the region and the rest of post-communist Europe where weapons from disintegrating or impoverished armies were easy to come by, but much more alarming in the Balkans was the emergence of serious, organized crime. When communism was in obvious danger of collapse some members of the nomenklatura had secreted funds abroad with which they established shadowy trading organizations or conglomerates. These played a powerful and at times very destructive role in a number of states.

If internal political reconstruction was relatively easy, internal economic transition was horrendously difficult. The goal in almost all cases was an economy advanced and healthy enough to secure closer association with the west and eventual admission to the EU. To this there seemed no alternative. The Soviet system was collapsing, an event which in itself inflicted considerable damage on those Balkan economies closely linked with it; the Black Sea Zone was little more than an idea; and closer association with the Middle East, the Caucasus and northern Africa could not offer the same prospects of trade, investment and prosperity as the west.

However, the switch to a market economy, which was the precondition for closer association with the west, could be achieved only at huge social cost. In a free market Balkan industries were not competitive. They were woefully inefficient and produced at high cost goods of poor quality which no one wanted to buy. To install modern, efficient plant was possible usually only with western loans which the Balkan states would be hard-pressed to service. The adjustment to the psychology of the free market was also difficult for generations which had been cocooned by price controls on staple commodities and subsidies to loss-making industries. The removal of price controls, albeit gradual, meant price inflation while the ending of subsidies meant more unemployment. The position of those dependent on pensions, welfare benefits and any form of fixed income was worst. Their plight and their financial naivety, together with a general lack of sophisticated fiscal regulation accounted for the prevalence in the Balkans of such dubious enterprises as the pyramid selling schemes. These seemed to offer the only hope of security in countries where forms of savings and investments such as stocks and shares, insurance policies and mortgages were unknown or little developed. But almost all of them collapsed inflicting real hardship on many of their investors in Bulgaria, Romania, Serbia, Macedonia and, above all, Albania. The schemes would have been impossible had the former communist states had any modern form of banking or personal financial services, but these had been considered hardly necessary under the universal welfareism of the communist days. At the same time the lack of banking facilities slowed commerce and the absence of bankruptcy laws meant there was no effective financial discipline which in turn threatened the stability of the banking system.

Even when the realities of the market system had been accepted psychologically their social impact remained hugely damaging. The problem of industrial inefficiency was compounded by the international financial institutions (IFIs) which insisted that subsidies to unprofitable and inefficient enterprises must be cut even in the service sector; this affected, among many other industries, those supplying cheap electricity, coal or other sources of energy. To subsidize such operations, said the IFIs, made for unfair competition. Yet to close them would only add yet more to the growing masses of the unemployed.

Given the difficulties they faced in the post-communist decade the surprising fact is not that upheaval, outside the former Yugoslavia, was so widespread but that it was so limited.

Chapter 14

THE YUGOSLAV CRISIS, 1989–1992, AND THE WAR IN BOSNIA, 1992–1995*

The collapse of the Soviet-style system in Eastern Europe and its own internal problems placed insupportable strains on the Yugoslav federation. Slovenia seized its chance to move closer to the more advanced states of central Europe while Serbia retreated into an old-fashioned state socialism and an even more old-fashioned aggressive nationalism. Slovenia's secession from the federation could be relatively easily managed not least because it had relatively few Serbs in its population. But if Slovenia left the federation Serbia would become totally dominant within it, and this Croatia's nationalists could not tolerate. Croatia, however, had a large Serb population which itself could not feel secure in a separate Croatia. The tensions this problem caused precipitated international intervention, first in an attempt to prevent the war and then to try and ameliorate its effects. When war in Croatia subsided the conflict moved to Bosnia and Hercegovina where it was more complex, more intense and more bloody. It was a conflict which did much to change the nature of international relations.

THE COLLAPSE OF THE POST-1945 FEDERATION, MARCH 1989 TO APRIL 1992

From the constitutional changes in Serbia in March 1989 until the outbreak of the Bosnian war in April 1992 three main political processes took place in Yugoslavia. First, at republican level there was political liberalization, which allowed nationalist parties to form and become active, including those among the ethnic minorities within the republics. Secondly, the institutions of central authority decayed or were debased and destroyed. And thirdly, the Yugoslav crisis became internationalized. The changes at republican level were mostly, but not always, quickened by developments in Serbia and Kosovo and were made easier by the decline in most federal institutions.

---

* Generally in this and subsequent chapters adjectives derived from 'narod' have been translated as 'national' rather than 'peoples''. The reason for this will be obvious from the context.

SERBIA AND KOSOVO

After the changes of March 1989 an entirely new constitution for all of Serbia was approved by referendum in July 1990 and came into force in September. It allowed multi-party elections and it removed the word 'socialist' from the republic's title, but it also removed most of the rights given to the provinces under the 1974 system.

Within Serbia itself Milošević continued to dominate the political scene. His League of Communists of Serbia merged with the umbrella group Serbian Socialist Alliance of the Working People to form the Socialist Party of Serbia (SPS) in July 1990 and not surprisingly this party emerged as the largest in the assembly after the Serbian elections of 9 and 23 December 1990. Milošević was also elected president of Serbia. In both the parliamentary and presidential elections the second strongest party was the fiercely nationalist Serbian Renewal Movement (SRM) led by Vuk Drašković.

No Albanian parties from Kosovo took part in the elections. This was hardly surprising. Since the changes of March 1989 Serbian nationalism was rampant and its primary objective appeared to be the subjugation of Kosovo, with Milošević moving swiftly to impose full Serbian control in the area. Serbo-Croat replaced Albanian as the official language and in February 1990 Milošević called for mass Serbian immigration into Kosovo, though few heeded his call. More serious was the agreement of the federal presidency, also in February 1990, that the JNA could be deployed against protesters in Kosovo. It was used in March to quell riots which followed a mysterious outbreak of stomach disorders amongst four hundred Albanian schoolchildren in Podujevo near Prishtina. On 17 April Milošević announced that the Serbian ministry of the interior had taken over from the federal authorities' responsibility for security in the province, sweetening the pill in the following week by releasing a number of detained Kosovan Albanians, including Vllasi and Adem Demaqi, the 'Kosovan Mandela' who had been in prison for no less than twenty-eight years. The April concessions also included the lifting of the state of emergency imposed in February 1989.

This relaxation was short-lived. In the summer there was full-scale constitutional confrontation. On 2 July the referendum on the new constitution took place. Resenting the loss of their privileges under the 1974 system the Kosovan Albanians boycotted the poll and on the day it was held 114 delegates of the Kosovo assembly issued a statement proclaiming Kosovo a separate republic within Yugoslavia. In retaliation the Serbian assembly voted on 5 July to dissolve the Kosovo assembly altogether, to dismiss the Kosovan government and to transfer all its responsibilities to Belgrade. On the same day the heads of the radio and TV services and the director general of the influential newspaper *Rilindja* were replaced. Albanian protests continued and the province was brought to a standstill by a general strike on 3 September. The strike was organized by the new Independent Trade Union Organization of Kosovo and among its grievances was the sacking of 15,000 Albanians who, since the imposition of direct rule from Serbia, had refused to sign pledges of loyalty or to work under police supervision; four fifths of the police and civil service had been sacked by this time. On 7 September 111 Albanian, Turkish and Muslim members of the Kosovo assembly met in Kaçanik and on 13 September proclaimed a 'Constitution of the Republic of Kosovo'.

The activists involved in drawing up the Kaçanik constitution came in large part from a new political class which had emerged in Kosovo in the 1980s. Its roots were in the intelligentsia produced by Prishtina university since 1968 rather than in the partisan veterans and their heirs. It was from this element that Ibrahim Rugova emerged. A quiet specialist in aesthetics and literary history with a Parisian training and a distinctive cravat, he had become the leader of the Democratic League of Kosovo when it was founded in December 1989. The League knew that direct confrontation with the Serbs would be suicidal and therefore preached passive resistance.

When calling for their own republic within Yugoslavia the Kosovan Albanians had two powerful arguments, one old and one new. The old posed the question: why should their 1.7 million constitute merely a *narodnost* or 'nationality' when the status of *narod* or 'nation' was enjoyed by approximately the same number of Slovenes, by the 1.3 million Macedonians and by the even less numerous Montenegrins? The new argument became valid in 1990 and 1991 and asked: why should the 1.7 million Albanians who formed 90 per cent of Kosovo's population be denied the minority rights within Serbia which the Serbian leader was demanding for the Serbian minorities in Croatia and Bosnia and Hercegovina, the more so when Croatia's 0.6 million Serbs were only 12 per cent and Bosnia's 1.2 million Serbs a third of the population? Neither the old or the new argument cut any ice in Belgrade.

The aggressive, assimilationist policies followed by Milošević in Kosovo alarmed the leaders of the other republics. So too did other manifestations of Serbian intentions as, for example, when Milošević insisted that the heads of all the republics join the million or so Serbs attending the six hundredth anniversary celebrations for the battle of Kosovo Polje held on 28 June 1989. In his speech, which was relayed throughout Yugoslavia, he spoke of the Serbs' gallant tradition of fighting for their independence and added that 'After six centuries we are again engaged in battles and quarrels. They are not armed battles, but this cannot be excluded yet.' The other republics and ethnic groups were put on their guard.

CROATIA

Croatia, remembering the reaction to the Croatian Spring, had been wary of radical reform and not until early 1989 did the leadership in Zagreb accept the notion of political plurality, conceding in December that multi-party elections should take place in the spring of 1990.

One of the new groups to emerge was the Croatian Democratic Union (HDZ) established in June 1989 under the leadership of Franjo Tudjman. Tudjman had fought with the partisans and by the end of the war was a major and a political commissar. He left the army in 1961 to become director of the Institute for the History of the Working-Class Movement in Croatia, moving in 1963 to Zagreb university. Here he published on the sensitive issue of the war dead, his conclusions predating those given wide publicity in the 1980s in their assertion that the number of deaths had been much exaggerated by the post-war partisan establishment. This earned him a spell in gaol and he was imprisoned again in 1971 this time for publishing in the west a book[1] which claimed that the wartime Independent State of Croatia (NDH) had acted as a salutary barrier against Serbian unitarist ambitions; it also claimed that the Bosnian Muslims were ethnic Croats, implying thereby that they belonged within a Croatian state. His views and his imprisonment made him a hero among the exiled Croat communities, and when the Croatian authorities allowed him an external passport in the 1980s he used it to visit many of those communities. It was an investment which was to pay huge dividends.

The foundation of the HDZ coincided with a rapid intensification of Croat nationalist feelings. Part of the impulse for this came from Milošević's Serbia and from the vitriolic attacks on Croatia in which its media were indulging. These, particularly the frequent invocation of the atrocities committed by the Ustaše in the NDH, had a disturbing effect upon many Serbs in Croatia. For the Croats themselves there was also cause for concern in a series of articles in the Italian press in July 1989 in which the Serbian nationalist novelist and one of the progenitors of the 1986 draft memorandum of the Serbian Academy of Sciences, Dobrica Ćosić, seemed to argue that Istria, Zadar and the Adriatic islands should be transferred to another Yugoslav republic. The issue of territorial integrity within Yugoslavia was to be one of the most sensitive and divisive in the turbulent years ahead.

It was the HDZ which most effectively exploited rising Croat nationalism. This, together with between four and five million dollars of exile money, the failure of the other parties to unite against it in the second round of voting, and the workings of the majoritarian system, enabled it in the elections of 22 April and 6–7 May 1990 to take 205 out of the 356 seats in the three chambers of the Croatian assembly.

Constitutional changes followed soon upon the elections. In May the sabor, or parliament, removed the word 'socialist' from the state's title and created the office of president of Croatia which was filled by Tudjman. On 22 December 1990 a new constitution vested considerable powers in the presidency.

The elections were also followed by signs of Croatian nationalist triumphalism. Streets and squares were named after figures from Croatian history and even after supporters of Pavelić; the use of the cyrillic alphabet was discouraged if not actually banned; the *šahovnica*, the chequered flag based on a mediaeval coat of arms but also used by the NDH, appeared everywhere; and the new Croatian currency, the kuna, bore the same name as that used in the wartime state. For supporters of federal Yugoslavia, inside and outside Croatia, however, the most alarming aspect of HDZ propaganda was its scarcely veiled assertion that Bosnia and Hercegovina were ethnically and historically part of Croatia.

Much of what happened in Croatia in 1989 and 1990 was viewed with great mistrust and suspicion by many of its 600,000 Serbs who formed 12 per cent of the population. For the Serbian activists it was almost impossible to dissociate a separate Croatian political entity from the NDH and its horrific wartime record. Tudjman did little to quieten their fears. He abolished the constitutional ruling which required a two-thirds majority in the sabor for any legislation affecting the rights of minorities. Even more alarming for the Serbs was the requirement that any Serb remaining in public office must take an oath of loyalty to the new regime. This was in part a legacy of the repressions of 1971–2 because at that time the number of Serbs in public office, and especially in the police, had become disproportionately high in order to prevent any recrudescence of the Croatian Spring. The question of who should police the Serbian areas of Croatia was soon to be of critical importance.

Serbian fears led to the formation of a number of Serbian political organizations, the most prominent of which was the Serbian Democratic Party (SDS) set up in February 1990 by a psychiatrist from Šibenik, Jovan Rašković. In May he pulled his supporters out of the sabor and in July organized a mass meeting to protest at the constitutional changes introduced in May and to proclaim the right of all Croatian Serbs to determine under what regime they should live. A hundred thousand Serbs attended. A Serbian National Council was formed which on 31 July demanded autonomy should changes in the Yugoslav federation lead to greater sovereignty for Croatia. At the same time the Serbian National Council announced that a referendum on cultural autonomy would be held in Serb areas on 19 August. The Croatian government banned the referendum but it went ahead and on the basis of its results the Serbian National Council on 1 October 1990 announced the formation of an 'autonomous region' comprising those districts in which the Serbs formed a majority of the population.

The tensions created by the referendum were greatly increased by disagreements over the question of the policing of Serbian areas, in some of which the Serbs had put their own armed men on the streets to preserve order. When rumours circulated that the Zagreb authorities were to disarm such forces and introduce their own police complete with uniforms with *šahovnica* badges panic seized a number of Serbian communities. One such was Knin where the Serbs barricaded the town. When the Zagreb government sent troops in helicopters to restore its authority they were turned back by JNA fighters. When the Croats made further attempts to disarm Serbian paramilitary forces there were clashes which involved casualties, though not as yet fatalities. The growing pressures perceived by the Serbs convinced many of them that they would soon become a minority, a *narodnost*, in the new Croatian state, whereas in federal Yugoslavia they had been a nation, *narod*. It was a demotion which few could tolerate. Nor could their most energetic champions in Serbia itself where opinion was being mobilized on their behalf, Drašković even calling for a declaration of war against Croatia.

The clash with the Croatian Serbs had embarrassed Tudjman; it had shown that the Serbs had friends in the JNA and presumably in Belgrade, and it had raised tensions between Croatia and Serbia to a dangerous degree. It had therefore moved Yugoslavia a step closer to disintegration.

BOSNIA AND HERCEGOVINA

The problems which faced Bosnia and Hercegovina were even more complex than those which plagued Croatia. In the first place Bosnia-Hercegovina, more than any other republic, depended for its viability on the continued existence of a Yugoslav entity. This was not least because more than any other republic it was torn between the Adriatic and the Danubian orientations which had done so much to separate Croatia from Serbia. Croatia, with its clear Adriatic dispositions, surrounds Bosnia on almost three sides, yet Bosnia has only one natural line of communication, the Neretva valley, with the Adriatic; the fact that the other rivers in Bosnia flow towards the Danube makes Bosnia dependent on Serbia. As long as Croatia and Serbia cooperated or were included in the same politico-economic unit, Bosnia could have both an Adriatic and a Danubian orientation. The problems came when Croatia and Serbia were separated. If Croatia dominated Bosnia, as it did during the Second World War, Zagreb could force Bosnia to face the Adriatic, whereas if Serbia had the upper hand it could insist that Bosnia orient itself towards the Danube. In the latter case one town, Brčko, would assume over-arching importance as it is the nexus between Bosnia and its links with the outer world via the Danube valley.

Bosnia and Hercegovina was also the only one of the six Yugoslav republics in which no one ethnic group formed an absolute majority, its three main groups, Muslims (44 per cent), Serbs (31 per cent) and Croats (17 per cent), being spread throughout the republic, though Croats predominated in western Hercegovina, the Muslims in the central core and the Serbs in pockets in the south- and north-east. The political reaction to events in other republics was slower in Bosnia than in Croatia. An electoral law, however, was passed in March 1990 allowing for a multi-party contest.

Political reaction was not only slower in Bosnia, it was also different. The local League of Communists was greatly discredited, a condition which ruled out the formation of the reform communist party which had appeared in all other republics. As a result parties were formed largely on an ethnic basis. In May the main Muslim party, the party of Democratic Action (PDA), was founded with Alija Izetbegović as its leader. In 1983 he had been gaoled for 'hostile and counter-revolutionary acts derived from Muslim nationalism', the main evidence against him being a fifty-page pamphlet, *The Islamic Declaration*, published in 1971; he was released in 1988. The PDA was anxious to stress the multi-ethnic, multi-faith nature of Bosnia, though another strand of Muslim opinion wanted to remove religion from the political agenda altogether; this faction established the Bosnian Muslim Organization (BMO) in September 1990 under the leadership of Adil Zulfikarpašić, a former partisan fighter and returned millionaire.

Attempts to downplay religion and to emphasize the multi-cultural and tolerant traditions of Bosnia were doomed to failure. The Serbs had established their own Serbian Democratic Party (SDS) as a branch of Rašković's Croatian organization in July, and in the following month the Bosnian Croats established their republican variant of the HDZ. In Bosnia, as in Croatia, a Serbian National Council and a Serb National Assembly were established. The latter was a form of parallel parliament, though the Serbs had not yet decided to divorce themselves from republican politics and did take part in presidential and parliamentary elections held in November and December. But there were massive pressures, usually mounted from outside Bosnia, for all politicians to align with their own ethnic comrades, and Croats and Serbs who attempted to campaign on an all-Bosnian programme were for the most part driven by these external pressures into the political wasteland.

In the November vote for the republican presidency six of the seven seats went to the ethnic parties; the exception was Ejup Ganić who was elected as a 'Yugoslav'. In accordance with a pre-electoral agreement the three main parties shared the major offices, Izetbegović becoming president of the presidency, Jure Pelivan of the HDZ prime minister and Momčilo Krajišnik of the SDS speaker of the assembly. This show of unity was skin deep. The three parties soon began installing their own supporters in the administrative machinery of the areas they controlled, and in so doing 'destroyed the intricate system of interethnic checks and balances that had been at the heart of the Titoist system',[2] while at the central republican level the three groups fell to a petulance over pretended national sensibilities which, had it not been a portent of such evil, would have been ridiculous: to take but one example, the Croats insisted that the oath of loyalty taken by deputies be translated into Croatian, which meant changing one letter in one word.

In general, however, ethnic peace was preserved in Bosnia and Hercegovina in 1990. This was to change in 1991.

MACEDONIA

For Macedonia a weakening of the Yugoslav federation was a daunting prospect. It needed federal funds for its backward and impoverished economy and it needed federal protection from neighbours whom history suggested might have claims upon its territory. It was also weak internally. The Macedonian nation had been late in forming. A literary language had not been agreed until 1947. The establishment in 1967 of the Macedonian Academy of Sciences and of the autocephalous Macedonian Orthodox Church were intended to solidify Macedonian national self-confidence, but by 1990 many Macedonians still doubted whether their republic could survive separation from Yugoslavia, the more so in that the Albanians, who formed around a quarter of the population, might not accept a Slav-dominated independent state.

Given these concerns the Macedonian establishment adopted few changes to its constitution other than to sanction the multi-party elections which were taking place throughout the federation. Provision was also made for some economic privatization.

Elections were held in November and December 1990. No party received a clear majority, the nationalist Internal Macedonian Revolutionary Organization – Democratic Party for Macedonian National Unity (IMRO-DPMNU) receiving 37 seats in the 120-strong unicameral legislature. Second came a party with almost as cumbersome a name, the League of Communists of Macedonia – Party for Democratic Change, with 37 seats; the two main ethnic Albanian parties accounted for a total of 25 seats and Marković's Alliance of Reform Forces 18.

After the elections a government of experts was formed, including some members of the previous communist regime but, squeezed between pressure from IMRO-DPMNU and the Albanians, it leaned more towards cooperation with the Macedonian nationalists. Its instincts remained for preserving the federation and for cooperation with Serbia but this the Milošević regime made difficult by such needless offences to Macedonian national dignity as the announcement by Belgrade that the Macedonian language was nothing but a dialect of Serbian which, observed a British expert, was 'palpable hogwash'.[3]

MONTENEGRO

Of the six republics Montenegro had the least complicated political life between 1989 and 1992. It legalized political plurality and in December 1990 staged elections for its 125-seat republican assembly. The League of Communists of Montenegro had an absolute majority with 83 seats, the next largest party being Marković's Alliance of Reform Forces with 17. The Democratic Coalition of Muslims and Albanians had 13 seats and the National Party 12. The communist candidate for the Montenegrin presidency, Momir Bulatović, defeated his Alliance of Reform Forces opponent in a run-off on 9 December. In 1992 the League of Communists of Montenegro changed its name to the Democratic Socialist Party and in elections at the end of that year it was still strong enough to secure more parliamentary seats than any other party, though it no longer enjoyed an absolute majority in the assembly.

Relations with Serbia featured more prominently in political debate. A referendum on 1 March 1992 had returned a huge majority in favour of continued association with Serbia in a reconstructed Yugoslav federation, but Montenegro's ethnic minorities had boycotted the poll and in subsequent months and years more and more Montenegrins began to question the wisdom of the association, especially because UN sanctions did massive damage to the republic's important tourist industry.

SLOVENIA

The differences between Slovenia and Serbia which had been decisive at the end of 1988 intensified in the subsequent two years and increased Slovenia's drive towards separation.

The only Yugoslav republic without a significant Serbian minority it did not wish to be involved in the growing disputes arising in Kosovo, Croatia and Bosnia, the more so because such involvement might impair its efforts to establish closer trading links with Italy, Austria and the EC. It also feared that the problems in Yugoslavia might lead to a federal declaration of emergency and via that the imposition of unitarist solutions to the federation's constitutional problems. When the Slovene assembly passed a number of constitutional amendments in September 1989, one of them was that only the Ljubljana parliament had the right to declare a state of emergency in Slovenia. Others allowed Slovenia to impose federal law selectively, gave the Slovene assembly the right to secede from Yugoslavia without the consent of the other republics, despite the fact that this was in contravention of the 1974 constitution, and declared Slovenia a 'sovereign and independent state' within the Yugoslav federation. The Serbian rulers disliked these moves but as it was they who had initiated the trend towards changes in the constitutions of the republics their complaints carried little weight. In February 1990 the League of Communists of Slovenia (LCS) cut its links with the federal party and renamed itself the League of Communists of Slovenia – Party of Democratic Renewal (LCS–PDR).

The September 1989 constitutional changes also prepared the way for multi-party elections which were held in April 1990. These were primarily a contest between the LCS–PDR and DEMOS, a six-party centre-right coalition which campaigned for greater separation from the rest of Yugoslavia. DEMOS took 55 per cent of the vote for the socio-political chamber to the LCS–PDR's 17 per cent. In the presidential elections Milan Kučan, who had become very popular during his spell as leader of the LCS from 1986 to 1989, defeated his DEMOS opponent, but immediately after being elected announced he would give up his party membership during his four years in office. On 16 May Lojze Peterle, of the Slovene Christian Democratic Party, a constituent party in DEMOS, was made prime minister.

The new government soon made clear its determination upon change. One of its first decisions was to close the nuclear power plant at Krško – the

Greens were also a constituent party in DEMOS – although this was a federal rather than a republican project. Other measures included a complete change of police personnel and the beginning of the reduction in the number of economic ministries and other agencies through which state control over the economy was exercised.

The government also acted on its election pledges to increase Slovene sovereignty. On 2 July 1990 the Slovene assembly issued a formal declaration of independence proclaiming the full sovereignty of Slovenia. Though no mention was made of secession the declaration called for a new constitution which would allow Slovenia to place its laws above those of the federation, control its own defence on its own soil, determine its own foreign policy, and introduce new legal and judicial systems. In September Slovenia placed the Slovenia Territorial Defence Force (TDF) under Slovene control, an act which provoked an unsuccessful attempt to seize its headquarters by the commander of the JNA's fifth army district which covered Croatia and Slovenia.

By the end of the year Slovenia had opened its first diplomatic mission abroad, in Brussels, had secretly placed an order with an Austrian company for the printing of notes for a new Slovene currency and, in December, had held a referendum on secession from Yugoslavia; in a turnout of 93.5 per cent 94.6 per cent voted in favour of full independence if no agreement had been reached on restructuring the federation within six months. The ties holding Slovenia to the old federation had become extremely tenuous.

THE DECLINE OF THE FEDERAL INSTITUTIONS

While the powers of the republics increased those of the federal authorities decreased. This affected the party, the presidency, the budget, the federal prime minister and, most critically, the army.

Surprisingly the first of the federal institutions to collapse was the one which had initially been the most dominant: the communist party. The fourteenth congress of the LCY, heralded as the 'congress of salvation', met on 20 January 1990 and was already committed to democratization, a mixed economy and even to participation in the European integration process. There was no problem with democratization, only 28 of the 1,654 delegates voting against a motion to end the leading role of the party, but there was no consensus on a Slovene proposal for the restructuring of the LCY itself and for the devolution of more power to the republican parties. When their proposal was rejected the Slovenes walked out of the congress. With the Slovenes gone and with Milošević controlling the Vojvodan, Kosovan and the Montenegrin votes, as well as that of Serbia, the Serbian-conservative faction had a secure majority. Not wishing to be subject to that, the Croats and the Macedonians followed the Slovene example and quit the congress. Attempts were made in March and May to resuscitate it but they failed. The once-mighty LCY had in effect ceased to exist.

The federal presidency scarcely fared any better. It had been discredited by Milošević's hijacking of the provinces in March 1989 because if they were integral parts of Serbia there was no real justification for their retaining their representation in the federal presidency. They did so because Milošević wanted their votes. In May 1990 a hardline Serb, Borisav Jović, took over as president of the federal presidency but not even this forceful figure could make it an effective instrument. He was mistrusted outside Serbia because he was Milošević's man, and his warnings on the dangers of civil war, though valid, would have been more effective had they been issued in less menacing a tone. His isolation was proved when he put before the federal assembly a thirteen-point programme for constitutional reform aimed at limiting the powers of the republics and increasing those of the federation. The deputies refused to vote on the proposal, arguing that they needed more time to decide what measures lay within their competency.

The presidency's ineffectiveness was even more glaring during the crisis which erupted in the autumn of 1990 with the confrontation between Zagreb and the Croatian Serbs over policing the Serb areas. Jović rushed back to Belgrade from the UN in New York in order to chair a presidency meeting on this critical issue. The meeting lasted fourteen hours and produced nothing more assertive than a call for the withdrawal of Croatian police from Serb areas.

Any viable state must have fiscal and budgetary cohesion. This Yugoslavia lost in 1990. Disagreements between Belgrade and Ljubljana had led in December 1989 to a Serbian embargo on Slovene goods and in retaliation Slovenia decided to withhold 15 per cent of its payments to the federal budget, this being the proportion set aside for subsidies to the Serbian economy. Later in the year Croatia, Serbia and the two provinces took similar action; by July 1991 15 per cent of federal bureaucrats had lost their jobs. Another fiscal casualty was FADURK, the agency for distributing development funds to the poorer republics. It was dissolved at the end of 1990. By far the most crippling blow to federal finances, however, was delivered by Milošević. With the Serbian elections of December in view he needed money to influence the voters; this could most easily be done by ensuring their jobs through continued subsidies to the loss-making enterprises which employed so many of them. There could be no better proof of his socialist credentials than this form of spending. The problem was that he did not have any money. Undeterred, he did what socialists usually do in such circumstances and helped himself to someone else's. He 'borrowed' the equivalent of between $1\frac{1}{2}$ and 2 billion dollars from a bank using as collateral money earmarked for the federal fiduciary issue for the coming year. He in fact stole from the federal budget almost the entire sum it had set aside for next year's increase in the money supply. This made any form of monetary restraint in 1991 impossible and exploded any faith in a federal fiscal system.

It also made the federal prime minister, Ante Marković, look ridiculous. In June 1990 he had urged republican leaders to cut their spending by up to

18 per cent, to restrict banknote issue, and to cooperate more fully with federal policy decisions; six months later Milošević raided the federal treasury without even consulting him. This was not the only indignity he suffered. Constitutional changes in Slovenia and Croatia decreased his authority in those republics, while in November 1990 the Serbs defied him by imposing import duties on Croatian and Slovene goods. Individual republics clearly had no concern for the federation's financial well-being and were acting purely in their own interests. Marković was so marginalized that when he delivered a ministerial address to the federal assembly on 15 November neither Croatian nor Serbian television bothered to cover the event.

The decay of almost all federal institutions was to intensify markedly in 1991 and this time was to affect also the JNA. The process began with political protests in Serbia. In March Drašković organized large-scale demonstrations against such ills as vote rigging in the December 1990 elections, the regime's control of the media and its increasing aggression towards non-communists and non-Serbs. The demonstrations began on 9 March and were quickly turned violent by the authorities' use of the police and the army. Order was not restored until 20 March. By then there had been a series of seismic political developments.

The army and the Serbian assembly had called for unspecified 'emergency measures' to be given to the army, but this the federal presidency refused. On 15 March the president of the presidency, Jović, and all its other Serb-controlled members resigned in an obvious attempt to wreck the institution and end its command of the military. Surprisingly, even the rump presidency then refused to endorse Milošević's demand for military action. Milošević was now in danger of seeing the presidency continuing to function without its Serbian members. On 20 March, therefore, the resignations were withdrawn.

The crisis had profound effects. Before he had been forced to reverse his policies over the military and the presidency Milošević revealed his true objectives in a statement on 16 March in which he said that the presidency had 'long since stopped functioning' and that Yugoslavia had 'entered the final stage of its agony'.[4] It seems Milošević had decided that the old Yugoslavia could no longer serve his needs and it would be better therefore if it were abandoned. This was a little premature. The JNA was not yet prepared to sacrifice the federation.

This was understandable. The officer corps had been favoured by Tito with huge privileges and these it did not wish to relinquish. Furthermore, Tito had bound the officers to him by a personal tie of loyalty and when he died the professional army saw itself as a form of collective successor to him and, more significantly, 'viewed socialism and the unified Yugoslav state as the prerequisite for its own existence'.[5] Its alliance with the old order had been underlined in November 1990 by the formation of a new Communist Party to replace the now defunct LCY; the new party, the League of Communists – Movement for Yugoslavia, was an alliance of top communists and retired senior military figures. On 19 March the army announced it would not be drawn into the political debate on the future of the country but at the same time it warned that it would not allow any inter-republican dispute to escalate into violence. If Milošević had ceased to believe in the utility of a unified Yugoslavia then he was on a collision course with the JNA but this was not to become apparent until the middle of the summer.

THE DESCENT INTO WAR IN SLOVENIA AND CROATIA

The immediate impact of the army's declaration of 19 March was felt most strongly in Slovenia and Croatia. On 12 February, with negotiations on the federal presidency making no progress towards a constitutional settlement, Kučan and Tudjman had conferred on the island of Krk; they had agreed that Yugoslavia could survive only as a free association of republics and had set a deadline of 30 June 1991 to reach an agreement without which they would seek UN arbitration. After the army issued its threat in March Kučan responded by saying that any attempt by the JNA to interfere in Slovene domestic affairs would precipitate immediate secession, and his parliament gave him full support. Tudjman followed suit. On 2 April he stated that he now favoured a confederation and that if Slovenia seceded Croatia would do the same and it would not allow the alienation of any Croatian territory.

The army leaders, together with Kučan and Tudjman were now all alarmed at the deteriorating situation in Croatia. Fighting had occurred at Pakrac in western Slavonia on 2 March, the cause being once again Croatian attempts to introduce their new police force into a Serb community. On this occasion the JNA intervened to end the conflict and there were no casualties. At the end of the month there were clashes in the Plitvice area but this time each side suffered one fatality. The crucial confrontation came on 1 May in the capital of eastern Slavonia, Osijek. During the 1 May celebrations young Croatian policemen attempted to replace the communist flag with the *šahovnica*; in the ensuing fracas two policemen were wounded and two captured. On 2 May colleagues who had set out to rescue their colleagues were ambushed at Borovo Selo and twelve of them killed. The Serb-Croat conflict was transformed. On 3 May Tudjman spoke on television and for the first time warned of war.

The Serbian response was to block the Croat candidate for chairman of the presidency, Stipe Mesić, on the assumption that this would prevent him from restraining the JNA which was now increasingly committed to the Serbs in the escalating conflict in Croatia. The enraged Croats held a snap referendum on independence. The Serbian areas did not take part but elsewhere it registered almost unanimous approval for a somewhat loosely worded demand for complete sovereignty.

In June the six-month deadline set by the Slovene referendum in December expired. There had been no progress towards a settlement of Yugoslavia's constitutional problems and accordingly, on 25 June, Slovenia declared it had seceded from the federation. Croatia followed suit. Two days later the JNA let loose the dogs of war in Slovenia. In this instance, however, their bark was much worse than their bite. The JNA action was limited; its main objectives were to seize control of the border posts and Ljubljana airport and no opposition was expected. But the Slovenes had retained some TDF equipment and were able to attack the JNA armour with anti-tank guns and armour-piercing rockets.

By this time the European Community had become thoroughly alarmed at the collapse of order in Yugoslavia. It sent a delegation consisting of the ministers of foreign affairs from the Netherlands, Italy and Luxembourg to try and end the crisis. The Yugoslav problem had been internationalized.

The delegation had three main objectives: to negotiate a ceasefire throughout Yugoslavia; to secure a moratorium on the implementation of the two declarations of secession; and to have Mesić installed as chairman of the collective presidency. Success seemed to have been achieved. The moratorium was agreed at a meeting on the island of Brioni on 8 July; the two states said they would suspend their declarations for three months but they would not withdraw them; and fighting would stop immediately and the JNA would withdraw to barracks. After Mesić had been installed as chairman of the presidency on 1 July it seemed that, on the surface at least, what was left of constitutional order in Yugoslavia had been restored.

The European troika had been leaning on an open door when it urged an end to the military operations in Slovenia. By the end of June the JNA was aware that without the deployment of large numbers of extra troops it could not impose its will on the breakaway republic. The presidency vetoed any further deployments and on 18 July ordered the army to leave Slovenia altogether. Slovenia was lost to the federation. This did not concern Milošević; on 3 July he said, 'Serbia has nothing against Slovenia's secession, it does no harm to our interests . . .'.[6] Quite the contrary: with Slovenia out of the federation Serbia would be its most powerful individual republic. Furthermore, Milošević could argue that with the old federation breaking up its former internal boundaries were no longer applicable; a new Yugoslavia should have new borders based on ethnic considerations. In this fashion all Serbs could be brought together in one republic.

The instrument for doing so would, if necessary, be the JNA. The departure of Slovenia from the federation meant that the JNA was in many people's estimation no longer a Yugoslav but a Serbian force. Its conduct did not belie that estimation.

When it withdrew from Slovenia the JNA moved mainly into Croatia. The fighting which had flared in May had continued and the arrival of the JNA posed a serious threat to the Croatians. Their main military force was the Croatian National Guard formed from police reservists in May; it was untrained and desperately short of anything but light weapons; and it was in no position to fight any war, least of all one against a well-equipped modern army such as the JNA.

But it had no choice. By August the Serbs were not only expanding their territory in Croatia but had begun to drive non-Serbs out of areas they had conquered. There was nothing new in this process beyond the name which the world now gave it: ethnic cleansing. The Croat response was to lay siege to JNA barracks in Croatia and to carry out occasional reprisals of their own. Much of the fighting was as senseless as it was nasty. On 1 October the Serbs attacked Dubrovnik; its port, airport and communications links to the interior gave it some strategic value, but the inept conduct of the assault and skilful propaganda on the part of the Croats made the attack seem no more than an act of pure malice, the poor peasants' revenge on the fleshpot port of the rich: why else use wire-guided missiles to destroy all the yachts in the harbour? The main theatre of operations, however, was in Slavonia where the pivotal point was Vukovar, which the Serbs subjected to a two-month siege and bombardment. During the siege the Croats were training their new forces and equipping them with weaponry from the increasing number of JNA barracks which they were starving into submission.

The Serbs were to take Vukovar on 18 November but nine days earlier the Belgrade leadership had written to the UN Security Council indicating its readiness to agree to a ceasefire and the sending of a peace-keeping force to Croatia. There were four main reasons for Belgrade's willingness to end the fighting. First, the JNA had taken heavy casualties and its morale had suffered from this and from the loss of many of its barracks in Croatia. Secondly, the raw recruits brought in from Serbia had little commitment to the Serbian cause in Croatia and did not perform well; the high rates of desertion and draft evasion seemed to indicate that Milošević's public was losing its stomach for the fight. Thirdly, it did not seem likely that the Serbs could take and hold much more territory in Croatia, while an international force might help preserve those recently acquired. Fourthly and most importantly, it appeared increasingly likely that the international community would recognize Slovenia and Croatia as independent states in which case the JNA in Croatia would be seen as an occupying force. The Croats were also ready for a ceasefire which was eventually signed on 2 January 1992.

The armistice agreement stipulated that JNA troops would leave Croatian territory and in the Serb-held areas they would be replaced by the UN Protection Force, UNPROFOR. There were two main but non-contiguous Serb-held zones, the Serbian Autonomous Region of Krajina based on Knin, and the Autonomous Region of Slavonia, Baranja and Western Srem. On 19 December they declared themselves united as the Serbian Republic of Krajina and elected as their president Milan Babić, the mayor of Knin, who had replaced Rašković as leader of the Croatian Serbs. Serbia recognized the new republic the following day.

A major consideration in Tudjman's and Milošević's willingness to accept UN intervention was the knowledge that Slovenia and Croatia would soon be granted international recognition. This was made public in mid-November when Chancellor Kohl stated that Germany would recognize the two states by Christmas. His decision derived from a number of domestic political considerations but also owed much to the argument that, if the reunification of the two Germanys and the secession of states from the former Soviet Union could be justified on the basis of self-determination, that same principle must allow independence for the two former Yugoslav republics.

On 16 December the EC agreed that any republic of Yugoslavia could be recognized as an independent state if it requested recognition and if it fulfilled certain conditions. Applications were to be submitted by 23 December and the vetting process would be carried out by a commission headed by Robert Badinter, a French lawyer. By the set date Bosnia and Hercegovina, Slovenia, Croatia, Macedonia, the Serbian Krajina in Croatia and the Kosovan Albanians had applied. The latter two were rejected, while Bosnia and Hercegovina and Macedonia were referred to the Badinter commission, but no action could be taken in the case of Slovenia and Croatia because Germany had gone ahead and recognized them on 23 December.

THE DRIFT TO WAR IN BOSNIA

The recognition of Slovenia and Croatia was a disaster for Bosnia and Hercegovina. It now faced three possible futures, none of which was acceptable to all three major groups. One was to remain in the federation, which would condemn it to permanent subjection to Milošević's Serbia, something which neither the Croats nor the Muslims could contemplate. It might be split into ethnically determined cantons which enjoyed a large measure of autonomy within an independent Bosnia. This, however, was almost impossible without local conflicts because so many local government entities had no clear ethnic identity and none of the three groups were advocates of this solution. The third option was partition. This was favoured by the Serbs who saw it as a prelude to union with Serbia itself, and it had some support among Croats who hoped thereby for some form of union with Croatia, but it was rejected out of hand by the Muslims who believed that a rump Muslim republic would not be viable and would in all probability fall prey to partition between Serbia and Croatia.

There was no doubt about Serbian intentions. In October 1991 the Bosnian assembly held a debate in camera on the question of sovereignty; when it seemed that the vote would be in favour of independence the seventy-three Bosnian Serb delegates walked out, their leader, Radovan Karadžić, warning that any attempt by Bosnia and Hercegovina to declare independence would lead to war.

The Serbs in Bosnia were well organized. They had followed Croatian examples and formed autonomous regions in areas where they were the dominant ethnic group, and from July 1991 they had taken measures to arm themselves, the weapons being supplied mainly by the ministry of the interior in Belgrade. In December Milošević gave orders for all non-Bosnian officers in the JNA to leave Bosnia and Hercegovina and for JNA soldiers of Bosnian

Serb origin to be concentrated in the republic; he was determined not to repeat the mistake of the Slavonian campaign when uncommitted conscripts from outside the republic concerned had impaired the effectiveness of the JNA.

The great fear of the Bosnian Serbs was the international recognition of Bosnia within its existing borders. That would prevent *enosis* with Serbia and leave the Serbs in a permanent minority. The Badinter commission's response to the Bosnian request for recognition had been that the republic should put the question in a referendum to all sections of its population. To this the Serbs would not agree and boycotted the vote when it was held on 29 February–1 March. The vote therefore produced a large majority in favour of independence which was declared on 3 March and the same evening the Bosnian parliament, minus its Serbian deputies, endorsed the declaration. On 27 March Serbian leaders proclaimed the Serbian Republic of Bosnia and Hercegovina and declared its loyalty to the 'all Serb state of Yugoslavia'.

The fragmentation of Bosnia had begun. By the end of March there had been clashes between Bosnian Serbs and Muslims, between Bosnian Croats and the JNA, between Bosnian Serbs and Bosnian Croats, and between Serbian units from outside Bosnia and forces loyal to the Bosnian government. On 6 April serious fighting began in Sarajevo. On that day the EC recognized Bosnia as an independent state. The USA did so on the following day; at the same time Washington reversed its previous policy and also recognized Slovenia and Croatia. Those two states, together with Bosnia and Hercegovina, were admitted to the United Nations on 22 May.

THE DISSOLUTION OF THE OLD YUGOSLAVIA

With the imminent recognition of Slovenia and Croatia Macedonia had also applied for recognition in December 1991, immediately drafting constitutional changes to meet EC requirements. It had held a referendum on the issue in September. Like the Bosnian Serbs, the Albanians of Macedonia took no part in the poll which had therefore shown a substantial majority for independence. According to the EC's criteria Macedonia's claims to recognition were at least as good as those of Bosnia and Hercegovina but they were blocked by Greece. Nevertheless, it was clear in Belgrade that Macedonia was going the way of the other republics and therefore the two remaining entities, Serbia and Montenegro, agreed on 27 April to re-establish Yugoslavia on a new basis. Tito's Yugoslavia, founded in 1944, had ceased to exist as a political entity.

If Tito's Yugoslavia had ceased to exist as a political entity it lived on in the many mixed marriages and communities, in the towns, villages and neighbourhoods which had emerged since the Second World War, and which in most cases were mystified and then revolted by the violence which was soon to rip through their country. Even in Slovenia an opinion poll in April 1990 revealed that 60 per cent of the population were in favour of some form of Yugoslav entity, while in June of the same year in Bosnia 69 per cent said they wanted the federation to continue. In July 1991 there were demonstrations in Belgrade, Sarajevo and Skopje calling for an end to inter-ethnic violence. After the breakaway of Croatia and Slovenia there were efforts to remodel the federation, the most viable idea seeming to be that pushed by the Bosnians and Macedonians of some form of 'asymmetrical federation' in which each member would have as much sovereignty as it wished to take.

Those who wished to see Yugoslavia continue were encouraged by the fact that it had been reborn once before; if it could re-emerge from the carnage of the Second World War, they argued, it could perhaps be reconstituted after the collapse of communism. They were not to know, of course, that the second collapse would produce horrors equal in kind if not in scale to those endured between 1941 and 1944. Furthermore, the first Yugoslavia fell primarily because of the action of external forces, aided to some degree by its internal foes. The second collapsed mainly because of internal contradictions aggravated by the opportunism of its leading political actors, and aided to some degree by external recognition of the successor states.

One of these contradictions, in the final years, was that the constituent republics held so many devolved powers that in most problem areas they could frustrate federal attempts to impose a solution. This applied critically in the economic sector where Abdić's cavalier behaviour in Agrokomerc and Milošević's irresponsible raiding of the federal treasury vitiated central attempts to impose fiscal discipline. But it was also a political problem. It is perhaps one of the great tragedies of Yugoslavia's demise that no simultaneous, coordinated, federation-wide, direct elections ever took place. This was in part because until June 1990 federation-wide parties, the LCY excepted, were illegal and by then both Croatia and Slovenia, whose representatives had frustrated efforts to change federal law on this issue, had staged republican elections. In those two elections it seemed the only alternative to the communists were the nationalists; there was no credible, non-communist, third option. This point was particularly important with regard to Croatia. Yugoslavia could have survived the loss of Slovenia with its different language and its more advanced economy. Yugoslavia could not, however, survive the loss of Croatia. Without Croatia no other republic could balance Serbia, especially one in full control of the two provinces.

A cardinal feature of the second Yugoslavia which is sometimes overlooked or forgotten is that it was a communist state. The communists had never been elected to office, nor did they ever subject their authority to the test of a free election. That authority had been taken by force of arms, and by force of arms it would if necessary be preserved, as was proved in Kosovo in 1981. The 1974 constitution enshrined the leading role of the party. That leading role was exercised most persistently via the SAWPY, especially through its control of both nominations for the myriad elections, and of appointments in state bureaucracies and the self-managing enterprises. The leading role of the party was a central feature of 'democratic centralism', the system which prevailed in the Soviet-style socialist states. But in Yugoslavia there was little centralism in the federal party. Careers were based on experience within an individual republican party; there was no federal, Yugoslav party cadre with officials moving from one republic to another, as there was in the Soviet Union. Once the founding fathers had gone Yugoslavia was a federal state without a federal élite.

This basic contradiction in the political structure of Yugoslav communism was reflected in the economic sector. As in all socialist systems the state was intended to perform distributive functions. Yet the central state, particularly after 1974, had little power over the units to which it was meant to be distributing; furthermore, the central government machinery, which was to supervise the distributive functions, itself consisted of representatives of the recipient units who had little interest other than to secure the best deal for their own particular republic. In the 1980s the powerlessness of the centre was highlighted when pressure from international financial institutions insisted to little effect that the central government adopt policies which frequently ran directly counter to the interests of those constituent units.

Yugoslavia's position was worse than that of the orthodox socialist states in that its open borders and its citizens' freedom to travel meant that many Yugoslavs who had worked abroad had enjoyed higher standards of living than they could find at home. Moreover, the economic recession of the 1980s hardened the resentment of the two north-western and most prosperous republics at being shackled to what they saw as the inefficient economies of the rest of the federation. The richer republics believed many of Yugoslavia's economic problems were the consequence of too little decentralization; their opponents, especially in Serbia, saw them as the result of too much decentralization. In effect, Yugoslavia had enough socialism to frustrate rapid economic modernization but not enough to impose rigid economic discipline from the centre. At the same time it had enough democracy to allow public expression of growing frustrations, but not enough to allow the formation of alternative political organizations which could have allowed those frustrations legitimate expression within the established political order.

These difficulties were compounded by two further, underlying weaknesses. The first was the complexity of Yugoslavia and its institutions. Yugoslavia between 1944 and 1991 was a state which had one ideology, two alphabets, three main religions, four constitutions, five major ethnic groups, six republics, seven land neighbours, eight members of its presidency, nine parliaments and ten communist parties. The constitutions became bywords for intricacy and obscurity, and there was no federal body with the independence and authority to arbitrate on constitutional issues, Yugoslavia's constitutional court, for example, never attained the stature of its Federal German namesake. Institutional instability was the second and perhaps the greater of Yugoslavia's two underlying weaknesses. The second Yugoslavia had as many constitutions as it did ministers of defence. There were constant modifications and amendments to each of the four constitutions and in such circumstances institutions never had sufficient time to bed themselves down. When institutions are able to become so embedded they tend to encourage continuity and almost to radiate calm. Yugoslavia had no such institutions; even the party frequently changed the composition of its leading body, the praesidium. Nor, after 1980, did Yugoslavia have a personality who could command respect or fear enough to act as a stabilizer when the ship of state hit ever more turbulent economic and political seas.

THE BOSNIAN AND CROATIAN CONFLICTS, 1992–5

From the spring of 1992 until the late autumn of 1995 Europe saw its most violent and destructive conflict since 1945, surpassing in horror even the Greek civil war. The fighting took place in the two former Yugoslav republics of Croatia and Bosnia and Hercegovina; the impact of conflict in one area was frequently felt in the other but that in Bosnia was the more protracted and the more extensive.

The fighting in Bosnia was not a war in the conventional sense; it was not a matter of one side battling against another. In Bosnia the three main factions, Muslim, Serb and Croat were all at war with each other at one point or another, and at one stage in Bihać the Muslims even fought each other. The complexity and absurdity of the conflict may be gauged from the fact that in 1993 Bosnian Croat soldiers were fighting alongside the Muslims in Sarajevo and against them in Mostar.

In the Bosnian conflicts cynicism reigned supreme. There seemed to be nothing which could not be done without money. Huge sums changed hands in order to allow the vital UN humanitarian convoys to move, while

> The duplicities of the war in Bosnia-Hercegovina have never been better illustrated than by a conversation between a Muslim commander and his Serb counterpart picked up by intercept radios during the Muslim–Croat war. First they bargained over the price in Deutschemarks of Serb shells which the Muslims wanted to buy from the Serbs to fire on the Croats in Mostar. After a price was agreed and routes for the supply in lorries arranged, the Muslim commander was heard to come back and ask if the Serbs could for a little extra money fire the shells if they were given the cross-bearings. After a brief haggle on the number of extra Deutschemarks this would involve, the Serbs duly fired on the Croats, paid for by the Muslims.[7]

Savagery was as widespread as cynicism. Much of the savagery was calculated and deliberate. The purpose of ethnic cleansing was obvious: to create ethnically homogeneous areas before a peace settlement. Rumours of ethnic cleansing, usually only too accurate, were deliberately spread by the Bosnian Serbs in order to terrify many into flight, this voluntary ethnic cleansing sometimes involving whole communities fleeing 'to avoid imagined future dangers that Serbian leaders planted in their minds'.[8] At the same time cultural heritages were destroyed in order to discourage the return of those who had been driven out, and hence the destruction of treasures such as the Gothic church at Voćin in Slavonia, the Ferhadija and other mosques in Banja Luka and, most famously, the bridge in Mostar, built in 1556.

There were also clear attempts by nationalist leaders to brutalize their followers and to increase their quotient of race hatred. For this reason each side demonized the other with Croats portrayed as Ustaše, Serbs as chetniks and Muslims as Islamic fundamentalists, which in the vast majority of cases they were not. Television relayed horror stories of the Second World War and at the same time lionized contemporary fighters who had put large numbers of the enemy to the sword; a Belgrade journalist told an American TV audience that watching Radio Television Belgrade in 1991 and 1992 'was as if all television in the USA had been taken over by the Ku Klux Klan'.[9] Many of the worst atrocity-mongers were poor, ill-educated youths brought into an area with which they were not familiar. Their small groups, frequently under the charge of a supposedly charismatic leader, were unconstrained by traditional military discipline, by any professional code of honour or by any evolved local habits of ethnic tolerance. Their savagery, and the public celebration of it, was in some ways 'a backhanded tribute to the Titoist vision of Yugoslavia'[10] because the atrocities were necessary to destroy the bonds which had united the differing ethnic groups, especially in Bosnia.

The complicated twists and turns of the military campaigns and alliances were not the only determinants in the Bosnian conflict. International engagement was equally vital and almost as riven with complexity.* To add yet more difficulty the two phenomena were closely related and interdependent.

By the summer of 1992 the Bosnian Serbs had formed their six enclaves into a political unit which was soon to be known as the Serbian Republic of Bosnia and Hercegovina, or more commonly Republika Srpska (RS). Its major stronghold was Banja Luka but its assembly met in Pale, near Sarajevo. The Bosnian Croats were not to be left out and established their own enclave of Herceg-Bosna which was declared a republic in August 1993.

Military organization preceded political. By the spring of 1992 all three factions in Bosnia had established their own armies with the Serbs inheriting a large amount of weaponry from the JNA which withdrew from the republic in May. The Serb objectives were twofold: to drive corridors through

---

* The European bodies which dealt with former Yugoslavia in 1992 and 1993 included: the EC Peace Conference under Lord Carrington which included representatives from the former Yugoslav states; The Conference on Bosnia and Hercegovina chaired by the Portuguese envoy to the EC, José Cutileiro; and Robert Badinter's Arbitration Committee. Before 1999 the Yugoslav problem was discussed also in the WEU, NATO, the Islamic Conference Organisation, CSCE (OSCE), UN Security Council, UN Human Rights Commission, the Central European Initiative, the G-7, the G-8, the International Court of Justice, the North Atlantic Council, the International Committee of the Red Cross, the Contact Group, the mini-Contact Group and the Consultation Group on the Former Yugoslavia.

Muslim or Croat regions to link the disparate Serbian krajinas, a process which gave rise to a great deal of ethnic cleansing; and to establish sufficient strength in Sarajevo to be able to dominate or divide the city. For that purpose the Serbs began the siege of the city in late April. It was to last almost without interruption until October 1995.

The Muslim leadership insisted that Bosnian unity had to be maintained and they therefore rejected any idea which smacked of partition. They were, however, militarily weak. They had few arms and the international community had imposed an embargo on their importing any more. In these circumstances Izetbegović's tactics were to try and secure maximum international intervention, a dangerous game because it might mean having to rely on the enemy becoming ever more savage.

The ultimate goal of the Croats was *enosis* with Croatia, an objective which Tudjman encouraged; he had always believed that Bosnia was an artificial creation which was ultimately not viable and which should therefore be partitioned between Serbia and Croatia. Until *enosis* had been achieved the Croats would fight to establish their own self-administered region in Bosnia.

Soon after the fighting began western news media were publishing reports of atrocities. Perceptive observers were already realizing that all sides in the conflict were culpable but it was the Serbs who received the most blame, especially after the revelation that they had established detention camps in areas conquered by them. It was against this background of moral indignation that the London conference convened in August 1992.

The conference was sponsored jointly by the UN and the EC. Those taking part included representatives of the EC, the five permanent members of the Security Council, the CSCE and other governments and interested groups, including representatives of the Kosovan Albanians and Vojvodina Hungarians. The Yugoslav delegation promised it would respect the internal boundaries of Tito's Yugoslavia and would not interfere in Bosnia and Hercegovina while Karadžić condemned ethnic cleansing and assured the conference that the detention camps would be closed. The conference widened the number of states involved in discussing the former Yugoslavia to include some Muslim countries and shortly after the London meeting the Western European Union (WEU) agreed to tighten the enforcement of the sanctions which had come into force at the end of May. A peace initiative sponsored by the EC and the UN was launched under the co-chairmanship of Lord Owen representing the EC, and Cyrus Vance the UN. Thereafter the focus of international activity turned to Geneva, the seat of the International Conference on the Former Yugoslavia (ICFY), which had been set up by the London conference and in which the dominant figures were Owen and Vance.

Early in 1993 the two statesmen produced the first systematic attempt to find a peace formula for the Bosnian conflict. Its main proposal was that Bosnia and Hercegovina should be divided into ten cantons. Three would be dominated by the Muslims, three by the Serbs, two by the Croats, and one would be mixed with Sarajevo becoming an open city. Bosnia and Hercegovina would have a rotating, three-member presidency, one from each major ethnic group, but the central government would have few powers. Most of the functions of government would be exercised by the cantons or provinces, but the latter would not have any international legal standing. That the Croats accepted the plan immediately was hardly surprising because it gave them virtually all they wanted short of union with Croatia itself. Izetbegović was more reserved but also accepted because the plan preserved Bosnian unity, at least in the international context. The problem lay with the Bosnian Serbs. Their military position was strong. They controlled about 70 per cent of Bosnia and Hercegovina and there seemed little sign that their grip might be loosened. At the beginning of May Karadžić and other Bosnian Serb leaders were brought to Athens where they were subjected to intense pressure from the Greek prime minister, Mitsotakis, Lord Owen and Milošević himself; after being told to accept the Vance–Owen plan or be bombed the Bosnian Serb leadership capitulated. Their parliament, however, did not. Despite the presence of Mitsotakis, the Yugoslav president Ćosić and Milošević, the voice which spoke loudest to the delegates in Pale was that of the Bosnian Serb military commander, Ratko Mladić. He produced maps to show that the Vance–Owen plan would involve considerable sacrifice of territory by the Serbs. On 5 May the Pale assembly voted against the plan, deciding to put it to a referendum on 15–16 May. This produced a 93 per cent majority in favour of rejection.

The Vance–Owen plan was an intelligent and fair-minded attempt to provide an answer to the Bosnian conundrum but it showed serious divisions among all those involved in the problem. The newly installed Clinton administration suspected it mainly because, they argued, it rewarded ethnic cleansing by allowing the Serbs to keep some areas they had seized and homogenized in brutal fashion. Of more impact in the short run was the division the plan created in the Serbian ranks. After the Pale assembly's rejection of the plan Milošević decided to impose his own sanctions on the Bosnian Serbs. He had concluded that they would never be able to gain more territory and that they should have settled for a decent offer when it was made. Furthermore, he had received assurances from Owen that vital links between Serbia and the Serbian enclaves in Bosnia, and between the enclaves themselves, would be policed not by Croats or Muslims but by the UN whose forces in these sensitive areas would include large numbers of Russians. Milošević was also given an assurance that in the three-member presidency decisions would be taken by consensus, thus relieving the Bosnian Serbs of the fear of being permanently subject to the dictates of a Muslim-Croat alliance; in effect each member of the presidency would have an absolute veto. Milošević no doubt also thought the Bosnian Serbs should accept the Vance–Owen plan because its very complexity would make it difficult, if not impossible, to implement. Above all, however, Milošević wanted to be seen to be cooperating with the international community as this would increase the prospect of sanctions against Yugoslavia being lifted. This was a critical consideration because in April those sanctions had been tightened into what was 'the most comprehensive set of mandatory sanctions yet imposed in UN history'.[11]

The failure of the Vance–Owen plan created a vacuum and threw the international community into confusion. American opinion hardened in favour of lifting the embargo on arms imports into Bosnia, wishing thereby to strengthen the Muslims against the Serbs; there were also some calls in the United States for air strikes against the Bosnian Serbs. Europeans were generally sceptical of both propositions, not least because the United States had no forces on the ground in Bosnia where, it was assumed, the fighting would intensify if the embargo were lifted and air operations launched. The British were not fully in line with European opinion, London admitting that some limited air strikes might be the 'least worst' option. President Yeltsin, preoccupied with the forthcoming referendum on his reform proposals for Russia, opposed further action.

With no one able to produce a new schema for Bosnia the UN assumed, almost by default, greater responsibility. The movement of some UNPROFOR units from Croatia to Bosnia had begun in the summer of 1992. The UN had also taken control of Sarajevo airport to ensure humanitarian supplies would reach the city, which they did with some interruptions, and had established land routes for the importation and distribution of the humanitarian aid without which many thousands of Bosnians would have starved.

After the Pale assembly had rejected the Vance–Owen plan the UN Security Council had decided to establish 'safe areas' protected by UNPROFOR in and around Sarajevo, Tuzla, Goražde, Žepa, Bihać and Srebrenica. The Bosnian Muslims opposed this idea because they believed it rewarded Serbian aggression and because they saw it as condemning Muslims to living in reservations in their own country, but it did mark an increase in UN involvement. So, too, did Security Council Resolution (UNSCR) number 816 of 31 March 1993. Passed after villages east of Srebrenica had been attacked from the air, this resolution declared the whole of Bosnia and Hercegovina a 'no-fly' zone and authorized NATO to take 'all necessary measures' to ensure compliance. The vital link between the UN and an effective military force had been established. UNSCR number 836 of 4 June went further and allowed the use of force, including air power, to protect the safe areas and the supply lines to them. As yet, however, the UN had committed itself to little more than a holding operation which preserved the status quo but which did not advance towards a settlement. Even though it had established links with NATO the international community was in effect politically inoperative.

The internal forces involved in the Bosnian conflict took advantage of this to intensify their action. Early in July 1993 the Muslims lost Maglaj in northern Bosnia to a joint Serb-Croat force and the Bosnian army suffered its worst military setback when Serb forces took two mountains which dominated Sarajevo. Both were relinquished by the Serbs early in August but the siege had tightened significantly, the Serbs using their new strength to refuse fuel supplies for the city's water pumps. In central Bosnia the Muslims enjoyed some success against Croat forces, while the Croats themselves intensified their ethnic cleansing near Mostar, a city which was to be under siege until September. By the end of 1993 it seemed no side was interested in peace, all believing that their cause would prosper by continued fighting.

There were significant changes in February 1994. On 5 February a mortar attack on a Sarajevo market left 68 dead and over 100 severely wounded. The responsibility for this outrage has never been unequivocally established but the effect was immediate and profound. All EU states with the exception of Greece agreed to the use of air strikes to end the siege. At the same time NATO said the Serbs' heavy weapons must either be removed from a 20 km belt around Sarajevo or placed under UN control. By the stated deadline, 20–21 February, enough heavy armour had been removed to avoid the use of force, the settlement being helped by Russian diplomatic intervention and by the promise that 800 Russian soldiers would be deployed in the 20 km exclusion zone.

In the same month negotiations in Washington produced a major change in the political and then the military constellations in Bosnia. The talks involved leading members of the Bosnian Muslim and Croat factions and the foreign minister of Croatia. The result was an agreement signed in the US capital on 18 March to establish a federation of Bosnian Muslims and Croats. The plan envisaged the cantonization of the federation with the central government having wide powers in defence, foreign affairs and economic policy. An agreement was then signed by Tudjman and Izetbegović for the setting up of a 'Confederative Council' which was to prepare gradual moves to bring Bosnia and Hercegovina and Croatia together in a lose confederation. On 30 May the constituent assembly of the Bosnian Federation of Muslims and Croats held its inaugural session and elected Haris Silajdžić as prime minister and Izetbegović as president. The formation of the federation was important in that it simplified the political structure of Bosnia thus rendering it less difficult to propose a division which would isolate the Serbs from the other two groups. In April in Geneva the USA, Russia and five EU states, including Britain and France, backed a plan to allot 51 per cent of Bosnia to the federation and 49 per cent to the Serbs. After much tortuous negotiation that division was eventually to be applied.

The creation of the Muslim-Croat federation also simplified the military picture and produced the first significant tilt in the military balance away from the Serbs. This was in part because the negotiations produced a ceasefire between Muslim and Croat forces leaving each with only one enemy upon whom to concentrate. The new federation was also helped by the fact that the USA turned a blind eye to a substantial arms delivery to the Muslims in Bosnia.

This shift in the military balance was by no means immediately effective or apparent. In April 1994 fighting intensified around the UN safe area of Goražde. So ferocious did the battle become that the commander of UN forces in Bosnia, Lieutenant-General Sir Michael Rose, overrode his previous concern at extending the UN's mission and asked NATO to launch air strikes against the besieging Serbs. It did so on 10 April. The action, taken, it was stated, to protect UN personnel, was the first time that NATO had fired a shot in anger, but the Serbs were unimpressed. On 22 April they took the town, handing it over to UN forces in September.

The siege and fall of Goražde had severely dented the prestige of the UN. The diplomatic initiative now passed to a new body, the Contact Group (CG). Consisting of the UK, the USA, Russia, France and Germany, the CG emerged from a meeting in London on 26 April. On 6 July it produced a peace proposal. Once again the territorial division envisaged was the 51–49 per cent split with the EU taking over the protection and administration of enclaves such as Sarajevo, Goražde, Srebrenica and Brčko. The Serbs were told that if they rejected the map sanctions on Yugoslavia would be tightened; the federation was told that if it rejected the map the sanctions would be eased. The plan produced much the same reaction in Bosnia as the Vance–Owen plan; it was accepted by everyone except the Bosnian Serb assembly in Pale. Milošević once again urged the Bosnian Serbs to fall into line and this time when his word was ignored he denounced the Pale's assembly's decision as 'senseless and absurd' and closed Yugoslavia's borders with the Bosnian Serbs. His reward was the partial lifting for a trial period of some of the UN sanctions on Yugoslavia.

The CG had not secured a peace settlement but Pale was now completely isolated, a condition of which their opponents soon took advantage. The Muslim army went on the offensive around Bihać and in November Muslim-Croat military cooperation brought real rewards in central Bosnia. In the previous month the Muslims had also gone on the offensive around Sarajevo. The gains they made on Mt Igman were denied them by UNPROFOR which, in an unprecedented operation, drove the Muslim soldiers off the mountain. The UN again extended its competence in November when it authorized NATO air strikes against Serbian bases in the Croatian Krajina; the amount of ordinance dropped was insignificant but the extension of the UN's and NATO's sphere of action was not. In December a four-month ceasefire was agreed by the main contestants and at the beginning of 1995 there was appreciable fighting only around Bihać where the Bosnian army was grappling with a motley force of rebel Muslims, Bosnian Serbs and Croatian Serbs who had not signed the ceasefire.

The fortunes of the federation forces seemed to be improving. In December 1994, to the anger of the Russians and the EU, the United States had announced that it would no longer enforce the arms embargo against Bosnia and in March 1995 an alliance was signed between the armies of Croatia, the Bosnian federation and the Bosnian Croats. When the December ceasefire expired on 30 April 1995 the Bosnian prime minister said his country was no longer interested in ceasefires: it wanted a settlement.

In Croatia too the leadership assumed a less accommodating posture. On 8 April Tudjman had said that Croatia was determined to liberate all Croatian territory and at the beginning of May his troops took a slice of western Slavonia which had been in Croatian Serb hands since September 1993. On 9 June he warned the Serbs that if they did not accept a peace settlement which acknowledged Croatian sovereignty throughout Croatia by 31 October then Serb territory would be taken by force.

The scene was being assembled for the final dénouement in Bosnia. A further element in this was the humiliation of the UN. By May 1995 Serbian guns were again at work within the 20 km exclusion zone around Sarajevo but NATO action against them had been overruled by the UN for fear that the Serbs would retaliate against UN personnel, 164 of whom had lost their lives by the end of that month. Such circumspection was needless because the Serbs took retaliatory action anyway. On 26 May they began seizing UN soldiers as hostages and by 1 June held 377 of them. By 18 June all had been released, but this had been brought about by the intervention of Milošević not of the UN. By the end of June UN authority around Sarajevo seemed to have collapsed entirely with Serbian guns firing at will from the exclusion zone and Serbian aircraft flying uncontested anywhere in Bosnia. The Bosnian Muslims had in the meantime launched an offensive of their own which, Izetbegović promised, would lift the siege of Sarajevo. It did not. The Bosnians were driven back with huge losses and morale in the city sank at the prospect of another winter under siege. Something, it was widely acknowledged, had to be done to prevent such a catastrophe, but what and by whom?

It had become clear in the early summer of 1995 that whatever was done was unlikely to be done by the UN. The hostage crisis had marked the end of its credibility as a military factor. Others, however, were appearing to take its place. At the end of May President Clinton said that he would send 2,000 marines to the Adriatic and would agree to the use of US ground forces to rescue UNPROFOR soldiers; in the summer fifteen NATO states met in Paris and agreed to set up a Rapid Reaction Force (RRF). Even the Germans at last expressed themselves ready to deploy their troops outside Germany's frontiers, a move which had been made possible by a decision of the German constitutional court in July 1994. Milošević had also become more than ever convinced that the Bosnian Serbs could make no more gains and was therefore prepared to do what he could to force them to a peace settlement, especially if a further lifting of sanctions were to be his reward.

If the increased willingness of the USA to engage in military operations and the formation of the RRF provided new mechanisms for enforcing the will of the international community, developments in Bosnia and then in Croatia increased the urgency for such action. Three events in midsummer 1995 changed the military and political situation irrevocably. The first was the capture of the UN safe area of Srebrenica by Bosnian Serb forces on 11 July. On the following day General Mladić supervised the separation of women and children from the menfolk. The former were sent to Tuzla, nearly 8,000 of the latter were taken away allegedly for questioning about war crimes. They were never seen again. It was the worst massacre in Europe since the Second World War and it completely demolished the UN's credibility as an effective force; President Chirac condemned it for 'congenital incompetence'. In fact the UN now virtually abdicated. On 21 July it agreed to end the so-called 'dual key' system by which it had to sanction any NATO operations in Bosnia. From now on NATO could operate alone. Two days later RRF units of British and French troops were deploying on Mt Igman.

The second major event took place in Croatia. Early in August the Croatian army launched a carefully prepared offensive against the Serbian Krajina and its capital Knin. Within a few days the Croats had achieved total success but at the cost of driving 152,000 hapless Serbs from their homes; in yet another grim record it was the largest single movement of refugees since the end of the Second World War. The collapse of the Serbian forces in Croatia profoundly affected Serbian troops everywhere. The myth of Serbian invincibility had been punctured and in many areas the morale of the Serbs was destroyed. Within days Bosnian forces had broken out of the Bihać pocket. This ensured that the Bosnian government would be able to rebuild its authority in western Bosnia, while for the Serbs it meant the rupture of all communications with those Serbs who remained in Croatia. In September federation and Bosnian Croat forces attacked Serbian positions in central and western Bosnia many of which surrendered without resistance. By the end of that month the map of Bosnia had been entirely changed with the Serbs now holding about half the territory rather than the 70 per cent which had previously been in their hands.

The loss of Knin and the defeats which followed it were not the only military blow to befall the Serbs. The third defining event in the summer of 1995 came on 28 August when a shell, this time universally recognized as having been fired by the Serbs, landed in the Markale marketplace in Sarajevo. It killed 37 people and put the international community into a frenzy. Its patience now completely exhausted on 30 August NATO launched Operation Deliberate Force, a series of heavy air raids on Serbian positions near Sarajevo aimed at forcing the Serbs to evacuate their positions around the city. The bombing, which continued until the middle of September, was extended to cover Serbian military installations throughout Bosnia and involved over 800 NATO bombing missions as well as the use of Tomahawk cruise missiles, a weapon only used before in the Gulf war. It was cruise missiles which destroyed the Serbs' communications network in the entire western part of Bosnia. The Serbs could not sustain such losses. They were saved from complete defeat, perhaps, by diplomatic moves which were to lead eventually to a settlement; what had been largely a diplomatic effort to restrain the Bosnian Serbs ended therefore by saving them.

Immediately after the Markale market bomb Milošević called a meeting in Belgrade of leaders from Serbia, Montenegro and the Bosnian Serbs, together with the head of the Serbian Orthodox Church, Patriarch Pavle. The so-called 'Patriarch's agreement' which emerged from the meeting allowed

Milošević to lead the negotiating team of the Bosnian Serbs. It was just what the international community, whose most active and able member was the American professional diplomat, Richard Holbrooke, wanted because it meant that meaningful negotiations could now be conducted with the Bosnian Serbs. The international community also knew that Milošević would take a hard line with Pale for whose politicians he had little respect: he described them to Holbrooke as 'shit'.[12]

The Patriarch's agreement was in fact the first step along the long and arduous road which led to Dayton. In Geneva in early September the Joint Agreed Principles upon which a settlement was to be based were worked out by representatives of the Contact Group and the ministers for foreign affairs of Bosnia, Croatia and Yugoslavia. The Joint Agreed Principles were vague in the extreme and said nothing on the vital question of the nature of the central government in Bosnia; it had been accepted, however, that Bosnia and Hercegovina would consist of two entities, the federation and the RS. This was a considerable advance in that it meant the Muslims had at last accepted a Serbian entity and that the Bosnian Serbs had at last acknowledged a unified Bosnia. By late September the negotiations had moved to New York where they continued to involve intensely detailed and frequently fruitless discussions on the future political structure of Bosnia, and on the map. On 5 October the announcement of a 60-day ceasefire cleared the way for the proximity talks for which Holbrooke had been preparing.

The eventual venue for these talks was the Paterson Air Base in Dayton, Ohio, an institution with a budget far greater than that of Bosnia and Hercegovina. The talks began on 1 November and involved the USA, the EU, Yugoslavia, Croatia, the Bosnian Muslims and the Bosnian Serbs, though the last were totally sidelined by Milošević. In many ways the Dayton talks symbolized many of the faults and idiocies of the wars of Yugoslav succession. The United States found itself frustrated and puzzled by the lack of unity among the EU which had no single spokesperson. The Europeans resented what they saw as American impatience and arrogance, while the translation booths pointed to the nonsense of much of the nationalist fervour which had destroyed so many communities and lives: there were six booths for translation into English, French, Russian, Bosnian, Croatian and Serbian, but only one person spoke for the last three channels.

Negotiation was far from easy. There was initial progress over the question of Slavonia. Serbian losses in Bosnia and elsewhere in Croatia left Serb-occupied Slavonia vulnerable and weak, for if he were not to lift a finger for Knin Milošević was unlikely to do so for Vukovar. Milošević exerted pressure on the Slavonian Serbs who put their signatures to an agreement on 12 November. In January 1996 UN troops of the United Nations Transitional Administration in Eastern Slavonia, Baranja and Western Sirmium (UNTAES) began to arrive in the area.

Agreement on Slavonia did not solve the difficulties over Bosnia. Some progress was made on the details of electoral procedures but until the very end the main problem was the map. On 18 November Milošević finally agreed that as long as the 49–51 per cent split was preserved the federation could have all of Sarajevo, a significant concession in that Sarajevo was, after Belgrade, the second largest Serb city in the former Yugoslavia. The Bosnian Muslims, however, remained extremely obdurate and not until presented with an ultimatum did they finally agree upon a territorial settlement which at last enabled the agreement to be initialled on 21 November. The Serbs were to retain Srebrenica and Žepa but Goražde and a connecting corridor to Sarajevo were to go to the federation. International arbitration was to decide the future of both Brčko, a vital link between Serbia and the Serbian areas of northern Bosnia, and of the Posavina corridor which linked Banja Luka with other Serb areas in northern Bosnia and with Serbia itself. Many of the constitutional details remained vague but there was to be a democratically elected central presidency in Sarajevo and a single currency and central bank. Indicted war criminals were to be barred from office. People were to be free to move where they wished and returning refugees were to have the right to repossess their former homes. The ceasefire and the division of Bosnia and Hercegovina into the federation and the RS were to be guaranteed by an Implementation Force (IFOR) of 60,000 troops under NATO rather than UN command. With the initialling of the agreement the latter agreed to lift sanctions on Yugoslavia and to phase out the arms embargo.

For reasons understood only by themselves the French leaders had all along insisted that any agreement reached at Dayton could only be initialled. The final signing of the agreement therefore took place in the Elysée Palace on 14 December. Before this a conference in London worked out details of the implementation plan and established itself as the Peace Implementation Council which was to have a steering board meeting every month under the chairmanship of a High Representative (HR). Carl Bildt, a former prime minister of Sweden, was appointed to this post.

A donors' conference under the joint chairmanship of the European Commission and the World Bank was held in Brussels on 20–21 December. The long and slow process of rehabilitation and reconstruction had begun. There was much to be done. The three and a half years of savagery had cost 200,000 lives; 250,000 refugees had fled to other parts of Europe and the world, while inside the former Yugoslavia there were 865,000 displaced persons, most of whom were homeless. The economic costs of the fighting were beyond realistic calculation.

Notes

1. *Nationalism in Contemporary Europe*, Boulder, CO: East European Monographs no. 76, distributed by Columbia University Press: New York, 1981.
2. Steven L. Burg and Paul S. Shoup, *The War in Bosnia-Herzegovina: Ethnic Conflict and International Intervention*, Armonk, NY and London: M. E. Sharpe, 1999, p.62.
3. Misha Glenny, *The Rebirth of History*, London: Penguin, 1990, p.137.

4. Keesings Record of World Events 1991, 38081.

5. Viktor Meier, *Yugoslavia: A History of Its Demise*, translated by Sabrina R. Ramet, London and New York: Routledge, 1999, p.5.

6. Quoted in Sabrina R. Ramet, *Nationalism and Federalism in Yugoslavia, 1962–1991*, 2nd edn, Bloomington and Indianapolis, IN: Indiana University Press, 1992, p.256.

7. David Owen, *Balkan Odyssey*, London: Indigo, 1996, pp.383–4.

8. Mark Almond, 'Learning from Our Mistakes and How to Make New Ones', in Sir Julian Bullard and Robert O'Neill (eds), *Lessons from Bosnia*, Summary Record of a seminar series of that title held in All Souls College, Oxford, Hilary Term 1996, private publication, pp.24–8, see p.25.

9. Noel Malcolm, *Bosnia: A Short History*, London: Macmillan, 1994, p.252.

10. Christopher Bennett, *Yugoslavia's Bloody Collapse: Causes, Course and Consequences*, London: Hurst, 1995, p.249.

11. Laura Silber and Allan Little, *The Death of Yugoslavia*, London: Penguin, BBC Books, revised edn 1996, p.276.

12. Richard Holbrooke, *To End a War*, New York: Random House, 1998, pp.105–6.

Chapter 15

YUGOSLAVIA AND ITS
SUCCESSOR STATES SINCE 1992

A fter the end of the war in Croatia and the construction of the new, smaller Yugoslav federation the successor regimes, Bosnia and Hercegovina excluded until the end of 1995, attempted to create functioning independent states. The most important dynamic in the area remained, however, the clash between Serbian nationalists and other ethnic groups. This time the *locus* of the conflict was within the Serbian republic, in Kosovo. The renewal of tension there after the end of the Bosnian conflict was to precipitate full-scale military action, in the air, by NATO. The Kosovo crisis so influenced the destiny of Serbia and the surrounding states that its evolution must be described before the affairs of those other states are examined. But even after the crisis had been contained peace did not come to the Balkans and a decade after the breakup of the post-1945 Yugoslav federation the one state which had departed that federation without a shot being fired, Macedonia, was plagued by a new ethnic conflict which threatened once more to destabilize the region.

KOSOVO SINCE 1992

After the upheavals and violence of 1989–91 Kosovo settled into what in retrospect may be regarded as a period of relative calm. In May 1992 the Albanians organized elections for the banned Kosovo assembly; Ibrahim Rugova's Democratic League of Kosovo (DLK) won most of the seats contested and Rugova was elected as president of the Republic of Kosovo. Under his leadership the parallel state established by the Kosovan Albanians in 1990 functioned smoothly. It was helped by generous donations from Albanians abroad and by the fact that the Belgrade authorities seemed willing to tolerate it; Rugova, for example, moved around Kosovo in a presidential Audi and travelled abroad freely on a Yugoslav passport.

For the Kosovan Albanians there seemed little alternative to Rugova's policy of passive resistance. They were unarmed and Bosnia provided a chilling example of what might be expected if armed combat were to be visited upon a region. Nor could the Serbs afford to disturb this uneasy calm. The Yugoslav government did not want any further international complications, especially in the later stages of the Bosnian war when Milošević was anxious to discipline the Pale Serbs and earn some relief from sanctions. In addition to this both Presidents Bush and Clinton had warned Belgrade that the United States might sanction military action if Serbia provoked conflict in Kosovo.

It was the Dayton agreement which wrecked the fragile calm in Kosovo. The Kosovan Albanians received nothing from the settlement. This was a huge disappointment, not least because the pro-American government of Sali Berisha in Tirana had argued that the United States was the natural protector of all Albanians. Furthermore, Dayton had confirmed that Kosovo was part of Yugoslavia; the Kosovan Albanians were resentful that they were now to be locked into a Serb-dominated Yugoslavia when the Slavs of Croatia, Slovenia and Macedonia had been allowed to flee the coop, as had the Albanians of Macedonia. In fact, the international community dared not allow Kosovo to leave Yugoslavia; if it did there could be no reason why the Serbs of Bosnia should not leave Bosnia and Hercegovina, in which case the Dayton settlement would be unravelled immediately. Nor could the Albanians of Kosovo reasonably expect relief via constitutional revision in Serbia or Yugoslavia. Were Belgrade to allow Kosovo republican status within a reconstituted Yugoslavia it would come under great pressure to do the same for Vojvodina, in which case inner Serbia would find itself in a permanent minority. Such concessions could be contemplated by no Serbian administration, least of all one which having made ethnic nationalism its leading legitimizing factor had then been forced to accept massive defeats for the Serbs of Croatia and Bosnia.

The mounting tensions broke surface in October 1997 when Albanian students demonstrated in Prishtina to demand the implementation of a 1996 agreement on education. They were violently repressed by the police. By the end of 1997 repression in Kosovo had increased so markedly that it was condemned by the Serbian Orthodox Church in January 1998. Rugova's passive resistance seemed to be leading nowhere and in April 1998 a rival political organization appeared in the New Democratic League of Kosovo (NDLK) under the leadership of Rexhep Qosja and former DLK deputy, Hyadjet Hyseni. More significant was the rise to prominence of the Kosovo Liberation Army (KLA).

The origins of this organization were to be found in the Kosovan Albanian émigré communities, especially in Switzerland, in the early 1980s. The KLA became rich, it is widely believed, through involvement in a number of international smuggling rackets involving prostitutes, cigarettes, stolen cars and above all narcotics. In the second half of the 1990s it amassed arms, some of which came from the mujaheddin in Afghanistan, but most of which were purchased during weeks of anarchy in Albania in 1997 when Kalashnikovs were on the market for no more than $10 a piece. The KLA made its first appearance in Kosovo when a group of masked men attended a funeral in November 1997, though at this stage the organization was still small with only around 200 members. In January 1998 it declared itself the armed force of the Kosovan Albanians while quietly announcing to influential sections of the world media that it was about to launch an armed insurrection in Kosovo.

This was the beginning of a process of KLA provocation, Serbian repression and Kosovan Albanian protest that was to destabilize Kosovo in 1998. The first serious incident took place on 28 February of that year when the KLA killed 4 Serbian policemen in Likosane in the Drenica region; in the next three days the Serbs killed 24 Albanians who, they said, were members of the KLA. A further operation in the Drenica region at the beginning of March was directed primarily at the Jashari clan and resulted in the death of their chief, Adem Jashari, the leader of the KLA, and 52 others, including women, children and old men, most of whom seemed to have been killed in cold blood. The KLA now had martyrs; the money and the volunteers flooded in. Within weeks it controlled most of the Drenica region and had established a supply corridor from the Albanian border. By May it was estimated that the KLA had 12,000 men under arms and controlled 40 per cent of Kosovo. In retaliation Serbian forces launched a major drive against KLA forces, burning villages where the insurgents might shelter and driving thousands of families from their homes in the process. Such campaigns continued throughout the summer until by September there were an estimated 300,000 internal refugees in Kosovo.

The escalating violence had been accompanied by intensifying political protest. On 13 March the Serbian authorities allowed the first officially sanctioned demonstration since 1988 in Prishtina and 50,000 appeared on the streets to denounce repression and demand political concessions. Pro-KLA demonstrations thereafter became a common occurrence.

Kosovan Albanian political demands were that the Serbian special police forces be withdrawn from Kosovo after which talks should be held with the Yugoslav rather than the Serbian government; the Albanians demanded that those talks also involve international mediation.

International concern over Kosovo had been growing with the tension in the region, not least because of the TV coverage of the refugee problem. A major concern was that the Albanian population in Macedonia might become involved, thus destabilizing Macedonia with all the dangers that entailed. The spring of 1998 therefore saw intense activity on the diplomatic front. The CG, NATO, the UN Security Council and other organizations debated the problem and further sanctions were imposed on Belgrade. Seasoned veterans of recent Balkan diplomacy, including Richard Holbrooke and the US ambassador to Macedonia, Christopher Hill, packed their overnight bags and set off once more on a series of wearying but largely unproductive negotiations.

With persuasion failing force became more likely. NATO began consideration of the Kosovo issue in March 1998. In May it announced plans for putting troops along the Albanian-Kosovo border and in August it staged Operation Cooperative Assembly, a large-scale exercise in Albania which was obviously meant as a warning to Belgrade. The British prime minister, Tony

Blair, also warned that air strikes were a possible option if Yugoslavia did not bend to international will.

In September, with little sign of an end to the fighting in Kosovo, international action at last seemed to have some impact. On 23 September UNSCR 1199 called for an immediate ceasefire in Kosovo and for negotiations between the Serbs and Albanians to end the conflict. It also demanded the withdrawal of 'security units used for civilian repression'. It did not specifically threaten the use of force but because it was passed under Chapter VII of the UN Charter it was widely assumed that such a threat was implicit. On 24 September NATO approved an 'activation warning' which meant that air strikes could be unleashed at short notice. Initially Milošević appeared unwilling to comply but after a further visit from Holbrooke, who left the Yugoslav leader in no doubt as to the imminence of NATO action, he agreed to limit his forces in Kosovo and to allow the OSCE to send 2,000 monitors to the area. This was hailed in the west as a victory for diplomacy backed by the threat of force.

It was a short-lived victory. By the end of the year tension was rising again and it exploded on 15 January 1999 when 45 bodies were discovered in the Kosovan Albanian village of Rachak. Most had been shot in the back of the head or in the neck and it was rumoured that western intelligence had learned from telephone intercepts that the atrocity had been sanctioned at a very high level in the Yugoslav capital. Ever since the October agreement the threat of NATO action had remained in the background, on what the British Foreign and Commonwealth Office called a 'soft trigger'. After Rachak the threat was brought to the foreground and solemn warnings were issued to both sides on 30 January. At the same time the CG had moved into top gear and insisted that the two sides appear for proximity talks in Rambouillet outside Paris on 6 February.

At Rambouillet the Serbs, who sent a very low-level delegation, were presented with a series of demands, two of which they could not possibly accept. The first was that a referendum be held in Kosovo after three years to determine the future of the province; the result could not have been in doubt. The second, contained in the military annex of the CG's plan, was that NATO should have 'free and unrestricted passage' throughout Yugoslavia; Belgrade had rejected an analogous demand from Austria-Hungary in 1914 and was unlikely to accept it now. Nor were the Albanians accommodating; they rejected the clause requiring the KLA to disarm within three months. The talks collapsed to reconvene on 15 March in the Palace Kléber in Paris. In the interim Serbian forces in Kosovo had been strengthened far beyond the limit laid down in the October 1998 agreement and a further 25,000 Kosovan Albanians had been driven from their homes. After three days of intense pressure the Albanians finally agreed to the terms drawn up by the co-chairmen of the discussions, the British and French ministers for foreign affairs. The Serbs, however, did not prove amenable to pressure and on 19 March the talks were abandoned.

On the following day the entire OSCE monitoring team was withdrawn from Kosovo. On 22 March Richard Holbrooke had made yet another journey to Belgrade while a NATO meeting had agreed to use force if necessary against Yugoslav military targets. Milošević had refused to listen to Holbrooke's warnings. Operation Allied Force therefore began on 24 March with NATO launching missile and bomber raids on Yugoslav air defences.

Not for the first time politicians plunged their people into war on the assumption that the conflict would be short. NATO leaders assumed their vast superiority would soon bring Milošević to his knees. But they were motivated by concern as well as confidence. There was fear that another Srebrenica might occur, a fear enhanced by Milošević's increasing willingness, when speaking off the record, to indulge in blood-curdling predictions of what he would do with, or to, the Albanians of Kosovo. Furthermore, there remained the danger that the crisis in Kosovo might destabilize Macedonia. Less laudably, there was concern that having demanded an end to the repression NATO would lose credibility if it did not act to enforce that demand. There were also reports that NATO had come by plans for an 'Operation Horseshoe' by which Serbia planned to cleanse Kosovo of its Albanians. It seems that what was involved was not a blueprint for definite, immediate action, but rather an academic assessment of how Kosovo might appear in fifteen years time, given present birth rates, and what might be done to preserve Serbia's grasp on its vital interests in the province: Prishtina, the Trepča mines and the historic monasteries. The plan involved securing a horseshoe-shaped area in the north and the north-east of Kosovo and along the eastern Montenegrin border.

NATO's campaign had surprisingly little effect on the Yugoslav forces. Despite regular assertions that the Yugoslav army's capacity to fight had been destroyed it remained stubbornly active, and at the end of the campaign it appeared NATO had destroyed no more than 14 Yugoslav tanks; it had also killed around 400 Yugoslav soldiers, roughly the same number as those killed by the KLA. The bombing, by and large, was surprisingly accurate but accidental damage could not be avoided, most famously when the Chinese embassy in Belgrade was hit on 7 May.

What the NATO action did achieve was a rapid intensification of Serbian action against the Kosovan Albanians. Within days thousands of refugees were being taken or driven to the Macedonian and Albanian borders; in the first eight days of bombing 307,500 left Kosovo and by the end of the campaign the UNHCR put their total number at 863,000. The rapidity and efficiency with which the refugees were forced from their homes immediately after 24 March indicates that plans for such a move had been long prepared. In fact, the NATO bombing changed the nature of the Serbian operations in Kosovo. Before 24 March these had been in essence an anti-insurgency campaign directed, albeit with great brutality, against KLA units and the areas which harboured them; after 24 March Serbian policy seemed to be to kill or expel all Albanians. At the same time the bombing provided

Milošević with the opportunity to wind up what was left of the parallel state in Kosovo.

The launching of Operation Allied Force was followed by intense diplomatic activity but not until President Yeltsin's personal envoy, Viktor Chernomyrdin, had a nine-hour negotiating session with Milošević on 28 May did any breakthrough appear likely. On that day the Yugoslav leader made his first real concession when he agreed to accept some deployment in Kosovo of troops from NATO states which had not taken part in the bombing. Chernomyrdin was soon back in Belgrade, this time with Finnish president, Martii Ahtisaari, who had been appointed as mediator for both the UN and the EU. They took to the Yugoslav capital a set of peace proposals drawn up by the G8, the G7 plus Russia, in Bonn. These Milošević accepted on 3 June, though both Blair and Clinton immediately made it clear that there would be no halt to the bombing until a Serbian withdrawal from Kosovo had begun. The bombing was suspended on 10 June when the first Serbian forces were pulled out and when the last troops left on 20 June the campaign was terminated.

Milošević had in effect accepted NATO's demands. All the gambles he had taken had failed. He had calculated that the NATO alliance would collapse under the strains created by the bombing campaign, and that his nation could survive the few days which this would take; his army, in the meantime, would be able to finish its allotted task of liquidating the KLA. Another disappointed expectation was that Russia would come to his aid. By late May there was also the danger that, rather than being crushed, the KLA might achieve a significant victory over the Serbian forces near the Albanian border where it was receiving strong support from NATO aircraft and artillery units of the Albanian army. Above all, however, Milošević had come to fear that NATO ground troops would be deployed against him. The Americans, burdened by memories of Vietnam and Somalia, had been very reluctant to go down this path, and when the bombing began Clinton had told the US people that he did not 'intend to put our troops in Kosovo to fight a war'. This had been a tremendous boost to Serbian morale. American resistance to the use of ground troops had continued through and beyond the fiftieth anniversary summit of NATO held in Washington at the end of April, but a month later, with Serbian resistance apparently unbowed, US attitudes began to harden. Milošević saw the deployment of ground troops as increasingly likely and, equally importantly, so did Russia, and the main reason why Moscow assumed such a positive role in the negotiations to achieve a ceasefire in early June was its conviction that the use of ground troops was imminent.

The settlement devised for Kosovo was complex and fragile. It was outlined in UNSCR 1244 of 10 June. It provided for the deployment of a force with substantial NATO participation under a unified command which was authorized 'to establish a safe environment for all people in Kosovo and to facilitate the safe return to their homes of all displaced persons and refugees'. Kosovo was to enjoy 'substantial autonomy' within Yugoslavia with an interim administration overseeing the development of provisional and democratic self-governing institutions. The KLA was to be disarmed while a limited number of Serbian police and troops were to remain to help clear mines, to guard 'patrimonial sites', and to monitor key border crossings. Further details of the interim administration were published on 14 June. The EU was to be placed in charge of reconstruction and the OSCE was to have the primary role in establishing democratic institutions, organizing elections and protecting human rights. The UNHCR would be in charge of the resettlement of refugees, and the UN Interim Administration in Kosovo, UNMIK, would administer the police, justice, schools, public transport, communications and power plants. An international police contingent of 2,000 was to supervise the setting up of a Kosovan police apparatus. In Brussels a meeting of NATO decided to send a 50,000 force to Kosovo, Kosovo-Force (K-FOR), and to divide the province into sectors under British, US, French, German and Italian control.

The first foreign troops to arrive in Kosovo, however, came not from a NATO state but from Russia. To the surprise and consternation of NATO a unit of Russian tanks sped from Bosnia to Prishtina airport. Here they were soon confronted by 100 British paratroopers. Attempts by Russia to send supplies and reinforcements to Prishtina were frustrated by the refusal of Bulgaria and Romania to allow Russian planes to overfly their territory, and the Russians were therefore left dependent for water and other essentials on their British minders. The Russian gesture had been made to remind NATO that Moscow could not be entirely excluded from the settlement and the potential crisis ended when it was agreed that 3,600 Russian soldiers should participate in K-FOR.

In subsequent months UNMIK and K-FOR imposed an imperfect order on Kosovo. They could not prevent systematic harassment of the Serbs by the Albanians, and by the end of 1999 an estimated 100,000 Serbs had fled the province. In towns where substantial numbers of them remained there was frequent tension between them and the local Albanians, especially in Mitrovica where both communities suffered casualties. The KLA declared that it had disarmed and transformed itself into the core of an unarmed, civilian police body, the Kosovo Protection Force. Nevertheless, arms caches were found, including a major haul in June 2000 near the headquarters of General Agim Ceku, a former commander of the KLA and then in charge of the Kosovo Protection Force.

In the second half of 2000 there were worrying developments in the Preševo valley in south-west Serbia on the border with Kosovo. The area had a large Albanian population but carries vital rail and road links from Serbia to Macedonia and Greece, and by the autumn there were indications that a new armed group had appeared with tactics and strategy very reminiscent of the KLA. The new force, the Liberation Army of Preševo, Medvedja and Bujanovac, threatened to attack Serbian policemen and injected a dangerous element of potential instability into the area.

Within Kosovo itself there were few indications that flourishing demo-cratic institutions were being created. The KLA remained the dominant, if unaccountable power in the Albanian communities and it was quite prepared to exercise that power to the detriment of any person or group who might pose a threat to its authority. The economic regeneration of Kosovo seemed as distant as that of Bosnia. The Stability Pact for South-Eastern Europe established by the OSCE in June 1999 did little in the subsequent two years but hold massive jamborees in Sarajevo in July 1999 and Lisbon in March 2000, though the latter meeting did pledge $1.6 billion in aid. Meanwhile, the economies of Bulgaria, Macedonia and, to a lesser degree, Romania were hobbled by the fact that NATO bombs had destroyed most of Serbia's bridges over the Danube and thereby blocked this vital water-way. Not until after the fall of Milošević in October 2000 did the EU agree to take action to lift the bridges.

These considerations did not dent the conviction of most western leaders that the Kosovo campaign had been a success. They remained oblivious or blind to the costs of their war in the area itself. They seem unconcerned that their action was judged of dubious legality by a British parliamentary en-quiry.[1] Nor were they troubled by the Human Rights Watch declaration that the use of cluster bombs near populated areas had been illegal, as had NATO's attacks on a number of targets of 'questionable military legitimacy'. They were apparently unaware or uninterested in the ecological legacy of their action. In addition to aggravating the existing problems of pollution of the Danube and other waterways, the bombing left scattered throughout the territory quantities of depleted uranium munitions which are thought to have contributed to illness among former participants in the Gulf war.

SERBIA SINCE 1992

Few leaders in history can claim a survival record to equal that of Slobodan Milošević. Between 1992 and 2000 he presided over defeats for the Serbian cause in Croatia, Bosnia and Kosovo. In 1999 his obduracy helped NATO launch an assault which wrecked most of his country's infrastructure. At the same time his regime became more and more entwined with organised crime, while members of his immediate family embarked on a campaign of self-enrichment reminiscent of the Ceauşescu clan.

Milošević's political longevity was all the more remarkable in that in addition to these humiliations Serbia under his rule suffered economic meltdown. The rot set in with the imposition of sanctions on Yugoslavia by the UN in May 1992. All trading links with the outside world were cut, an oil embargo was imposed, government assets abroad were frozen and Yugo-slavia was excluded from international cultural and sporting events. There was some relaxation early in 1998 but the relief was soon ended by the intensi-fication of the crisis in Kosovo. The economic damage caused by sanctions was compounded by the government's unwillingness to cut expenditure or relinquish control of the economy, the result being inflation which reached 'haemoglobin numbers'.★

The deterioration of the economy produced periodic protests. Anti-Milošević demonstrators took to the streets of the Serbian capital in June 1992. There were strikes in Belgrade against declining living standards in March 1993 when the economy and the fiscal confidence of the nation had been further damaged by the collapse in the previous month of the Jugoskandik Bank which had attracted investors with its irresponsibly high interest rates.

The major confrontations between the authorities and its opponents, however, were political rather than economic. The most serious occurred in late 1996 and early 1997. In local elections in November 1996 'Zajedno' (Together), a loose coalition of anti-government parties, had won control of thirteen of Serbia's largest urban centres, including Belgrade. The Milošević regime refused to accept the results. The ensuing protest, led by Vuk Drašković, the head of Serbian Renewal Movement, garnered massive popular backing with an estimated ¼ million people taking part in a march through the capital on 15 December. In the new year the Serbian Orthodox Church aligned itself with the demonstrators, Patriarch Pavle leading another huge march through Belgrade on 27 January. In February Milošević gave way. An OSCE meeting in Vienna on 3 January had called on the Serbian government to accept the results of the November local elections, OSCE's own investigations having confirmed Zajedno's claims of victory. Milošević decided, as he told the Serbian prime minister, Mirko Marjanović, that 'relations with the OSCE and the international community surpass by far the importance of any number of council seats'.[2] On 11 February the Serbian assembly passed the necessary legislation which gave Zajedno control of Belgrade and thirteen other towns.

The local election results and the public support offered to Zajedno had revealed the strength of the opposition. Zajedno, however, was unable to capitalize on this. Its constituent groups, and even more so the leaders of those groups, found it impossible to cooperate and compromise. The anti-government coalition began to crumble even at its moment of triumph and by July it had ceased to exist, the final rupture coming when no agreement could be reached on a joint candidate when the federal parliament had to nominate a president of Yugoslavia.

The chronic divisions within the opposition obviously strengthened Milošević's position, as did his own skills in institutional manipulation.

No authoritarian leader with pretensions to longevity can disregard the army. Early in 1992 Milošević had removed a number of generals who had been trained under Tito and replaced them with those who had been promoted under the nationalist regime. More were replaced in July 1993. The

---

★ For an explanation of this phrase see Richard Dawkins, *The Blind Watchmaker*, London: Penguin Books, 1998, p.45.

defeats suffered by the Serbs in Croatia and Bosnia depleted Milošević's stock in military circles and in the confrontation of 1996–7 student leaders claimed that they had been assured by the chief of the general staff, Colonel-General Perišić, that the army would not move against them as it had against the demonstrators of March 1991. The cool relations between the government and the army were also reflected in, and caused by, Milošević's increasing reliance on the special police, an élite, professional force of dedicated Milošević supporters which received far better equipment than the conscript regular army. The special police, a virtual private army of Milošević, became his favoured instrument for operations in Kosovo.

Control or manipulation of the media is the dream of every politician. Milošević was not completely successful in this sector and the Serbian media, traditional and electronic, showed great ingenuity and courage in maintaining a public platform for opposition opinion. When the government attempted to take over the influential Belgrade daily, *Borba* (Struggle), in January 1995 the journalists responded by issuing their own version which they renamed, *Naša Borba* (Our Struggle). In March 1997 the Serbian government introduced a new media bill which limited private ownership of daily newspapers to 20 per cent of the shares and which enacted that private radio and TV stations could broadcast to no more than a quarter of the population, but in this case the government was thwarted by the courts and the proposed legislation was dropped. The NATO bombing of 1999 provided Milošević with a pretext for further restrictions on the media, including the temporary closing down of B-92 Radio, a popular anti-government station.

On the political front Milošević showed as much acumen as his opponents did incompetence. In June 1992, shortly after the formation of the new Yugoslav federation, Dobrica Ćosić was elected president. He chose as his prime minister Milan Panić, a Serb who had returned to his native land after a successful career in the pharmaceutical industry in North America. At the London conference in August Ćosić and Panić overshadowed Milošević, even refusing to allow him to address the other delegates. Milošević neither forgot nor forgave the humiliation. By the end of the year he was using his position as president of Serbia, which was confirmed by elections in December, to castigate the Ćosić-Panić team for the conflict in Bosnia. Panić was the first to fall, brought down by a vote of no confidence in the federal assembly on 29 December; he was succeeded by Radoje Kontić, a Montenegrin. In June 1993 Ćosić went, again following an adverse vote in the federal assembly.

Meanwhile, Drašković and his Serbian Renewal Movement had joined with the Democratic Party and two other opposition groups in June 1992 to form Depos, the Democratic Movement of Serbia. There was also opposition on the right, represented chiefly by the ultra-nationalist Serbian Radical Party led by Vojislav Šešelj. It was the latter which spearheaded an attack on Milošević in late 1993, citing economic mismanagement, war profiteering and general incompetence as grounds for removing him. Milošević called an election to head off a parliamentary debate on Šešelj's proposed censure motion. In the elections Depos was hamstrung by an inability to agree on electoral lists, but despite this it secured 45 seats and was the second largest group in the assembly, the largest being Milošević's Socialist Party of Serbia with 123. The anti-Milošević vote had been depleted by a refusal to take part in the polls by the Kosovan Albanians and by the Muslims of the Sanjak of Novi Pazar which straddles the border of south-western Serbia and Montenegro.

By the early summer of 1997, though he had weathered the storm of the local elections protest, Milošević was faced with a constitutional problem. His term of office as president of Serbia was soon to expire and the constitutional rules forbad him a third term. When the federal assembly was required to elect a president of Yugoslavia in July Milošević put his name forward and was elected unopposed by both houses; he promised that his four-year presidency would be one of 'peace, progress and prosperity'. His position seemed to strengthen further in March 1998 when Šešelj agreed to take part in a new coalition government formed in Serbia. Further consolidation came in May when Milošević removed Kontić as federal prime minister and also introduced a new law which allowed the government to appoint senior academic personnel in Belgrade university.

Perhaps the most important factor in strengthening Milošević's hold on Serbia, however, was the NATO campaign of 1999 which, on patriotic grounds, made it impossible for the domestic opposition to oppose the regime.

After the virtual loss of Kosovo there was some backlash against Milošević in which the Serbian Orthodox Church took a prominent part. The Church grieved for its lost sites in Kosovo and on 15 June the Holy Synod backed a call from Bishop Artemije of Kosovo for more protection for the Serbs and their churches and monasteries in the province; it also endorsed Artemije's call for Milošević's resignation and for the formation of a government of national salvation. A conference of bishops in August repeated the call for Milošević to go and the same demand was put forward by the 100,000 who demonstrated in Belgrade on 19 August. The political opposition to Milošević, however, was still fractured and feeble.

It remained so for a year. There were large-scale rallies in Belgrade on 14 April and 26 May and protest marches in Novi Sad and Niš. A united opposition youth group, *Otpor* (Resistance), was also formed in May, but neither the demonstrations nor the new group had much impact on the regime. Milošević certainly had no fear of opposition in July 2000 when he pushed through a set of important constitutional changes. The first was that the president should be elected directly rather than by parliament; such a president would be allowed to serve two terms of four years. This meant in effect that Milošević, who would be barred from re-election as federal president under the old system, would be able to put himself forward under the new one; in effect, the proposed constitutional adjustment would give Milošević another eight years in power. The second amendment stated that members of the upper house of the federal parliament should be directly elected by popular vote in numerically determined constituencies. Under the existing system the upper house had equal numbers from Serbia and Montenegro, and the changes would obviously greatly enhance the influence of Serbia, the population of which was ten times larger than that of Montenegro; Serbia was also more strongly in favour of Milošević. The third amendment allowed parliament to appoint and remove individual ministers, the existing rules stating that the cabinet must be approved or removed as a body. The changes would allow Milošević to remove any minister who might become an embarrassment or a threat.

The prospect of continued rule by Milošević at last concentrated the minds and coordinated the actions of the opposition. By mid-August fifteen groups had come together and agreed to back a single candidate in the presidential elections due in September. Their choice was Vojislav Koštunica of the Democratic Party of Serbia. He had first come to prominence as the joint author of a work on communist political tactics during the immediate post-war period.[3] His electoral appeal was that he was an anti-Milošević Serbian nationalist with a clear dedication to the rule of law; he had supported the Serbian national cause in Bosnia and had been a fierce critic of NATO action against Serbia, but at the same time he had maintained a political level-headedness which had escaped other anti-Milošević nationalist leaders.

Koštunica secured his expected easy victory in the election of 24 September. Milošević initially refused to accept defeat, the electoral commission declaring on 27 September that Koštunica, although the victor, did not have over 50 per cent of the poll and therefore a second round of voting would be necessary. The opposition did not believe it. They were convinced that Koštunica had over 50 per cent and they refused to take part in a second round. Pressure on Milošević mounted rapidly. On 27 September a massive demonstration in Belgrade backed the opposition's stance and the following day the electoral commission reversed its decision and announced Koštunica had won the elections. It was also made clear in the world's powerful capitals, not least in Washington, that should Koštunica take office the question of sanctions would immediately be reviewed. But the pressure which toppled Milošević was internal rather than external. On 29 September strikes began and on 2 October a general strike was declared. Two days later the miners at Kolubara faced down police sent to intimidate them: even the most favoured sons of Serbian socialism had forsaken Milošević. On 6 October over ½ million people congregated in the centre of Belgrade. There were some clashes between the demonstrators and the police and there were a few acts of violence but by and large the demonstration was peaceful. The crowd proclaimed Koštunica as president and no one seriously contested the proclamation.

The thirteen years of rule by Milošević were over. In April 2001, under considerable pressure from the west and especially the USA, the new Yugoslav authorities seized the nettle and arrested him. Finally, on 28 June, the anniversary of Kosovo Pole in 1389, of the assassination of Franz Ferdinand in 1914, of the enactment of the ill-fated Vidovdan constitution of 1921, and of the expulsion of Yugoslavia from the Cominform in 1948, Milošević was sent to The Hague. The following day in Brussels a conference of potential donors agreed to offer Yugoslavia $1.28 billion in grants and loans.

In the long term Milošević's fall has to be explained by his failures in Slovenia, Croatia, Bosnia and Kosovo. The international sanctions which his aggressive policies called down upon Yugoslavia also inflicted huge privation upon his people. There was little surprise that they found the prospect of eight more years of his kleptomaniac rule uninviting and therefore turned eagerly to the first credible alternative to appear. In the short run Milošević's fall had two important causes. In the first place neither the army nor the police were prepared any longer to back him against the populace. The chief of the general staff, General Pavković, had made this clear shortly before the election when he stated that the army would be loyal to whoever was lawfully elected. And when the police faced the huge crowds, especially on 6 October, it was obvious that they too could no longer be counted upon. The second cause for Milošević's fall was that the whole country united against him in unprecedented fashion. Opposition was no longer confined to the intelligentsia of the larger towns and now involved workers such as the miners at Kolubara. But above all it involved thousands of ordinary people whose feelings were personified in the mayor of Čačak who led a column of demonstrators from his town to Belgrade, clearing road blocks en route with a strategically placed bulldozer. Actions such as his were not as spontaneous as they were made to appear but their appeal was none the less real. Against such a combination of forces not even Milošević's special police would be effective.

After the removal of Milošević Koštunica moved with great circumspection. He rejected external pressures for the extradition of his predecessor and he refused to bow to internal demands for the immediate sacking of the heads of the army and the political police, both Milošević appointees. He also handled the question of forming a new federal government with considerable care. This was a complicated issue. In Montenegro the main opposition party had boycotted the elections with the result that the Montenegrin representation in the federal parliament was dominated by the pro-Milošević Socialist Peoples' Party (SPP). The federal constitution required that if the president were a Serb then the prime minister must be a Montenegrin, but given the Montenegrin representation in the federal parliament the only Montenegrin who would command loyalty in that assembly was the SPP leader, Zoran Žižić. After almost a month of careful and not always calm negotiation Koštunica accepted him as federal prime minister. On 23 December 2000 elections in Serbia gave victory to the Democratic Opposition in Serbia led by Zoran Djindjić, who formed a new Serbian administration in January 2001.

Even after the formation of new federal and Serbian governments many questions remained to be solved. Koštunica's relations with the west, especially the Americans, were not without difficulties, there was the ominous build-up of tension in the Preševo valley of which the nationalist opposition were quick to take advantage, and there were huge internal problems. The extradition of Milošević had been the work of the Serbian rather than the federal authorities and it created further tensions between Djindjić and Koštunica. The economy was still in tatters and there was a major constitutional issue over relations with Montenegro; there was the further problem that if Montenegro decided to leave the federation Yugoslavia would cease to exist and Koštunica, as president of Yugoslavia, would no longer have a constitutional position. But however great the problems one obstacle on the road to their solution would be removed: neither Yugoslavia nor Serbia were any longer international pariahs and there would be external help available should they wish to comply with the conditions on which it was offered. The need for such help was pressing: in April 2001 Yugoslavia had an unemployment rate of around 40 per cent, an external debt of $13 billion and a shrinking GDP.

MONTENEGRO SINCE 1992

Relations with Serbia were the dominant feature of Montenegrin political affairs after the formation of the new Yugoslav federation in April 1992. In January 1993 the incumbent Momir Bulatović won the second round of the elections for the presidency of Montenegro. He was a dependable supporter of the federation and of Milošević. Milo Djukanović, who became prime minister in March 1993, was neither. He was resentful of the increasing power of Serbia within the federation, as manifested in developments such as the abolition of the separate Montenegrin ministry of defence and a law allowing the federal assembly to declare a state of emergency in any province without reference to the assembly of that province. There was also the consideration that were Montenegro to disengage from the federation it might then escape the crippling economic sanctions imposed on Yugoslavia.

Djukanović turned more and more towards the idea of resurrecting the independence of Montenegro which had been given up at the end of the First World War when the tiny mountain state joined the new Kingdom of the Serbs, Croats and Slovenes, or Yugoslavia as it was known after 1929. A growing segment of Montenegrin opinion seemed to share Djukanović's view. On 30 September 1993 Bulatović's car was stoned by protesters demanding separation from Serbia, and separatist sentiments were again much in evidence in the following month when a meeting of several thousand in Cetinje, the old Montenegrin capital, proclaimed the re-establishment of the separate Montenegrin Orthodox Church.

The Bosnian war restricted the Montenegrins' ability or willingness to push further down the road to looser ties with Serbia but by 1997 the momentum had been regained. In a press interview in February Djukanović attacked Milošević as incompetent and called for his removal from office; as a result Djukanović was replaced as vice president of the majority Democratic Party of Socialists of Montenegro. Djukanović's fortunes changed in October when he defeated Bulatović in the second round of the elections for the presidency of Montenegro. Djukanović told a German newspaper that he would use his presidency to ensure that Milošević did not interfere where he had no right to do so.

In 1998 relations between Djukanović and Belgrade deteriorated further. In June elections to the Montenegrin assembly brought victory to his supporters and setbacks for the Bulatović camp, after which all twenty Montenegrin representatives in the upper house of the federal assembly were replaced by Djukanović loyalists. This was an attempt, unsuccessful in the long run, to ensure that Milošević did not have the two thirds majority he needed for constitutional changes. Bulatović in the meantime was made federal prime minister in May, after which the Montenegrin regime withdrew its recognition of the federal government.

The Kosovo emergency was to deepen the rift between the two states. In August 1998 Montenegro refused to supply more recruits for the Yugoslav army and when the NATO campaign was launched Podgorica said it did not regard itself as bound by Belgrade's severance of diplomatic relations with the NATO states; in April the Montenegrins refused orders from the commander of the Second Army in Montenegro to place their police under his command. Djukanović angered the Serbs yet again in May by visiting a number of NATO capitals, and in the same month Montenegro put forward proposals to replace the federation with a loose 'Association of the States of Serbia and Montenegro', adding that if the Milošević government refused this plan Montenegro would hold a referendum on the question. Actual separation seemed a step closer in November when Montenegro, fearful of renewed inflation in Serbia, adopted the Deutschemark as a parallel currency alongside the Yugoslav dinar, a move which the Yugoslav constitutional court declared illegal in January 2000.

Djukanović also cultivated links with the west, warning Tony Blair in January 2000 that Montenegro was in imminent danger of attack. No such attack materialized but Milošević's constitutional proposals of July threatened to relegate Montenegro to permanent subservience to Serbia. On 7 July, the day after the constitutional proposals were presented to the federal parliament, the Montenegrin assembly went into emergency session. Those Montenegrin delegates to the federal parliament who had voted for the amendments were denounced as traitors and a resolution passed declaring the Yugoslav parliament's moves 'illegal and illegitimate'. Djukanović denounced them as a brutal attempt to end Montenegrin statehood and he feared that civil war was about to break out.

This did not happen but the constitutional revisions greatly complicated the political situation during and after the Yugoslav elections of September 2000. Djukanović's party boycotted the federal parliamentary and the presidential elections on the grounds that they had been made possible by the constitutional changes of July which had been enacted without the participation of Montenegro.

This complicated relations between Koštunica and Djukanović. These had never been easy. Djukanović made little secret of his suspicion of Koštunica's Serbian nationalist past while Koštunica resented the boycott of the elections which he had denounced as a virtual vote for Milošević. During the elections he referred to Montenegro in disparaging terms and soon after his victory he declared that Montenegrin independence was 'impossible'. He soon modified his tone. He ceased referring to 'Yugoslavia' and spoke rather of 'the federation of Serbia and Montenegro' and said that although he believed most Montenegrins wanted to retain some links with Serbia he would respect the decision of the Montenegrin people if it were to be expressed in a referendum. Djukanović meanwhile was somewhat discomposed by the fact that the Yugoslav president was no longer a pariah but the favoured son of the western powers; to frustrate him might anger those powers.

Koštunica's estimation of Montenegrin opinion appeared justified. Opinion polls in November showed that though most respondents wanted independence, even more wanted independence and the retention of some links with Serbia. For his part, Djukanović seemed determined to push along the road to separation. When, in November 2000, Yugoslavia was re-admitted to the UN he complained that this had been done without Montenegro being consulted; in any case, he argued, Montenegro should have separate representation in the world forum. He made a similar claim in other international meetings, including the EU-sponsored Balkan summit in Zagreb in the same month. In December 2000 Montenegro announced that it wished to expand its representation to the USA and the EU and to establish new diplomatic missions in Macedonia, Croatia, Germany, the UK and France. He spoke of federal Yugoslavia as being a 'fiction' and stressed that Montenegro was in reality an independent state. He gave substance to this assertion by dropping the dinar as legal tender in Montenegro; now the Deutschemark was the only medium of exchange, and in April 2001 Montenegro applied to financial transactions with Serbia the regulations for dealings with foreign countries.

The referendum threatened in November 1999 had not been forgotten. Towards the end of 2000 Djukanović promised that it would be held after Montenegrin parliamentary elections which he called for April 2001. In fact, to the surprise of many, not least Djukanović himself, the elections failed to produce the unambiguous endorsement for secession which he had sought and confidently expected.

BOSNIA AND HERCEGOVINA SINCE 1995

What the international community hoped to see emerge after Dayton was a peaceful, democratic, multi-cultural, united, war-criminal free, economically healthy and viable state of Bosnia and Hercegovina.

A relatively peaceful and democratic Bosnia was created. Very soon after Dayton the respective forces had withdrawn to leave the 4 km gap between the federation and the RS as stipulated by the agreement and no serious clashes between military forces have taken place since 1995. Prisoners of war were also exchanged without difficulty. If reasonably free and fair elections are accepted as a measure of democracy then Bosnia and Hercegovina has become a democratic state. By the summer of 2000 there had been three rounds of elections.

Another noteworthy achievement of the international community was to secure an apparent settlement over the highly dangerous question of Brčko. The Serbs had insisted that they could not allow the town to pass into Muslim hands because it controlled the links between Serbs in Serbia and eastern Bosnia and those in northern Bosnia. The Dayton agreement had left the city's fate to be decided by international arbitration but in February 1997 the international arbitrators decided the question was still too sensitive to settle and that the area should remain under supervision until March 1998. No change in fact was made until March 1999 when a multi-ethnic local government was imposed by the Peace Implementation Committee's High Representative (HR). A year later Brčko was made a self-governing neutral entity, an ingenious solution which would be unlikely to survive should Bosnia be once again destabilized.

In its other objectives the international community has been much less successful. There have been few signs of a return to the multi-culturalism and ethnic tolerance which was once a distinctive feature of Bosnia, and which it was hoped would be recreated by the mass return of refugees to their former homes and communities. In fact in the first months after the Dayton accord the movement seemed to be in the opposite direction. In March 1996 a number of Serbian districts in Sarajevo were to be handed over to federation control. Instead of leading to a renewed mixture of groups this produced another spasm of ethnic cleansing; the Pale authorities intimidated local Serbs into destroying their homes before they were to be handed over, and an estimated 100,000 Serbs fled as a result of the transfer of authority away from Pale. In November 1996 attempts to return Muslims across the inter-ethnic boundary line to their original homes had to be abandoned because of the worst outbreak of Muslim-Serb violence since the end of the war. In sub-sequent years further attempts to return people to their original places of residence produced much the same effect. Inter-communal tension in fact remained endemic if at a reduced level. Srebrenica had to be placed under OSCE administration in April 1998 after the local Serbs had refused to assist Muslims returning to their former homes, and there were ugly scenes in Banja Luka in the spring of 2001 when attempts were made to rebuild mosques in the town. In political terms the power of ethnic identity has been revealed in all the elections held since Dayton, with most voters casting their ballot on national lines.

The international community has put great store on the necessity for sending all accused war criminals for trial in The Hague. The International Criminal Tribunal for the Former Yugoslavia (ICTFY) had been established by UNSCR 827 and inaugurated on 17 November 1993. It was to have 'jurisdiction over persons accused of grave breaches of the Geneva Conventions, of violations of the laws and customs of war, of genocide, or of crimes against humanity, committed within the territory of the former Yugoslavia after 1 January 1991'. There were many, both important and insignificant, who came under that definition and it was believed, particularly in the Clinton administration, that without their detention, trial and incarceration a healthy democracy could not be constructed in any part of the former Yugoslavia. But the determination to capture war criminals was not always apparent and when it was it could, particularly in the early years, complicate relations between the international forces and local political authorities, usually to the embarrassment of the former. By the turn of the century a change was perceptible and the ICTFY celebrated a major success with the extradition of Milošević in June 2001.

On the other hand it was difficult to argue that Bosnia and Hercegovina was either a unified political entity or a functioning, sovereign state in the generally understood sense of the phrase. Despite the introduction of some features of a cohesive state, for example a common currency and a unified system of vehicle licence plates, Bosnia-Hercegovina was in effect a partitioned state, and it was more a protectorate of NATO and the OSCE than a functioning state. Bosnia was a federation in little but name.

It seemed also to be a condensed version of the old Yugoslav system if political complexity were to be considered. The elections held in 1997, 1998 and 2000 were 'in all probability the most complex set of elections in modern history'.[4] They involved the selection of: the three-member federal presidency; the assembly of the union of Bosnia and Hercegovina; a 42-member chamber consisting of 28 deputies of the (Muslim-Croat) Federation Chamber of Deputies and 14 from the RS Chamber of Deputies; the 140-strong House of Representatives of the Muslim-Croat federation; the chambers of the 10 cantons; and the 83-member Peoples' Assembly of the RS, together with the presidencies of both the federation and the RS.

It was not the multitudinous assemblies which had effective power, however. They seemed unwilling or unable to decide on any matter of importance concerning Bosnia's internal governance. As a result power rested with the HR. Carl Bildt remained the HR until June 1997 when he was succeeded by Carlos Westendorp, a former Spanish minister for foreign affairs. In August 1999 he in turn was succeeded by Wolfgang Petritsch, an Austrian. It was the HR who enforced decisions on a host of issues including, in January 1998, the adoption of the common currency which had been stipulated at Dayton. Indicative of Bosnia's lack of political cohesion was Westendorp's decree of July 1998 which stated that a law on privatization prepared by his office had taken effect although it had been rejected by the Bosnian parliament. Over two years later, in November 2000, Petritsch introduced a Bosnia-wide state court, pension reforms requested by the World Bank and a series of changes demanded by the EU. Although the reforms were essential for the issuing of a World Bank credit of $24 million the local Muslim, Serbian and Croatian politicians had refused to pass them. Indeed, by the end of 2000 the all-Bosnian parliament, which had served two full two-year terms, had not passed a single law.

Political life within the RS was much more lively than within the federation, the main issue in the former being the contest between on the one hand the Pale diehards grouped around Karadžić and his Bosnian Serbian Democratic Party (SDS) and, on the other, the moderates who had their headquarters in Banja Luka. The latter were represented by Biljana Plavšić who had made her name during the war as a hardliner but who after Dayton, while retaining her nationalism, abandoned her secessionist aspirations having become convinced that the only hope for the Serbs of Bosnia was within the framework laid down by Dayton. Once again the determining factor in the dispute was the international community. Karadžić was removed from the presidency of the RS following a threat from IFOR and the HR that if he remained the SDS would not be allowed to take part in the elections. Plavšić owed much of her strength to the backing of SFOR★ which at one point closed down the TV transmitters operated by her opponents. Plavšić lost the presidency of the RS in the September 1998 elections to the diehard Nikola Poplašen, but he was removed by Westendorp in the following March.

While these political charades were being enacted, Bosnia's economy had little chance of revival. The problems were prodigious. Fifty years of socialism and five years of war are hardly a recipe for economic health, but the patient was not much helped by the international financial institutions' (IFIs) prescribed medicine of immediate privatization. In reality remedial measures could not always be applied for fear of their social consequences, and thus the Tuzla coal mines, accounted by the World Bank as the most inefficient on the planet, were kept working to prevent unemployment levels rising even further. Another difficulty was that the aid promised by western governments and, to a lesser extent the IFIs, was slow in coming. In the summer of 1996 it was still the case that the United States government had disbursed less money in Bosnia than the private benefactor, George Sőrős. Funds did flow more frequently in later years but they were never enough to meet all the demands for them and there was a further problem for which the external world could not be held accountable: corruption. The closer their acquaintance with local conditions the greater was the despair of external donors. In August 1999 the HR stated that up to a billion dollars of aid money, a fifth

---

★ IFOR, the Implementation Force ceased to exist when its mandate expired in December 1996; it was replaced by another UN-backed body, the Stabilization Force, or SFOR.

of the total, had been stolen by local officials, and at a donor's conference in May of the same year the OSCE chief of mission in Sarajevo advised donors not to invest in Bosnia until real attempts at reform had been made: 'I wouldn't', he said, 'be putting money down a rat hole.'[5]

Further dangers appeared following elections in March 2001 when Ante Jelavić, the leader of the Croatian Democratic Union (HDZ), and the Croat member of the Bosnian state presidency, declared that the Croat National Assembly of Bosnia would establish a separate state in areas with a Croat majority. A few days later he was sacked by Petritsch but his supporters remained unintimidated and within days there were reports that ethnic Croat soldiers had deserted their barracks. In early April SFOR troops and local police took over by force the administration of the Hercegovačka Banka to remove the financial basis of the HDZ. Even if the following protests were less well attended than their organizers had hoped the incident, like the desertions from the barracks, showed how fragile the political settlement in Bosnia remained.

CROATIA SINCE 1992

From 1992 until the end of 1995 the dominant question in Croatian public life was inevitably the war; from 1995 to 1999 the main feature was the growing disillusionment with Tudjman and his style of government; and since the beginning of 2000 the most noticeable feature has been the attempt to distance the country from the old regime and its failings.

Croatia had a good war. Of all the states involved in the wars of Yugoslav succession it gained most. Its own territory was little damaged; it retrieved all the lands lost in 1991 and 1992; it broke the Serbs by driving them out of the country; and its protegées in Bosnia emerged from the war relatively unscathed.

Franjo Tudjman understandably made political capital out of his nation's involvement in the war, insisting that the HDZ was the only party which could guarantee national unity. Nevertheless, in the elections to the newly created upper house of parliament in February 1993 the HDZ did less well than expected, while its showing in the simultaneous local polls was worse. In the general elections of October 1995 it failed to secure the two thirds majority it needed to enact constitutional changes.

In the following month it lost control of Zagreb city council to a coalition of seven opposition parties. The victors duly chose a mayor and other officials but early in December Tudjman announced that he could not allow Zagreb to have an authority which would oppose state policy and that 'all democratic means' would be employed to prevent such an eventuality. The HDZ and the Party of Croatian Rights withdrew their delegates from the municipal council which, the government argued, had been rendered inquorate. The constitutional court upheld the government view. The confrontation was to continue for over a year during which the Tudjman regime rejected four mayoral candidates proffered by the opposition which in return refused to accept his nominee. Not until HDZ gains in the elections of April 1997 did a settlement seem likely and even then it was delayed until May when two delegates from other parties joined with the HDZ to support its candidate.

The president's and the government's behaviour over the Zagreb municipality affair was typical of its arrogance. This had long been apparent, especially in its disdain for the opposition and the media. Early in the war the Tudjman government had established tight, but not total control over the electronic media, declaring for example that Croatian TV was to become 'A Cathedral of the Croatian Spirit', whatever that might mean. Even after the war independent broadcasters could operate only with difficulty. In 1996 two provincial radio stations were closed but when the government attempted to silence the one remaining independent national station, Radio 101, it was confronted by demonstrations and abandoned the idea.

The authorities were more pertinacious, though no more successful, in their dealings with the press. Here their tactics were not overt censure or total closure but rather underhand, quasi-legal means. Early in the war they took control of the weekly *Danas* and turned it into a docile mouthpiece of the HDZ, but the two largest weeklies, *Globus* and the Split-based satirical *Feral Tribune*, remained beyond their grasp. The latter was a particular thorn in the HDZ's side; in January 1994 its editor was conscripted into the army and six months later the government declared the journal a pornographic publication and therefore liable to an extra 50 per cent sales tax. The Croatian government came under considerable international pressure as a result of these decisions but it was not outside intervention but a decision of the Croatian constitutional court the following year which reversed the decision and saved the journal. A more general attack on the opposition press was launched after March 1996 when a new law made it an offence to criticize or pass satirical comment upon the president, the prime minister, the parliamentary speaker or the chief magistrates. Action was initiated under this legislation against *Feral Tribune* and also against *Nacional*, another weekly which was often critical of senior officials, and against *Novi List*, the country's only independent daily. The authorities made little headway. The courts twice dismissed slander actions brought against the editor of *Feral Tribune*, nor were libel suits any more successful, even though one of them was brought by Tudjman's daughter, Nevenka Košutić, who, said the weekly, had set up a profitable business using government connections.

The accusation against Košutić was only one in a series intended to show how the Tudjman family and HDZ prominenti were enriching themselves while the rest of the population faced declining living conditions. There was much to the charges. Tudjman appointed his son as director of the intelligence service in 1995 and although he resigned in 1998 he was reappointed in the following year. More serious was the revelation in October 1998 of a bank account in the name of Tudjman's wife, Ankica. The account held 440,000 Deutschemarks; when complying with recent legislation requiring the listing of his wife's assets the president had mentioned only a car, and her explanation that the money came from royalties on the sales of Tudjman's books carried little conviction. In May 1999 it was revealed that the Komercijalna Banka, which had recently declared itself bankrupt, had connections with a charity run by Mrs Tudjman.

These accusations made little impact on a regime which by the end of the 1990s appeared increasingly arrogant and divorced from the nation it ruled. Its arrogance was symbolized by Tudjman's personal and entirely unconstitutional diktat that the leading Zagreb soccer team should be named 'Croatia' rather than 'Dinamo'; to vast popular rejoicing it reverted to its original name on St Valentine's Day 2000.

Tudjman responded to criticism by falling back on nationalism. He never gave up his insistence that the institutions of the Croat semi-state in Hercegovina should be maintained even after the creation of the federation in Bosnia and Hercegovina. He consistently refused to end the system he had introduced whereby Croats living abroad could participate in Croatian elections and be represented in the sabor. And when, after 1995, Croatia had no enemies on the battlefield he created them in the guise of his foreign and domestic critics. He directed particularly heavy fire at foreign-based institutions or individuals who supported his critics, mentioning among others the Sőrős-financed Open Society Institute, the BBC and the Voice of America, as well as, within Croatia, *Feral Tribune*, *Novi List* and Radio 101. He even attacked individual scholars or journalists such as the Croatian-American academic Ivo Banac and the respected British-Croatian journalist Christopher Cviić, denouncing them as enemies who 'have spread their tentacles throughout our society'. Early in 1998 Tudjman accused opposition politicians and independent journalists of being 'genetically predisposed against Croatian independence'.

Sustained opposition to the HDZ in the early years of its rule had been confined mainly to the intelligentsia and to the regions, especially Istria and Dalmatia, where particularist feelings were strong. By the end of the 1990s it had become nationwide. The HDZ and its leader had brought the nation to independence and had won great gains for it in the wars of the first half of the decade, but thereafter it was increasingly outmoded. There was growing concern at the lack of modernization; the HDZ and its leader still behaved as if they were in the old world of the one-party state and the all-powerful first secretary, while their nationalist rhetoric had become jaded and jejune. The HDZ's stated objective of integrating Croatia into European and world organizations was unlikely to be achieved until there had been systematic efforts to separate party from state. It was significant that in April 1996 when Croatia was at last admitted to the Council of Europe, hardly the most selective of clubs, the Council's parliamentary assembly took the unprecedented step of insisting that admission be conditional upon Croatia's allowing basic democratic liberties such as a free press and accepting the terms of the Dayton accord, especially over the return of Serbian refugees to Slavonia.

In addition to the sustained opposition of the intelligentsia the Tudjman regime also had to face periodic protests from a working class angered by declining standards of living and rising unemployment. Over 400,000 workers staged a 4-hour stoppage in March 1993, securing some concessions in pay and an improvement in workers' rights; there were further strikes in subsequent years by a variety of workers, including the railwaymen who were on strike for a month in late 1996 and early 1997.

Little had been done to redress these grievances when President Tudjman died on 10 December 1999, a victim of stomach cancer. In parliamentary elections already arranged for 22 December victory went to a coalition of the Social Democratic Party of Croatia (SPH) and the Croatian Social Liberal Party (HSLS) which took 47 per cent of the vote, the HDZ receiving 31 per cent. Ivica Račan of the SPH was appointed prime minister of a government drawn from six separate parties. In the presidential elections on 24 January and 7 February 2000 Stipe Mesić, the deputy leader of the Croatian People's Party (HNS), emerged the winner.

Both president and prime minister pledged themselves to policies less nationalist and less authoritarian than those of Tudjman and the HDZ, and they both reaffirmed the commitment to seek membership of NATO and the EU. The shift away from nationalism was registered when official support of the Croats in Bosnia and Hercegovina ceased. The new rulers also ended the exiled Croats' rights to vote for and be represented in the sabor. Račan's government went on to amend the law on the representation of minorities so that any ethnic group which formed 8 per cent of the population was to be guaranteed seats in parliament. But the most dramatic turn away from the nationalism of former years was a willingness on the part of the Zagreb authorities to cooperate with the International Criminal Tribunal in The Hague, even though this policy caused considerable bitterness, especially among war veterans.

The move away from authoritarianism was less obvious. Although both the president and the prime minister remained committed to a reduction in the former's powers it was not long before there was tension over who should control the intelligence service and Mesić was complaining about plans to abolish presidential powers which he said should be merely restricted.

Croatia received some reward for its new attitudes when it was admitted in May 2000 to the Partnership for Peace Programme, the wheeze invented by NATO to keep embarrassing would-be members in the entrance lobby.

On becoming prime minister Račan declared that another of his priorities was to tackle unemployment and stimulate the economy. His room for manoeuvre, however, was limited by a crisis in the banking system in March 2000 when the Istarska Banka seemed about to fold. In a gesture which showed that regionalism was still a powerful factor in Croatian politics, the Istrian Democratic League threatened to pull out of the ruling coalition if the bank were allowed to go under. It was bailed out by the government in April. Not until May was Račan able to introduce a reform plan aimed at stimulating investment.

President Tudjman had attempted to distance Croatia from the Balkans, even to the extent of declaring it an offence to advocate Croatian participation in or membership of a Balkan organization. His successors, on the other hand, played host in November 2000 to an EU-sponsored summit of the Balkan states.

SLOVENIA SINCE 1992

Immediately after independence Slovenia made clear its objective to become part of the European system. It had a strong case: its economy could compare with the weaker brethren in the EU; it was blessedly free of ethnic divisions; and its political life soon settled into a modified version of *transformismo*. Government was by coalition but the lack of a parliamentary majority did not much disturb the functioning of the administration, months sometimes intervening between the collapse of one governing coalition and the formation of another. There were some protests at the failure to separate the judiciary from the legislature, and at the government's influence over the media, and Slovenia, like other states, experienced social tensions in the transition to a market economy, tensions which were manifested in a number of strikes by professionals such as teachers as well as by the traditional working class. The Catholic Church remained a powerful factor in Slovene affairs and has raised its voice over abortion and other 'pro-life' issues.

The major obstacle in Slovenia's path towards Europe was not internal but external. Italy claimed compensation for property seized from Italians who had fled or been forced from Slovenia immediately after the Second World War. In March 1995, however, after long negotiation Italy agreed to lift its veto on Slovenia being admitted to associate membership of the EU, and in 1998 an agreement was signed whereby Italy dropped its claim for the return of property and agreed to accept monetary compensation. Aspirations towards closer association with the EU, which makes it a condition of membership that a state has no frontier disputes, was made easier by the settlement of a long-running argument with Croatia over territory between Koper and the Istrian peninsula; the two governments also came to an interim agreement over ownership of the Krško nuclear power station.

In December 1997 an EU summit in Luxembourg included Slovenia in a list of six states with which substantive negotiations for accession to the European Union would begin in 1998.

MACEDONIA SINCE 1992

Macedonia occupies a key point in the Balkans. Were it to be destabilized there could be a scramble for territory with conflicting claims from Albania,

Bulgaria, Serbia and Greece. A fundamental change in the Balkan balance of power could also cause Turkey to intervene, in which case the whole of the eastern Mediterranean basin, with its access to the Suez canal and the Black Sea, would be threatened with chaos. NATO's cohesion would be endangered by Greek–Turkish disagreements and in the worst of scenarios world peace could be threatened.

To contain these dangers the international community decided in December 1992 to send 700 troops to monitor the Macedonian border. The United Nations Preventive Deployment Force (UNPREDEP) was the first preventive deployment ever by the UN. In June 1993 the United States agreed to add 300 of its own service men and women to UNPREDEP, the first time Washington had agreed to commit its troops to the Balkans.

The danger facing Macedonia did not arise from its departure from Yugoslavia which was smooth and orderly, Macedonia being the only one of the four republics to leave the Yugoslav federation without a shot being fired in anger. By April 1992 the JNA had left the republic with no greater bones of contention than those which arose from its attempt to take with it more equipment than the withdrawal agreement allowed, the most serious of these disputes being over the army's attempt to remove the radar facilities at Macedonia's main airport. Macedonia's smooth exit from Yugoslavia was helped by the fact that the republic contained few Serbs. There were small demonstrations by the Association of Serbs and Montenegrins in Kumanovo in February 1992 and there were rumblings in the Serbian chauvinist press when, during New Year celebrations at the end of 1992, the Macedonian police manhandled some Serbs displaying pictures of Milošević; but neither of these incidents, nor the occasional reference to border claims by Belgrade, posed any serious threat to Macedonia. Indeed, most Serbs in Macedonia felt some affinity with the Macedonian Slavs given their shared fear of the local Albanians.

The major difficulty facing Macedonia was not Serbia but Greece. The Greeks believed that the existence of a state called Macedonia posed a threat to the integrity of Greece, one of whose provinces bore the same name, and Athens therefore refused to recognize any state which used the word 'Macedonia' in its title. The Macedonian government would not give up its name; it did not have another and, in any case, it insisted it had no territorial claims on anyone. The Greeks were not convinced. They pointed out that in 1990, before Macedonia left the federation, Macedonian protesters had blocked frontier crossings into Greece demanding the latter recognize the existence of a Macedonian minority on its territory. After the formation of the Macedonian state the Greeks resented the fact that it had adopted as its national symbol the Star of Vergina, the burial place of Philip of Macedon which is in Greece. This was undoubtedly insensitive or naive on the part of the Macedonians, and there was further cause for Greek concern in the appearance of signs in Macedonia declaring 'Salonika is Ours'.

Quite how Greece, a nation of 10 million, and a member of the EU and NATO, was to be deprived of territory by an impoverished, backward state of 2 million with virtually no army and no allies was never explained, but Greek fears reached hysterical proportions. Huge demonstrations took place in Athens, Salonika and other cities; foreign visitors were subjected to a barrage of propaganda, and streets, squares, ships and airports were renamed to stress that Macedonia had always been Greek. More serious was Greek retaliation against the new Macedonian republic itself. In January 1992 97 tons of medicine and food destined for Macedonia were detained in Greece despite a serious influenza epidemic in Macedonia, and in August 1992 Athens closed the border and imposed an oil embargo. The European Union was seriously embarrassed and shortly before 1 January 1994, when Greece was due to assume the presidency of the Union, most EU states announced that they would recognize Macedonia under the title, 'The Former Yugoslav Republic of Macedonia', FYROM. In February 1994 Greece declared a total ban on trade with Macedonia, items of humanitarian need excepted; this, said the Greek prime minister, Andreas Papandreou, was to remind Macedonia that Greece remained 'the primary guarantor of peace, stability and security' in the Balkans.[6] The EU condemned this as a violation of European law and in an unprecedented move decided to institute legal proceedings in the European Court of Justice. It was a mistake. The Court embarrassed the EU by deciding that the urgency of the case had not been established and that no decision, therefore, could be expected before 1996.

Before then the Greeks and Macedonians had at last found a partial solution to the problem. After twenty-eight months of desultory negotiations an 'interim accord' was signed in September 1995 in New York; the Greeks were to lift the embargo and stop vetoing Macedonian entry into international organizations while the Macedonians were to end using the Vergina symbol on their flag. The vexed question of the name of the new state had not been resolved but relations between Athens and Skopje at last emerged from the ice age. They did not become warm but in 1997 the Greek minister for foreign affairs paid a surprise visit to the Macedonian capital; he said little about the name problem but, understandably, urged cooperation between the two states in face of the anarchy then raging in Albania.[7] Trade across the border and Greek investment in Macedonia expanded rapidly and in November 1999, after another and greater crisis had threatened the Balkans, the two states agreed to build an oil pipeline from Salonika to Skopje, while in December of the same year they signed a military accord and a bilateral security agreement, the growing tension in south-west Serbia giving both states cause for concern.

In historical terms the neighbour which was most likely to react in hostile fashion to Macedonian independence was Bulgaria. Ever since 1878 Macedonia had been regarded by most Bulgarians as *Bulgaria irredenta* and few Bulgarians believed there was a separate Macedonian nation or that the Macedonian language was anything more than a dialect of Bulgarian. In 1992, however, Sofia was surprisingly quick to bury most of its historical hatchets; the Bulgarian administration agreed – and it was the first government to do so – to recognize the independent Macedonian state. It was also rumoured that shortly after Macedonia declared independence President Zhelev of Bulgaria had scuppered a Greek-Serbian plan for a Greek-Serbian-Bulgarian partition of Macedonia. By 1999, with Kosovo about to erupt into war, the Bulgarians buried their last hatchet. In an agreement signed in February they virtually recognized the existence of a Macedonian language, culture and nation separate from the Bulgarian; the Macedonians in return renounced any claim on Pirin Macedonia.

The threats to Macedonia's stability were not entirely external. The large Albanian minority, officially recorded at 23 per cent of the population but this in a census boycotted by many Albanians, inevitably presented a threat of destabilization, as did the fact that there was no tradition of parliamentary democracy. In these circumstances Macedonia was well served by its first president, Kiro Gligorov, who in the early years of independence held a series of wide-ranging talks in which all major parties took part. As in inter-war Czechoslovakia an informal government by consensus emerged from procedures which had no constitutional standing.

This did not mean that internal political problems were absent. Macedonia's electoral processes did not win widespread commendation. In the legislative elections of October and November 1994 there were allegations of widespread irregularities and IMRO-DPMNU, which had been the largest single party in the outgoing assembly, boycotted the second round of voting after it had failed to win any seats in the first because, it said, of fraudulent practice by its opponents. In the presidential vote of October and November 1999 malpractice forced a re-run in about a tenth of the constituencies while the local elections on 10 September 2000 were roundly condemned by OSCE observers.

Like most impoverished former communist states Macedonia suffered from crime, corruption and violence. Even in the inter-war years Macedonia had been an important conduit for narcotics and there seems little doubt that the trade continued after 1992. This was also the case in other Balkan states where, as in Macedonia, crime and corruption were encouraged by the smuggling opportunities created by the imposition of sanctions on Yugoslavia. What was singular in Macedonia, however, was that it was the first state in which a leading political figure was attacked by what were assumed to be representatives of the criminal gangs. In October 1995 President Gligorov was seriously injured in an assassination attempt. He was treated by French, Serbian and Greek doctors who rushed to Macedonia. A Greek minister sent him wishes for a speedy recovery.

Macedonia's greatest internal weakness remained the ethnic divide between the Slav Macedonians and the Albanians. The Macedonians see their state as one primarily of the Macedonian people; they are the new state's constituting *narod*; the Albanians fear they are being condemned to the permanent second-class status of the former Yugoslav *narodnost* or national minority. In November 1992 rumours that the police had killed an Albanian youth during a raid on black marketeers led to riots in which three Albanians and a Macedonian died. A year later a number of prominent Albanians, including the deputy minister of defence, were arrested on suspicion of plotting to overthrow the government, dismantle the state and create a greater Albania. In 1994 the Albanians refused to take part in a census and at the end of the same year a serious dispute arose over the Albanians' intention to establish an Albanian-language university in Tetovo, an Albanian majority town in north-west Macedonia. The authorities demolished the building in which the university was to be established but this did not prevent the project going ahead.

This, together with government decrees which forbad the flying of the Albanian flag and the use of Albanian in official documents such as identity cards and passports, brought ethnic tensions to a dangerous level. They were diffused in sudden and surprising fashion. In the legislative elections of October and November 1998 a right-wing coalition of IMRO-DPMNU and the Democratic Alliance secured enough seats to form a government led by IMRO-DPMNU's Ljubčo Georgievski. When it did so Georgievski included in his cabinet representatives of the Democratic Party of the Albanians and then promised government money for Tetovo university. He also released the mayor of Gostivar, another predominantly Albanian town, who had been imprisoned for allowing the Albanian flag to be flown. When President Gligorov rejected this amnesty, parliament overrode the presidential veto. A year later Gligorov was defeated in presidential elections by Boris Trajkovski of IMRO-DPMNU who enjoyed massive backing from the Albanians.

A less successful decision by the new government had been to recognize Taiwan. The anticipated bonanza of investment failed to materialize and in retaliation the People's Republic of China used its UNSC veto to prevent the renewal of UNPREDEP's mandate.

Macedonia was greatly affected by the Kosovo crisis of 1999 when it was temporary host to hundreds of thousands of ethnic Albanian refugees. That crisis emphasized Macedonia's critical position in the centre of the Balkans and raised fears which had prompted the despatch of UNPREDEP in 1992. Following a sudden outbreak of ethnic unrest in western Macedonia in the early spring of 2001 tension rose not only on Macedonia's borders but between the two main ethnic groups within the country. By the midsummer armed units of the Albanian National Liberation Army were active even near Skopje.

The country seemed to be on the brink of civil war and were that to break out it would be probably the last of the wars of Yugoslav succession and certainly its most dangerous. In all previous conflicts the local forces pulled into them had all been from areas which had formerly been part of the

Yugoslav federation. Were Macedonia to explode there would be the danger that the forces drawn in would be from states outside the former Yugoslavia. Some of these states have military machines far stronger than any of the local forces and some of them also have additional disputes which could be enflamed by serious disagreements between them over Macedonia.

Sensing these dangers NATO backed a peace plan put forward by the Macedonian president in June 2001. Intense negotiations in Ohrid eventually produced an agreement under which the Albanians were to disarm in return for a series of concessions. These included increased recognition for the Albanian language, an expansion of local self-government, more ethnic Albanians in the police force and more extensive rights to higher education in Albanian. Furthermore, in future laws affecting the ethnic minorities would have to be approved by a parliamentary majority that included 'a majority of the votes of representatives claiming to belong to the communities not in the majority of the population of Macedonia'. To ease the process of disarmament the Albanians surrendered their weapons not to Macedonian forces but to NATO troops.

Despite this encouraging success the Macedonian parliament still had to ratify the constitutional changes, and as national elections were due at the beginning of 2002 many Macedonian politicians feared the electoral consequences of making concessions to the Albanians. Nor was there unassailable proof that all Albanian weapons had been surrendered.

The dangers of a Macedonian explosion, though diminished, had not been entirely dispelled.

Notes

1. House of Commons, Session 1999–2000, Foreign Affairs Committee, Fourth Report, *Kosovo*, vol. i, *Report and Proceedings of the Committee*, London: The Stationery Office, 23 May 2000.
2. Keesings Record of World Events 1997, 41503.
3. See above, p.141.
4. Carl Bildt, *Peace Journey: The Struggle for Peace in Bosnia*, London: Weidenfeld and Nicolson, 1998, p.256.
5. Keesings Record of World Events 1999, 42961.
6. Ibid., 1994, 39872.
7. See pp.304–5.

Chapter 16

ALBANIA SINCE 1991

Although integration into international institutions was relatively easy, in internal affairs Albania moved slowly and with considerable difficulty from its hardline socialist position. Domestic politics rapidly became concentrated into a struggle between the communists' successors in the Albanian Socialist Party and their opponents in the Democratic Party of Albania. Neither side found it easy to abandon the habits and aspirations of one-party domination. In 1997 the country suffered a total internal collapse from which it has slowly recovered, but formidable problems, above all those of crime and corruption, remain.

THE SEMI-TRANSITION, MARCH 1991 TO MARCH 1992

The elections of March/April 1991 did not bring about stable government to Albania. Although Ramiz Alia remained president there were to be two changes of prime minister within a year. Fatos Nano, who had been appointed after the student demonstrations of February, kept his post until May when, after further disturbances, a 'government of national solidarity' was formed under the leadership of Ylli Bufi. He lasted only until December when, in the face of still further disorders, he was replaced by a non-party figure, Vilson Ahmeti, who announced that fresh elections would be held in March 1992.

The 1991 administrations did introduce some lasting changes. In April an interim constitution guaranteed some of the newly granted freedoms and changed the country's name to the 'Republic of Albania'. At its tenth congress in June the APL also altered its name, becoming the Socialist Party of Albania (SPA). But such cosmetic changes could not save the successive administrations from mounting unrest on a number of issues. Supporters of the Democratic Party of Albania (DPA) were convinced that the elections had been rigged and immediately after the first round of voting demonstrators had taken to the streets to express their anger; in Shkoder they had been met by police whose violence led to the deaths of four protesters, one of them being the leading DPA activist in the city. The call for a full enquiry into the deaths of the 'Shkoder martyrs' was added to the demands of the anti-government protesters. Their demands already included the abolition of the Sigurimi, the depoliticization of the civil service and the removal of government influence from the media. In effect, the protesters were demanding the full transition from authoritarianism which was taking place elsewhere in the former communist bloc. The Albanians were experiencing the social dislocation of transition without many of its compensating political changes. The trade unions, however, had been freed from party control and with prices and unemployment soaring they contributed as much as any other discontented element to the growing public unrest.

This unrest, however, did not prevent the holding of the country's second post-communist elections in March 1992.

THE BERISHA/MEKSI REGIME,
MARCH 1992–JUNE 1996

The elections of March 1992 were held under a new electoral system according to which 100 members of the assembly were to be chosen by single-member constituencies on the majoritarian system, and a further 40 were to be elected by PR with a 4 per cent threshold for securing seats in the parliament. The new regulations outlawed parties based on ethnic allegiance. This forced Omonia to regroup as the predominantly Greek Human Rights Union (HRU). The HRU won two seats but, as has always been the case in post-totalitarian Albania, the main contest was between the SPA and the DPA. This time the latter was the winner, emerging with 92 seats to the SPA's 38. Alia resigned as president and the parliament elected as his successor Sali Berisha, a cardiologist, of the DPA. A predominantly DPA cabinet was formed with Aleksander Meksi, an engineer, as its head.

The immediate problem facing the new government was food. Shortages and the soaring prices of what was available had reduced parts of the country to near anarchy in 1991 and shortly before the elections had led to attacks on shops and warehouses. After the formation of the new government unrest continued with a rash of strikes in the summer, most of them fuelled primarily by the food shortage. Meksi's government had contributed in part to the problem. It was determined to de-communize the economy and had therefore made moves towards decollectivization and the privatization of agriculture which inevitably caused uncertainty and disruption in production and distribution. By the second half of 1992 Albania was dependent on foreign aid. The G24 agreed to supply food at least until the 1993 harvest had been taken in, the USA gave $95 million worth of aid, and Greece promised a loan of $70 million for agricultural development. In 1993 production and distribution became more stable but remained inadequate and still gave rise to intermittent protest. The improvement continued in 1994 with more foreign aid which included $10 million from the World Bank for irrigation, while at home the government came to an agreement with the trade unions and the employers whereby all three parties would meet every six months to review wages and pensions in the light of recent price movements. Despite the drought of 1994, the worst for a century, a degree of social stability had at last been achieved.

The amelioration of the food problem was accompanied and furthered by Albania's reintegration into the international community after its years of isolation. The Berisha–Meksi regime assiduously cultivated the west and in particular the United States. In 1995 Albania became a member of the Council of Europe. In February 1994 it had become a member of NATO's Partnership for Peace programme, as a result of which American troops took part in manoeuvres on Albanian soil in March and in July Albanian soldiers did the same in Louisiana. The Americans were allowed to use Albanian bases to launch unmanned reconnaissance craft over Bosnia during NATO operations there and at all points in the Bosnian conflict Albania cooperated fully with NATO.

Its determination to remain on good terms with the leading western powers and above all the United States meant that Berisha's Albania had little impact on the Kosovan crisis of the early 1990s. Despite its use of artillery in the border areas the Albanian army had almost nothing in the way of modern equipment and even if it had the terrain would have made direct intervention extremely difficult; and most importantly the country was near bankrupt and could not afford foreign adventures no matter how inflamed nationalist passions might become. This military, economic and financial weakness similarly prevented any serious Albanian action on behalf of the Albanian minority in Macedonia. Poverty and enfeeblement, however, did not prevent serious disputes with Greece which arose primarily over the Greek minority within Albania.

Relations between the two states declined rapidly in 1993 when the Albanian government expelled an ethnic Greek Orthodox priest whom they accused of trying to hellenize Albanians in southern Albania; in June ethnic Greeks and Albanian police came to blows near the southern town of Gjirokaster. The government in Athens likened the position of Greeks in Albania to that of Albanians in Kosovo, and then expelled thousands of illegal Albanian immigrants in Greece. This, said Berisha, was a deliberate attempt to undermine the Albanian economy; Greece also blocked a $43 million credit the EU had agreed to give Albania to ease its trade deficit. Tensions rose even further in 1994 when two Albanian soldiers were killed during a raid on an arms store in southern Albania. Five ethnic Greeks, all of them members of the HRU, were arrested and imprisoned, in response to which Greece withdrew its ambassador and, after expelling a further 70,000 illegal Albanian immigrants, sealed its border with Albania. At the end of 1994 the Germans, who at the time occupied the EU presidency, intervened, following which the sentences on the imprisoned Greeks were reduced, one of them actually being released. The remaining four were released in 1995 which enabled a gradual thaw in relations to take place, and by March 1996 there was enough warmth for a treaty of friendship to be signed. This regulated the status of the

Greek minority in Albania and offered a little more security to Albanians in Greece. Later in the year another Greek grievance was addressed when Greek schools were opened in three towns in southern Albania.

The pressure on the Greek communities which had done much to precipitate the crisis in Albanian-Greek relations was only one sign of the DPA's seeming intention, despite its name, to introduce its own form of party-based authoritarianism.

As soon as it took office the Meksi government placed former president Alia under house arrest and banned all parties loyal to Hoxha. It also banned all graduates of the former communist party school from entry into the legal profession, while many members of the former communist secret police were jailed. So too were a number of prominent political figures. In 1993 Alia was given a nine-year prison sentence for abuses of power under the old regime, and other prominent socialists were also imprisoned on charges relating to the totalitarian era. Hoxha's widow, Nexhimije, was one of them; she had received a nine-year sentence which, on appeal, was increased to eleven years. The non-party former prime minister, Ahmeti, was also jailed for the abuse of power, but the most sensational arrest came in July 1993 with the detention of Fatos Nano, the incumbent leader of the SPA and a member of parliament; he was accused of mishandling $8 million of aid from Italy. Other leading SPA figures soon followed him into the dock. The arrests provoked huge demonstrations and the SPA organized a petition which, they claimed, had almost ¾ million signatures. The total population of the country was 3.4 million.

The government was undeterred. It continued its pressure not only on non-DPA politicians but also on the non-government media. In February 1993 the editor of *Kohe Jone* was detained under the provisions of the old, communist-era, penal code, though he was later released after which he emigrated. Editors of independent or opposition papers were subjected to threats and occasionally to actual violence; the home of a subsequent editor of *Kohe Jone* was fire-bombed in November 1995 while one of his journalists was badly beaten by the police who advised him against writing any more articles critical of the president. In 1996 the press came under further pressure after a bomb in Tirana had killed four bystanders. The authorities implied that the opposition press was indirectly inciting such acts and financial measures were introduced which severely limited its operations; weekly journals associated with *Kohe Jone*, for example, were classified as dailies and therefore subjected to crippling backdated additional taxation.

There were two main reasons for the intensifying pressure on the opposition during 1995 and 1996. The first was the constitutional referendum Berisha insisted upon holding in November 1994. That constitutional change was needed was scarcely at issue. Apart from the interim constitution introduced in April 1991 there had been no significant change since communist times when the president reigned supreme. The powers of the presidency were still great but there was now an assembly elected, in theory at least, on a democratic basis, and the powers of the two institutions needed to be defined. Berisha's scheme, predictably, favoured increasing the authority of the president even further. This and other changes were necessary, he argued, to break with the communist past, to make it easier for Albania to join European organizations and to attract foreign investors. He announced his plan only in October which left little time for discussion and consideration, but there was time enough for the socialists to denounce it and for many non-socialists to question its wisdom. It is hard to escape the conclusion that had Berisha and Meksi ruled with a lighter hand fewer non-committed voters would have become as concerned as they did. In the event, they turned the vote against the president's scheme, a clear majority, 54 per cent, rejecting the proposals which were therefore scrapped.

His defeat in the referendum left Berisha furious and seemingly determined to limit the opposition's freedom of manoeuvre yet further. This was seen not only in increasing pressure on opposition politicians and their press but also in an attack upon the judiciary. The head of the supreme court and parliamentary deputy, Zef Brozi, had opposed the constitutional reforms put forward in the November 1994 referendum and early in 1995 he further angered Berisha by objecting to the release of the remaining four ethnic Greeks imprisoned for the killing of the two Albanian soldiers in the previous year. Brozi, who had been appointed by Berisha with an explicit mandate to combat corruption, added yet more fuel to the fire by accusing the president himself of involvement in shady financial practices, and in May successfully countered government plans to increase the power of the ministry of justice at the cost of that of the courts. The DPA's patience broke. After further confrontations, most of them won by Brozi, parliament voted in September to remove his parliamentary immunity. Two months later police surrounded his house and confiscated his passport. American intervention and a Fulbright award saved him and he left Albania for the USA at the end of the year.

The second reason for the intensification of totalitarian tendencies on the part of the government was the approach of the general election due in 1996. Shortly before Albania was admitted to the Council of Europe in June 1995 Alia had been released from detention. He was soon rearrested, this time on charges of having used undue force against would-be refugees in 1990 and against demonstrators in 1991. At the same time Fatos Nano's sentence was increased by a year which would mean, as the socialists were quick to point out, that their party leader would still be in prison when the elections were held.

A further restriction on potential opposition at the polls, and elsewhere, came in September 1995 with the so-called 'genocide act'. This decreed that anyone who had held senior office in the APL would be banned from public office until 2002; this would affect many who intended to stand as parliamentary candidates for the SPA. A further enactment was even more restrictive. It required that seven-member commissions should vet the police files of all those appointed to state and local government office, of all persons employed by the law courts and of all persons working in the state media or for independent newspapers with circulations of over three thousand, a category devised to include the main socialist dailies. Anyone who was found to have had any connection with the communist police apparatus would also be excluded from public office until 2002.

The genocide act led to the disqualification of 139 candidates in the 1996 elections, almost all of them from the SPA. Another blow to the opposition was a change in the electoral system which decreased the number of PR seats from 40 to 25. During the election campaign itself opposition meetings were frequently frustrated or disrupted, and the government decided that the DPA should be given as much air-time on public radio and TV as the other parties combined.

If the auguries for an orderly and open election were not good, the vote itself was worse. The first round was held on 26 May and so blatant was government interference that the SPA refused to take part in the subsequent rounds. The DPA therefore secured an easy victory with 122 seats to the SPA's 10. Meksi immediately formed a new government but his credibility was gravely damaged. The OSCE declared that no fewer than 32 of the 79 clauses of the electoral law had been infringed, and the Americans were equally critical.

Despite the electoral debacle the Albanian economy did surprisingly well in 1996. Inward investment reached $2,500 million with a further $500 million coming from remittances, all of which helped to keep inflation down to around 6 per cent and the budget deficit to 7 per cent, even if the relaxation of controls on the price of more commodities, including bread, did cause demonstrations and a one-day general strike in October. A more portentous indicator of approaching trouble came in December when two pyramid investment schemes failed.

THE COLLAPSE OF 1997

In January 1997 it became obvious that more pyramid schemes were in serious trouble and on 23 January the parliament agreed to freeze the assets of two of them and then further decided that to avoid inflation future payments were to be made gradually rather than in lump sums. Serious rioting broke out in Tirana because so many of its inhabitants were affected by the new regulations and were now terrified that their savings might be lost entirely. As a result of the riots parliament granted Berisha special powers. It was a fateful decision. February saw the collapse of two of the largest investment schemes, Vefa Holdings which was based mainly in Tirana, and Gjallica which was centred upon Vlore. The ensuing riots persuaded Berisha to declare a state of emergency and to deploy armed police and specialized military units.

This was a disastrous development, especially outside Tirana where the use of these units confirmed atavistic suspicions that national government was nothing more than a device for imposing the will of a few politicians in the capital upon the reluctant provinces. The disorders therefore intensified and spread to such a degree that the country was virtually ungovernable. The crowds, incensed by the use of the military units, took advantage of the prevailing anarchy and simply helped themselves to weapons from the armouries. The more bizarre items taken, tanks, guided missiles and a jet fighter, were returned, but most of the small arms and ammunition were not. The prisons were also emptied, one beneficiary being Fatos Nano who walked out of gaol on 13 March and was pardoned two days later. Even the national gold reserves were raided and $2.8 million worth of coins taken.

The Berisha regime was swept away by the storm. Meksi had been sacked early in March and Berisha had agreed to the formation of a government of national reconciliation and to the holding of a general election in June; an interim cabinet was formed under a socialist, Bashkim Fino, on 11 March. But the restoration of order was by then beyond the capabilities of any Albanian government; with the armouries looted it had no military force to call upon. Help therefore had to come from without and although both NATO and the EU turned a deaf ear to Fino's pleas for help a number of states with an interest in the region, primarily Italy, knew they could not allow the disorders to continue. An international force, the main component of which was Italian, was formed and began deploying in Albania on 11 April. The OSCE also appointed the former Austrian chancellor, Franz Vranitzky, as its special representative. He made a number of visits to Albania and was instrumental in removing the difficulties in the way of a new electoral law.

All the major parties had by now recognized that new elections were essential before any full restoration of order could be achieved. The poll took place on 29 June and 6 July with two constituencies having a third round on 13 July. There were now 155 seats in the assembly and the number to be filled by PR had been returned to 40. The DPA paid a heavy price for the arrogance and incompetence with which it had yielded power. It was reduced to 29 seats with the SPA having 101. The first round of the voting also saw a referendum on the monarchy, prompted by the presence in the country of the claimant to the throne, the six-foot-seven, gun-toting Leka I. He returned to South Africa after 66.74 per cent of the voters had decided in favour of remaining a republic.

ALBANIA SINCE JUNE 1997

After the defeat of the DPA Berisha resigned as president on 23 July, the assembly nominating Rexhep Mejdani of the SPA as his successor. Fatos Nano returned to office as prime minister and to make absolutely sure of the two thirds majority necessary for constitutional change he included a number of minor parties in his government.

The new administration faced challenges huge even by the exacting standards of post-communist Albania. It committed itself to restoring order, eliminating corruption and crime, reconstructing the armed forces and reforming the administration. The need for such improvement was acknowledged by all, but the difficulties this involved were equally obvious. In the first instance the government was desperately short of money. During the meltdown earlier in the year it had been impossible to collect internal revenues while trade and overseas aid had stopped, yet the government had continued to pay salaries. Inflation and the budget deficit therefore had slipped the leash. This in turn meant that external aid was more essential than ever but also that the conditions on which it would be offered would be more exacting than ever. A donors' conference in Brussels agreed to lend Albania $600 million but only on condition that taxes were increased, government expenditure was decreased and the pyramid schemes were liquidated. The last condition was met in November 1997 and in December, despite a socialist administration's reluctance to take such steps, 15,000 government jobs were axed. VAT had also been increased in October from 12.5 to 20 per cent.

But Albania's difficulties were not merely fiscal. The collapse of 1997 had created new and exacerbated existing problems. One of the latter was the intense, seemingly unbridgeable gap between the two major political factions. In 1998 a report into the chaos of the previous year laid the blame squarely on Berisha's shoulders in response to which he led his party in a walkout from parliament. Tensions became much greater on 11 September when Azem Hajdari, a DPA deputy and close associate of Berisha, was murdered. Two days of intense rioting followed in which a number of people were killed and the prime minister's office was ransacked; the government chose to interpret the events as a failed putsch by the DPA. However, the disorders did persuade Nano that he no longer enjoyed the confidence of the nation or of his party and in October he resigned, making way for Pandelj Majko. Majko made few changes in the cabinet but he represented a new generation, being so young that he had had no connections with the communist regime.

Majko inherited from Nano draft legislation on a new constitution. This was passed by the assembly in October and put to a national referendum in the following month. It received an overwhelming majority from those voters who went to the polling booths but they were only about half of the eligible electorate because, in another indication of the hostility between the two groups, the DPA had called upon its supporters to boycott the vote. The main provision of the new constitution was greatly to reduce the authority of the president.

Majko's tenure of office turned out to be short-lived, his demise being the consequence of tensions within his own party rather than between the SPA and its opponents. Nano had not reconciled himself to the loss of power and in October 1999 challenged Majko for the leadership of the SPA. Nano won and Majko decided he could not continue as prime minister after what amounted to a vote of no confidence by his own party. It was not Nano who became head of government, however, but the deputy prime minister, Ilir Meta, who was even younger than Majko.

The greatest damage inflicted on Albania by the disorders of 1997 was that it diminished even further the respect which central government enjoyed in the country. The most pernicious effect of this was an explosion of crime with many criminals holding, and using, weapons seized from armouries in 1997. Particular crimes expanded with great rapidity, most notably smuggling, the main commodities being drugs, cigarettes, stolen cars and human beings, especially young women from Moldova, Ukraine, Belarus and Russia, most of whom were destined for the whorehouses of the western world. The vast fortunes to be made in crime, together with the power of the criminals, meant that many law enforcement officers and other civil servants became involved either in the crimes themselves or in protecting the criminals. In October 1999 the minister for public order acknowledged that a number of unidentified politicians had put pressure on police and justice officials which had led to the release of several gang leaders arrested and imprisoned in the summer. It was to combat such practices that in September 1999 the government had ordered that all civil servants must disclose their own and their family's wealth, together with the sources of that wealth. But such decrees had little impact and the intimidatory power of the gangs persisted, even spreading to affect officials from international organizations; in November 2000 the official spokesman of the OSCE left Albania after his life had been threatened.

Its reputation for crime and collusion with the criminals helped to deprive Albania of much of the moral credit it had earned by its uncomplaining acceptance of 350,000 refugees during the Kosovo emergency of 1999. During that crisis Albania had not only accepted the refugees but had also steadfastly supported NATO action in Kosovo. While it did so a number of leading western politicians made encouraging statements about the rewards Albania might expect for its cooperation. EU officials in Luxembourg in April had promised that Albania would be able to sign an association agreement with the EU 'very soon'; on 25 May that body's commissioner for external affairs told Majko that the EU would discuss the timetable for Albania's accession to the EU and at the end of September the United States government said it would support Albania's efforts to join the World Trade Organization (WTO). Such fine words soon proved hollow. In October France vetoed Albanian membership of the WTO and an EU spokesman back-tracked on the promises of an association agreement; before that could be signed Fabrizio Barbaso, the head of the EU department for the western Balkans, said there had to be more structural change. There was no doubt that he meant, among other things, more effective measures to combat crime and to root out collusion between public servants and criminals.

Without rooting out such evils it is difficult to see how Albania will attract the foreign aid and loans necessary to repair its tarnished image and its shattered administration. It is equally difficult to see how the second of those two objectives can be achieved without the first. In the five and a half decades since the end of the Second World War Albania, despite its many experiments, had not succeeded in escaping from its dependence on external assistance.

Chapter 17

BULGARIA SINCE 1989

——————

Bulgaria's movement away from political totalitarianism was relatively easily achieved, but its progress towards economic modernization on the western pattern was much slower and more painful. For half a decade after the fall of Zhivkov the dominant ideology was that of the Union of Democratic Forces, even when that group did not form the government. From 1995 to 1997 the successors of the communists, the Bulgarian Socialist Party, dominated parliament but the period was one mired in corruption. This led in 1996–7 to an economic crisis so severe that it brought about an early general election and forced Bulgaria to hand much of its economic sovereignty to an externally-imposed currency board. This produced a slow return to economic health under the Union of Democratic Forces but after its administration had run its full constitutional term it lost power in one of the Balkans' most remarkable elections, after which its former king became Bulgaria's prime minister.

THE UDF YEARS, DECEMBER 1989 TO DECEMBER 1994

In the year before the ousting of Todor Zhivkov on 10 November 1989 a number of opposition organizations had appeared in Bulgaria, including ecological lobby groups, reborn and new political parties, and an independent trade union, Podkrepa (Support). On 14 November 1989 a number of these groups came together to form a loose federation, the Union of Democratic Forces (UDF). The UDF was anti-totalitarian, anti-monopolist, anti-communist and pro-western. Its ideas were to dominate the first five years of post-totalitarian Bulgaria, even though the federation itself was to be in office for only one of those five years.

After 10 November 1989 the ruling communists, now headed by the former minister for foreign affairs, Petŭr Mladenov, were quick to make concessions. A plenum on 11–13 December acknowledged the manifold sins and wickednesses of authoritarian rule and also admitted that the foreign debt was not the $3 billion given in previous official statements, but a crushing $12 billion. The party promised that it would introduce a more open, democratic and pluralist system, and on 29 December it proclaimed an end to the regenerative process aimed at the Turkish minority.

This concession produced a backlash. Large numbers of protesters poured into Sofia from the provinces on 7 January 1990, obviously with the blessing of local BCP officials who alone could have sanctioned the use of so much rationed petrol. A week later a counter-demonstration was staged and the prospect of continued confrontation persuaded Bulgarian politicians of all stripes to initiate conversations to contain the crisis. Bulgaria's round-table discussions had begun. The purpose of the discussions was to plot the course for the country's escape from totalitarianism.

Shortly after the beginning of the round-table discussions the BCP subjected itself to major reform. At the fourteenth congress at the end of January its leading organs, the politburo and the central committee, were made more accountable to the membership and the party committed itself to economic restructuring on the basis of privatization, decentralization and demonopolization. A multi-party political system was to be introduced and the party was to be divorced from the state. To emphasize the latter point Mladenov renounced the leadership of the party and became state president; the new party leader was Aleksandŭr Lilov; a reformist communist, Andrei Lukanov, became prime minister. At the beginning of April the BCP changed its name to the Bulgarian Socialist Party (BSP).

The fourteenth congress had shown that important reforms in state affairs could still be promulgated by the ruling party, but within the round table significant advances towards pluralization and the end of one-party rule were made. The trade unions, the youth movement and eventually the Fatherland Front cut their links with the party; it was agreed that the secret political police would be abolished; strikes were to be legalized within set limits; private ownership of land was to be permitted, as was the employment of wage labour by individual employers; and to confirm the abandonment of the regenerative process it was agreed that all citizens should be allowed free choice of their own names. The last principle was enshrined in legislation in March.

The most important issue addressed by the round table was that of the leading role of the party which remained embedded in the constitution. Some professions had already unilaterally dissolved party organizations in the workplace, and after tense debate the communists finally agreed to relinquish their privileged position. Having cleared that hurdle the round table could then proceed to its second function, that of deciding how to move towards drawing up an entirely new constitution. It was agreed that Bulgaria should revert to the pre-communist device of a Grand National Assembly (GNA) which would be almost twice as large as an ordinary sŭbranie (parliament) with half the delegates being chosen by PR and half by the first-past-the-post system.

The elections were held on 10 and 17 June 1990. They were, in the words of the UDF leader, Zheliu Zhelev, 'free but not fair'. The unfairness arose first from the fact that the BSP was better provided with logistical support in terms of office equipment and transport, and secondly from the BSP's cynical exploitation of ungrounded fears, especially in rural areas, that a UDF victory would mean the end of pensions and other state-funded welfare benefits. The BSP emerged from the poll with 211 seats, the UDF with 144, the mainly Turkish Movement for Rights and Freedoms (MRF) with 23 and the Agrarians with 16. Lukanov remained prime minister but there was a change of president after tapes had been uncovered which seemed to show Mladenov urging the use of tanks during earlier demonstrations; he resigned and the GNA eventually elected Zhelev as his successor.

The GNA was intended to devise a new constitution but it made only slow progress in that direction because it was distracted by more immediate concerns, above all that of the economy. Lukanov wanted the UDF to join him in a coalition government. He argued that the economic situation required such drastic remedies that an administration of national unity was necessary to ensure they were accepted. The UDF refused his overtures on the ground that the BCP/BSP was responsible for the mess and it alone should bear the opprobrium of clearing it up. Lukanov also faced dissatisfaction from many UDF supporters, especially students, who believed the BSP victory at the polls had been rigged; the protesters formed a 'tent city' in the centre of Sofia and at the end of August set fire to part of the BSP headquarters.

The main difficulty facing Lukanov, however, remained economic contraction and the social tensions this created. A major cause of the economic collapse was that Comecon was in dissolution and therefore Bulgaria's trade was severely disrupted; this was aggravated by the fact that Lukanov had suspended repayment of foreign debt in March and of interest on it in June which meant that western credits were denied the country; and most crucially, Bulgaria's observance of UN sanctions against Iraq meant that it lost the 600,000 tons of oil which that country was to pay to clear its debt to Bulgaria. Though much of its source of income had dried up the government nevertheless continued to meet its internal obligations which meant in effect it had to print money and thereby fuel inflation. At the same time, the dislocation of trade sent unemployment rates soaring. To make matters worse, the harvest was bad, not least because large areas had been left unsown after the departure of the Turks in the previous summer; food shortages were so severe that rationing had to be introduced in the countryside and extended to Sofia in September. By late autumn popular anger was rising dangerously and when trade unionists joined students in street protests in November Lukanov resigned. A month later his successor was agreed; he was Dimitŭr Popov, a lawyer without party affiliation.

Popov's task was, he announced, 'to guarantee the peaceful transition to a democratic society'. Once again progress to the declared goal was slow. It was checked by futile squabbles over minor issues and long and frequently inconclusive deliberations on major ones. Nevertheless, some reforms were enacted. The price of a number of commodities was deregulated, causing panic among many consumers for a while; the land was to be decollectivized, though as yet little was done to implement this declaration of principle; small enterprises were made eligible for privatization; and the Bulgarian National Bank was made accountable to parliament rather than to the government. On the other hand, the government had to retreat from a proposal to introduce immediately teaching in Turkish in some schools in Turkish areas; so sharp was the reaction by teachers and many ethnic Bulgarian parents that the plan was delayed until the beginning of the new academic year in September. Another stormy issue was that of police files and what they revealed of the past of many politicians. Although open access to files was not yet conceded enough information was disclosed to destroy a number of political reputations. One was that of the current leader of the UDF, Petŭr Beron, who had replaced Zhelev. Beron, a quiet zoologist, resigned after admitting he had given harmless information on foreign academics visiting Bulgaria. He was replaced by Filip Dimitrov.

These various squabbles and diversions delayed the process of defining a constitution which was not ready for final discussion by the GNA until the summer of 1991. It was approved on 12 July. The head of state was to be a president who was to be directly elected every five years; a clause requiring that the president had to have been resident in Bulgaria for the previous five years was inserted to prevent the exiled King Simeon II from presenting himself for election. The unicameral ordinary sŭbranie was to consist of 240 members chosen by PR with a threshold of 4 per cent of the national electorate. The constitution gave overwhelming power to neither president nor parliament and a new institution, the constitutional court, was to play an important part in mediating any disputes which might arise between executive and legislature.

Having voted through the constitution the GNA dissolved itself and the first general election under the new system was held on 13 October 1991. The UDF secured the most seats, 110, but the BSP was close behind with 106 which left the MRF with its 24 seats holding the balance. Over 20 per cent of the votes cast had been for parties which did not surmount the 4 per cent hurdle.

The delicacy of its parliamentary position doomed the UDF government formed by Filip Dimitrov to frustration and ultimately to destruction. It did, however, manage to push through some important legislation. Foreign ownership of Bulgarian enterprises and the export of profits was legalized in February 1992; in March it was decreed that collective farms must be dissolved by 1 November the same year; and in April, against bitter hostility from the BSP, a law was passed restoring to its former owners property confiscated by the communists between 1947 and 1962. The military establishment was slimmed down with the dismissal of some 750 officers, this being the work of Dimitŭr Ludjev, Bulgaria's first civilian minister of defence since 1934. The slimming down of the officer corps reduced government expenditure but it was less a financial measure than one of lustration, i.e. restrictions on or revenge against the former rulers. Other such acts included the Penev law which excluded from university administration anyone who had been a party secretary or equivalent official under the old regime. Another act of lustration, though not one for which the government was responsible, was the seven-year sentence passed on Zhivkov. The first former East European communist boss to be convicted, he was allowed to serve his sentence under house arrest rather than in prison and was released in 1997, dying aged 86 in the following year.

Despite these acts Bulgaria was changing only slowly, and too slowly for many foreign observers and would-be investors. But for many Bulgarians change was too rapid, too apparent and above all too painful. By January 1992 price levels were in the region of five times higher than a year before and inflation for that month alone was 30 per cent; unemployment continued to rise inexorably and had reached 400,000 by the same month. The trade unions, both Podkrepa and the Confederation of Independent Trade Unions in Bulgaria (CITUB), the descendant of the old communist trade union body which took very seriously the adjective 'Independent' in its title, organized protest strikes which in the summer forced the government to concede an inflationary 26 per cent wage increase for civil servants.

As conditions deteriorated for many Bulgarians one of the country's most important institutions descended into a demeaning and depressing debacle. On 9 March 1992 the head of the Bulgarian Orthodox Church, Patriarch Maxim, was sacked by the government because, it was alleged, his election in 1971 had been, by a strict interpretation of the Church's statutes, irregular. It was also alleged that once in office Maxim had acted as a 'collaborator' with the communist regime. His opponents nominated Metropolitan Pimen as his successor. Both accusations against Maxim probably had a grain of truth but in June the constitutional court decided that, even if they were true, the lay authorities had no right to intervene in Church affairs. Maxim's removal may have been a desirable end but the means used to secure it were unjustified. Pimen's supporters refused to accept the ruling of the constitutional court or to vacate the headquarters of the Holy Synod. The Bulgarian Church was reduced to the spectacle of rival groups of priests indulging in fisticuffs on the steps of the Aleksandŭr Nevski cathedral in Sofia, and not until 1998 was an uneasy compromise between the two factions reached.

In foreign affairs the Dimitrov government did succeed to some degree in overcoming Bulgaria's previous isolation from the west. In May 1992 Bulgaria was admitted to the Council of Europe and remarkably warm relations were established with Turkey, the most notable expression of which was the signing of a military agreement in December 1991. Even more surprising was the fact that the emergence of a separate Macedonian state was accepted by the Sofia regime. Despite the historical sensitivity of this subject the Bulgarian government was the first to recognize the Macedonian state when it declared its independence in January 1992, though the recognition was only of the

Macedonian state, the Bulgarians still not being prepared to recognize the existence of a separate Macedonian nation.

The recognition of Macedonia was due to the initiative of President Zhelev and his advisers. The government acquiesced in the President's initiative but relations between the two were seldom easy. There was a long-running conflict on who had control over the intelligence services and what role the latter should play in the new Bulgaria. By the late summer Zhelev's patience was running thin on this and on a number of other issues. He thought the government had done too little to advance economic reform or reduce social distress; he even held Dimitrov partially responsible for the debacle in the Church, as well as for needlessly alienating the trade unions, the press and a number of other anti-communist political parties. Zhelev's frustrations burst forth in a vicious attack on Dimitrov in the late summer when he accused him of 'seeking confrontation with everyone' and suggested the formation of a national government.

To lose the confidence of the president was dangerous for Dimitrov, to lose that of the MRF was fatal. The MRF had serious problems. The Turkish population had suffered even more than most Bulgarians as a result of the recent social changes, partly because of the way in which the land privatization scheme operated and partly because of a general decline in the demand for tobacco, the crop on which many Turkish families depended. In desperation many Turks left and this second wave of emigration threatened so to reduce the Turkish population that the MRF was in danger of not passing the 4 per cent hurdle in future elections. The MRF wanted concessions and when the UDF administration showed reluctance to grant them the Turkish party withdrew its parliamentary support. At the end of October Dimitrov resigned. When the next administration was formed it was one sponsored by the MRF and led by a professor of economic history, Liuben Berov.

Berov came to office promising to speed up the process of economic reform and in February 1993 he published a 'plan of action' to bring this about. There was more planning than action. But to the UDF even talk of economic plans seemed like a regression to communist days. So too did the new government's attempts to control appointments in the media and to reinstate many figures prominent under the communists. In fact, Berov's government was able to do very little. Berov himself was not well and had to undergo major heart surgery in 1994. In the sŭbranie his support grew less and less secure. The MRF which had sponsored his government at the outset suffered a number of defections early in 1993 and therefore lost its controlling balance in the assembly. In the spring and summer both the UDF and the BSP suffered similar losses and two new factions emerged in parliament, as a result of which intrigue and plotting increased to such a degree that politics seemed completely to have ousted government at the centre of the nation's affairs. In 1994 Berov further angered the UDF by introducing a judiciary bill which insisted that only those who had five years' legal experience were eligible for high judicial office; in other words the only people who could take the highest legal posts were those trained under the communists. The bill was referred to the constitutional court.

While these largely pointless political games were being played the economy deteriorated. A serious new factor was the imposition in May 1992 of UN sanctions on Yugoslavia which Bulgaria loyally observed even though it meant that its main trading artery to central and western Europe was severed; by September losses caused by the new embargo were estimated at $2.71 million. But it was not only external factors which were causing stagnation. The Berov administration did nothing to hasten the privatization of land which was essential to effective restructuring in the agricultural sector, and progress towards the privatization of industry was equally slow: throughout 1993 there was only one major privatization, that of a maize-producing enterprise near Razgrad which was purchased by a Belgian company. The IMF expressed its displeasure at this lack of progress and at the high levels of government spending which were increasing the budget deficit.

To no one's surprise and most people's relief the Berov government finally collapsed in September 1994 and a caretaker administration was formed under Bulgaria's first female prime minister, Renata Indjova. She remained in office until elections were held in December. Those elections gave a clear victory to the BSP which since its defeat in the 1991 poll had been led by Zhan Videnov. It had 125 sŭbranie seats to the UDF's 69. Videnov formed a government dominated by the BSP but including some representatives of minor groups.

BSP GOVERNMENT AND ECONOMIC CATASTROPHE, JANUARY 1995–APRIL 1997

Many, even those who were not natural BSP supporters, after the December 1994 elections hoped that government would finally replace politics and that real action on the reforming front would be taken. Videnov confirmed these hopes in his inaugural speech as prime minister when he asserted that his aims were to reverse the economic decline, to further Bulgaria's integration into European institutions and to combat crime. In May 1995 he introduced an action programme in which he reaffirmed these commitments and his belief in the benefits of the 'social market economy'.

In foreign policy the new government continued its predecessor's commitment to Europe but it did not share its enthusiasm for NATO. The BSP in fact resumed the pro-Moscow line of its BCP predecessor, albeit less slavishly. In May 1995 a number of agreements were concluded increasing cooperation between Bulgaria and Russia in the fields of trade, defence and energy policies. There were significant developments in the last when it was agreed that pipelines would be constructed from the Bulgarian port of Burgas to Alexandroupolis in Greece and to other points in the Balkans, the object being to distribute Russian oil via Bulgaria. A new joint company, Top-

Energy, was created to implement the scheme; its head was the former prime minister, Lukanov.

The new government's distaste for NATO and its desire for closer relations with Russia complicated its relations with the pro-NATO and pro-western President Zhelev. These were not the only points of difference between president and government. Soon after entering office the BSP began to replace a number of leading military personnel and media figures, the apparent intention being to remove personalities installed by the anti-socialist administrations and to reinstitute political controls over the media. There was little Zhelev could do in most cases but he was more effective in blocking government plans to water down the land reform act of 1991. The proposed amendments encouraged the formation of new cooperatives and after Zhelev had objected to the bill it was referred to the constitutional court which decided in favour of the president on the grounds that the proposed changes were an infringement of the rights of private property.

Zhelev at this juncture provided the most forceful opposition to the Videnov regime. The UDF had suffered a severe electoral defeat in 1994 and was adapting to its new leader, Ivan Kostov, a former minister of finance. There was worse to come in 1995 when in local elections the UDF, though winning control of the three major cities – Sofia, Plovdiv and Varna – gained fewer mayoralties than the MRF. The BSP won all but 60 of the 255 mayoralties.

The BSP was clearly in a stronger position than any administration since the fall of Zhivkov and in its first year in office it seemed that some progress might be made towards economic regeneration. GDP increased by 3 per cent in 1995 and the first half of that year produced a trade surplus of $106.3 million. Another positive feature was the decline in inflation, particularly in the first half of the year; the monthly figure for June, 0.5 per cent, was the lowest since economic reforms were inaugurated in 1991, and the overall figure for the first half of the year was 15.2 per cent compared to 59.4 per cent for the same period in 1994. These encouraging circumstances enabled the Bulgarian National Bank (BNB) to lower interest rates no fewer than seven times in 1995. At the same time the rise in the value of the lev during the year had meant that interest payments on the foreign debt would be about 2 to 2.5 billion leva less than predicted.

There were other, less satisfactory indicators. At the end of 1995 the minister of finance admitted that the budget deficit for the coming year would be greater than previously anticipated. Furthermore, despite Videnov's pledge to reverse the economic decline, in 1995, on the government's own figures, the standard of living in Bulgaria fell by 6 per cent. In what was later to be seen as a highly significant pointer to future problems 1995 had also seen a bread shortage, caused primarily by the sale of the grain surplus by the Orion group of companies which had close associations with the highest figures in the BSP. There were accusations that the export of grain had been illegal; the nexus of social and economic crisis, criminal activity, the conglomerates and the BSP was to dominate Bulgarian affairs in 1996 and was to bring the country to the verge of popular revolution.

Crime had been a growing concern ever since the overthrow of Zhivkov. The police lost their former powers and petty crime expanded rapidly but with the coming of sanctions against Yugoslavia crime expanded exponentially. The sums to be made in smuggling banned commodities were so huge that few could resist the temptation. The need to cover up such large-scale crime meant the involvement of officials from the lowest customs officer and policeman to the highest civil servants and their political masters. Also involved, it was generally believed, were the conglomerates, known colloquially in Bulgaria and elsewhere in former communist lands as the mafia.

The origins of the conglomerates are obscure but it is widely assumed that when the communist regimes began to crumble in the late 1980s there were many able apparatchiks in Bulgaria and other socialist states who could see what was happening. They are reported to have used their positions within the power structures to shift money out of their native countries to safe havens in Switzerland and elsewhere. After 1989 this money was sometimes used to establish companies which traded domestically and internationally, a number of companies merging into loose confederations or conglomerates.

The Bulgarian companies, given the links the BCP had had with the CPSU, had close relations with their Russian equivalents. In both countries the leaders of the conglomerates, having inside knowledge of how the communist economic system worked, knew that considerable profit was to be had from manipulating the subsidies given to loss-making state enterprises. This gave the conglomerates a vested interest in preserving those enterprises and therefore in frustrating the privatization and reform processes which aimed at closing the loss-making concerns. At the same time the wealth of the conglomerates made it easy for them to purchase influence over legislators, more especially those of the BSP who had in many cases been party comrades of the racketeers in the old BCP. If pressure from the IFIs meant, as eventually it did, a restriction of direct subsidies from the state to the loss-making enterprises then an alternative was soon found in bank loans. Those who ran the banks were also frequently old BCP appointees and could easily be persuaded to extend to loss-making enterprises loans which they knew could never be repaid. As long as the politicians could be relied upon to make sure the BNB bailed out any bank that might find itself under pressure the conglomerates could go on making money.

Crime and violence attended the growth of the conglomerates and they took fearsome revenge on those who crossed their path. The murder of former prime minister Andrei Lukanov outside his house in Sofia on 2 October 1996 was widely believed to have been the consequence of his threat to reveal the involvement of some leading BSP figures in illegal or semi-legal activities. But before then the activities of the conglomerates had been revealed as a threat not only to individuals but to the entire country.

Early in 1996 the Bank for Agricultural Credit 'Vitosha' had found itself in difficulties; in January it had received $33 million dollars from the BNB but not even this could keep it afloat and it therefore attempted to call in a number of non-performing loans. The money was not forthcoming and at the end of February the BNB took it over; in effect the Vitosha Bank had failed. There had been concern at the condition of the economy since the turn of the year and since the minister of finance's annual statement on the budget deficit. Concern rapidly became panic. Interest rates were raised a number of times in an effort to bolster the declining currency but it had no effect because such measures addressed only the symptoms and not the cause of the disease which lay in the weakness of the banking system and its exploitation by the mafia; in March Zhelev declared that the banks were 'plundering' the nation.

As the crisis deepened pressure mounted on the government to tackle the root cause which meant in effect shutting down the loss-making enterprises from which the mafia, by courtesy of the banks and their political allies, were making their profits. Finally, on 15 May, the government announced it was to close 64 large loss-making state enterprises and 70 more were to be 'isolated', i.e. they were to be denied any further loans from the banks and were to be given a year in which to put their house in order. By that point the leva had lost 70 per cent of its dollar value of 1 January; two days later, on so-called 'Black Friday', two more banks folded and precipitated a run on other banks with depositors desperate to withdraw their savings and turn them into goods or solid currencies.

External donors remained unconvinced that real action would be taken against the 64 or the 70 enterprises and late in the summer the IMF announced that it would not provide the second tranche of a loan agreed in July until action had been taken to end the subsidies to the loss-making enterprises. This caused yet another loss of confidence and in September a further nine banks had to be placed under the supervision of the BNB and interest rates were increased yet again, this time to 300 per cent. Not even this could save the lev and in November it was once again in apparent free fall with the IMF remaining adamant that no further help would be provided until real structural change had been introduced.

The social costs of the crisis were enormous. Not only did inflation far outstrip salaries but in many instances the latter were long overdue, and therefore much devalued when they were eventually received. To make matters worse food exports had not stopped and shortages were once again experienced. By December soup kitchens had been established in Sofia and a number of other towns. Not even in the terrible winter of 1991 had recourse had to be made to such emergency measures.

There was a political as well as a social price to be paid for the crisis, and it was the BSP which paid it. Public anger was expressed in demonstrations, particularly that of 7 June when an estimated million people marched in Sofia, while prevailing fears and uncertainties were reflected in August when rumours of an imminent military coup ran through the capital. But the main vehicle for revenge was neither the demonstration nor the coup but the ballot box.

Presidential elections were due in the autumn. In the summer Zhelev lost a primary organized by the UDF which had been wary of him since his duel with Dimitrov, and his elimination from the race enabled the UDF to give full backing to Petŭr Stoyanov, an anti-socialist lawyer who also had the support of the MRF and other smaller parties. He was forced to a second round but in that he secured 60 per cent of the poll to the BSP candidate's 40 per cent; the BSP vote was a million less than that of the parliamentary elections of 1994, albeit in the lowest turnout yet recorded in post-communist Bulgaria. A further expression of disapproval came when nineteen prominent BSP figures signed an open letter calling for the formation of a new government under a different leader. Videnov could not survive and on 21 December resigned as both prime minister and leader of the BSP. At the end of the year the outgoing president apologized to the people for the state of the nation, admitting that he was 'ashamed of the Bulgarian political class'.

Bulgaria was fast approaching paralysis. The public had expressed no confidence in the ruling party; the prime minister had resigned but no successor had yet been found; and there was a lame duck president. The opposition parties and a growing section of the population wanted fresh elections so that a start might be made in recovering from the disaster. The IMF had insisted since the summer that it would support Bulgaria only if it agreed to introduce a currency board which would tie the amount of money in circulation strictly to the reserves of the BNB. The UDF announced on 3 January 1997 that it was ready to support such a solution, but only if new elections were held before their due date in 1998; the drastic remedies and the reduction of national sovereignty which a currency board entailed could be imposed, said the opposition, only by a government which enjoyed national confidence and the presidential elections had proved that the BSP did not. On the evening after the UDF statement crowds gathered to demonstrate in favour of early elections; they were to some extent inspired by contemporary events in Belgrade where the crowds were gently forcing Milošević towards acceptance of the popular will as expressed in the Serbian local elections.

Initially the mood of the demonstrators, like those in Belgrade, was good-humoured but things turned sour on 10 January. On that day UDF deputies, frustrated at the apparent immobility of the administration, walked out of parliament; in the evening some demonstrators tried to force their way into the sŭbranie building and in the ensuing clashes with the police over a hundred protesters, including the former prime minister Filip Dimitrov, were injured. Tension rose further on 22 January. On that day the incoming president, against his inclination, bowed to constitutional convention and asked the candidate nominated by the largest faction in parliament, the BSP's Nikolai Dobrev, to form a new government. The demonstrators were enraged. Not only was this a continuation of BSP rule, it was rule by a figure whom they regarded as little different from Videnov: it was old wine in old bottles. The protests intensified with demonstrations and strikes across the country. By the end of the month energy supplies were limited and there was a threat of an indefinite general strike. Civil war seemed a real possibility until, on 4 February, Dobrev conceded. He accepted a ruling from the supreme committee on national security, a presidential body, and agreed not to form a government but to call a general election in April. Until then an interim administration, the third in post-communist Bulgaria, was to be formed under the UDF mayor of Sofia, Stefan Sofiyanski. The concession had an immediate effect. The demonstrations subsided, the threat of a general strike receded and the IMF rode back into town. On 24 February it resumed negotiations on the assumption that a currency board would be introduced, and in March it gave approval in principle to a financial support package worth $167 million.

THE SECOND UDF GOVERNMENT, BULGARIA SINCE APRIL 1997

Before the elections of 19 April some party realignment took place. The UDF joined with a smaller right-of-centre group, the People's Union, to form the United Democratic Parties, though the UDF remained by far the dominant partner and the new grouping was still usually referred to as the UDF. The leadership of the MRF meanwhile joined with a number of other small parties, including some monarchists, to form the Alliance for National Salvation (ANS); this evolution puzzled many observers and not a few MRF members and led to a revolt by MRF organizations in the north of the country which concluded local agreements to cooperate with the UDF. The BSP suffered a number of defections, the defectors forming a new party, the Euro-Left.

These realignments did not make any difference to the final outcome of the election. The UDF secured an absolute majority at the polls of 52.36 per cent and took 137 seats in the sŭbranie. The BSP had 22.07 per cent of the votes and 58 seats. The ANS emerged with 19 seats and the Euro-Left 14, while 12 seats went to the Bulgarian Business Bloc, whose colourful leader, Georgi Ganchev, had been a fencing master at Eton.

On 19 May a new government was formed under UDF boss, Ivan Kostov. Its first priority was to return the economy to working order, while in the longer term it had the traditional UDF goals of greater privatization, the elimination of crime and corruption, and moves towards integration into the EU and NATO.

It made obvious progress towards its first objective. In June a currency board was established and the Bulgarian leva pegged to the Deutschemark; the government was forbidden to issue any more notes unless Bulgaria's foreign currency reserves had increased by a similar amount and this had an immediate effect upon inflation; a year after its coming to office the Kostov government had brought the rate down from the 300 per cent of January 1997 to 11 per cent; in 1999 it was down to 6 per cent. Food shortages had also been largely overcome by tough measures against speculation and exporting, the encouragement of sowing, and the relaxation of price controls to provide an incentive to producers. Unemployment was a more difficult nut to crack but at least its rate of increase fell. The country also attracted considerable sums in loans and grants, even if private foreign investors proved reluctant to commit themselves to Bulgarian projects.

In terms of privatization progress continued to be slow. Kostov announced an ambitious programme in 1997 but at the beginning of 2000 a third of industry remained in public ownership. This was one reason why the president of the European Commission, Romano Prodi, stated that although the EU was prepared to extend to Bulgaria grants of 1.8 billion Euro ($1.84 billion) in the period up to 2006 the country would need to make further efforts to reform its economy.

To achieve its long-term aim of combating crime and corruption the Kostov government took energetic measures. Shortly after coming to office it tightened the laws on gun control, imposed stiff sentences for membership of criminal gangs and increased the penalties for smuggling and tax evasion. In November 1997 the police service was reorganized and made more accountable to parliament. Penalties against other crimes were increased in 1998, including that of the production of and trade in pirate CDs, the elimination of this flourishing activity being a particular demand of the United States. In April 2000 legislation was announced requiring all civil servants to reveal their incomes and their expenses. But so deeply engrained a deformity as Bulgaria's crime and corruption could not be removed rapidly. Turf wars between rival groups were still breaking out in the first decade of the new millennium and corruption also continued to embarrass the government; in June 2000 Bulgaria's chief negotiator with the European Union was required to resign after being accused of financial irregularities.

The campaign against corruption and crime led at times to international complications. In August 2000 Bulgaria ordered the expulsion of five foreign businessmen, four of them Russians. In the sharp exchanges which followed the Bulgarian minister for foreign affairs reminded her Russian counterpart that the Warsaw pact no longer existed.

This exchange was an extreme example of the generally cool relations which the Kostov government had with Moscow. Bulgaria sought to decrease its dependence on Russian supplies of energy by developing links with the oil-producing states of the Caucasus. In the military sector the Kostov administration used Russia's failure to abide by the terms of an agreement to pay off some of its $100 million debt to Bulgaria with spare parts for fighter planes as an excuse to explore the possibility of buying F-16s from the USA.

This was part of the government's strategy of moving closer to NATO. Its greatest chance to do this came with the Kosovo crisis of 1999–2000. It was not a chance which the Kostov government was likely to miss, despite the opinion of the majority of the Bulgarian public which remained opposed to NATO action against Serbia. Undeterred the government allowed NATO free use of Bulgarian airspace and denied Russia permission to overfly Bulgaria when it wanted to reinforce and supply the troops it had rushed to Prishtina airport at the end of the NATO campaign.

Another service Bulgaria had performed, perhaps unwittingly, to the NATO alliance was to improve its relations with Macedonia. After the recognition of the Macedonian state relations between Sofia and Skopje had remained prickly on the issue of Macedonia's claim to be a separate nation, a Bulgarian minister of education cutting short an official visit when translators appeared at an official meeting. While the Macedonians regarded such gestures as insulting, the Bulgarians sometimes expressed a fear that the claim by a handful of Bulgarians in the Pirin region to be of Macedonian nationality could lead to a Macedonian claim upon the area. Early in 1999 these long-standing suspicions were overcome in two agreements of enormous, but generally underestimated importance. On 22 February the two governments announced that neither had a territorial claim upon the other, and the Bulgarians officially stated for the first time that they recognized the existence of a separate Macedonian nation. In March an accord was signed under which Bulgaria agreed to supply Macedonia with military equipment; the two armies were also to hold joint manoeuvres. The rapprochement had been made possible primarily by the advent of the coalition government in Skopje whose major partner had close links with the UDF, but whatever the origins of the agreement one of its most important results was that when NATO took action in Kosovo and Serbia it could feel confident that the area to the east and south of any battle ground would be stable. When Albanian insurgents threatened the stability of Macedonia in the early spring of 2001 Bulgaria rushed military equipment to the Skopje government in an attempt to strengthen its army.

Bulgaria received little tangible reward for its services to NATO, nor for the economic losses inflicted by further sanctions on Yugoslavia and then the closing of the Danube. A visit from President Clinton in November 1999, the first time a ruling US president had ever set foot in the country, was welcomed but it did little to compensate for the knowledge that accession to NATO had been effectively ruled out for at least half a decade.

There were initially disappointments too in the attempts to move closer to the EU. From March 1998 Bulgaria had begun to adapt its legislation to meet the requirements of Brussels but in July the country was excluded from the fast-track accession states, a not entirely unexpected outcome given the delays in Bulgaria's transition process. At the end of 1999 there was more encouraging news when Bulgaria was included in the list of states with which accession talks were to begin. But difficulties remained. Bulgaria found European pressure to close the nuclear power station at Kozlodui irksome and took even greater umbrage at the EU's refusal until December 2000 to remove Bulgaria from the list of states whose citizens must have visas to enter the EU.

The chief obstacles to Bulgaria's closer association with the EU, however, remained economic and financial, a fact which led Kostov to admit in April 2000 that Bulgaria's accession may not come until 2010. Within a year the picture had changed considerably. There was proof of increased political stability in the fact that it was clear the Kostov government would be the first since 1989 to run its full constitutional course of four years. Its tough economic policies were also paying dividends and this was increasingly recognized outside Bulgaria. By the end of 2000 the currency had been stabilized and exports had increased by almost a quarter over the 1999 figure, a fact which enabled Bulgaria to report a positive annual trade balance in 2000, the first since the fall of communism. Kostov himself became more confident and assertive, telling *Financial Times Deutschland* on 16 January 2001 that Bulgaria's financial and monetary systems had been 'radically changed' and that the country ranked second only to Hungary in terms of harmonizing its legislation with that of the EU; Bulgaria, he added, was not being given sufficient credit for its efforts or its achievements. That recognition soon came. An influential OECD report on agriculture praised Bulgaria warmly, particularly for its liberalization of the market in grains, but even more exciting was a statement on 21 March by the EU commissioner for enlargement, Guenther Verheugen, to the effect that Bulgaria had made such rapid progress that its accession talks could be completed by 2004. This was the earliest date yet mentioned.

If Kostov believed he and the UDF would reap electoral reward for these improvements he was to be disappointed. In April 2001 Bulgarian politics were suddenly and radically changed. At the beginning of the year there were rumours in the media that the exiled King, Simeon II, might run for president in elections due later in the year. The constitutional provision requiring candidates to have been resident in the country for the five years preceding a presidential election prevented this but in April Simeon returned to Bulgaria and announced he would establish a new 'Simeon II National Movement' (SSNM) which would contest the parliamentary elections due to take place within a few months.

Simeon's programme was avowedly populist. He promised that within 800 days of being elected his movement would bring about fundamental changes in the economic and political life of all Bulgarians. There were few precise details on how this was to be done, though there were promises of tax cuts for small businesses and other measures to encourage the entrepreneur. In addition there was great emphasis on the movement's determination to eliminate corruption. The latter was an extremely powerful weapon. Despite its other successes Kostov's government had been coming under increasing criticism for its failure to eliminate graft and corruption. Simeon, on the other hand, was absolutely free of any suspicion on this score. It was probably his strongest electoral weapon. It was not, however, his only one. He gained enormously from the fact that he was associated with neither of the two groups which had dominated the country since 1990, the UDF and the BSP, added to which he had considerable personal charm, proven business acumen and potentially valuable links with the financial circles of the west. During the election campaign he insisted he was not considering any restoration of the monarchy, a wise move in view of public opinion polls which showed that support for such a move was very limited.

On the other hand the polls showed that in the electoral contest the SSNM was far ahead of its rivals and this was confirmed at the polls on 17 June. The SSNM took 42.74 per cent of the vote which gave it exactly half the 240 deputies in parliament. The UDF was left with 51 seats, three more than the Coalition for Bulgaria, a group dominated by the BSP; the mainly Turkish MRF had 21 seats. In July Simeon agreed to take the post of prime minister at the head of a cabinet supported by his own party and the MRF and including two members of the BSP. He was henceforth known officially as Simeon Saxecoburggotski, from the Saxe-Coburg-Gotha dynasty, though in common parlance he is almost always referred to as 'tsarya', the king.

Simeon's victory was a populist victory. Populism can be a raw and dangerous phenomenon but it need not necessarily be so. The SSNM had appealed to all sections of society and to all ethnic groups. The SSNM may have made promises which it will be difficult to keep but it avoided any attempt to whip up popular emotions; apart from the corrupt politicians of the previous decade it had few bogeymen. If populism is unavoidable it is better that it be mobilized by a movement which attempts to secure support in all sections of society rather than one which sets out to exploit and deepen divisions.

Chapter 18

ROMANIA SINCE 1989

For the first two years after the fall of the Ceauşescus the new regime retained a form of paternalist, semi-authoritarian rule. Civil liberties were allowed but the authorities were still capable of exploiting nationalism and violence for political purposes. That there was not greater popular pressure for further reform was primarily because the motive force of the Romanian revolution had not been a desire to change the system but rather a simple desperation to remove the Ceauşescus and to secure enough food and heat to survive in reasonably tolerable conditions. The 1990s were to show, however, that Romania's leaders were reluctant to commit themselves to thorough-going reform. This was in part because the economic situation in Romania was even more difficult than in other post-communist states. Romanian manufacturing was characterised by huge, state-controlled, heavy-industrial concerns. These had been promoted by Ceauşescu as part of his drive to make Romania economically self-reliant and had become bywords for inefficiency, pollution and waste; the situation had been made even worse by the debt-repayment crusade of the 1980s which had prevented investment in new technology. In the first post-communist decade successive Romanian governments showed little inclination to tackle this problem, and their reluctance to do so was intensified by the violent reaction which even moderate reform provoked among the work-force. The 1990s also showed great instability within political parties and within ruling coalitions; frequently the country's leaders appeared more concerned with politics and politicking than with administration and government.

THE NATIONAL SALVATION FRONT AND MANAGED TRANSITION, DECEMBER 1989 TO SEPTEMBER 1991

The new rulers of Romania were the National Salvation Front (NSF) headed by Ion Iliescu, an educated, sophisticated, modernizing, Moscow-trained reformist communist who had been a student associate of Gorbachev whose political outlook he shared. The NSF had been formed in the summer of

1989 by Iliescu and other reformists who were or had been relatively high in the ranks of the RCP. The original NSF had consisted of 39 members and in January 1990 it was expanded to 145 but real power remained where it had always been, with a small inner group of 11 all of whom had been in the RCP. As prime minister the new rulers nominated Petre Roman, a member of the younger generation of RCP apparatchiki who, it was assumed, would be amenable to guidance from the inner circle of power-holders. Also, early in 1990, the NSF reneged on a promise not to form itself into a political party or to contest elections.

This about face, and even more so the speed and efficiency with which the NSF had assumed power in December 1989, aroused suspicions that the revolution and the civil war had not been all that they seemed to be and a number of interesting questions were raised: if the Securitate had been assisted by Arab terrorists why was it that none of the latter had been wounded, killed, or even seen? Why was the only building in Bucharest's Palace Square not to be splattered with bullets the one containing the NSF leaders? Why did the supposedly super-trained, fanatical Securitate units guarding Ceauşescu not attack the TV tower which became the centre of the new government? And why when Iliescu created a new Romanian Intelligence Service (RIS) in the early months of 1990 did former Securitate officers fill the majority of its posts? Why, too, in subsequent years, did so many former Securitate personnel land powerful and lucrative jobs, why were the whereabouts of the Securitate funds and archives not disclosed, why was there no thorough investigation of Securitate activities, and why when the few prosecutions against former Securitate personnel were brought did they never concern events before December 1989?

Even if, as many suspected, the NSF had stage-managed the revolution to ensure power remained in the hands of the communists, this did not mean the new regime was not committed to change. Its purpose, said the NSF, was to manage the transition from one-party rule to democracy with caution and sensitivity. Accordingly, no significant change of local government personnel was undertaken, nor were organizations such as the official trade unions reformed. Furthermore, the NSF said it would not sell out the economy to wealthy foreign capitalists and that, in keeping with Romanian historical tradition, national control of the economy would be defended. It rejected the free-market system on the grounds that this would lead to vast differentiations of wealth in which the majority would suffer great hardship.

The most hated aspects of the Ceauşescu regime, however, were done away with immediately; the systematization programme was abandoned, the export of food ceased temporarily and foreign food imports were permitted. The new regime also recognized the civil liberties which had been assumed and seized by many during the revolution. The press and the electronic media were allowed much greater freedom of action, and broadcasting in the minority languages was sanctioned. Many organizations previously proscribed were allowed public existence once more, including the Uniate Church whose remarkably rapid revival proved the strength it had retained while underground. Political parties of the pre-communist era also reappeared, most notably the National Peasant Party and the National Liberal Party. The NSF tolerated this and committed itself to a multi-party system and free elections. On the other hand, there was little confidence that the NSF would admit the opposition into government, the attitude of Iliescu and his associates seeming to be that the NSF should form a type of Directory which would tolerate freedom but which would reserve unto itself the right to interpret and implement the general will.

When the first post-communist elections were held in May 1990 the NSF won an easy victory in both the parliamentary and the presidential contests; it secured two thirds of the seats in both houses of parliament and in some areas of Wallachia and Moldavia it received suspiciously high percentages of the vote. The poll had not been entirely fair. The NSF controlled the media and in rural areas where election monitors did not penetrate there was considerable fraud. More serious than this were two indications that Romania was susceptible to a violence which its rulers were prepared to tolerate and exploit, and perhaps to initiate.

The first violent incidents occurred in March 1990, before the elections. One of the immediate advances achieved by the NSF government was to relieve pressures on the national minorities. For the remaining Germans this meant immediate emigration and it was not long before almost all of them had left. The most noticeable improvement for the Hungarians came in broadcasting and even more so in education. In predominantly Hungarian areas it was decreed that schooling should be in that language and those Romanians presently attending such institutions would be bussed to other, Romanian-language schools. Plans were also produced to reintroduce tertiary education in Hungarian by splitting once more Cluj university and the medical university in Tîrgu Mureş in Transylvania. This enraged extreme nationalist Romanians, particularly those who had joined Vatra Româneăsca (Romanian Hearth) established in December 1989. Vatra Româneăsca was strong in ethnically mixed areas, attracting both professionals who feared their jobs might be lost to members of other ethnic groups, and immigrants from elsewhere in Romania who tended to be uneducated and chauvinistic. It had a strong following in Tîrgu Mureş which had been the focus of large-scale immigration of Romanians in the previous two decades. On 19 March supporters of Vatra Româneăsca, with the connivance of local officials and of at least one Orthodox priest, attacked Magyars living in the town. On the following day Magyars from outlying villages, together with a number of Roma, marched on Tîrgu Mureş and attacked the Romanians. Order was not fully restored for another three days by which time, according to official figures, which were almost certainly an underestimate, there were 3 dead and 269 injured. Plans to introduce Hungarian-language teaching in schools were put off until the following year and the schemes for tertiary education shelved.

The second outbreak of violence occurred in Bucharest after the elections. Disappointment at the lack of real change had intensified and was particularly strong among the students who wanted a 'second revolution' and an end to the neo-communist 'survivalist' regime. On 22 April they began a permanent protest near the university, the protest receiving fresh impetus from the elections in May which many held to be fraudulent. The protesters were eventually cleared from University Square, or 'the Anti-Communist Zone' as the students had called it, by police and workers' militia on 13 June. On the same day unidentified figures attacked a number of government buildings, including those of the RIS. Iliescu appeared on television to appeal for help from all 'conscious and responsible forces'. Even before he began speaking 10,000 'conscious and responsible' miners in the Jiu valley were boarding trains for Bucharest. On 14 and 15 June they trashed the headquarters of the principal opposition parties and large sections of the university; when they had finished there they laid about a Roma settlement just outside the city.

That so many trains had been available in the Jiu valley on 13 June, the speed with which they reached Bucharest, and the fact that when they arrived helpers were awaiting them with maps and lists of whom to arrest, shows beyond doubt that the miners' action was organized by the government. It confirmed the worst fears of the protesters and the opposition.

The violence, especially that in Bucharest, did much to discredit the new government which Roman had formed after the May elections. Roman's cabinet also lost popularity because it could not resist pressures, mainly from external sources of loans, for some economic reform. In November huge price increases in clothing and transport were introduced and the leu devalued by 70 per cent. Public anger forced the postponement of further price increases and compelled the government to take powers to manage the economy by decree. In April 1991 it removed controls from all but twelve food-stuffs and enacted that wages must not rise by more than 60 per cent of the increase in food prices. At the same time income tax ranging from 6 to 20 per cent was introduced and in August a law was passed allowing for 30 per cent of the assets of state enterprises to be given to Romanian citizens in the form of vouchers, the remaining 70 per cent being available for private purchase. Public anger was profound and nowhere more so than in the socialist heartland of the Jiu coalfields where privatization was feared as much as the declining standard of living was resented. In September the miners returned to Bucharest and indulged in savage violence in which a number of Bucharest residents died.

The immediate political casualty was Roman who was disgraced and resigned to be replaced by Theodor Stolojan, an economist. In the long run Romania itself was also a casualty of the September 1991 events. The shadow cast by the miners' action stretched over all subsequent administrations, all of which knew they had to reform the economy and all of which were constrained by the fear that the social consequences of effective reform could precipitate another violent political crisis.

Stolojan constructed a coalition government with the National Liberal Party, his non-RCP background and his willingness to accept free-market ideas making this possible. His first major task was political rather than economic. He had to push through parliament the new constitution drawn up under Roman. This was done in November with public endorsement following in a referendum on 8 December. The constitution by and large confirmed the political status quo, retaining the considerable presidential powers enjoyed by Iliescu. Two years after the revolution, it was hoped, Romania had achieved political stability.

THE NEO-COMMUNIST GOVERNMENTS, SEPTEMBER 1992 TO NOVEMBER 1996

Between September 1992 and the elections of November 1996 Romania achieved continuity but not stability. Patterns of political and economic activity had been established which were to carry over into the subsequent regime. Those patterns were: considerable instability in the composition of the political parties; intense hostility between those parties, even when they were fellow members of a ruling coalition; great instability within the ruling coalitions, a condition which made for regime instability; caution if not pusillanimity in economic policy; and, consequently, a failure to integrate Romania into world organizations.

By 1992 public resentment at the post-revolutionary regimes was increasingly sharply articulated and was registered in February in the first multi-party local elections since 1945. There was a large swing away from the NSF towards the new Democratic Convention of Romania (DCR), an alliance of centre parties. The NSF was further weakened in March when a minority of economic reformers under Roman split from the main body of the party. The secessionists retained the name NSF, the majority faction under Iliescu changing its title to the Democratic National Salvation Front (DNSF). Despite these setbacks the ruling faction was able to retain power in national elections held in September 1992 when the DNSF emerged with the most seats and the DCR pushed Roman's NSF into third place. In the presidential elections Iliescu was surprisingly forced into a second round of voting before he secured victory over Emil Constantinescu, the rector of Bucharest university.

After the elections Stolojan resigned to take up a position with the World Bank. His place was taken by another economist, Nicolae Văcăroiu. His administration was composed of a number of non-party experts seasoned with a few experienced party managers from the DNSF. Văcăroiu was to remain prime minister until 1996, a surprisingly long term in Romanian post-revolutionary politics. He was not, however, free from worries about his coalition's cohesion. Initially he found it easiest to work with nationalist or neo-communist groups such as the Socialist Labour Party (SLP) and the Party of Romanian National Unity (PRNU). In July 1993 Văcăroiu decided to give the DNSF a new image, and one which was intended to reassure possible foreign donors of his party's political acceptability: the DNSF became the Party of Social Democracy in Romania (PSDR). Despite this, in January 1996 he sought more unsavoury company when he concluded a deal with the chauvinist Greater Romania Party (GRP), though the latter did not seek seats in the cabinet, agreeing to support the administration in return for junior government posts. The association did not last long. Within months the GRP press was attacking President Iliescu, accusing him of treasonably trying to run down Romania's armed forces at the behest of NATO, of being a former KGB agent, and, typically of GRP rhetoric, of being involved in an anti-Romanian zionist conspiracy. After breaking with the GRP the PSDR went on to sever its links first with the SLP and then with the PRNU.

Chauvinists in the GRP and the PRNU were angered in 1996 by a state treaty signed by Romania and Hungary under which Hungary agreed to recognize existing state borders as permanent and Romania undertook to observe its international obligations with respect to minority rights. After the confrontations in Tîrgu Mureş tensions between Hungarians and Romanians in Transylvania had subsided; but they had not disappeared. The election of Gheorghe Funar as mayor of Cluj in 1992 alarmed Hungarians as did the appointment of Romanian prefects in the two overwhelmingly Magyar counties of Covasna and Harghita. Funar indulged in a number of anti-Magyar antics, such as trying to remove the statue of the Hungarian King Martin Corvinus in Cluj to allow, it was alleged, for archaeological excavations. Hungarian interests were defended by the Hungarian Democratic Union of Romania (HDUR) but even this party, despite all the external pressures which urged unity and cohesion, showed dangers of splitting into moderate and extreme wings, the latter faction being led by László Tőkés.

In economic policy the Văcăroiu administration was avowedly gradualist, not least because of its fear of the miners. Privatization, which had progressed in some sectors of the service industry, slowed down and by the end of 1994 the official target of having 50 per cent of the economy in private hands was nowhere near being achieved. The government also continued to pour money into loss-making enterprises, to give large subsidies to agriculture and to tolerate an alarmingly high level of inter-enterprise debt. In retaliation the IMF and the World Bank decided in 1994 to delay the issuing of an agreed loan until the following year. Nevertheless, in 1993 and 1994 the economy, if unreformed and virtually stagnant, was in relative terms stabilized, thanks in no small measure to the efforts of the Romanian National Bank.

The Văcăroiu regime, like its immediate predecessors, proclaimed its desire to join the European institutions and NATO. Its performance did not encourage the other side. Its record on human rights was open to criticism from Brussels, especially the fact that there had been no investigation into the Securitate. Matters were not helped by remaining legal sanctions on homosexuality; when the Romanian assembly voted early in 1996 to retain this ban the European parliament approached Iliescu directly and only after his intervention was the ban lifted as long as homosexual acts did not cause a public scandal. Some credit, on the other hand, was earned by sending Romanian troops to participate in the NATO-led IFOR, while the treaty with Hungary made approaches to the EU more credible, given Brussels' determination not to import frontier disputes into the EU.

On its north-eastern border post-revolutionary Romania was faced with the conundrum of Moldova. This new, and in ethnic terms predominantly Romanian state contained most of the former Bessarabia over which Romanian passions had many times been roused. In relations with Chişinău Romania's rulers showed extreme caution, not least because the last thing Romania could afford was a foreign entanglement which would anger the western powers and the IFIs. Successive Romanian governments were content therefore to recognize that Moldova contained a large Slav minority which would not welcome rule from Bucharest and when that minority attempted to secede from Moldova in 1993 Romanian caution was intensified; it increased even more after a referendum in March 1994 revealed that a majority even of the ethnic Romanians in Moldova wished to remain independent.

With Russia and Ukraine Romania's relations were complicated by Bucharest's insistence that any agreement between Romania and those states must include an explicit renunciation of the Molotov-Ribbentrop pact of 1939 which assigned Bessarabia and the northern Bukovina to the Soviet Union. Both Moscow and Kyiv feared that this could be the first step to Romania's demanding the return of those territories. Relations with Russia were further complicated by Romania's demand that Russia return the gold sent there for safe keeping by the Romanian government during the First World War.

If neither the foreign nor the domestic policies of the Văcăroiu regime greatly enhanced its chances of admittance to the European or NATO clubs, in Romania itself it was domestic issues which preoccupied voters' minds as the parliamentary and presidential elections of November 1996 approached. Meanwhile, the government set out in traditional style to enhance its own chances of victory. The breaking of the links between the PSDR and its former coalition partners in 1995 and early 1996 had left the PSDR free to remove all county prefects who were not PSDR party members; it was the county prefects who would control the vital electoral bureaux. In the pre-election months the Văcăroiu administration also kept price increases to moderate levels. It was no use; none of these manoeuvres could save the ailing ministry. The majority of the electorate was deeply disappointed at the painfully slow pace of economic reform, at the continuing decline in living standards, and at the fact that Romania was being left behind other post-communist states in the process of international integration. The voters took their revenge. The share of the poll taken by the DCR and its ally, the Social Democratic Union (SDU), increased by 13 per cent while that of the PSDR fell by 6 per cent. The DCR had 122 deputies in the lower house, the PSDR 91, the SDU 53, the HDUR 25, the GRP 19 and the PRNU 18. Văcăroiu could not remain in office and resigned. It was the first time since 1937 that a change of government in Romania had been brought about through the ballot box.

In the presidential elections Iliescu lost to the man he had defeated in 1992, Emil Constantinescu.

CENTRE-RIGHT GOVERNMENT, NOVEMBER 1996 TO DECEMBER 2000

The formation of the first truly post-communist government in Romania may well turn out to be the turning point at which Romanian history failed to turn. A series of prime ministers, each torpedoed in turn by petty-minded and petty-fogging disputes within the ruling coalitions and the parties of which they were made, tried and failed to set Romania on the road to reform.

The new president appointed as his first prime minister Victor Ciorbea, a member of the National Peasant Party – Christian Democratic (NPPCD) and a lawyer who had been elected mayor of Bucharest in the preceding summer; his opponent in that contest had been the former tennis star, Ilie Nastase, one of a number of prominent Romanians put up by the PSDR in an effort to retrieve its sinking popularity. In his short time as mayor Ciorbea had made a favourable impression by his energetic attack upon corruption in the city. His government was of the centre right although his cabinet included members of the SDU; it also included two members of the HDUR, one of them as minister for national minorities, this being the first time the HDUR had been in government. Hope returned to a jaded population. Ciorbea was committed to change and to breaking with the communist and the neo-communist past, and he had a 60 per cent majority in the lower house of the legislature to enable him to do it. He also let it be known that he would henceforth insist upon unity within the cabinet.

Initially the hopes seemed justified. In January 1997 Ciorbea applied on a national scale the anti-corruption drive he had conducted in Bucharest, including the arrest of those who had been responsible in 1994 for the collapse of the Caritas pyramid scheme. In April the director of the RIS was sacked after a parliamentary commission of inquiry into his activities; his replacement was a close associate of Constantinescu.

It was not long, however, before the faults which had plagued the previous administrations were again apparent. Ciorbea's cabinet was soon facing dissention and defection. There were disagreements about how to tackle the economic problems facing the country and many cabinet members were irked by Ciorbea's style of 'leadership', it being not unusual for cabinet meetings to last over twelve hours and to do nothing more than indulge in rambling discussions of general issues.

In 1997 two of the main parties within the DCR fell out over land reform. In January 1998 the SDU left the government, though continuing to support it in parliament. The SDU accused Ciorbea of incompetence, inefficiency and doctrinaire conservatism, but it did not escape notice that the prime minister had refused the SDU a senior financial appointment. In March Ciorbea suffered a much more serious blow when he lost the support of a portion of his own party; he resigned. His successor was Radu Vasile, also of the NPPCD, who formed a multi-party cabinet which included the SDU which now had the ministry of industry. Vasile promised speedier reform and more privatization, even issuing a timetable, but once again little transpired and it was soon obvious that back-stairs intrigue, party squabbles and personal rivalries had more influence than national needs. Vasile's cabinet began to crumble. The first to leave was the Hungarian minister of health who, it was revealed, had once signed an agreement to act as an informer for the Ceauşescu-era Securitate, though he had signed under duress and had never informed on anyone. In September Vasile dismissed the minister of finance who disagreed with the government's and the president's enthusiasm for an agreement with the Bell-Textron concern in the USA under which Romania was to buy 96 helicopters for $1,500 million and Bell-Textron was to invest in the heli-copter plant in Braşov. Soon after that Vasile dismissed the minister for privat-ization whom he blamed for the slow disposal of state assets.

Despite these setbacks and notwithstanding difficulties with the HDUR, the Hungarians being frustrated by the lack of progress towards re-establishing tertiary education in Hungarian, Vasile managed to cling to office until December 1998 when cabinet members of his own party resigned en bloc. He was replaced by Mugur Isarescu, the non-party governor of the Bank of Romania who had an excellent record in defending the independence of the Bank and in masterminding the stabilization of the economy in 1993 and 1994. By the middle of 2000 his administration had suffered two defections, the departure of the defence minister in March coming about after yet another unseemly squabble between two coalition partners.

In the economic, as in the political sector the post neo-communist govern-ments repeated the mistakes and sins of their predecessors. They were quick to promise reform and slow to deliver it because they feared social unrest.

Ciorbea had set out to eliminate price subsidies and controls on energy and foodstuffs, to liberalize the foreign exchange markets, to speed up privatiza-tion and to restructure the tax system. He had little success. Nor did Vasile. His policies were similar but by the end of 1998 had proved equally ineffect-ive: privatization was only 20 per cent of the projected total; GDP, which had been targeted at zero percentage growth had fallen by 4 per cent; officially recognized unemployment had risen from 7 to 9 per cent; inflation at 40 per cent, though much reduced, was well above the targeted level; the leu had declined rapidly again; and the average real wage was down to just over $100 a month. The IMF finally lost its patience. When the existing loan package lapsed in May 1998, with much of the money unused, the IMF insisted that if any further credits were to be extended then the Romanian government had to adopt strict budgetary controls and actually implement the restructuring programmes it was constantly putting forward. There were to be no substantive talks on further aid until 1999.

That year at last saw progress. There were real moves towards restoring land to its pre-1944 owners with priority going to those who had suffered persecution at the hands of the communists. The new legislation also provided at last for the breakup of the communist-created collective farms, though the whole reform was to cost a massive $2 billion. In 1999 there was a major success in privatization when Renault acquired a majority holding in the Dacia car-manufacturing plant, although the deal included tax concessions which the IMF deemed *ultra vires* and insisted must not be repeated. That insistence scuppered a project to sell the Petromidia refinery to a Turkish company. In August the IMF relented on its March decision to suspend talks on a stand-by credit and agreed to lend $547 million in four tranches in 1999–2000. At the end of the year Brussels announced a huge three-year aid package worth $2,400 million. In January 2000 the Isarescu government introduced a major reform programme which included much tighter budgetary control, the reduction of the budget deficit to 3 per cent of GDP, an overhaul of the tax system and a scheme to contain inflation at 25–30 per cent per annum. In May, to meet IMF conditions, the government undertook to increase gas and electricity prices by another 20 per cent, to reduce the workforce in the state sector by 20,000 and to privatize the national oil company, Petrom. Similar promises had been made and broken before but the IMF seemed convinced that real action would be taken and agreed to issue the second tranche of the $547 million loan.

Real economic reform meant, as elsewhere in post-communist Europe, social suffering. And social suffering provoked protest. In the first part of 1997 the government faced strikes in the mines, the health service and among engineering workers; there were further protests in August when the government announced its intention to close seventeen loss-making enterprises, including three of the country's nine oil refineries. 1998 saw strikes in transport, the mines, the steel mills, the car assembly plants and by the garbage collectors of Bucharest. The unrest continued in the following year with stoppages in the tractor and helicopter plants in Braşov, the steel industry, the health services and on the Bucharest metro, although the one-day general strike called for 24 May had far from universal support.

The most important clash of all, however, was the confrontation in January between the forces of law and order and the miners of the Jiu valley. Angered by pit closures and inadequate pay increases, and under the direction of Miron Cozma who had led them in 1991, the miners set out to march once more on Bucharest. They broke through one security cordon before being stopped at a second a hundred miles north of the city where a compromise was agreed.

The appeasement of the miners removed a great danger but it did little to salvage the government's sinking political credit. By the end of 1999 a public opinion poll revealed that 60 per cent of the population considered that life had been better under the communists and President Constantinescu was booed when he visited Alba Julia on 1 December for the traditional celebrations commemorating the union of Romania and Transylvania in 1918. Less than two weeks later the collapse of the Vasile cabinet further discredited the country's political establishment.

In foreign policy the post-1996 administrations fared somewhat better. In 1997 Romania contributed troops to the Italian-led operation to restore order in Albania, although this did not prevent Romania being excluded from the states who were to join NATO in 1999. In 1997 an agreement was signed with Ukraine by which Romania accepted the inviolability of the Ukrainian–Romanian border, thereby acknowledging the loss of Bessarabia. The agreement also committed the two states to coming to an accommodation within three years on the demarcation of the Black Sea shelf and other border disputes. During the Kosovo crisis of 1998–9, Romania, like Bulgaria, remained steadfast in its support of NATO policy, allowing NATO planes the right to use Romanian airspace, a right refused to Russia when it wanted to fly troops and supplies to Prishtina. As in Bulgaria the government's stance met with widespread popular disapproval.

The major success in foreign policy was in relations with the EU. In July 1997 the EU had failed to include Romania in the states with whom it was prepared to begin talks on accession. In December 1999 the Helsinki conference of the EU reversed that decision, making Romania one of the six additional countries with which accession negotiations were to begin in 2000.

It is difficult to see what changed the mind of the EU, if the decision were taken on Romanian factors alone. The Romanian economy was nowhere near the standards usually needed for accession talks; the human rights situation, especially for Roma and for homosexuals, was below European standards; and Romania had done little to remedy its appalling record on ecological degradation. It is difficult to avoid the suspicion that the EU, and to a lesser degree the IMF, have acted on the unspoken assumption that Romania, the largest state in the Balkans, simply cannot be allowed to collapse.

The poor record of the centre-right administrations not surprisingly led to the defeat both of the Isarescu government and President Constantinescu in the elections of November 2000. If there was no surprise there was considerable concern because the chauvinist GRP was returned as the second largest party in both houses of the assembly, the largest being the PSDR. At the same time the GRP leader, Vadim Tudor, forced the presidential contest to a second round. In that contest he was easily defeated by Ion Iliescu.

Disillusioned by the failures of the centre-right the Romanian electorate had turned back to the old neo-communists of the PSDR. But should the latter fail yet again the elections of 2000 indicated that next time the disillusioned would turn not to the left but to the extreme right.

Chapter 19

GREECE SINCE 1990

In the 1990s three main themes dominated Greek politics: the necessity of adapting to the momentous changes in the former communist states to the north; the need to discipline the economy sufficiently to conform with the standards required for full integration within European structures; and, inevitably and depressingly, relations with Turkey.

NEW DEMOCRACY IN POWER, APRIL 1990 TO OCTOBER 1993

Old political habits as well as old problems persisted in Greece in the 1990s. After scraping home in the elections of April 1990 Konstantinos Mitsotakis's ND decided to adjust the electoral system yet again, this time bringing back reinforced PR. The new regulations required a party to reach a threshold of 3 per cent of the total national vote before it could secure any seats in the assembly, and it was also decided that no coalition parties would be included in the third redistribution of votes. The latter regulation was intended to thwart any PASOK–communist alliance, while the former ruling had the effect of rendering impotent any party based on an ethnic minority.

In foreign affairs Mitsotakis set about proving Greece's commitment to the west, first with the EC and then with the USA. He visited every state belonging to the former and in June 1990 became the first Greek prime minister to journey to Washington for a quarter of a century. In the following month he renewed the Greek–US defence cooperation agreement for a further eight years, an act made somewhat more palatable to the still predominantly anti-American Greek public by the fact that the US decided to reduce the number of its bases on Greek soil from four to two. Greece further pleased the United States by at last recognizing the state of Israel *de jure*, though this recognition did not extend to the occupied territories. When the Gulf crisis erupted in the summer of 1990 Greece immediately allowed transit rights to troops being sent to Saudi Arabia and contributed a frigate to the international naval contingent. In July 1991 President Bush made a brief visit to Athens while en route for Ankara.

Relations with Turkey could not be so easily improved. The Cyprus sore continued to irritate, and Greek hackles were raised in 1990 both when the Turkish consul in Komotini in Thrace referred to local Muslims as his 'fellow countrymen', and in 1992 when Turkey moved quickly to recognize the new republic of Macedonia.

The Macedonian question generated a great deal of passion in Greece in the early 1990s. The main public complaint was that the existence of a state named Macedonia implied a territorial claim on the Greek province which bore the same name. But there was also the less well-publicized fear that a Macedonian state would confirm the existence of a Macedonian nation which might in turn encourage the small Slavophone minority in Greece to demand recognition as a national minority; Greece had consistently denied that there were any ethnic as opposed to religious minorities in the country. In 1991 the minister for foreign affairs, Antonis Samaras, declared that Greece would never recognize a state calling itself Macedonia, and this marked the beginning of the frenetic anti-Macedonian campaign launched by the Athens government. Mitsotakis effectively lobbied his European partners, convincing them that if they did not accept his tough line on Macedonia Greek public opinion would drive him from office which would mean a return to power of the even more chauvinistic Andreas Papandreou and PASOK. That there was substance to Mitsotakis's threat was shown by huge popular demonstrations in Salonika in February and in Athens in December 1992.

Relations with Albania were also troubled. The focus of the problem was the Greek minority in Albania which Greek estimates put at 300,000 and which the Albanian authorities said numbered between a fifth and a sixth of that figure. The end of communist rule had allowed the minority to voice its grievances and officials in Athens could not but hear what was said. The problem was compounded by the relaxation of frontier controls in Albania with the result that thousands of ethnic Greeks, and many Albanians, poured into Greece; in January 1991 Mitsotakis went to Albania to urge the local Greeks to stay where they were, while periodically the Greeks would round up illegal immigrants and send them back to Albania, particularly if Athens were anxious to underline a diplomatic point.[1]

In internal affairs the ND hoped to reap some political benefit from the Bank of Crete trial which began in March 1991. Andreas Papandreou was among the accused but he refused to attend the trial and charges against him were later dropped. Two of his former ministerial colleagues did not escape so lightly and were sentenced to long spells in gaol, while the former owner of the Bank, Koskotas, having claimed that PASOK had blackmailed him with threats of nationalizing his bank if he did not hand over money, was sent down for five years for forging a document implicating Papandreou in the scandal.

Mitsotakis's main task on the domestic front, however, was not to persecute the former administration but to prepare Greece for further integration into the European economic system and this demanded tough action to reduce inflation, debt, the state profile in the economy, and, most important of all, budget deficits. Retrenchment and austerity became the order of the day. To this end the government pushed up the price of petrol and alcohol and imposed differential rates of VAT. The social costs of retrenchment were soon made clear. The indexing of pay to the cost of living was abandoned, as were official controls on wages. The extraordinarily complex system of pensions was also put under review and the privatization of a number of state enterprises was mooted. The prime targets in this exercise were the 'problematic' enterprises; not only did these make a loss, and therefore contribute to the budget deficit, but they employed far too many workers, many of whom were there not because they were needed but because they had been given jobs as a reward for loyalty to a particular political party.

In 1992 Mitsotakis was greatly helped by a huge, 2.2 billion ecu stabilization loan from the EU which in all probability saved the economy and the government from collapse. But the stabilization package had a price tag which demanded yet more discipline in the economy and society. The government froze wages for an entire year and for the same period it suspended recruitment into the civil service. New taxes were introduced and, with shades of earlier decades of dependence, United States Internal Revenue Service advisors were brought in to help combat tax evasion. At the same time most restrictions on price movements were removed. The effects were predictable; inflation rose to 15.5 per cent and unemployment to 10 per cent.

Public discontent had been mounting since the beginning of the austerity programme in 1990. Strikes became more numerous and more widespread as industrial action was taken not only by manual workers but also by professionals such as teachers, medics, pilots and civil servants, all of whom were on the public payroll and who therefore bore the brunt of government retrenchment. In October 1992 a further cause for discontent arose when King Constantine was given a generous settlement for properties lost to the crown.* Anger at the government's policies was expressed not only in strikes but in a series of massive protest meetings, while the terrorists of 'November 17' added to the general tension by attempting to assassinate the minister of finance. Within the ND leadership the main fear was less the assassin's bullet than the electors' revenge; so great did the discontent become that in December 1992 Mitsotakis sacked his entire cabinet in order to give his government a new image.

In fact by the middle of 1993 Mitsotakis's policies were beginning to pay dividends. Inflation, though still too high, had fallen to 12.8 per cent, the numbers on the government payroll had decreased, the labour market had

---

* The king did not consider it generous enough. He went to the European Court of Human Rights in Strasbourg with a claim for a further $800 million in further compensation. In 2000 the Court decided in his favour but when he tried to persuade the government in Athens to part with the extra cash they retaliated by demanding back-dated taxes of an equal or greater sum.

become freer, some privatization had been effected – for example of Athens's buses – and foreign currency reserves had increased. There had also been some tax cuts on the assumption, mistaken in the Greek case, that lower rates would increase receipts by decreasing evasion. But many Greeks were still more conscious of their pains than their pleasures and strikes and demonstrations continued. So too did rumblings within the ranks of ND. In June 1993 Samaras, who had been dismissed from his post as foreign minister in March 1992 because of his extreme attitudes over Macedonia, formed a new party, Political Spring. In September 1993 three disgruntled ND deputies, angry over government plans to privatize the Greek telephone system, defected to Samaras and in so doing deprived Mitsotakis of a working majority in parliament.

Elections were held on 10 October 1993. PASOK conducted an avowedly populist campaign, castigating the government for its austerity programme and pushing for an ultra hard line on Macedonia. Papandreou's party secured 47 per cent of the vote and, thanks to Mitsotakis's changes in the voting system, was given a comfortable working majority in parliament with 170 seats to ND's 111, ND having taken 39 per cent of the votes.

PASOK GOVERNMENT, GREECE SINCE APRIL 1993

Papandreou's new government suspended the privatization of the state telephone company and re-nationalized Athens's buses, much to the rage of many drivers who had bought their own vehicles, but the new administration dared not go any further in reversing ND's austerity programme for fear that the EU might rule against Greece's further integration into the European structures, from which the country was deriving so many benefits.

In foreign policy, however, there was less restraint. Old PASOK leftist and populist sympathies combined in huge demonstrations outside the United States consulate in Salonika after the USA had said it would recognize Macedonia, and on 16 February 1994 Greece imposed its trade embargo on Macedonia. Not until after the signature of the New York agreement in September 1995 was there any sign of a let-up in Greek hostility to the new state, but thereafter relaxation followed quickly.[2]

Relations with Albania also eventually improved. Initially they were soured by the internment in Albania of the five Greeks[3] in retaliation for which the Greek government vetoed EU aid for Albania and at the same time expelled 50,000 Albanian illegal immigrants. In 1995, however, relations began to improve with the release of the five detainees and the setting up of joint commissions to discuss problems between the two states, and in 1996 an agreement was signed allowing Greek schools and consulates to open in Albania and for the legal status of some 300,000 Albanians in Greece to be regularized. Much greater reconciliation came with the collapse of central authority in Albania in 1997. Greek forces, with those of Italy, took a leading part in restoring calm and order, remaining on Albanian territory from mid-April to early August. In September three agreements for defence cooperation were signed, after which Greek-Albanian relations remained reasonably stable and cordial.

Those with Turkey were seldom either stable or cordial. The Cyprus issue remained unresolved and Turkey took exception to the promulgation of a Greek-Greek Cypriot 'unified defence doctrine' which allowed for joint exercises by Greek and Greek-Cypriot forces, the first such manoeuvres taking place in October 1994. The question of the Aegean also generated great tension. In June 1995 the Greek parliament ratified the 1982 UN convention on the law of the sea. Turkey feared that under this convention Greece would declare a twelve-mile limit. Had it done so the medial line between Greek and Turkish territorial waters would in some cases have been less than six miles from the Anatolian coast and Ankara therefore responded by stating that any such declaration would be regarded as a *casus belli*. The Greeks made it clear that they would not make such a declaration, though they retained the freedom to do so. Things became more serious in December 1995 when a Turkish ship ran aground on the uninhabited islet of Imia, or Kardak in Turkish. The Turks refused the offer of salvage from a Greek vessel because, said the Turks, this was Turkish territory. The dispute escalated rapidly. It had many of the characteristics of *opéra bouffe* with Greek and Turkish marines charging around raising their own flags and lowering those of the other side, but this seeming pantomime disguised a very serious development in which outright hostilities were only narrowly averted; for the first time since 1947 Greece and Turkey were at odds over actual territory. It persuaded the Greek government in November 1996 to announce a huge ten-year programme to modernize and expand its forces, and this in a country where defence spending already accounted for 4.6 per cent of GDP, the highest proportion for any NATO state, and which was desperately trying to reduce government spending and budget deficits.

By the time the Imia crisis had reached its height a major change had come about in Greek politics. Papandreou had been in questionable health ever since he resumed the premiership in 1993 and at the end of 1995 it became obvious that he could not remain as head of government. He resigned on 15 January 1996 and died six months later. His successor was Kostas Simitis who had considerable ministerial experience and was a pragmatic reformer in the European social democratic tradition. At 60 he was also a comparative youngster for a Greek premier.

Simitis, like Karamanlis two decades before him, wanted elections to give him a fresh mandate to tackle the Turkish problem and to make another major step towards Europe, this time the integration of Greece into the European Monetary Union (EMU). Elections were therefore called for 22 September 1996. Simitis fought a restrained campaign, promising the Greeks little but continued austerity, the reward for which would be the prosperity to be gained by eventual inclusion in the EMU. It was ND which ran on a populist ticket, promising to scrap PASOK's proposed tax and welfare reforms. PASOK's share of the vote fell from the 47 per cent of 1993 to 41 per cent but it still had an absolute majority in the assembly with 162 seats; ND had 38 per cent of the vote and 108 seats.

Under Simitis the Turkish problem ebbed and flowed with, at times, the government more prepared than the population at large for compromise. In 1997 both governments agreed to the EU's suggestion that a committee of 'wise men' be set up to investigate possible solutions to Greek-Turkish problems, and in July in Madrid the two states agreed to keep the peace, to respect each other's sovereignty and to do all they could to promote friendly relations. By the end of October the Greeks had declared the agreement void after Turkish fighters had buzzed a plane carrying the Greek defence minister on his journeys to and from Cyprus, and in the following month Greece blocked the inclusion of Turkey in the list of states to be considered for admission in the next round of EU enlargement. In 1998 serious disagreement arose over a decision by the Greek Cypriot administration to install Russian S-300 missiles on their part of the island. The Turks threatened to remove them by force. In this particular spat the Greek delegation to the Cardiff summit of the EU vetoed humanitarian aid from the Union to Turkey. The issue was only partially resolved when the Nicosia government agreed to place the missiles not in Cyprus but in Crete where they would be much further from Turkish territory.

A constant complaint from the Turkish side, always energetically denied by Athens, was that Greece was giving aid to the Kurdish separatist organization, the PKK. In February 1999 the leader of the PKK, Abdullah Öcalan, was seized by Turkish agents in Kenya; he had been smuggled into Greece by a retired Greek army officer and had subsequently somehow found sanctuary in the Greek embassy in Nairobi. A number of Greek diplomatic missions were seized by enraged Kurds.

This somewhat bizarre episode saw the beginnings of a change in Greek attitudes. A government reshuffle led to the sacking of the outspoken minister for foreign affairs and his replacement by Georgios Papandreou, the son of the late prime minister. Papandreou upset nationalists by stating that it would not worry him if the Muslim minority in Greece chose to describe itself as Turkish; its own minister for foreign affairs had seemingly overthrown the convention by which Greece had always insisted that its minorities were religious not ethnic. Unusually close and easy cooperation between the two countries followed over the problems caused by the refugees from Kosovo but it was two acts of God which brought about the most surprising changes. On the morning of 17 August 1999 a severe earthquake struck north-western Turkey. Greek rescue teams were operating on Turkish soil that evening and Greece immediately lifted its embargo on EU humanitarian aid for Turkey. There seemed this time a genuine warmth among both officials and the public and this was reciprocated when another, though less serious 'quake struck north of Athens on 7 September, with this time Turkish rescue teams rushing to Greece. By the end of the year Georgios Papandreou had spoken of Greece becoming the 'locomotive which would pull Turkey into the EU' and at the Helsinki summit in December there was no Greek veto on giving Turkey candidate status for the EU. In the autumn of 2000 there were disagreements again over participation in NATO exercises in the Aegean but the 'earthquake diplomacy' of 1999 had at least proved that good relations between Greece and Turkey were possible.

Simitis had visited the United States shortly after assuming the premiership and official relations with Washington remained correct. The largest strain placed upon them came with the NATO campaign in the Balkans in 1999. Greece had a traditionally pro-Serbian attitude but this did not prevent the government in Athens from remaining solidly, if unenthusiastically loyal to the general will of NATO. The public was less restrained and hostility to the NATO action was much stronger in Greece than any other state in the alliance. So much so in fact that a visit by President Clinton in late 1999 had to be first postponed and then shortened on security grounds. The president, however, disarmed criticism by apologizing for the stance taken by the United States during military rule and by showing sympathy with the Greek demand that the Parthenon frieze be returned from the British Museum to Athens.

The recurrent disagreements with Turkey and later the Kosovo emergency complicated Simitis's main domestic task, the preparation of Greece for entry into the EMU. His policies were much the same as those of Mitsotakis and Papandreou. So were the difficulties they caused. The difference was that Simitis was able to reap some benefit from the sacrifices exacted by his two predecessors. Already in 1995 inflation had been brought below 10 per cent for the first time in twenty-three years and two years later it was down to 5.6 per cent. This was still too high for the Maastricht convergence criteria and further austerity was needed; it was introduced in 1998 in the form of a decrease in welfare benefits and overtime working by state employees and by a 14 per cent devaluation of the drachma in March 1998. But the Simitis regime had a more sophisticated approach to the problem, not least in its decision in May 1997 to launch a 'social dialogue' to explain its policies, the dialogue involving setting up tripartite commissions of employers, government officials and trade unionists. This had little lasting effect but it improved the government's image. So too did the fact that it was less prone to the scandals to which the Papandreou administration was sometimes prone, not least that of the 'pink villa' constructed at public expense for Andreas Papandreou's wife.

The Simitis government could not avoid some reaction against its tough policies. Teachers, policemen and health workers had all protested in 1997 and early in 1998 farmers, angry at high fuel prices and declining subsidies, blocked roads cutting links between northern and central Greece for a week. In April and May 1998 24-hour general strikes were called. In 1999 public protest shifted from the economic to the political front with large public demonstrations against NATO's action against Serbia.

In fact by 1999 there was less reason for economic discontent. By the middle of the year inflation had been brought down to almost 2 per cent with an expected budget deficit of only 1.5 per cent of GDP. By February 2000 inflation had at last come down to within the limits set by Maastricht and Greece had met the final requirement needed for admission to the Eurozone. Official application was made on 9 March and was soon accepted, the entry date being 1 January 2001.

Simitis understandably thought this an appropriate moment to go to the country. PASOK's share of the poll did not increase appreciably, rising from 41 to almost 44 per cent and giving it 158 parliamentary seats. ND, led since March 1997 by Kostas Karamanlis, a nephew of the former prime minister and president, polled almost 43 per cent and took 125 seats.

If PASOK had not greatly increased its share of the vote it had done what no party in modern Greek history had done: it had won a third consecutive term in office. The third PASOK victory also marked almost a quarter of a century of democracy and relative stability in Greece, the longest period for over a century without war, revolution or coup.

Notes

1. See above, pp.301–2.
2. See above, pp.294–5.
3. See above, pp.301–2.

Chapter 20

EPILOGUE

_____

In the decade since 1989 the former communist Balkan states were tragic victims of their own and other peoples' histories. The majority of the domestic problems they faced derived from the unnatural processes of rapid and illogical industrialization and enforced collectivization which the communists had imposed. Without them Balkan agriculture would have been in a much more healthy state and the industries created would have been better adapted to local resources and markets; whatever the ideological compulsions there was no economic logic in building steel mills in Albania.

These problems were compounded by the fact that the upheavals of 1989 produced no new ideology. Socialism, it was assumed, had failed, but there was no new blueprint for social and political salvation. If there was no prescription for the future, there was relatively little guidance from the past. With the collapse of the authoritarian, one-party socialist system the Balkan states had little in terms of helpful historic memory to fall back upon. As was stated at the beginning of this book the 1930s and the war had destroyed whatever vestiges remained of political pluralism and parliamentary democracy in the Balkan states, and if Greece had rediscovered those phenomena the other states had not. For them the only port of historical call was the brief period of relatively open government in the 1920s. Thus ideologies and parties of that time were resurrected. The ideologies were not always compatible with modern western thinking and in most cases tended to be discouraged by incumbent governments, while most of the resurrected parties proved to be anachronistic; the social, economic and cultural conditions in which they had originally developed were no longer extant, and with very few exceptions these parties withered on their new, inhospitable vines.

In these circumstances, the former communist Balkan states might revert to the closed societies and dirigiste economies of the recent past, but this was an unwelcome choice when the dynamic of the 1989 revolutions had been to liberate society and the individual from such a system. The only alternative therefore was to embrace the western model. Unfortunately, the west did not always show the requisite sensitivity when dealing with the former communist states of the Balkans.

Immediately after the fall of the communist regimes there was a widespread assumption that all that had to be done was to abolish one-party rule, end government subsidies to rust-bucket industries, give the land back to the peasants and wait for everything in the garden to bloom. The transition needed much more careful oversight. This might have been realized if the attention of the west in the crucial early years had not been so engaged by the Gulf war, by the collapse of the Soviet Union and then by the intensification of internal European cohesion enshrined in Maastricht. When Europe did address the problems of the Balkans seriously it did so with a surprising lack of subtlety. Although association agreements were eventually signed with most Balkan states there were unconscionable delays in implementing them, delays arising usually from disputes between member states rather than from the actions of the Balkan countries. When negotiations for entrance did begin, after the EU summit in Helsinki in December 1999, too little regard was paid to local conditions, local requirements and local difficulties; instead Brussels seemingly retreated into a bureaucratic fetishism which required the Balkan states to go into huge contortions if they were to adapt their systems to the minutiae of the regulations laid down in the *acquis communautaire*.

This created a long-term danger that the Balkan peoples would become disillusioned with the European aspirations of their leaders. By the turn of the century the majority of the populations were already depressed by years of rising unemployment, high inflation and falling living standards. In similar circumstances the Weimar Republic had collapsed into authoritarianism; that the Balkan states had endured such sacrifices while moving towards rather than away from a more open and democratic system showed a political sophistication and a social forbearance which, the Balkan peoples understandably felt, were seldom recognized in the west.

There were other less encouraging signs. Crime rates soared and a number of fortunes were made in smuggling and sanctions busting. But even where fortunes had been legitimately made many people in the Balkans found it difficult to accept domination by this new 'aristocracy' of wealth as opposed to the old élite based on power, and social resentment smouldered on this and other accounts.

Even more serious, long-term difficulties were to be seen in demographic trends. Birth rates and life expectancy had fallen, while emigration rates had soared. Between the 1992 and 2001 censuses Bulgaria's population fell by over half a million, a net decline of 6.01 per cent; although the birth rate in the same period had fallen from 10.4 to 9.0 per thousand, the main reason for the decline was emigration, an estimated 700,000 people having left the country since the end of 1989. More serious was the fact that those emigrating were among the most highly qualified. By the end of 1998 in Albania almost a third of those who had been in university teaching or research posts in 1990 had left the country.

Even more dangerous was the fear that the decline in population was ethnically differentiated. The fears, sometimes exaggerated to a hysterical degree, of the Serbs in Kosovo had been a major factor in the rise of tension there. The president of Macedonia was more sober when he warned in September 1999 that given the current birth rates among Albanians and Macedonian Slavs in Macedonia the republic would have a majority Albanian population by 2015. Another major ethnic issue, and again one in which fears arising over differential birth rates were common, was that of the Roma. Their numbers were difficult to establish but they were to be found in virtually all Balkan states, and everywhere their low standards of living, poor education and the resultant propensity to crime posed problems to which few governments could find convincing answers.

Greece was insulated from these dangers by the cocoon of the EU and NATO but the remainder of the Balkan states, with the exception of Slovenia, entered the twenty-first century facing enormous dangers. Perhaps the greatest of these was that, feeling forsaken by and therefore abandoning any hope in the west, they would eventually revert to the introspective and destructive ethnic nationalism which had inflicted such appalling suffering on the former Yugoslavia in the last decade of the twentieth century.

Although the difficulties facing the Balkan states are enormous there are indications that they are not insuperable. The development of new communications networks could help bring closer cooperation and a number of major developments are planned or are already being introduced. One is to construct a road from Durres in Albania to Skopje, Sofia and the Aegean coast; it will follow the line of the old Roman Via Egnatia and will be the first major east–west transportation project since that road was built, the railways in the peninsula running basically north to south or north-west to south-east. The trans-Balkan highway has the energetic support of both Italy and Turkey at either end of it. However, it is less favourably regarded by the states to the north and south, Romania and Greece, who fear they might lose trade and be somewhat isolated by the new route. Their preference is for a new north–south road which is also being considered; a major link in that new chain would be a second bridge over the Danube from Bulgaria to Romania and an agreement to construct such a bridge was signed after long negotiations in 2000. Another form of inter-Balkan or cross-Balkan communication will come with the new Burgas–Alexandroupolis gas and oil pipelines.

The Kosovo emergency also produced a move towards some form of regional military cooperation in the form of the Balkan Multinational Peace Force established in January 1999 and consisting of forces from Italy, Greece, Albania, Bulgaria, Macedonia, Turkey and Romania, with headquarters for the first four years in the Bulgarian city of Plovdiv. The first commanding officer was to be a Turk and the first head of the political secretariat a Greek, and during the Macedonian crisis of March 2001 the Greek and Bulgarian foreign ministers discussed the possibility of deploying troops from the Multinational Force along the Macedonian border.

The Balkan Peace Force is not yet capable of containing dangers such as those presented by the threat of insurgency on the borders of Macedonia, but the substantial deployment of UN forces in the centre of the Balkan region should be sufficient to control such threats to the stability of the area.

Without such stability, be it guaranteed by internal, regional, or external agencies the Balkans will continue to be the victims of history, both their own and that of the wider world.

The opening paragraph of this book pointed out the difficulties of finding a starting point. Its closing sentences face the even more difficult problem of identifying an end point. The problem is in fact insoluble. A work of history which strays into contemporary affairs cannot be nicely rounded off with confident conclusions. The historical forces which determined the fate of the Balkans in the fifty years after the end of the Second World War have largely disappeared, perhaps only temporarily, from the political arena. Those which dominated the 1990s are still in play. It is as yet impossible to say where these forces will lead the Balkans. It is hoped that the preceding pages have at least indicated the direction in which the Balkans are moving.

BIBLIOGRAPHY

The following bibliography makes no claim to be exhaustive. It lists those works which have been most helpful to the author in preparing this book. Most of the works cited are in English and many of them contain further, more detailed bibliographies.

General

Allcock, John B.
'Constructing the Balkans', in John B. Allcock and Antonia Young (eds), *Black Lambs and Grey Falcons: Women Travellers in the Balkans*, Bradford: Bradford University Press, 1991, pp.170–91.

Cullen, Robert
Twilight of Empire: Inside the Crumbling Soviet Bloc, London: The Bodley Head, 1991.

Cviic, Christopher
Remaking the Balkans, Chatham House, Papers, London: Pinter Publishers for the Royal Institute for International Affairs, 1991.

Dawisha, K. and Parrott, B.
Politics, Power, and the Struggle for Democracy in South-East Europe, Democratization and Authoritarianism in Postcommunist Societies, no. 2, Cambridge: Cambridge University Press, 1997.

Djilas, Milovan
The New Class: An Analysis of the Communist System, Introduction by Robert Conquest, London: Unwin Books, 1966.

Djilas, Milovan
The Imperfect Society: Beyond the New Class, translated by Dorian Cooke, London: Unwin Books, 1972.

Eyal, Jonathan
Vicious Circles: Security in the Balkans, Whitehall paper, 0268-1307, London: Royal United Services Institute for Defence Studies, 1992.

Eyal, Jonathan (ed.)
The Warsaw pact and the Balkans: Moscow's Southern Flank, London: Macmillan, 1989.

Gibianskii, Leonid
'The Soviet Bloc and the Initial Stage of the Cold War: Archival Documents on Stalin's Meetings with Communist Leaders of Yugoslavia and Bulgaria, 1946–1948', in David Wolff

	(ed.), *Cold War International History Project Bulletin* (Woodrow Wilson International Center for Scholars, Washington DC), no. 10 (March 1998), pp.112–34.
Glenny, Misha	*The Balkans 1804–1999: Nationalism, War and the Great Powers*, London: Granta Books, 1999.
Glenny, Misha	*The Rebirth of History*, London: Penguin, 1990.
Gsovski, Vladimir and Grzybowski, Kazimierz	*Government, Law and Courts in the Soviet Union and Eastern Europe*, London: Stevens, 2 vols, 1959.
Jelavich, Barbara	*History of the Balkans*, vol. 1, *Eighteenth and Nineteenth Centuries*, vol. 2, *The Twentieth Century*, Cambridge: Cambridge University Press, 1983.
Kaser, M. C. (ed.)	*The Economic History of Eastern Europe*, 3 vols, Oxford: Clarendon Press, 1985, 1986.
King, R. R.	*Minorities under Communism: Nationalities as a Source of Tension among Balkan Communist States*, Cambridge, MA: Harvard University Press, 1973.
Lampe, John R. and Jackson, Marvin R.	*Balkan Economic History, 1550–1950: From Imperial Borderlands to Developing Nations*, The Joint Committee on Eastern Europe Series, no. 10, Bloomington, IN: Indiana University Press, 1982.
Larrabee, F. Stephen (ed.)	*The Volatile Powder Keg: Balkan Security after the Cold War*, Washington DC: The American University Press, 1994.
Lendvai, Paul	*Eagles in Cobwebs: Nationalism and Communism in the Balkans*, London: Macdonald, 1970.
Linz, Juan and Stepan, Alfred	*Problems of Democratic Transition and Consolidation; Southern Europe, South America, and Post-Communist Europe*, Baltimore, MD/London: The Johns Hopkins University Press, 1996.
Lory, Bernard	*L'Europe balkanique de 1945 à nos jours*, Paris: Ellipses, 1996.
Mazower, Mark	*The Balkans*, New York: Random House, 2000.
Norris, H. T.	*Islam in the Balkans: Religion and Society between Europe and the Arab World*, London: Hurst, 1993.
Pavlowitch, St. K.	*A History of the Balkans, 1804–1945*, London/New York: Longman, 1999.
Poulton, Hugh	*The Balkans: Minorities and States in Conflict*, with a foreword by Milovan Djilas, London: Minority Rights Publications, 1991.

Pridham, Geoffrey and
Lewis, Paul G. (eds)
Stabilising Fragile Democracies: Comparing New Party Systems in Southern and Eastern Europe, London/ New York: Routledge, 1996.

Ramet, Pedro (ed.)
Eastern Christianity and Politics in the Twentieth Century, Christianity under stress, no. 1, Durham, NC/London: Duke University Press, 1988.

Stavrianos, L. S.
The Balkans since 1453, Hinsdale, IL: Dryden Press, 1958.

Stoianovich, Traian
Balkan Worlds: the First and Last Europe, Sources and Studies in World History, series editor Kevin Reilly, Armonk, NY/London: M. E. Sharpe, 1994.

Todorova, Maria
Imagining the Balkans, Oxford: Oxford University Press, 1997.

Wolff, Robert Lee
The Balkans in Our Time, Cambridge, MA: Harvard University Press, 1956.

Yasamee, H. J. and
Hamilton, K. A. (eds)
Documents on British Policy Overseas, series I, volume VI, *Eastern Europe August 1945 – April 1946*, London: HMSO, 1992.

Albania

Bartl, Peter
Albanien: Vom Mittelalter bis zum Gegenwart, Regensburg: Friedrich Pustet, 1995.

Biberaj, Elez
Albania: A Socialist Maverick, Boulder, CO/ Oxford: Westview, 1990.

Costa, Nicholas J.
Albania: A European Enigma, Boulder, CO/New York: East European Monographs no. 413, distributed by Columbia University Press, 1995.

Griffith, William E.
Albania and the Sino-Soviet Rift, Cambridge, MA: MIT Press, 1963.

Halliday, Jon (ed.)
The Artful Albanian; The Memoirs of Enver Hoxha, London: Chatto & Windus, 1986.

Hibbert, Reginald
Albania's National Liberation Struggle: the Bitter Victory, London: Frances Pinter, 1991.

Hoxha, Enver
The Khrushchevites: Memoirs, Tirana: '8 Nentori', 1980.

Logoreci, Anton
The Albanians: Europe's Forgotten Survivors, London: Victor Gollancz, 1977.

Marmullaku, Ramadan
Albania and the Albanians, translated from the Serbo-Croat by Margot and Bosko Milosavljević, London: Hurst, 1975.

Milo, Paskal
'Albania in East-West Relations, 1944–1945', paper presented to the conference on 'The

	Establishment of Communist Regimes in Eastern Europe, 1945–1950: A reassessment', Moscow, 29–31 March 1994, Tirana: Tirana University Press, no date.
Pano, Nicholas C.	*The People's Republic of Albania*, Integration and Community Building in Eastern Europe, Series Editor Jan F. Triska, Baltimore, MD: The Johns Hopkins University Press, 1968.
Pipa, Arshi	'The Political Culture of Hoxha's Albania', in Tariq Ali (ed.), *The Stalinist Legacy: Its Impact on Twentieth-Century World Politics*, London: Penguin, 1984, pp.435–64.
Pollo, Stefanaq and Puto, Arben	*The History of Albania from its Origins to the Present Day*, translated by Carol Wiseman and Ginnie Hole, London/Boston, MA: Routledge & Kegan Paul, 1981.
Prifti, Peter	*Socialist Albania since 1944: Domestic and Foreign Developments*, Cambridge, MA: MIT Press, 1978.
Skendi, Stavro (ed.)	*Albania*, East-Central Europe under Communism, Series Editor Robert F. Byrnes, New York: Praeger for the Mid-European Studies Center of the Europe Committee, Inc, 1956.
Smiley, David	*Albanian Assignment*, with a foreword by Patrick Leigh Fermor, London/Sydney: Sphere Books, 1984.
Tönnes, Bernard	*Sonderfall Albanien. Enver Hoxhas 'eignener Weg' und die historischen Ursprünge seiner Ideologie*, Munich: Oldenbourg, 1980.
Vickers, Miranda	*The Albanians: A Modern History*, London and New York: I. B. Tauris, 1995.

Bulgaria

| Bell, John D. | *The Bulgarian Communist Party from Blagoev to Zhivkov*, Histories of the Ruling Communist Parties, series editor, Richard F. Starr, Stanford, CA: Hoover Institution Press, Stanford University, 1986. |
| Bell, John D. | 'Bulgaria' in Stephen White, Judy Batt and Paul Lewis (eds), *Developments in East European Politics*, Basingstoke and London: Macmillan, 1993, pp.83–97. |

Black, Cyril E. — 'The Start of the Cold War in Bulgaria: A Personal View', *Review of Politics*, vol. xli, no. 2 (1979), pp.163–202.

Boll, Michael M. — *Cold War in the Balkans; American Foreign Policy and the Emergence of Communist Bulgaria 1943–1947*, Lexington, KY: The University Press of Kentucky, 1984.

Boll, Michael M. — 'Pro-Monarchist to Pro-Muscovite: The Transformation of the Bulgarian Army, 1944–1948', *East European Quarterly*, vol. 20, no. 4 (January 1987), pp.409–28.

Bristow, John A. — *The Bulgarian Economy in Transition*, Studies in Communist Transition, series editor, Ronald J. Hill, Cheltenham, England/Brookfield, VT: Edward Elgar, 1996.

Broun, Janice — 'The Schism in the Bulgarian Orthodox Church'; *Religion, State and Society: The Keston Journal*, vol. 21, no. 2 (1993), pp.207–20.

Brown, J. F. — *Bulgaria under Communist Rule*, London: Pall Mall Press, 1970.

Crampton, R. J. — *A Short History of Modern Bulgaria*, Cambridge: Cambridge University Press, 1987.

Crampton, R. J. — *A Concise History of Bulgaria*, Cambridge: Cambridge University Press, 1997.

Crampton, Richard J. — '"Stumbling and Dusting Off" or an Attempt to Pick a Path through the Thicket of Bulgaria's New Economic Mechanism', *East European Politics and Societies*, vol. 2, no. 2 (1988), pp.333–95.

Dimitrov, Vesselin Tzvetanov — 'The Failure of Democracy in Eastern Europe and the Emergence of the Cold War, 1944–1948: A Bulgarian Case Study', PhD thesis, University of Cambridge, 1997.

Hatschikjan, Magarditsch A. — *Tradition und Neuorientierung in der bulgarischen Aussenpolitik 1944–1948; die 'nationale Aussenpolitik' der Bulgarischen Arbeiterpartei (Kommunisten)*, Munich: R. Oldenbourg, 1988.

Horner, John E. — 'The Ordeal of Nikola Petkov and the Consolidation of Communist Rule in Bulgaria', *Survey*, vol. 20, no. 1 (90) (Winter 1974), pp.75–83.

Horner, John E. — 'Traicho Kostov: Stalinist Orthodoxy in Bulgaria', *Survey*, vol. 24, no. 3 (108) (Summer 1979), pp.135–42.

Karpat, Kemal H. (ed.)   *The Turks of Bulgaria: The History, Culture and Political Fate of a Minority*, Istanbul: The Isis Press, 1990.

Lampe, John R.   *The Bulgarian Economy in the Twentieth Century*, London/Sydney: Croom Helm, 1986.

Markov, Georgi   *The Truth that Killed*, translated by Liliana Brisby with an introduction by Annabel Markov, London: Weidenfeld & Nicolson, 1983.

Oren, Nissan   *Revolution Administered: Agrarianism and Communism in Bulgaria*, Baltimore, MD/London: The Johns Hopkins University Press, 1973.

Raikin, Spas T.   'The Bulgarian Orthodox Church', in Pedro Ramet (ed.), *Eastern Christianity and Politics in the Twentieth Century*, Christianity under Stress, no. 1, Durham NC/London: Duke University Press, 1988, pp.160–82.

Şimşir, Bilâl N.   *The Turks of Bulgaria (1878–1985)*, London: K. Rustem & Brother, 1988.

Slavov, Atanas   *The 'Thaw' in Bulgarian Literature*, Boulder, CO/New York: East European Monographs no. 74, distributed by Columbia University Press, 1981.

Slavov, Atanas   *With the Precision of Bats*, Washington DC: Occidental Press, 1986.

Zhivkova, Liudmila   *Liudmila Zhivkova: Her Many Worlds; New Culture & Beauty; Concepts & Action*, London: the Pergamon Press, 1982.

Greece

Alexander, George   *The Prelude to the Truman Doctrine: British Policy in Greece, 1944–1947*, Oxford: Clarendon Press, 1982.

Blinkhorn, Martin and Veremis, Thanos   *Modern Greece: Nationalism and Nationality*, London/Athens: Sage, 1990.

Chandler, Geoffrey   *The Divided Land; an Anglo-Greek Tragedy*, Wilby: Michael Russell, 1994.

Chircop, Aldo E., Gerolymatos, André and Iatrides, John O. (eds)   *The Aegean Sea after the Cold War, Security and Law of the Sea Issues*, International Political Economy Series, Basingstoke: Macmillan, 2000.

Clogg, Richard   *A Short History of Modern Greece*, Cambridge: Cambridge University Press, 1979.

Clogg, Richard   *A Concise History of Greece,* Cambridge: Cambridge University Press, 1992.

Clogg, Richard (ed.)   *Greece in the 1980s*, London: Macmillan in association with the Centre of Contemporary

	Greek Studies, King's College, University of London, 1983.
Clogg, Richard and Yannopoulos, George (eds)	*Greece under Military Rule*, London: Secker & Warburg, 1972.
Close, David	*The Origins of the Greek Civil War*, Origins of Modern Wars series, London: Longman, 1995.
Close, David (ed.)	*The Greek Civil War, 1943–1950: Studies of Polarization*, London: Routledge, 1993.
Crawshaw, Nancy	*The Cyprus Revolt: An Account of the Struggle for Union with Greece*, London/Boston: G. Allen & Unwin, 1978.
Eudes, Dominique	*The Kapetanios: Partisans and the Civil War in Greece*, translated from the French by John Howe, London: NLB, 1972.
Hitchens, Christopher	*Hostage to History: Cyprus from the Ottomans to Kissinger*, 3rd edn, London: Verso, 1997.
Iatrides, John O. (ed.)	*Ambassador MacVeagh Reports: Greece 1933–1947*, Princeton, NJ: Princeton University Press, 1980.
Iatrides, John O. and Wrigley, Linda	*Greece at the Crossroads: the Civil War and its Legacy*, Philadelphia, PA: Pennsylvania State University Press, 1995.
Kofas, Jon V.	*Intervention and Underdevelopment: Greece during the Cold War*, University Park, MD/London: Pennsylvania State University Press, 1989.
O'Balance, Edgar	*The Greek Civil War, 1944–1949*, with a foreword by C. M. Woodhouse, London: Faber, 1966.
Stavrakis, Peter J.	*Moscow and Greek Communism 1944–1949*, Ithaca, NY: Cornell University Press, 1989.
Veremis, Thanos	*The Military in Greek Politics: from Independence to Democracy*, London: Hurst, 1997.
Vlachos, Helen	*House Arrest*, London: André Deutsch, 1970.
Vlavianos, Haris	*Greece 1941–1949 from Resistance to Civil War; the Strategy of the Greek Communist Party*, London: Macmillan in association with St Antony's College, Oxford, 1992.
Volkan, Vamik D. and Itzkowitz, Norman	*Turks and Greeks: Neighbours in Conflict*, Huntingdon: Eothen Press, 1994.
Wittner, Lawrence S.	*American Intervention in Greece, 1943–1949*, Contemporary American history series, New York: Columbia University Press, 1982.
Woodhouse, C. M.	*Karamanlis, The Restorer of Greek Democracy*, Oxford: Clarendon Press, 1982.
Woodhouse, C. M.	*The Rise and Fall of the Greek Colonels*, London/New York: Granada, 1985.

Woodhouse, C. M.   *The Struggle for Greece, 1941–1949*, London: Hart-Davis, MacGibbon, 1976.

Romania

Almond, Mark   *Decline without Fall: Romania under Ceausescu*, European Security Study, no. 6, London: Alliance for the Institute for European Defence and Strategic Studies, 1988.

Behr, Edward   *Kiss the Hand You Cannot Bite; The Rise and Fall of the Ceauşescus*, London: Penguin, 1992.

Brucan, Silviu   *The Wasted Generation: Memoirs of the Romanian Journey from Capitalism and Back*, Boulder, CO/San Francisco, CA/Oxford: Westview, 1993.

Carothers, Thomas   *Assessing Democracy Assistance: The Case of Romania*, Washington DC: The Carnegie Endowment, 1996.

Castellan, Georges   'The Germans of Romania', *Journal of Contemporary History*, vol. 6, no. 1 (January 1971), pp.51–75.

Deletant, Dennis   *Ceauşescu and the Securitate. Coercion and Dissent in Romania, 1965–89*, London: Hurst, 1995.

Deletant, Dennis   *Communist Terror in Romania: Gheorghiu-Dej and the Police State, 1948–1965*, London: Hurst, 1999.

Fischer, Mary Ellen   *Nicolae Ceauşescu: A Study in Political Leadership*, Boulder, CO: Lynne Rienner, 1989.

Fischer-Galati, Stephen   *Twentieth Century Romania*, New York: Columbia University Press, 2nd edn, 1991.

Fischer-Galati, Stephen   'Myths in Romanian History', *East European Quarterly*, vol. 15, no. 3 (September 1981), pp.327–33.

Fischer-Galati, Stephen   '"Autocracy, Orthodoxy and Nationalism" in the Twentieth Century: The Romanian Case', *East European Quarterly*, vol. 18, no. 1 (March 1984), pp.25–34.

Floyd, David   *Rumania: Russia's Dissident Ally*, London: Pall Mall Press, 1965.

Gallagher, Tom   *Romania after Ceauşescu: The Politics of Intolerance*, Edinburgh: Edinburgh University Press, 1995.

Gallagher, Tom   'A Feeble Embrace: Romania's Engagement with Democracy, 1989–94', *The Journal of Communist Studies and Transition Politics*, vol. 12, no. 2 (June 1996), pp.145–72.

Galloway, George and Wylie, Bob	*Downfall: the Ceauşescus and the Romanian Revolution*, London: Futura, 1991.
Georgescu, Vlad	*The Romanians, A History*, Columbus, OH: Ohio State University Press, 1991.
Gilberg, Trond	*Nationalism and Communism in Romania: The Rise and Fall of Ceauşescu's Personal Dictatorship*, Boulder, CO/Oxford: Westview, 1990.
Gilberg, Trond	'Ceauşescu's Romania', *Problems of Communism*, vol. 23, no. 4 (July–August 1974), pp.29–33.
Gill, Graeme J.	'Rumania: Background to Autonomy', *Survey*, vol. 21, no. 3(96) (Summer 1975), pp.94–113.
Giurescu, D. G.	*Romania's Communist Takeover: the Radescu Government*, Boulder, CO/New York: East European Monographs, no. 388, distributed by Columbia University Press, 1994.
Hale, Julian	*Ceauşescu's Romania: A Political Documentary*, London: George Harrap, 1971.
Hitchins, Keith	*Romania, 1866–1947*, Oxford: Clarendon Press, 1994.
Ionescu, Ghita	*Communism in Rumania, 1944–1962*, London: Oxford University Press, 1964.
Jowitt, Kenneth	'Political Innovation in Rumania', *Survey*, vol. 20, no. 4(93) (Autumn 1974), pp.132–51.
King, Robert R.	*A History of the Romanian Communist Party*, Histories of the Ruling Communist Parties, series editor, Richard F. Starr, Stanford, CA: Hoover Institution Press, Stanford University, 1980.
King, Robert R.	'The Problems of Romanian Foreign Policy', *Survey*, vol. 20, no. 2/3(91/2, Spring/Summer 1974), pp.105–20.
King, Robert R.	'The Blending of Party and State in Romania', *East European Quarterly*, vol. 12, no. 4 (Winter 1978), pp.489–500.
Kristov, Ladis K.D.	'On Comparing East European Political Systems: Romania', *Studies in Comparative Communism*, vol. 4, no. 2 (April 1971), pp.36–42.
Lee, Arthur G.	*Crown against Sickle*, London: Hutchinson, 1950.
Nelson, Daniel N. (ed.)	*Romania in the 1980s*, Westview Special Studies on the Soviet Union and Eastern Europe, Epping: Bowker, 1981.
Nelson, Daniel N. (ed.)	*Romania After Tyranny*, Boulder, CO/London: Westview, 1992.
Nelson, Daniel N.	'Worker-Party Conflict in Romania', *Problems of Communism*, vol. 30, no. 5 (September–October 1981), pp.40–9.

Pachepa, Ion Mihai — *Red Horizons*, London: Heinemann, 1986.

Quinlan, Paul D. — *Clash over Romania: British and American Policies towards Romania: 1938–1947*, Los Angeles, CA: American Romanian Academy, 1977.

Rady, Martyn — *Romania in Turmoil; A Contemporary History*, London: I.B. Tauris, 1992.

Rates, Nestor — *Romania: The Entangled Revolution*, New York: Praeger, 1991.

Roberts, Henry L. — *Romania: Political Problems of an Agrarian State*, New Haven, CT and London: Yale University Press, 1951.

Saiu, Liliana — *The Great Powers and Rumania, 1944–1946; A Study of the Early Cold War Era*, Boulder, CO/ New York: East European Monographs, no. 335, distributed by Columbia University Press, 1992.

Schöpflin, George — 'Romanian Nationalism', *Survey*, vol. 20, no. 1/2(91/92) (Spring/Summer 1974), pp.77–104.

Shafir, Michael — *Romania: Politics, Economics and Society; Political Stagnation and Simulated Change*, Marxist Regimes Series, series editor Bogdan Szajkowski, London: Frances Pinter, 1985.

Sislin, John — 'Revolution Betrayed? Romania and the National Salvation Front', *Studies in Comparative Communism*, vol. 24, no. 4 (1991), pp.395–411.

Stuart, Anthony — 'Ceauşescu's Land', *Survey*, vol. 16, no. 76 (Summer 1970), pp.112–21.

Sweeney, John — *The Life and Evil Times of Nicolae Ceauşescu*, London: Hutchinson, 1991.

Turnock, David — *The Romanian Economy in the Twentieth Century*, London/Sydney: Croom Helm, 1986.

The Yugoslav lands

General

Akhavan, Payam and Howse, Robert (eds) — *Yugoslavia, the Former and the Future; Reflections by Scholars of the Region*, Washington DC: The Brookings Institution; Geneva: The United Nations Research Institute for Social Development, 1995.

Alexander, Stella — *Church and State in Yugoslavia since 1945*, Cambridge: Cambridge University Press, 1979.

Allcock, John B.	*Explaining Yugoslavia*, New York: Columbia University Press, 2000.
Auty, Phyllis	*Tito, A Biography*, London: Longman, 1970.
Banac, Ivo	*With Stalin against Tito: Cominformist Splits in Yugoslav Communism*, Ithaca, NY/London: Cornell University Press, 1988.
Banac, Ivo	*The National Question in Yugoslavia: Origins, History, Politics*, Ithaca, NY/London: Cornell University Press, 1984.
Beloff, Nora	*Tito's Flawed Legacy; Yugoslavia and the West: 1939 to 1984*, London: Victor Gollancz, 1985.
Bennett, Christopher	*Yugoslavia's Bloody Collapse; Causes, Course and Consequences*, London: Hurst, 1995.
Bertsch, Gary K.	'Currents in Yugoslavia. The Revival of Nationalisms', *Problems of Communism*, vol. 22, no. 6 (November–December 1973), pp.1–15.
Carter, April	*Democratic Reform in Yugoslavia; The Changing Role of the Party*, London: Frances Pinter, 1982.
Cohen, Lenard J.	*The Socialist Pyramid: Elites and Power in Yugoslavia*, Oakville, ON: Mosaic Press, 1989.
Cohen, Lenard J.	*Broken Bonds: Yugoslavia's Disintegration and Balkan Politics in Transition*, Boulder, CO: Westview, 1995.
Dedijer, Vladimir	*Tito Speaks; His Self-Portrait and his Struggle with Stalin*, London: Weidenfeld & Nicolson, 1953.
Dedijer, Vladimir	*The Battle Stalin Lost: Memoirs of Yugoslavia 1948–1953*, New York: Grosset & Dunlap, 1970.
Djilas, Aleksa	*The Contested Country: Yugoslav Unity and Communist Revolution, 1919–1953*, Russian Research Center Studies, 85; Harvard Historical Studies, 108, Cambridge, MA; Harvard University Press, 1991.
Djilas, Milovan	*Conversations with Stalin*, translated by Michael B. Petrovich, London: Penguin, 1969.
Djilas, Milovan	*Tito, the Story from Inside*, translated by Vasilije Kojić and Richard Hayes, London: Weidenfeld & Nicolson, 1981.
Djilas, Milovan	*Rise and Fall*, London/Basingstoke: Macmillan, 1985.
Dyker, David	*Yugoslavia: Socialism, Development and Debt*, London/New York: Routledge, 1990.
Glenny, Misha	*The Fall of Yugoslavia: the Third Balkan War*, London: Penguin, 1992.
Halperin, Ernst	'Revisionism in Yugoslavia', *Survey*, vol. 8, no. 42 (June 1962), pp.48–58.

Heuser, Beatrice — *Western Containment Policies in the Cold War: The Yugoslav Case, 1948–53*, London/New York: Routledge, 1989.

Irvine, Jill A., Bokovoy, Melissa and Lilly, Carol (eds) — *State-Society Relations in Yugoslavia, 1945–1992*, Basingstoke: Macmillan, 1997.

Kardelj, Edvard — *Reminiscences; the Struggle for Recognition and Independence: The New Yugoslavia, 1944–1957*, London: Blond & Briggs with Summerfield Press, 1982.

Koštunica, Vojislav and Čavoški, Kosta — *Party Pluralism or Monism; Social Movements and the Political System in Yugoslavia, 1944–1949*, Boulder, CO/New York: East European Monographs no. 189, distributed by Columbia University Press, 1985.

Lampe, John R. — *Yugoslavia as History: Twice there was a Country*, 2nd edn, Cambridge: Cambridge University Press, 2000.

Lendvai, Paul — *National Tensions in Yugoslavia*, Conflict Studies, no. 25, London: Institute for the Study of Conflict, 1972.

Lydall, Archibald — *Yugoslavia in Crisis*, Oxford: Clarendon Press, 1989.

Magaš, Branka — *The Destruction of Yugoslavia: Tracking the Break-up, 1980–92*, London/New York: Verso, 1993.

Meier, Victor — *Yugoslavia: A History of its Decline*, translated by Sabrina Ramet, London/New York: Routledge, 1999.

Meier, Viktor — 'Yugoslavia's National Question', *Problems of Communism*, vol. 32, no. 2 (March–April 1983), pp.47–60.

Novak, Bogdan C. — *Trieste, 1941–1954; the Ethnic, Political, and Ideological Struggle*, Chicago, IL/London: The University of Chicago Press, 1970.

Palmer, Peter — 'The Communists and the Roman Catholic Church in Yugoslavia, 1941–1946', D Phil thesis, University of Oxford, 2000.

Pavlowitch, Stevan K. — *The Improbable Survivor: Yugoslavia and its Problems, 1918–1968*, London: Hurst, 1988.

Pavlowitch, Stevan K. — *Tito: Yugoslavia's Great Dictator, A Reassessment*, London: Hurst, 1992.

Ramet, Pedro — 'Yugoslavia's Debate over Democratization', *Survey*, vol. 25, no. 3 (112, Summer 1980), pp.43–8.

Ramet, Sabrina P. — *Nationalism and Federalism in Yugoslavia, 1962–1991*, Bloomington IN: Indiana University Press, 2nd edn, 1992.

Ramet, Sabrina P. — *Balkan Babel: the Disintegration of Yugoslavia from the Death of Tito to the War for Kosovo*, Sabrina P. Ramet, with a foreword by Ivo Banac, 3rd edn, Boulder, CO/Oxford: Westview, 1999.

Ramet, Sabrina Petra and Adamovich, Ljubiša S. — *Beyond Yugoslavia: Politics, Economics, and Culture in a Shattered Community*, Eastern Europe and Communism, series editor, Sabrina Petra Ramet, Boulder, CO; San Francisco, CA; Oxford: Westview, 1995.

Rusinow, Dennison L. — *The Yugoslav Experiment, 1948–1954*, London: Hurst for the Royal Institute of International Affairs, 1977.

Schöpflin, George. — 'Nationality in the Fabric of Yugoslav Politic', *Survey*, vol. 25, no. 3 (112) (Summer 1980), pp.1–19.

Sharp, Samuel L. — 'The Yugoslav Experiment in Self-Management: Soviet Criticism', *Studies in Comparative Communism*, vol. 4, no. 3/4 (July/October 1971), pp.169–78.

Shoup, P. — *Communism and the Yugoslav National Question*, New York/London: Columbia University Press, 1968.

Silber, Laura and Little, Allan — *The Death of Yugoslavia*, London: Penguin, BBC Books, revised edn, 1996.

Ulam, Adam — *Titoism and the Cominform*, Cambridge, MA: Harvard University Press, 1952.

Wilson, Duncan — *Tito's Yugoslavia*, Cambridge: Cambridge University Press, 1979.

Woodward, Susan L. — *Balkan Tragedy: Chaos and Dissolution after the Cold War*, Washington DC: The Brookings Institution, 1995.

Woodward, Susan L. — *Socialist Unemployment: the Political Economy of Yugoslavia, 1945–1990*, Princeton, NJ: Princeton University Press, 1995.

Zimmerman, Warren — *Origins of a Catastrophe; Yugoslavia and its Destroyers*, New York: Times Books, Random House, 1999.

Bosnia

Almond, Mark — 'Learning from Our Mistakes and How to Make New Ones', in Sir Julian Bullard and Robert O'Neill (eds), *Lessons from Bosnia*, Summary

Record of a seminar series of that title held in All Souls College, Oxford, Hilary Term 1996, private publication.

Bildt, Carl — *Peace Journey: the Struggle for Peace in Bosnia*, London: Weidenfeld & Nicolson, 1998.

Bringa, Tone — *Being Muslim the Bosnian Way: Identity and Community in a Central Bosnian Village*, Princeton, NJ/Chichester: Princeton University Press, 1995.

Burg, Steven L. and Shoup, Paul S. — *The War in Bosnia-Herzegovina: Ethnic Conflict and International Intervention*, Armonk, NY/London: M.E. Sharpe, 1999.

Cigar, Norman — *Genocide in Bosnia: The Policy of 'Ethnic Cleansing'*, Eastern European Studies, no. 1, series editor Stjepan Meštrović, College Station, TX: Texas A&M University Press, 1995.

Donia, Robert J. and Fine, John V. A. Jr. — *Bosnia and Hercegovina: A Tradition Betrayed*, London: Hurst, 1994.

Dyker, David A. — 'The Ethnic Muslims of Bosnia – Some Basic Socio-Economic Data', *Slavonic and East European Review*, vol. 50, no. 119 (April 1972), pp.238–56.

Friedman, Francine — *The Bosnian Muslims: Denial of a Nation*, Boulder, CO/Oxford: Westview, 1996.

Gow, James — *The Triumph of the Lack of Will; International Diplomacy and the Yugoslav War*, London: Hurst, 1997.

Holbrooke, Richard — *To End a War*, New York: Random House, 1998.

Malcolm, Noel — *Bosnia; A Short History*, London: Macmillan, 1994.

O'Balance, Edgar — *Civil War in Bosnia, 1992–4*, Basingstoke/London: Macmillan, St Martin's Press, 1995.

Owen, David — *Balkan Odyssey*, London: Victor Gollancz, 1995.

Pinson, Mark (ed.) — *The Muslims of Bosnia-Hercegovina: Their Historic Development from the Middle Ages to the Dissolution of Yugoslavia*, with a foreword by Roy P. Mottahedeh, Harvard Middle Eastern Monographs, no. 28, Cambridge, MA, Harvard Center for Middle Eastern Studies, 1996.

Rose, General Sir Michael — *Fighting for Peace: Lessons from Bosnia*, London: Warner Books, 1998.

Croatia

Cuvalo, Ante — *The Croatian National Movement: 1966–1972*, Boulder, CO/New York: East European

	Monographs no. 282, distributed by Columbia University Press, 1990.
Goldstein, Ivo	*Croatia, A History*, translated by Nikolina Jovanović, London: Hurst, 1999.
Irvine, Jill A.	*The Croat Question: Partisan Politics in the Formation of the Yugoslav Socialist State*, with a foreword by Ivo Banac, Boulder, CO/Oxford: Westview, 1993.
Pusić, Vesna	'Constitutional Politics in Croatia', *Praxis*, vol. 13, no. 4 (January 1994), pp.389–404.
Schöpflin, George	'The Ideology of Croat Nationalism', *Survey*, vol. 19, no. 4(86) (Winter 1973), pp.123–46.
Tanner, Marcus	*Croatia: A Nation Forged in War*, New Haven, CT/London: Yale University Press, 1997.

Macedonia

Barker, Elisabeth	*Macedonia; Its Place in Balkan Power Politics*, London/New York: Royal Institute for International Affairs, 1950.
Kofos, Evangelos	*Nationalism and Communism in Macedonia; Civil Conflict, Politics of Mutation, National Identity*, published under the auspices of the Speros B. Vryonis Center for the Study of Hellenism, New Rochelle, NY: Aristide D. Caratzas, 1993.
Livanios, Dimitris	'Bulgar-Yugoslav Controversy over Macedonia and the British Connection, 1939–1949', D Phil thesis, University of Oxford, 1996.

Serbia and Montenegro

Judah, Tim	*Serbs: History, Myth and the Destruction of Yugoslavia*, New Haven, CT/London: Yale University Press, 1997.
Popov, Nebojša (ed.)	*The Road to War in Serbia; Trauma and Catharsis*, Budapest: Central European University Press, 2000.
Thomas, Robert	*Serbia under Milošević; Politics in the 1990s*, London: Hurst, 1999.

Slovenia

Gow, James and Carmichael, Cathy	*Slovenia and the Slovenes: A Small State and the New Europe*, London: Hurst, 2000.

INDEX

Abdić, Fikret, 144, 256
ACC (Allied Control Commission)
 Bulgaria, 5, 54, 57, 59
 Romania, 5, 73, 75, 76, 80, 84, 86n7
ACP (Albanian Communist Party), 39, 41, 43,
 45, 48, 156
ADF (Albanian Democratic Front), 43, 45, 46
Aegean littoral, 29, 38, 63, 95, 99, 206, 345
Aegean Sea, 99, 220, 223, 227, 339, 341
Afghanistan, 196, 271
agrarians, 51, 52, 53, 54, 55, 57, 58, 59, 60,
 61, 62, 66, 71, 168, 310
Agrarian Union, 20, 23
agriculture, collectivization and
 decollectivization, 8, 9, 107, 108, 343
 Albania, 43, 45, 158, 161, 300
 Bulgaria, 64, 168, 169, 171, 173, 174, 311
 Romania, 184, 185, 187, 200, 333
 Yugoslavia, 26, 114, 116, 118
Agrokomerc, 144, 256
Ahmeti, Vilson, 299, 302
Albania
 and First World War, 39
 and Germany, 165
 and Great Britain, 47, 47fn, 165
 and Greece, 27, 45–6, 158, 163, 165, 301–2
 and Italy, 4, 39, 305
 and Macedonia, 293, 301
 and PRC, 159–63, 165
 and Second World War, 4, 39–40, 157
 and Soviet Union, 43, 45, 46–9, 156–60,
 163, 165
 and the west, 40, 46–8, 49n6, 109, 158,
 162, 163, 301, 303, 307
 and USA, 42, 46–8, 49n6, 165, 271, 301,
 303, 304, 307
 and Yugoslavia, 39, 44, 45, 47–9, 156, 158,
 163, 164, 165
 disorders in, 271, 295, 299–300, 303–7
 Greek minority in, 45–6, 158, 165, 219,
 301–2
 monarchy, 7, 305
Albanian National Liberation Army
 (Macedonia), 40, 297
Alexandroupolis, 219, 314, 345
Alia, Ramiz, 165, 166, 299, 300, 302, 303
Anatolia, 88, 92, 339

Ankara, 118, 212, 224, 227, 335, 339
Antonescu, Marshal Ion, 70, 82, 192, 194
APL (Albanian Party of Labour), 156, 158,
 160–4, 166, 299, 303
April Line (Bulgaria), 170, 174, 179
ARF (Alliance of Reform Forces) Yugoslavia,
 145, 246
aristocracy, 7, 42, 50, 53, 67, 68, 69, 71, 218
army, 7, 237
 Albanian, 40, 49, 162, 163, 275, 301
 Bosnian Muslim, 264
 British, 16, 90–1, 93, 209
 Bulgarian, 51, 52, 53, 55–7, 60, 62, 63, 64,
 171, 172, 178, 321
 Croatian, 252, 266, 290
 German, 4
 Greek, 89, 90, 92–5, 98–101, 210, 211, 213,
 214, 217, 220, 222, 223, 225, 229, 295,
 339, 340
 Democratic Army of Greece (DAG), 99,
 100, 102, 103, 226
 Macedonian, 295
 Ottoman, 50, 87, 149
 Romanian, 70–1, 72, 73, 75, 76, 77–8, 80,
 191, 202, 203
 Turkish, 88, 222, 223
 Yugoslav, 11, 12–13, 17, 20, 21, 28, 33, 34,
 113, 114, 118, 123, 133, 134, 143, 144,
 147, 152, 153, 154, 240, 243, 244, 248,
 250–5, 259, 262, 274–5, 278, 279, 282,
 284, 294
Aspida (Shield), 213, 214
Atatürk, Kemal, 88, 208
Athens, 28, 88, 93, 94, 96, 99, 100, 165, 205,
 207, 209, 213, 217, 218, 219, 220, 222,
 224, 225, 226, 227, 229, 261, 294, 295,
 301, 335, 336, 338, 341
Australia, 133, 199, 207
Austria, 23, 35, 130, 138, 186, 247, 287, 305
Austria-Hungary, 22, 67, 68, 273
AVNOJ, 13, 15, 16, 19, 90

Badinter commission, 254, 255
Bakarić, Vladimir, 127, 134
Balkan conferences, 165, 223, 224, 285, 293
Balkan federation, 28–31
Balkan Multinational Peace Force, 345–6